Bible Study Notes

Volume Two

Bible Study Notes

Volume Two

EXODUS
LEVITICUS
NUMBERS
JOSHUA
JUDGES

by Anita S. Dole
Edited by William Ross Woofenden

Swedenborg Foundation Press
West Chester, Pennsylvania

First printed in 1977 – 1979 by the American New Church Sunday School Association.
Published with editing by William Ross Woofenden, 2001; reprinted in 2011.

ISBN for the six-volume set: 978-0-87785-357-2
Volume 1 (Genesis): 978-0-87785-358-9
Volume 2 (Exodus, Leviticus, Numbers, Joshua, Judges): 978-0-87785-359-6
Volume 3 (I and II Samuel, I and II Kings, Psalms): 978-0-87785-360-2
Volume 4 (Isaiah, Jeremiah, Ezekiel, Daniel, Joel, Amos, Jonah, Micah, Haggai, Zechariah, Malachi): 978-0-87785-361-9
Volume 5 (Mark, Luke): 978-0-87785-362-6
Volume 6 (John, Revelation): 978-0-87785-363-3

Cover image: "The Discovery of Moses" by Julius Schnorr von Carolsfeld from *Treasury of Bible Illustrations* (Mineola, N.Y.: Dover Publications, Inc., 1999)
Printed in the United States of America.

For information on the Swedenborg Foundation, contact:
Swedenborg Foundation
320 North Church Street
West Chester, PA 19380
or
www.swedenborg.com

Contents

CONTENTS

INTRODUCTORY NOTES FOR TEACHERS

As we may see by the accompanying chart, this program was planned as a four-year Bible course, but it was originally arranged so that the whole Word was covered by periods each year, in order that the child might early realize that the Bible is one book—not only a continuous story but a completed one—and also that children might not so often enter the Sunday School for the first time in the middle of the Bible story with no idea of what has gone before. While this plan might in any one year seem to leave many important stories untouched, the retelling of the background of the successive periods from year to year in the context of different stories built up gradually in the child's mind both a surer knowledge and a better understanding of the whole letter of the Word. The plan insured that the beginning of the Bible story was not forgotten before the end was reached, and that the Old and New Testaments were seen in their proper relation and proportion. Although the lessons are now arranged in Bible sequence, it is still possible, by using the chart, to use the original four-year plan.

The notes for the various age groups are written with two purposes in view. It is *not* intended that the teacher should read them to the class. Neither is it intended that copies should be given out to the pupils in advance. Only the Bible reading should be done in advance. For the teacher, the notes are meant to suggest the points to be covered in the lesson, a possible order of presentation, and the general level of meaning which pupils in the particular age group may be expected to comprehend. For the pupil, if he has his own set of the books, they are meant to be taken home, read as a review during the week, and preserved for future reference.

It is very important that the teacher plan his use of the class time carefully. Five minutes or less at the beginning of the period are enough for review questions. Then give five minutes to a carefully thought-out covering of the background of the lesson for the day before going into the lesson proper. In the Old Testament build the background as far as possible about persons and places in order to fix these in their proper sequence in the pupils' minds. In the New Testament the background should be the factual story of the Lord's life on earth.

The writings of the church tell us that "generals" must be grasped before "particulars" can be understood in their proper context; so we may feel sure that our first object in the Sunday School should be to impress the general outline of the whole Bible story on the minds of our pupils. The covering of the whole story each year has this objective in view.

The two survey lessons (nos. 22 and 24 on the accompanying chart) are general lessons but are based on a different passage each year in order to give the pupils a wider variety in the study of the Prophets than has been possible in previous courses. They are also optional lessons, written in such a way that Sunday Schools with a school year of less than forty sessions may omit them without losing continuity. Each series also contains fifteen lessons from the New Testament. A different Gospel is studied each year. Two of the fifteen lessons are written as optional lessons; three are the special lessons for Christmas, Palm Sunday, and Easter; and three are from the book of Revelation.

FOUR-YEAR LESSON COURSE FOR NEW CHURCH SUNDAY SCHOOLS

Assignments in the Old Testament

Lesson	*Subject*	*Series I*	*Series II*	*Series III*	*Series IV*
1.	The Creation	General View	First Four Days	Days Five and Six	The Seventh Day
2.	The Most Ancient Church	The Garden of Eden	Helpmeet for Adam	The Serpent	Cain and Abel
3.	The Ancient Church	Noah Builds an Ark	End of the Flood	The Rainbow	Tower of Babel
4.	Abraham	The Call of Abram	Abram and Lot	Birth of Ishmael	Abraham & the Angels
5.	Isaac	Birth of Isaac	Sacrifice of Isaac	Isaac and Rebekah	Isaac & Abimelech
6.	Jacob	Jacob & Esau	Jacob's Dream	Wives & Sons	Jacob's Return
7.	Joseph	Joseph & Brothers	Joseph in Prison	Ruler of Egypt	Sons and Death
8.	Moses	Birth of Moses	The Burning Bush	The Ten Plagues	The Passover
9.	Escape from Egypt	Crossing Red Sea	Marah & Elim	Quails and Manna	Rephidim & Amalek
10.	Mount Sinai	Ten Commandments	Ark of Covenant	The Tabernacle	The Golden Calf
11.	Wilderness Wanderings	Nadab & Abihu	The Twelve Spies	Korah, Dathan, Abiram	Aaron's Rod
12.	Entering the Holy Land	Balaam	Call of Joshua	Crossing the Jordan	Gilgal
13.	Conquest of Holy Land	Jericho	Ai	The Gibeonites	Conquest & Division
14.	The Judges	Deborah & Barak	Gideon	Jephthah	Samson
15.	Samuel	Birth of Samuel	Lord Calls Samuel	Capture of the Ark	Asking for a King
16.	Saul	Choosing of Saul	Saul's Impatience	Saul & Jonathan	Sparing Agag
17.	David	Anointing of David	David & Goliath	Ark to Jerusalem	David & Bathsheba
18.	Solomon	Wisdom of Solomon	Glory of Solomon	Building the Temple	Decline & Death
19.	Kingdom of Israel	Elijah & Ahab	Elijah at Horeb	Elijah's Mantle	Elisha & Naaman
20.	Kingdom of Judah	Reign of Asa	Hezekiah & Isaiah	Josiah	Zedekiah & Jeremiah
21.	Book of Psalms	Psalm 1	Psalm 19	Psalm 91	Psalm 119

*22.	Major Prophets—Survey	Isaiah 6	Jeremiah 1	Ezekiel 47:1-12	Daniel 5
23.	Major Prophets	Fiery Furnace	Ezekiel's Vision	Daniel & the Image	Daniel & the Lions
*24.	Minor Prophets—Survey	Micah 6	Joel 3:9-21	Amos 8	Zechariah 4
25.	Minor Prophets	Haggai 1; 2	Jonah & the Fish	Malachi 3; 4	Jonah & the Gourd

Assignments in the New Testament

Lesson	*Series I*	*Series II*	*Series III*	*Series IV*
26.	Matthew 1:18-25; 2:13-23	Mark 1	Luke 1	John 1
27.	Matthew 3	Mark 2	Luke 7:1-30	John 2:1-11
28.	Matthew 4:1-11	*Mark 3	Luke 9:1-36	*John 3:1-21
29.	*Matthew 4:12-25	*Mark 4	Luke 10:25-42	John 4:1-42
30.	Matthew 5; 6; 7	Mark 5	*Luke 11	John 5:1-16
31.	Matthew 8	Mark 6	Luke 14	John 9
32.	*Matthew 13	Mark 10	Luke 15	*John 10
33.	Matthew 17:1-13	Mark 14	*Luke 16	John 11:1-46
34.	Matthew 26; 27	Mark 15	Luke 24:13-53	John 15
35.	Revelation 1	Revelation 4	Revelation 6	Revelation 12
36.	Revelation 2; 3	Revelation 5	Revelation 8; 9	Revelation 13; 19:11-21
37.	Revelation 21; 22	Revelation 20:11-15; 21:1-7	Revelation 21:9-16	Revelation 22:8-21
Special Lessons				
Christmas	Matthew 2:1-15	Luke 2:1-20	Matthew 2:1-15	Luke 2:1-20
Palm Sunday	Matthew 21:1-27	Mark 11	Luke 19	John 12:12-50
Easter	Matthew 28	Mark 16	Luke 24:1-12	John 20; 21

*Optional Lessons

Bible Study Notes

Exodus

Leviticus

Numbers

Joshua

Judges

THE BIRTH OF MOSES

Exodus 1; 2:1-10

The book of Genesis ends with the death of Joseph. At that time the Israelites were settled comfortably in Egypt and still respected because of Joseph. But as the years passed, and the Hebrews grew in numbers, the Egyptians began to resent them until one of the Pharaohs ordered that all male children born to the Hebrews were to be killed. This is where the story begins in the book of Exodus.

Doctrinal Points

"To be led by the Lord is freedom." –A. 5660[e]

Notes for Parents

It is widely recognized that the land of Canaan represents heaven or a heavenly character, but few realize that all the countries mentioned in the Bible picture specific planes or states of our minds. There are three countries especially which are mentioned over and over again in the Bible: Canaan, Assyria, and Egypt. There are three major planes of mind in each of us: the inmost plane, where we feel the promptings of the Lord, the plane of our rational thinking, and the plane of our natural knowledge and thought. In the Bible, Canaan pictures the inmost plane, Assyria pictures the rational plane, and Egypt the outmost or natural plane. It is in this outmost plane that all our sense impressions are registered, the things we see and hear, what we read, and what we learn from other people. All these things are stored up in our memories, as Joseph stored up grain in Egypt, against the time of famine–the time when we become conscious of our need of knowledge for use in life. Again and again in the Bible story people go down into Egypt, and this always pictures a learning period.

But learning is not particularly valuable in and of itself. It is meant for use. Jacob and his family came down into Egypt to be nourished in the time of famine, but they should have gone back to the land of Canaan when the famine was over—back to the service of the Lord. Instead, they found themselves comfortable and prosperous in Egypt, and settled down there, forgetting their true home and eventually coming to worship the gods of the Egyptians instead of their own God.

People do the same today. They begin to study in order to master the knowledge necessary for a profession, a trade, or a business, and then often fall in love with the knowledge itself and simply try to keep on learning, not applying their knowledge to the service of the Lord and the neighbor. A man may become so absorbed in building up his business or improving his farm that he has no time or thought for his family and friends, much less for the church. A woman may become so intent on taking care of her house and improving it that she forgets that its only real value is as a home for her family, where they can be happy and safe and from which they can go out eager to perform their uses in the world. Such a man or woman has become a slave in Egypt, as the Hebrews did.

The Lord raised up Moses to lead the people back to the Holy Land. In each one of us He preserves some knowledge of the Word of God, which we have perhaps learned in childhood. He takes care of it and brings it back to our conscious memory when we finally realize into what bondage we have fallen. Under divine providence, Moses was brought up in the court of Pharaoh in all the learning of the Egyptians, but he was nursed in infancy by his true mother, so that he felt himself to be a Hebrew and knew the traditions of his people. No one of us is without his "Moses," prepared by the Lord and ready to lead him back to the Holy Land when he wants to go.

Primary

The littlest ones can understand most of this simple story. Be sure they know that it was really the Lord who saved Moses by bringing Pharaoh's daughter to the river just at the right time. Impress upon them the name *Moses*. Show them what a mistake the Israelites made when they stayed in Egypt instead of going back to the land the Lord had given them, when the famine was over. The trouble they got into as a result leads directly to the story of Moses, which is always interesting to children and easy to tell.

During the days of Joseph, Pharaoh gave the Hebrews the best part of Egypt to live in, and they became so prosperous and comfortable there that they did not go back after the famine in Canaan was over, as they should have done. This proved a foolish mistake. For after Joseph died, the kings of Egypt became less friendly to the Hebrews, and finally the Egyptians became so afraid of this growing nation of strangers in their land that they decided to make slaves of them and keep them down in other ways.

What happened about two hundred years after Joseph died?
What order did the new Pharaoh give?
What child was saved?
How was he saved?
Who adopted him?
Who was his nurse?

Let us read the story from the Bible. [Read Exodus 1:6-22; 2:1-10.] We shall hear much more about Moses in our next lessons; so you want to be sure to remember his name. You see the Lord took care of Moses just as He had taken care of Joseph.

Junior

The Juniors are old enough to be interested in the fact that the Hebrew people increased in Egypt until the Pharaoh became afraid of them and tried to prevent them from producing any more fighting men. Stress the Lord's protection of the infant Moses. Also show them how important the double education of Moses—(1) in the learning of the Egyptians, and (2) in the traditions of the Hebrews—would be when it came time for him to deliver his people from the Egyptian bondage.

Joseph at first had had a very hard time in Egypt, but the Lord was with him and helped him to rise until he became a very great man, ruler of the whole land, subject only to the Pharaoh, as the king of Egypt was called. In time of famine Joseph's brothers came to Egypt to buy food and were very much afraid when they discovered that the ruler they had to deal with was actually the brother they had wronged. But Joseph forgave them and, with Pharaoh's consent, invited his whole family to move down into Egypt for the duration of the famine.

Who before this in the Bible story had come to Egypt because of famine?

Pharaoh gave Jacob and his family the best of the land to live in and they liked it so well that they did not go back, as they should have, after the famine was over. They lived in Egypt a great many years—long enough to multiply into a numerous people. We read in Genesis 46:26-27 that sixty-six men in all came down to Egypt at Joseph's invitation, and in Exodus 12:37-40 we read that when they finally left there were about six hundred thousand men, besides children.

During this long time a great change had taken place in the condition of the Hebrews in Egypt. Our chapter says, "There arose up a new king over Egypt, which knew not Joseph." This was really a whole new line of kings. They did not see the Hebrews as friends, but as possible enemies because they were an alien people—not Egyptians. So the new Pharaohs tried to hold the Hebrews down and made slaves of them. You know that the Egyptians built great temples and tombs, such as the pyramids. They used the Hebrews as laborers in these works. They did not have building machinery such as we have. Men had to do all the heavy lifting and building.

What cruel command did Pharaoh give?

The people naturally tried in every way to save their baby boys, and the Lord helped them. The Lord even made use of Pharaoh's harsh command when He wanted a man trained to lead the Hebrews out of Egypt.

Who was this man?
How did his mother try to save him?

An ark is a container made for the safekeeping of something precious. There are three famous arks in the Bible, of which the ark of Moses is the second.

What was the first?
Do you know what the third ark was?

The ark which held the baby Moses was made of bulrushes. The bulrushes of Egypt were the stalks of the papyrus plant, from which paper also was made. Notice that this little ark, just like Noah's ark, was covered with pitch to keep it afloat. The sister of Moses, who was set to watch and see what happened to him, was probably Miriam, of whom we learn later.

Who came to the river and found Moses?
What did she decide to do?
Whom did his sister bring to nurse him?

So you see that Moses, when he grew up, would have the knowledge of his Hebrew birth and all the Hebrew traditions from his mother, and he would also have the advantage of the best schooling in the world, which at that time was to be had in Egypt, and would also know at first hand a great deal about government. So the Lord prepared him to lead the Hebrews out of Egypt, organize them into a nation, and lead them back to their true home in Canaan.

Intermediate

With this age group it may be well to discuss the fact that we each have a higher and a lower nature which are constantly at variance with each other. At this age children have their serious and thoughtful times, but they are liable to be swept away quickly by claims of exercise and play. They need to understand that their everyday pleasures and activities are good in their place but that they should lead to and not away from the establishment of a genuinely good character. Any activity of which in their better moments they are ashamed is questionable. The commandments are the test, the only laws which can be trusted to lead to a good and happy life here and in heaven. A helpful thought to give them is that if they cannot say "no" to temptation, they are really slaves.

Exodus 12:40 says that the Israelites were in Egypt four hundred and thirty years, and four hundred is the number given in Genesis 15:13 and in Acts 7:6. Scholars have estimated that the actual time was something over two hundred years. Swedenborg says in the *Arcana Coelestia*, n. 1502 that the years "were not reckoned from Jacob's going down into Egypt, but from the sojourning of Abram in Egypt, counting from which the years were four hundred and thirty." However, in the Word numbers are important for their correspondence rather than for their historical accuracy.

The Pharaoh who set Joseph over the land had urged him to bring his father and his brothers and their flocks down to Egypt and had given them the best of the land to live in, the fertile delta of the Nile. But after Joseph's death, as the Hebrews increased in numbers (during the time they were in Egypt their numbers increased from seventy persons to more than six hundred thousand), the Pharaohs began to be afraid of these strangers in their midst, and in the time of our lesson for today the Pharaoh took drastic steps to limit their increase, especially the increase of fighting men.

The history of the Israelites in the Word was so recorded by inspiration from the Lord that it might throughout represent the history of the church in man, a man's relation to the Lord. The Israelites came down to Egypt in time of famine to be nourished and cared for by Joseph. The Pharaoh who made Joseph ruler of his land is a picture of our external memory when it is orderly and used in the service of the Lord.* So the coming down of the Hebrews to Egypt at that time pictures an orderly state of acquiring knowledge under the protection of a true spiritual affection. But Joseph died and was embalmed and put in a coffin in Egypt. Sometimes we become absorbed in the pursuit of knowledge for its own sake and forget its spiritual purpose. We come under the domination of a principle which recognizes only worldly aims. This is the Pharaoh "which knew not Joseph." Then, although we

---

*although it may not be so used by us *consciously* or *deliberately*. —*Ed.*

may seem to ourselves to be leading an independent life, doing as we please, we are really servants under a hard master, working very hard to build up wealth and power, and driven by ambition and greed. People often work themselves to death to acquire things which at death they have to leave behind them. Swedenborg says, "To be led by the Lord is freedom."

In the Word the birth of sons pictures the development of new truth. Pharaoh's ordering all the male children killed at birth pictures the fact that worldly ambition in the end seeks to destroy every spiritual thought which may come to us. But Moses was saved. Moses, because he was to lead the people out of Egyptian bondage and be the Lord's instrument in the giving of the commandments, pictures divine law. Most of us in our childhood become at least somewhat familiar with the ten commandments. Those who are not taught them directly from the Bible get many of them indirectly, because they are implied in all the laws which we have to observe in order to keep out of trouble even in a worldly sense. This knowledge of the commandments is what leads us out of our Egyptian bondage. Moses had an Israelitish mother and an Egyptian foster mother. That is, the divine law really comes from the Lord, but even our affection for getting along in the world makes us see that it is desirable and to be preserved. This is pictured, too, by the fact that the ark of bulrushes was daubed with slime and pitch to keep it afloat. The ark which Noah built was daubed with pitch also. Pitch represents selfishness. We are often saved from doing something wrong by our selfish fear of consequences. The rushes which grow at the river's edge, which in this case were probably the papyrus plant, represent the simplest ideas of what is right and fitting.

In a more particular sense the ark of bulrushes pictures the letter of the Word, and in this sense Pharaoh's daughter stands for the natural love of knowing about everything, which sometimes leads people to read the Bible even before they see any higher use in it than to be able to talk about it. But the little infant is nourished and cared for by his own mother. Divine truth is fed and cherished in us by means of love for the Lord and His truth which is a part of our inheritance from our heavenly Father, the "remains" planted in us in infancy and early childhood.

Moses growing up in the court of Pharaoh pictures the letter of the Word growing up in us as a part of our worldly education, but fostered under the Lord's providence by a deeper feeling of which we are hardly conscious.

Basic Correspondences

rushes	=	the simplest ideas of right
pitch	=	selfishness
Moses	=	the divine law

Senior

The young people should be impressed by the spiritual meaning of the bondage in Egypt. They know people who are slaves to their appetites, to their business, to their housework, to their intellectual pursuits, and even to their bridge parties. We spoke recently of higher and lower values. This is a good thought to keep constantly before them. In this lesson show them that when our "Joseph" dies in us, we easily become slaves to external considerations.

The word *Genesis* means "beginning." We can think of the whole book of Genesis as treating of the beginning of our lives. Swedenborg tells us that as infants we are surrounded and protected by celestial angels, angels of the third or highest heaven. So at that time we are in the sphere of the celestial plane of life. As we grow and become conscious of ourselves as individuals and begin to think and reason, the celestial angels recede and spiritual angels surround us. And finally, as we begin to try to act for ourselves, independently from our parents, we are associated with angels of the natural heavens, for that is then the plane of thought and feeling in which we are most interested.

So when we reach the point of being really grown up, our thoughts and feelings are centered about our external activities and uses. Spiritually we are in Egypt. But within us are stored up, like the body of Joseph in its coffin (Genesis 50:26), what Swedenborg calls the "remains"—all the states and knowledges of a celestial and spiritual character which we have acquired from our earlier heavenly surroundings.

Joseph had told the children of Israel that they would someday go back to the land of Canaan. No man can be permanently satisfied with merely worldly living because as a human being instead of an animal he has higher possibilities within him. The old hymn which begins "I'm but a stranger here; heaven is my home" is based on a fundamental truth. The Hebrews were strangers in Egypt to the very last of their stay there. Sooner or later the man who has immersed himself in the business or pleasures of the world wakes up to find himself a slave, and looks for a deliverer.

Moses is the deliverer provided by the Lord to break the bonds and lead the soul back to its true home. Moses represents divine law. But this law does not come to us at first full-fledged. The person seeking a way out of his bondage is conscious first only of a small stirring of life in the recollection of the simple truths concerning what is right and fitting which are stored up in his memory from his innocent childhood—pictured by Moses in his little basket of rushes at the river's edge. Pharaoh's daughter symbolizes the desire to examine this new awakening, but the new life must be nourished by a deeper and more genuine affection. The Lord sees to it that the sister and the mother of Moses are at hand.

In the literal story Moses received providentially everything necessary to his preparation for his great task—the instruction from his Hebrew mother and the learning of the Egyptians. The Lord sees to it that when any young man or woman wakes to the realization that a merely worldly and selfish life is bondage and longs for the freedom of the spiritual life, the first stirrings of thought deep down in his mind are fed and protected and supplied with the necessary knowledge until they become strong enough to attempt the actual work of reformation.

Spiritual character is not developed overnight. It comes in clear stages, called by Swedenborg repentance, reformation, and regeneration. Repentance is the acknowledgment that we have been wrong, together with the sincere effort to change ourselves. Reformation is the actual correction of our external lives according to the teachings of the Word. Regeneration is a new birth, the birth of a new will which is in accord with the Lord's will. This is something we do not create ourselves. It flows in from the Lord as we make the necessary preparation for it by repentance and reformation. Repentance and reformation are our part; regeneration is the Lord's. So the Israelites had to groan under their bondage until they were ready to make the effort to escape, to accept Moses as their leader, and to make the long, hard journey through the wilderness to the land of Canaan, the Holy Land which was their true home.

Adult

The difference in meaning between Egypt under Joseph and Egypt under a Pharaoh "which knew not Joseph" should be clearly pointed out. Then give the correspondence of Moses and, with this as a basis of interpretation, take up the general outline of the life of Moses and its meaning.

When Jacob and his family came down into Egypt and were given the best of the land to live in because of Pharaoh's gratitude to Joseph and confidence in him, we have the picture of an orderly learning period, when the Lord is supreme in our thoughts and recognition of Him directs our acquisition and ordering of facts. It is a peaceful, happy, profitable state. We are in such a state not only in our childhood but also in adult life when we read the Word daily, when we study the writings of the church, when we attend Sunday school and church, and also when for the sake of our use to the Lord and the neighbor we study or refresh our minds on subjects other than the Word which we feel will help us.

This learning state is essential to progress, but it is not to be our constant state. The Lord had promised Jacob that He would bring the children of Israel out of Egypt again. Joseph before he died had exacted a promise from them that when they returned to the Holy Land they would take his bones with them—a promise which they fulfilled (Exodus 13:19 and Joshua 24:32). The land of Canaan was their true home. The Lord, when He called Abraham to leave Ur and go to the land of Canaan, had promised it to him and his seed forever, and had repeated this promise to Isaac and to Jacob.

Canaan has always been called "the promised land," and recognized as a symbol of heaven. Heaven is the inheritance the Lord wishes to give each one of us. But the Lord tells us, "The kingdom of God is within you." We do not go to heaven when we die unless heaven is within us when we die. So our Canaan is a heavenly character, and that is the object of our whole journey through life.

When the Israelites settled in Egypt, they prospered and increased greatly in numbers and possessions and, as we are all apt to do when everything goes well with us, they presently forgot that they were merely sojourners in Egypt and made no effort to return to Canaan. Then Joseph died, and his body was embalmed and put in a coffin in Egypt. So when we become wholly satisfied with our worldly prosperity, our higher spiritual perceptions are laid away out of sight in the memory, and we become more and more absorbed in the pursuit of the things of this world. The Israelites eventually became slaves to the monarchs who succeeded those who had originally befriended them, the later Pharaohs, who as time went on "knew not Joseph." They themselves at last forgot even the name of their own God–Moses had to be told the name *Jehovah* by the Lord when He spoke to him at the burning bush. So if we fall in love with knowledge for its own sake or for the sake of what it can do for us in a worldly way and forget that it is given us by the Lord as a means to help us to serve Him and the neighbor, we come under the rule of a selfish and worldly principle and become slaves to it; our higher natures are made to serve worldly ends. But the Israelitish people had been chosen by the Lord to serve as a representative of His church on earth, and their history was so regulated by Him that it should represent the course of a person whose mind is not wholly closed to spiritual lessons. So they began to groan under their bondage and to long for deliverance from it. Every person who really intends to lead a good life eventually becomes restless and dissatisfied with his bondage to the world.

The command of Pharaoh that all the male infants of the Hebrews should be killed may be compared with Herod's slaying of all the babes in Bethlehem. It is the effort of the worldly nature into which all of us are born to destroy every seed of spiritual truth which might grow up to threaten our selfish interests. But the Lord sees to it that a saving element is preserved—knowledge of his law. Moses represents divine law. There are two elements necessary to the preservation of this knowledge. One is a genuine affection for it, represented by the mother of Moses, which is part of the "remains" implanted in us during infancy and early childhood. The other is an affection for the material rewards of keeping the law, self-esteem and the esteem of others, represented by Pharaoh's daughter. The ark of bulrushes, covered with pitch like Noah's ark, portrays a knowledge of the mere letter of the law—the rudiments of understanding it—preserved by love of self, since ignorance of the law gets one into trouble. The timing—which brings Pharaoh's daughter down to bathe just when Moses in the ark has been left at the water's edge—is the Lord's. So our opportunities are always timed by divine providence to give us the best possibility of correcting our mistakes. Moses grew up as the foster son of Pharaoh's daughter. We might think here of the rich young man who had kept all the commandments from his youth up and came to the Lord feeling that his orderly life should be sufficient. But Moses had his own mother always in the background, and was not allowed to lose sight of his birth and allegiance.

The life of Moses is divided into three periods of forty years each: (1) The first period was spent in Egypt. It begins with his birth and preservation in the ark of bulrushes. We may see that this ark represents the simplest knowledge of what is right and fitting held together and kept afloat by the sense that one must observe the standards of his community if he is to succeed. Moses was brought up—as many of us are—in the learning of the Egyptians but in the tradition of the Hebrews; that is, in worldly knowledge but with some knowledge of the Word also. This period closes with the flight of Moses after he slew an Egyptian whom he saw smiting a Hebrew—our first impulsive attempt to preserve what we feel is important to our spiritual life. (2) The second period was spent in the land of Midian, tending the flocks of Jethro, a priest of Midian, who became Moses' father-in-law. Midian was the son of Abraham by Keturah, whom he married after Sarah's death. In a good sense Midian represents a state of simple good, a thought which is further carried out by Moses' occupation there. A temporary return to the simple belief and resolution of our childhood is a necessary part of our preparation for the escape from bondage. This period closes with the call of Moses at the burning bush. (3) The third period Moses spent in the actual deliverance of his people and in leading them from Egypt to Canaan through the wilderness.

We may think of the story of the Hebrews from the time of the Exodus as the story of our attempt to attain a heavenly state of character, once we have realized that we cannot stay in mere memory-knowledge of what is good and true but must really apply it to our own personal life. This story proceeds under a series of great leaders of whom Moses is the first. The wilderness journey pictures the period of reformation when we are trying to bring our external lives into order from a principle of simple obedience to the ten commandments.

From the Writings of Swedenborg

Arcana Coelestia, n. 6751: "The law Divine in a wide sense signifies the whole Word; in a sense less extended the Historic Word; in a close sense, what was written through Moses; and in the closest sense, the ten commandments written on the tables of stone upon Mount Sinai. Moses represents the law in the less wide sense, also in the close, and likewise in the closest sense."

Arcana Coelestia, n. 6723: "*And she took an ark of rush.* That this signifies what is of low value round about, but nevertheless derived from truth, is evident from the signification of 'an ark,' as being what is round about, or that in which anything is enclosed; and from the signification of 'rush,' as being what is of low value, but nevertheless derived from truth. . . . As it was provided that Moses should represent the Lord as to the law Divine, or the Word, specifically the historic Word, it was therefore brought about that when he was an infant he was placed in a little ark, but in one of low value, because he was in his first rising, and because his being there was only a representative; but that afterward when the law Divine itself had shone forth from Mount Sinai, it was placed in an ark which was called the 'ark of the testimony.' "

Suggested Questions on the Lesson

J. What was the condition of the Hebrews when they first settled in Egypt? *honored guests*

J. How did it change as the years went on? *became slaves*

P. What was the Pharaoh of our lesson today afraid of? *numerical strength of Hebrews*

P. How did he try to keep the Hebrews from increasing? *ordered death of newborn sons*

P. What was the name of the baby boy who was saved? *Moses*

P. What did his mother do in order to save him? *made "ark," hid in rushes*

P. Who found him? *Pharaoh's daughter*

J. What did she decide to do? *adopt him*

P. Who was called to nurse Moses? *Moses' mother*

I. What does Egypt represent? *state of acquiring knowledge*

S. What is pictured by the bondage in Egypt? *becoming enslaved to worldly knowledge or principles: e.g., business or pleasure*

I. What does Moses represent? *divine law*

THE BURNING BUSH

Exodus 3

In order to connect with the last lesson, the point to emphasize is that Jacob and his family went down into Egypt to be fed and protected by Joseph just for a time, and then yielded to the temptation to stay there in comfort instead of going back where they belonged. It is another example of taking the easy way instead of the right way—like the choice Lot made. Reference to Lot will also give an opportunity for a brief review, which is always useful. Even the littlest children can get the idea that the thing which looks easiest is not always the right thing, and that to choose anything but the right thing always leads to trouble.

Doctrinal Points

The Lord is the only one who can truly say, "I am."

Knowledge of truth may be misused, as the knowledge of correspondences was turned into magic by the Egyptians.

The Lord at the right time calls each one of us to the particular work He wants us to do for Him.

Notes for Parents

The story of Moses is another of the great stories of the Bible with which most people are familiar; but usually when we think of Moses, we think of some one incident in his life—some, who have not been taught beyond the beginner stage in the Sunday school, think only of Moses as a little baby in the bulrushes on the brink of the Nile. The Lord saved Moses then, and the story is a touching and beautiful one, but it is only the beginning of his life, for he was saved in order that he might perform a great task. Our children, when they are little, love the story of the baby Moses and it makes a deep impression on them, but they should even then be taught something of the great work which that baby was to do.

The children of Israel, who had gone down into Egypt to live during the seven years of famine in the time of Joseph, had become too well satisfied with their ease and prosperity there, and had forgotten to go back to their own country. So in time they got into difficulties with the Egyptians and were made slaves. When everything is going well with us, we are likely to forget that we are created not just to enjoy the good things of this world, but that the Lord has a place for each one of us and a work which we should be doing for Him. The Holy Land represents heaven or a heavenly character, and that is the true home of every one of us. All our occupations are really our opportunities for serving the Lord and the neighbor, and if we think of them in this way, we shall come to love our work not for the money or acclaim it brings us but because it is useful to others. This is the only way in which we can really find happiness in our work. Unhappiness always comes from thinking about ourselves, because we are never satisfied then, our work seems hard and our pay small, and we are always thinking about what other people should do for us. This is slavery, the kind of slavery into which the children of Israel fell in Egypt when they forgot the country in which they were supposed to be living.

We are apt to think that people who have things we do not have are the happy ones—but are they? Are all the rich people you know really happy? If you look about you honestly, you will see that the people who really are happy are always the ones who are not thinking about themselves; and we can all be such people if we will. The Lord's call to Moses at the burning bush, the lesson the children have for today, is the call which comes to every one of us if we are willing to listen, the call to turn our thoughts and our lives away from our own wants and toward the Holy Land of unselfish, heavenly living.

Primary

The story of the burning bush is a dramatic story and one which is easy to tell. The children can understand that the Lord was giving Moses a hard thing to do, but that the Lord will always help us if we do right. Review briefly the story of the birth of Moses and of his early life in Egypt and the cause of his going to Midian. Moses will be the leading figure for several lessons, and the children need to understand how he was chosen and prepared by the Lord for his task.

Joseph became a very great man in Egypt. He was next to the king in the government. When a time of famine came, his father and his brothers and their families all came down to Egypt to get food. Joseph forgave his brothers, and Pharaoh allowed him to give them homes in the best part of the land.

When the famine was over, they should have gone back to the Holy Land, but Egypt seemed to them an easier country to live in and so they stayed on, and for a long time they prospered and their numbers increased greatly.

But after Joseph died, there was no one in Egypt to protect them, and little by little the people of Egypt came to be anxious because these strangers were increasing so fast in their land. The Pharaohs began to oppress them and finally made them slaves. Their lives became harder and harder.

About two hundred years passed and they forgot all about their own country and even forgot the name of their own God. But God had not forgotten them. He provided that one of them, whose name was Moses, should be specially protected and trained until he could be their leader. Moses grew up in Egypt but when he was grown up, Pharaoh became angry with him and he had to run away.

Moses fled to the land of Midian and lived there for forty years.
He married the daughter of Jethro, the priest of Midian.
Where was Moses when the Lord called him?
What was he doing?
Where did the Lord's voice seem to come from?
What did the Lord tell him?
Was Moses eager to undertake the task the Lord gave him?

How did the Lord reassure him?
What name did the Lord give Himself?
The name *Jehovah* is a form of the Hebrew for "I am."
Moses was afraid he would not be able to persuade Pharaoh to let the people go.
So the Lord gave Moses power to work miracles.
He also told Moses that his brother Aaron would help him.
Then Moses was willing to obey the Lord.

Junior

Have the Juniors study a map for the relative locations of the Holy Land, Egypt, and the land of Midian. Have them look up Genesis 25:1-2 to find the birth of Midian, and Judges 6:1-6 to see how the Midianites later turned against the children of Israel. The Juniors can understand the meaning of being so prosperous that we forget all about the Lord, and that we sometimes have to get into trouble before we realize our need of going back to the Holy Land where we really belong. It is good for the children to get into the habit of thinking of the Holy Land as meaning a truly good life. Have them look up also Deuteronomy 6:10-12.

Jacob died in Egypt, but Joseph took his body back and buried it in the cave of Machpelah where Abraham and Sarah, Isaac and Rebekah, and Leah were buried. On this journey he was accompanied by many of the rulers and elders of the Egyptians as well as by his brothers. When Joseph himself died, he made his relatives promise that when they went back to the Holy Land to live, they would take his body back with them. His body was "embalmed" in Egypt. This meant that it was preserved by being treated with certain aromatic oils. The Egyptians in those days knew how to do this, and that is why archaeologists sometimes find "mummies," or preserved bodies, in the ancient tombs in Egypt even today.

But the children of Israel were comfortable and prosperous in the land of Goshen, and forgot that they ought to go back to the Holy Land. When everything is going well in our lives, we are liable to forget that we are in this world to serve the Lord and the neighbor and not just to get things for ourselves. They stayed there more than two hundred years, and after a while the Egyptians began to be anxious because these strangers were increasing so fast. They were afraid they might become strong and turn against the Egyptians. So finally a Pharaoh arose "who knew not Joseph" and made the children of Israel slaves, loading them with heavy work and trying to prevent them from increasing. He even ordered all the boy babies to be killed as soon as they were born. Moses, however, as we have learned, was saved by his mother by being put into an "ark" or covered basket of bulrushes on the brink of the river, where he was found and adopted by Pharaoh's daughter.

Moses was brought up in the court of Pharaoh and educated in all the learning of the Egyptians, but his own mother was his nurse and from her he learned about his own people and their traditions and came to feel as an Israelite. We learn from another part of the Bible (Acts 7:23) that he lived in Egypt for forty years. Then one day while trying to defend one of his own people, he killed an Egyptian and had to flee from Egypt. He went to the land of Midian. On the map you will find this land at the southeastern corner of the Sinai Peninsula. Midian, from whom this people took their name, was a son of Abraham by Keturah, whom Abraham married after the death of Sarah; so the people of Midian were related to the children of Israel. Moses was received into the home of the priest of Midian. His name was Reuel, but he is usually called Jethro, which means "his excellence" and was probably an honorary title. Moses married his daughter and settled down to tend the flocks of his father-in-law, wandering about the country to find pasture for them, as the shepherds did in those days. He remained in Midian for the second forty years of his life.

Now comes our story for today.

Where do we find Moses?

Horeb is the name of a group of peaks, of which one is Sinai, from which later the commandments were to be given (verse 12).

What strange sight did Moses see there?
Who spoke to him from the bush?

From the Hebrew tradition which his mother had taught him, Moses knew that the Hebrews had a God of their own who had made promises to the patriarchs Abraham, Isaac, and Jacob, but that had been hundreds of years before. It looked as though their God had forgotten them. Think what it must have meant to Moses when the voice from the burning bush said, "I am the God of thy father, the God of Âbraham, the God of Isaac, and the God of Jacob"! The children of Israel had been in Egypt so long that Moses did not even know the Lord's name.

What name did the Lord give Himself when Moses asked Him?

This seems a strange name, doesn't it? But if you think a little, you will see what it means. No one made the Lord or gave Him life. He is Life itself, from whom all life comes to the world and to each of us. He is really the only one who can say, "I am." The Hebrew word *Jehovah* is one form of this same word, "I am."

What did the Lord tell Moses he was to do?
Moses was afraid he would not be able to accomplish so great a task.
What did the Lord tell him? (verse 12)

He also gave Moses the power to perform miracles, and gave him the help of his brother Aaron. And He promised still another kind of help to the people. Read verses 21 and 22 and see what they were to be allowed to take with them out of Egypt. When you read in later chapters of the gold and silver and jewels which were used in the making of the tabernacle and its furnishings, and the materials used for the curtains of the tabernacle and the clothing of the high priest, you will remember where they got these things. And when you are older you will understand what this "borrowing" from the Egyptians means. Moses was to live another forty years during which he did lead his people out of Egypt and back to the point where they could enter the Holy Land.

Intermediate

The meaning of the call of Moses and of the burning bush should be brought out with this class, as well as the relationship of the Midianites to the Israelites and why Moses fled from Egypt to Midian and lived there so long before he was called to his real task. Emphasize the fact that the Lord never asks us to do something until He sees that we are really able to do it, and that He is always with us when we obey him. When we do wrong, it is easy to say, "I couldn't help it," but that is never true.

Every time we face some new task for which we are not properly prepared, we have to go down into Egypt. And this is just as true of our spiritual progress as it is of our occupations in the world. We often come to problems which we do not know how to solve. We say, "I don't know what is really right for me to do in this matter." Then we search our memories to find the right answer, and there we find Joseph. You remember that Joseph pictures the desire to do right in the Lord's sight. Joseph gave his brothers grain from the stores which had been laid up for just this time of famine. Our "Joseph" draws instruction for us from the letter of the Word where the Lord has stored it up for us. Then, you remember, Jacob and all his family came down into Egypt, and Pharaoh–because of his gratitude to Joseph–gave them the rich land of Goshen, the Nile delta, to live in. And there they settled down to live in plenty under Joseph's protection until the famine should be over.

Sometimes people find that answers to all life's problems can be found in the Bible; but they get so fascinated studying the Bible they forget why they went to it in the first place. Some people go to college and fall in love with learning, and go on learning all their lives and forget that learning is of no value unless we use it as a means to help other people. All knowledge is meant to be used in service to the Lord and the neighbor, and if we become absorbed in just acquiring more and more knowledge, we are like the children of Israel who were so well fed and so contented in the land of Egypt that they forgot to go back to the Holy Land. You know the story of how they finally became slaves there. People can become slaves to learning.

The children of Israel stayed in Egypt for many, many years–possibly more than two hundred. They had forgotten the Lord, but the Lord had not forgotten them. When they finally realized their unhappy condition and longed to be freed from it, He raised up Moses to lead them back to their true home. Everyone knows the story of how Moses was saved when he was a baby by being put into the little basket of rushes on the river brink, and being discovered by Pharaoh's daughter when she went down to bathe. He was brought up in the Egyptian court as Pharaoh's daughter's adopted son, and was given the education of an Egyptian ruler at a time when Egypt was the center of learning of the world. But Moses also had his own mother as his nurse, and from her he learned the traditions of his own people and so came to feel himself a Hebrew. And when he was a man, his sympathies were with the Hebrews. He lived in Egypt for forty years, and then had to flee because he killed an Egyptian who was striking a Hebrew slave.

He spent his next forty years in the wild, mountainous region called Midian, the southeastern tip of the Sinai Peninsula, tending the flock of his father-in-law, the priest of Midian. Midian, for whom this country was named, was the son of Abraham by Keturah, whom he married after Sarah died, and the Midianites had remained in the wilderness and had preserved the simple faith and worship of Abraham's day. In one of our earlier lessons we learned that they were merchantmen traveling through the surrounding regions and engaging in trade. They had a part in the Lord's plan for saving Joseph. They picture the kind of simple belief in God which we have when we are children; and sometimes, when we realize that our worldly learning is becoming too absorbing, we have to go back to that state of simple faith for a time until we have stored up enough spiritual strength to face the world in a better way. But we are not meant to stay in Midian. In religion as well as in everything else, our minds are given us to use.

There came a day when Moses was feeding his flocks in the wilderness near Horeb, the range of mountains of which Sinai is one, and his attention was attracted by a strange sight: a bush that was apparently on fire but was not being burned up. You may remember from the Creation story that vegetation pictures the springing up of thoughts in our minds. A bush is not a short-lived plant like grass; neither is it a tall tree. It pictures an idea which has developed in our minds over a period of time but has not yet become big enough to seem very important. Sometimes at the right moment such an idea inspires us to go out and do something really great. It seems suddenly to be on fire. And when we examine it more closely, we feel that the Lord is really speaking to us in that idea. So as Moses approached the bush, he heard the Lord's voice saying, "Put off thy shoes from off thy feet, for the place whereon thou standest is holy ground." Our shoes in which our feet walk from day to day represent our everyday, practical considerations. If we really feel inspired to do something big for someone and feel that the Lord has put the thought into our minds, we must put aside our ordinary, selfish ideas, and prepare ourselves to obey the Lord. The Lord tells us, just as He told Moses, that if we obey Him, He will be with us and help us to accomplish what we undertake to do for Him.

Now read verse 14. Moses and his people had even forgotten the name of their God, although they knew that their fathers had worshiped a different God from the god of the Egyptians. You are familiar with the name *Jehovah*. That is one form of the Hebrew word meaning "I am." What does "I am" mean? We know that everything in the world had a beginning. Each of us, even though we are to live forever, had a beginning. We did not make ourselves. The Lord made each of us and everything in the world, as we learned in our first lesson. But who made God? Verse 14 is the answer: No one made God—God *is*. He is Life itself, the first and the last, as the book of Revelation tells us. Everything else comes from Him. Moses knew that the Egyptians made their gods, which were idols. But the God of the Hebrews was not an idol, but the living being who was the source of all life in the world. We call Him our heavenly Father and know that centuries after the time of Moses He came into the world in person as Jesus Christ so that we can know just what kind of person He is.

Chapter 4 tells us of certain signs which the Lord gave Moses so that he would feel perfectly sure that the Lord's power was with him. Moses did not feel very sure of himself and he needed this reassurance. We sometimes think we are not strong enough or wise enough to do what the Lord asks us to do, and we need to be reassured in the same way. We hear the Lord's voice in our consciences and we learn our duty.

Basic Correspondences

Midian = a simple, childlike belief
shoes = our everyday, "practical" thoughts

Senior

The difference between carrying on our occupations for the sake of worldly prosperity, and carrying them on as a means of serving the Lord and the neighbor, is the important lesson for this age. They are about to enter the Egyptian period and should be warned to keep always in mind that their real home is the Holy Land, and that all they learn should be regarded in the light of its possible service to the Lord and the neighbor. They can also be serving the Lord and the neighbor every day in their relations with others, if they have this in mind.

The slavery into which the children of Israel fell through their long stay in Egypt is a picture of the slavery to worldliness into which we may fall if we forget what the real purpose of life is. Eventually almost everyone recognizes this slavery: the businessman is seen to be a slave to his office, the housewife a slave to her housework, and so on. Only when we think of our occupations as means of serving the Lord and the neighbor can we find true freedom and happiness in our daily work. The Israelites had forgotten their true home and even the name of their God, but the Lord had not forgotten them. The Lord is always at hand watching for openings in our armor of self-satisfaction and worldly living, and prepared to raise up a Moses to lead us back to our true home.

We learn from Acts 7:23 that Moses remained in Egypt at the court of Pharaoh for forty years. The number *forty* pictures a full state of temptation or testing. Egypt at that time was the world's center of learning. The greatest library in the world was being gathered in Egypt. Parts of the Ancient Word may have been there in the time of Moses. (Swedenborg tells us that the first eleven chapters of our Bible were taken by Moses from the Ancient Word.) Correspondences were well known in Egypt. This knowledge was the basis of their hieroglyphic writing, and—perverted—was the power which enabled the so-called "wise men" of Pharaoh to duplicate several of the miracles of Moses.

But Moses, in spite of the learning of Egypt, still felt himself a Hebrew, and we recall that it was through his slaying of an Egyptian for smiting a Hebrew slave that he fell under Pharaoh's displeasure and was forced to flee to the land of Midian, where our lesson for today finds him. His first attempt to serve his people had shown him his own weakness and timidity. He was not ready for his great call. The Midianites in a good sense picture a simple, childlike state of faith and obedience. Moses remained in Midian for another forty years, keeping the flocks of his father-in-law, Jethro, the priest of Midian. In this period nothing hard was given him to do; it was a time of preparation—not of further learning, but of establishing the habit of trust and obedience. The Lord always withholds temptations from us until we are strong enough to meet them if we will (see I Cor. 10:13).

Then Moses one day came to Horeb (the range of mountains of which Mount Sinai is one) and saw the burning bush. Bushes—small vegetable growths—represent ideas that are in our minds from the knowledges we have acquired. The flame in the bush is divine love speaking to us through these truths, calling us to do more than save our own souls. In every sincere life the time comes when we hear such a call: when we realize that there is something for us to undertake for others. Moses was reluctant, as we are often reluctant, to leave his quiet, solitary, safe wanderings and undertake a bold and difficult task. But the Lord promised to be with him and went on to give him practical demonstrations of the power that would be his if he obeyed. Chapter 4 teaches us how the Lord leads us to feel the reality of the power which only He can give us.

A name signifies the quality of a thing. The name which the Lord gave Himself—"I am" (the Hebrew *Jehovah*)—expresses the essential quality of the Lord, for He is Life itself, the only person who can truly say, "I am."

Adult

The excuses given by Moses are perhaps the most fruitful source of discussion material for adults. Their Egyptian period should be over, and the question is, what are they doing with their lives? what are they doing for the Lord and the church?

The Israelites came down into Egypt to be protected and fed by Joseph during the years of famine. But because they were given the best of the land to dwell in and prospered in a worldly sense better than in their own land, they did not go back, and eventually, although they preserved their national identity, they forgot their home and even the name of their own God. We do this when we feel the lack of knowledge necessary to a useful life but, when we find it, become so interested in the knowledge of itself and so self-satisfied that we forget the true purpose of life altogether.

The life of Moses is divided into three periods of forty years each, and we remember that the number forty represents fullness of temptation. His first forty years was spent in Egypt in the court of Pharaoh, where he was educated in the learning of the most intellectually active nation in the world at that time, and also, through his mother, in the traditions of the Hebrews. The second forty were spent in the land of Midian, in the southeastern portion of the Sinai Peninsula. Midian in a good sense represents a state of childlike faith and obedience—Midian was a son of Abraham (Genesis 25:1-4). When worldliness threatens to master us and we awake to the necessity of saving our higher nature, our first need and impulse is to go back to the simple trust and obedience of our childhood, and to reestablish the good habits developed in that state.

But we cannot remain in the Midian state. Many people today try, as they say, to go "back to Jesus," back to an unreasoning acceptance of the finite human picture of Christ, closing their minds to the real problems involved in a rational consideration of the claim and teachings of Christ and to the need of the modern world for just such rational understanding, and imagining that this is the only way to save their souls. But when we remain too long in blind faith, Midian becomes an enemy, eating up the new developments and opportunities which are presented to us which ought to lead us to greater spiritual insight and usefulness, as the Midianites of Gideon's time spread over the land like grasshoppers and destroyed the harvest. The Lord has more for us to do than merely to save our own souls alive. Moses was called to go back to Egypt and free his people. Moses, as we know, represents divine law. It is divine law which leads us out of bondage to worldliness and materialism.

The call to undertake this "going out" comes as a sudden prompting from divine love in the rudimentary truths we have stored in our memory: the fire in the bramble bush. It is significant that when Moses saw the burning bush, he was at Horeb, close to Sinai, and was feeding the flock. The call comes to us in moments when we are thinking of the commandments and trying to preserve something of the innocence which the Lord has stored up deep within us in the "remains" of our childhood states. The writings tell us that without these remains no one could be saved. Whenever we have sufficiently prepared the way in ourselves and the Lord sees that we are mature and strong enough to take a forward step, He brings to our consciousness something out of these remains to make us feel that He is present with us and urging us to new endeavor. But the first thing the voice said to Moses was: "Put off thy shoes from off thy feet, for the place whereon thou standest is holy ground." If the Lord is to communicate with us, we must first put aside the everyday, selfish considerations which we call "practical," and be ready to listen to His voice even though it may point us to unexpected and difficult undertakings.

We do not hear the Lord speaking when we are bent on listening to the voice of the world.

Moses was not eager to accept the commission offered him. He raised several objections. The first was a legitimate one: "Who am I" that I should do this great thing? His sense of his own weakness and unworthiness was praiseworthy and was answered by the Lord's assurance: "Certainly I will be with thee." Then he pleaded ignorance: he did not know even the name of his God. We often do this when we are asked to teach Sunday school or to lead a discussion group, or to make some new missionary effort: "I don't know enough myself." We should recognize this as an excuse, not a reason. The Lord answered it by telling Moses His name, a name signifying the quality of a thing. The Lord is giving us as well as Moses the simplest and most comprehensive information about Himself when He says: "I AM THAT I AM . . . Thus shalt thou say unto the children of Israel, I AM hath sent me unto you." In the Hebrew *Jehovah* is another form of "I am." *Jehovah* is the name of the Lord which, we learn from Swedenborg, is always used in the Word when the divine love is under consideration, just as *Elohim* (translated "God") is used to express the activity of the divine truth. If we know that in the King James version of the Bible* *Jehovah* is almost always translated "the LORD" (in small capitals) and *Elohim* "God," we shall find the use of these names a very enlightening study. When we read "the LORD God," the Hebrew is *Jehovah Elohim*, and the emphasis is on the activity of divine love and divine wisdom together. When, therefore, the Lord tells Mose's that His name is I AM, He is saying that He, divine love, is Life itself—the one reality and source from which everything in the universe has its life and its existence. To recognize this is basic to any belief in God and trust in Him. In the chapter which follows our lesson the Lord gives Moses the power to work certain miracles which will help to convince his people, as well as Pharaoh,

---

*A similar device is followed in the Revised Standard Version. See RSV footnote at Exodus 3:15.

that he is really commissioned by the Lord. Then Moses raises a final objection. He says that he is not eloquent but is "slow of speech, and of a slow tongue." How often we raise this objection when we are asked to approach others with the message of our church! And the Lord says to us, as to Moses: "Who hath made man's mouth? or who maketh the dumb, or deaf, or the seeing, or the blind? have not I, the Lord? Now therefore go, and I will be with thy mouth, and teach thee what thou shalt say." Read here Luke 12:11-12. And the Lord gave Moses Aaron his brother to go with him and to speak for him. We are told in the writings (AC 6998) that Moses here represents the truth as it proceeds from the Lord and Aaron the "doctrine of good and truth of the church." When we are called either to amend our own lives or to engage in missionary efforts for the church, we need to realize that if we recognize that the work is the Lord's work and the truth His truth and sincerely desire to serve Him and the neighbor, not looking to ourselves for wisdom and power, He will be with us and put the right words in our mouths. Our failures come from self-consciousness and from trust in self rather than in the Lord.

Another incident in our chapter for today should be noted. The Lord told Moses (verses 21, 22) that when the time came for them to leave Egypt, He would give them favor in the eyes of the Egyptians and that every woman should "borrow of her neighbor, and of her that sojourneth in her house, jewels of silver, and jewels of gold, and raiment." This promise was carried out (Exodus 12: 35, 36), and the things received from the Egyptians in this way were later used in the construction of the tabernacle. When we turn from worldly living to begin our journey to the promised land of heavenly character, we do not discard everything we learned in our former life. We take with us all the knowledge we have acquired which can be serviceable to our new life. To "spoil" the Egyptians is to remove these knowledges from their merely worldly context so that they can be made to serve their true use. Knowledge is power: power for evil or power for good, according to the use we make it serve.

From the Writings of Swedenborg

Charity, n. 158: "When a man sincerely, justly, and faithfully does the work that belongs to his office or employment, from affection and its delight, he is continually in the good of use, not only to the community or public, but also to individuals and private citizens. But this cannot be unless he looks to the Lord and shuns evils as sins; for . . . to look to the Lord and shun evils as sins is the 'first' of charity; and the 'second' of charity is to do goods. And the goods that he does are goods of use, which he does every day, and which, when he is not doing, he thinks of doing. There is an interior affection which inwardly remains and desires it. Hence it is that he is perpetually in the good of use, from morning to evening, from year to year, from his earliest age to the end of his life. Otherwise he cannot become a form, that is, a receptacle of charity."

Suggested Questions on the Lesson

P. Where was Moses brought up? *palace in Egypt*
J. How long did he live in Egypt? *forty years (Acts 7:23)*
J. Why did he have to flee? *killed Egyptian*
P. Where did he go? *land of Midian*
J. Who was Midian? *son of Abraham and Keturah*
J. How long did Moses stay in the land of Midian? *forty years*
P. Near what mountain was he when the Lord called him? *Horeb (Sinai)*
P. What was he doing there? *tending sheep*
P. How did the Lord call him? *burning bush*
J. What did He tell him he was to do? *lead Israelites out of Egypt*
J. Was Moses eager to undertake this great task? *no*
J. What did the Lord tell him? *"I will be with you"*
J. What did the Lord tell Moses to have the women do before they left Egypt? *"borrow"*
I. What does Egypt represent? *state of acquiring knowledge*
I. Why did the Israelites become slaves when they stayed there too long? *knowledge must be used in service to Lord*
S. What does the land of Midian represent in a good sense? *simple faith*
I. Why did Moses stay in each land forty years? *full state of testing*
S. What is pictured by the burning bush? *Lord's speaking to us through our memory*
I. What does Moses represent? *divine law*
S. In what ways do we sometimes act like Moses? *hate to start serving the Lord, make excuses*

THE TEN PLAGUES

Exodus 7-10

Cover the necessary facts connecting this lesson with the last one as briefly as possible at the beginning of the lesson period. The teacher must use his own judgment in choice of details. Be sure to point out that if the children of Israel had gone back to the Holy Land after the famine was over as they should have done, they would never have become slaves in Egypt and would have been spared much hardship and suffering.

Doctrinal Points

What happens when we lose sight of our spiritual purpose.
How worldliness can gradually destroy our higher nature.
Why we so often stubbornly persist in evil.

Notes for Parents

The Egyptians never forgot that the Hebrews were "outsiders" and after a while became afraid of their growing numbers, and the Pharaohs began to try to curb them. They made them slaves, and at last one Pharaoh ordered that all the male children of the Hebrews should be killed as soon as they were born. Everyone remembers the familiar story of how the infant Moses was saved.

Moses was preserved by the Lord and finally commissioned by Him to lead the children of Israel out of Egypt and back to their true home in the Holy Land. Pharaoh naturally wanted to keep his slaves, and the story of the ten plagues, which is our lesson for today, is the story of how his stubborn resistance to the Lord's will was gradually broken.

What does this teach us about our own lives? All who love the Bible have recognized the Holy Land as a symbol of heaven. Heaven is our true home. We live on earth for a few years and find the earth beautiful and full of pleasures, but if our life here is too easy, we are likely to forget that after all we are only strangers in the earth and "sojourners, as all our fathers were." If we let the world make slaves of our higher faculties, our character deteriorates, just as the land of Egypt was progressively devastated by the plagues brought on by Pharaoh's stubborn determination not to let the children of Israel go home and worship God. All the good things which the Lord gives us in this world—and they are many—are meant for use, to help us develop the love to the Lord and the neighbor which make heaven in our souls both here and hereafter.

Primary

Review briefly the birth and call of Moses, but be sure to leave time for reading part of the current lesson from the Word. Read at least Exodus 8:1-15. If you can leave sufficient time, the list of the ten plagues may be read to the class from the Junior Pupils' notes, although you cannot discuss any but the second in detail.

The children of Israel stayed on in Egypt after Jacob and Joseph had died, and they had many children and became a very numerous people. After a while the Egyptians became jealous of these strangers in their land and began to be afraid that they were enemies. The Pharaohs forgot Joseph and all he had done for Egypt. They began to make slaves of the Hebrews. So then the Hebrews remembered their own land and wanted to go back there. The Lord told Moses that he was the one who should lead them out of Egypt.

He gave Moses power to work miracles, and his brother Aaron to help him.
Pharaoh did not want to let the Hebrews go.
It took ten terrible plagues to make him consent to their departure.
In the first plague Moses turned all the waters of Egypt to blood so that the people could not drink it.
What was the second plague?
How did Moses and Aaron bring it about?
Who else showed the same power to bring frogs out of the river?

But the first and second plagues were the only ones in which the magicians could do what Moses did.

What did Pharaoh ask Moses to do?

What did Pharaoh promise?

Did he keep his promise?

We ourselves often go on stubbornly doing wrong in spite of the lessons we have had.

It was only after the tenth plague, when all the firstborn in the land died in one night, that Pharaoh actually let the Hebrews go.

Don't you think he was very foolish? Did you ever suffer from being naughty and then go right back and do the same thing over again? We are sometimes just as foolish as Pharaoh was.

Junior

Part of the connecting story has been given to the Juniors in the form of questions. Looking up in class the references given after the questions may take too much time. If the pupils cannot answer any given question, the teacher should answer it briefly, but the pupils should be encouraged to look up and read the Bible passages afterward at home. The lesson to be emphasized is suggested in the last paragraph of the pupils' notes.

The word *exodus* means a "going out," and the book of Exodus is the story of how the children of Israel were finally let out of Egypt and of the first part of their journey in the wilderness. The story of Moses is another very familiar story and you will probably be able to remember it.

What command had Pharaoh given? (Exodus 1:15-16)

What did Moses' mother do to save him? (Exodus 2:1-4)

Who adopted Moses? (Exodus 2:5-10)

Why did Moses have to flee from Egypt? (Exodus 2:11-14)

Where did he go? (Exodus 2:15)

Who was Moses' father-in-law? (Exodus 2:16-21)

Where was Moses when the Lord called him? (Exodus 3:1-6)

What did the Lord tell him to do? (Exodus 3:10)

What signs did the Lord give Moses? (Exodus 4:1-5)

Who did the Lord tell him would be prepared to help him? (Exodus 4:14-17)

What request did Moses and Aaron make of Pharaoh? (Exodus 5:3)

How did Pharaoh answer? (Exodus 5:4-9)

Now comes our lesson for today. Moses first showed Pharaoh the sign of his power which the Lord had taught him. Aaron cast his rod down and it became a serpent. Pharaoh called in the magicians and sorcerers of Egypt and they were able to do the same thing; only Aaron's rod swallowed up their rods. These men knew how to do magic because they understood how things in nature are produced by things of the spirit or mind. This knowledge of correspondences had come down to the Egyptians by tradition, and it was one of their favorite studies. Because they and people like them used this knowledge for evil purposes, it was afterwards lost. Bad men can often do things which outwardly seem like the deeds of good men; but there are many things they cannot do because they are not good and the Lord's power is not available to them. So the magicians of Egypt could do only the simplest of the things Moses did.

Our lesson today shows us how the Lord through Moses and Aaron and the rod sent one plague after another upon the Egyptians. There were ten plagues in all:

1. All the water in the land was turned to blood.
2. Millions of frogs came up from the river and got into everything.
3. The dust of the earth was turned into lice (or gnats).
4. Swarms of flies covered everything in the land.
5. A murrain (a deadly disease) killed all the animals.
6. Everyone—even the magicians—had boils.
7. A terrible hailstorm and fire destroyed the young crops.
8. Locusts ate up everything that was left.
9. Absolute darkness was upon the land for three days.
10. The firstborn of everyone in the land died in one night.

None of these plagues afflicted the Hebrews. You would think that Pharaoh would soon have realized that he must let the Hebrews go. Several times when a plague was at its height, he promised to let them go, but when the plague was over, he would change his mind. Do we ever do that? When we do wrong things and get into trouble, we usually determine to do better, but when the trouble is over, we often forget.

From time to time as the plagues went on, Pharaoh's magicians and his servants begged him to give in, but he was very stubborn. It is always hard for someone who is used to having his own way in everything to admit that he is wrong. The tenth plague finally broke his resistance and he let the children of Israel go, although you may remember that he afterward changed his mind again and pursued them and had to be overcome by the power of the Lord at the Red Sea.

When you come into the Intermediate class, you will study the deeper meaning of the plagues. Each one teaches us a particular lesson about what happens when we persist in refusing to obey the Lord. Everything good in our souls is gradually destroyed until the time comes when nothing can save us from spiritual death.

Intermediate

For this class the connection should be made by calling attention to the fault of the Hebrews in not returning to their true home, noting the death of Joseph in Egypt, and explaining the meaning of the difference between the Pharaoh who made Joseph ruler and the later Pharaoh who "knew not Joseph." This will make it easy to take up the general meaning of the plagues and of Pharaoh's stubbornness.

Recently we had a lesson in the right use of our memory-knowledge. The Pharaoh of Joseph's time represents a good principle ruling in the outmost plane of our mind, a principle which recognizes the wisdom which comes only with knowledge of the Lord and His purposes and is willing to put the desire to serve the Lord above all other motives, as Pharaoh set Joseph over the whole land of Egypt. Then in the Bible story Jacob and all his family were brought down into Egypt and settled in the land of Goshen in the rich Nile delta, where they could be preserved through the seven years of famine.

But today our picture is very different. Jacob and Joseph died in Egypt. You remember that Jacob pictures goodness in the outward or natural plane of life; and Joseph, the interior goodness which should develop in us if we live rightly, and which is what connects us with the Lord. But sometimes when a person has reached the point where he lives a good outward life and perhaps by joining the church has made the acknowledgment that his life should be lived in service to the Lord, he settles down right there and feels that he is now a pretty good person and doesn't need to go any further.

The children of Israel, when they left the Holy Land, expected to go back to their true home as soon as the famine was over. But Joseph died, and they were too comfortable and too indifferent to go back. And gradually they forgot their own land and even their own God. When the Lord spoke to Moses from the burning bush (Exodus 3), Moses had to ask Him by what name He should be called. In the story the children of Israel represent the higher part of our nature in which the Lord can dwell. The Egyptians represent the side of our nature which connects with the physical world. So you can guess what is meant by the time when the Egyptians had made slaves of the Hebrews. A Pharaoh has come to the throne who "knew not Joseph."

Chapters 7 through 11 of the book of Exodus tell the dramatic story of the ten plagues which were visited upon the Egyptians because of Pharaoh's hardness of heart. These plagues were not punishments, although Pharaoh felt them to be. Neither was it the Lord who "hardened" Pharaoh's heart, even though the letter of the Word says so. You remember that the letter of the Word often speaks in the language of "appearances," that is, it expresses the truth as the evil see it. Just as the Hebrews in the story blamed Moses for their troubles, so it seemed as if the Lord must be keeping Pharaoh from seeing his own folly. But Pharaoh's stubbornness was all his own, and the plagues were only outward manifestations of the evils in his own heart and of the falsities in his own mind.

When a person settles down to enjoy an easy natural life and forgets his duty to the Lord, the love of self and the world gradually perverts all good and destroys all truth in his heart and mind. This is what the plagues picture. The turning of the waters into blood pictures the falsification of truth, that is, the use of truths to support evils of which we are fond. So, for example, people who do not want to go to church or think about religion but are quite willing to give a little something to charity, may point to their "good deeds" and quote the Lord's saying, "Inasmuch as ye have done it unto one of the least of these my brethren, ye have done it unto me." The frogs, lice, flies, and boils are particular types of evil and falsity which overrun the mind; the destruction of the crops and cattle is the killing out of goodness in the heart; and the darkness which finally covers the land is the final inability of such a mind to see anything spiritual. The final plague, the killing of the firstborn, pictures the fact that a person who has reached this state cannot produce any real and lasting truth or goodness in his life. Each plague is a wonderful study in correspondence.

One would think that Pharaoh would have been convinced long before he was, but his conduct is typical of those who do not want to change their selfish ways. When they are in trouble, they make promises of amendment, but once the trouble is past, they fall back into their former state. That explains why Swedenborg says that no one is regenerated in a state of physical illness or by the prospect of immediate death. Fear merely serves to check the accomplishment of evil desires. It does not really change the desire. Such change must be of our free choice.

Basic Correspondences

Pharaoh	=	when good, the principle of right living; when evil, the principle of worldliness
the children of Israel	=	our spiritual possibilities

Senior

The meaning of the individual plagues can be discussed in this class. The important lesson is the danger of allowing oneself to fall captive to worldly and materialistic reasoning because of its insidious effect on the mind and heart.

"The natural in the man who is being created anew, that is who is being regenerated, is entirely different from what it is in the man who is not being regenerated." (AC 5326) This is a key to the meaning of our present lesson. The Pharaoh who made Joseph ruler of Egypt stands for the natural side of the person who is being regenerated, and the Pharaoh who stubbornly insisted on keeping the Hebrews as slaves, in spite of the plagues with which his land was afflicted, represents the natural side of the person who is not being regenerated. We need to remember that it is of our own free choice that we are or are not regenerated.

Egypt is the plane of memory-knowledge, and the Egyptians represent that part of us which lives on that plane and depends upon it for regular subsistence. The children of Israel—here and throughout the rest of the Old Testament—represent "the church" in us, that higher plane of our nature in which the Lord properly dwells. So the story of how the Pharaohs gradually forgot Joseph and came to make slaves of the Hebrews is the story of how, even in a life which has recognized the Lord and been set in outward order according to the Lord's truth, worldliness can creep in and take possession, enslaving the higher nature.

We wonder sometimes how people become criminals, how anyone growing up can fail to see that "crime does not pay." The Pharaoh of this lesson gives us the answer to this question. In the mind of a person who thinks himself wiser and more powerful than anyone else, any effort to show him the Lord's truth—as pictured by the appeal of Moses and Aaron—awakens more and more stubborn resistance, and as the effort continues it reveals his inner state more and more deeply.

The ten plagues picture this progressive appearance of deeper and deeper falsities and evils which have developed in the inner life of the wholly materialistic and worldly person. The turning of the waters into blood is his turning of truth into falsity by making it support his selfish purposes. The frogs which were brought up out of the river afterward are the enjoyment he takes in his selfish reasoning. It is not hard to see why the magicians of Egypt could reproduce these two miracles, but we should notice that Pharaoh had to appeal to Moses to get rid of the frogs. The magicians could not undo their work.

The plague of lice or gnats is a picture of how the mind of such a man is infested by sensual desires which spring from "the dust of the earth"—the same dust which the serpent was condemned to eat, you remember—and the swarms of flies which followed are the countless false thoughts which fly about and settle in his mind as a result of these sensual desires. The next discovery is that all his natural good desires have wasted away—the murrain or plague on the cattle—and his interior evils begin to break out on the surface, as boils reveal the presence of poison within the system. Then follow the hail and the locusts, the destruction of everything true and good in the outward life, and finally the plague of darkness, picturing the mind no longer able even to see truth. The last plague, the killing of the firstborn, represents the fact that there is no life left in any of the things in which such a person puts his faith, because there is no good left in the heart.

This picture of degeneration is a dark one, but it is very true, as anyone can testify who has tried to speak of spiritual things to a confirmed materialist. The only bright spot in the picture is the fact that the children of Israel are restless under the yoke of Egypt and that Moses and Aaron have been commissioned by the Lord to lead them out. As we have seen, we have to "go down into Egypt" many times during our lives, but we must always keep in mind the purpose for which we have gone there and the fact that our proper home is the Holy Land of spiritual living. And if we are captivated by the apparent advantages of a life in Egypt, we must break the chains that hold us there and take the difficult road back. In this journey it is Moses, the law of the Lord, who is our leader.

Adult

There are plenty of discussion topics here: the change in Egypt from the time of Joseph to the captivity, the ten plagues themselves, the power of the magicians, Pharaoh's stubbornness. The quotations at the end of the lesson may also be used.

For anyone without a knowledge of correspondence, the chapters of Exodus which recount the story of the plagues present unanswerable questions. In the letter the Lord instructs Moses to lie to Pharaoh by telling him that the Hebrews merely want to go three days' journey into the wilderness to sacrifice to their God. In the letter it is said that the Lord hardened Pharaoh's heart. The murrain, or plague, is said to have killed all the cattle of Egypt, but immediately afterward those Egyptians who fear the Lord are told to take their cattle into their houses to protect them from the hail. A question is raised, too, by the fact that the magicians of Egypt were able to perform some of the miracles which Moses performed.

But a knowledge of the essential nature of the letter of the Word, as revealed by the Lord in His Second Coming, not only answers all these questions but makes the whole story of the plagues a wonderful study in the specific evils inherent in a materialistic philosophy of life and their destructive effects.

In the first place we recognize that the letter of the Word took its form from the impact of divine truth upon the minds of those through whom it was written. Thus, the deception practiced by Moses represents the measure of his ability to comprehend and fulfill his mission. His own fearfulness intervened to twist the message, just as later his own pride prompted him to take credit for bringing water out of the rock and so condemned him to die without entering the Holy Land. The Lord permitted these appearances in the literal account for our instruction. In the same way, Pharaoh's stubborn resistance to enlightenment is permitted to appear as an act of God, because there are people who can be restrained only by fear of God and of punishment by Him. Pharaoh's repeated changes of mind were foreseen by the Lord indeed, but they were the result of Pharaoh's free choice.

We recall that the Pharaoh who made Joseph ruler over Egypt

pictures the principle which rules the natural level of the mind of the person who is regenerating—what Swedenborg calls the "new natural." Recent biblical research tells us that this Pharaoh was of the line called the "shepherd kings." The Pharaoh of our lesson today—who was of a different line—represents the principle of worldliness which rules the natural level of the mind of the person who is not regenerating. This principle resists with all its power any effort to set free in the mind those higher spiritual faculties which are represented by the children of Israel. Perhaps we have had the experience of trying to introduce New Church teachings into the mind of some thoroughly worldly person and have been shocked at our inability to make any impression and at the revelation of what lay back of an apparently orderly and pleasant exterior. The story of the plagues is the story of such a revelation.

There were ten plagues, preceded by the miracle of the rod becoming a serpent, and followed by the "spoiling" of the Egyptians. These plagues were not in any sense arbitrary manifestations of divine power. Pharaoh, stubbornly insisting upon the bondage of the Israelites, pictures the natural level of the mind insisting on keeping the spiritual level in subjection. When a person is in this state, true order is inverted and power from the Lord flowing into his will and understanding is turned to destruction, the destruction of what is good and true. This destruction proceeds gradually, by successive steps, represented by the successive plagues; at first only annoying for a time, but later beginning to destroy the necessaries of life and finally depriving him of all that is dearest to him. Swedenborg tells us that all noxious things are created through evils in men.

The plagues in Egypt actually took place, but they were wrought not as punishments from the Lord but as materializations—for our instruction—of the actual, inevitable results in the soul of centering one's affections and thoughts on the natural world and on self-gratification through it. In reading the story we note that the magicians of Egypt were able to reproduce the first two plagues but no further ones, and that as soon as their power was insufficient, they recognized that Moses had power from the divine (Exodus 8:18-19). We learn from the writings that the magic practiced in the eastern countries was accomplished by means of the knowledge of correspondence which they had by tradition from the Ancient Church.

A point which always strikes us in this story is Pharaoh's seeming stupidity in requiring so many disasters to convince him. But our own experience may be cited in answer. Have we, for example, never suffered from overeating, and did we learn from one such experience? When we are suffering from the effects of some physical indulgence, we think how foolish we were to do it and resolve to change our habits, but how quickly we forget once the suffering is over! We are taught that no one is regenerated through punishments. Punishments, however, are inevitable results of wrongdoing, and the plagues are a wonderful study in the progressive devastation wrought by persistent materialism, one of the most universal temptations of our modern world.

The meaning of the various plagues can be studied in detail only by reading the *Arcana*, but we should note that they follow each other logically. For example, the first plague, the turning of the water into blood, represents the falsification of truth—what we do when we use truth or twist it to support what we want to believe—and when this is done, the next step is to derive enjoyment from constant reasoning from this falsity. This is the plague of frogs. Swedenborg develops the meaning of each of the plagues and gives many illuminating illustrations.

The Plagues

1. All the water in the land was turned into blood: Truth being falsified.
2. Frogs were brought up from the river and filled everything in the land: The mind becoming full of the enjoyment of arguing from falsity.
3. The dust of the earth was turned into lice (or gnats): Sensual desires excited by the contemplation of earthly pleasures.

4. Swarms of flies settled on everything in the land: All sorts of false thoughts filling the mind.
5. A murrain—a wasting disease—killed all the cattle: All natural good impulses being gradually destroyed.
6. The people broke out with boils: Interior evils manifesting themselves on the surface of the life.
7. The hail and the fire following it destroyed the young crops: Falsity from evil destroying in the mind the truths of the church learned in childhood.
8. Locusts ate up the later crops: Falsity on the outermost plane destroying all remaining goodness.
9. Absolute darkness was upon the land for three days: The mind having become unable to see any genuine truth.
10. The firstborn of everyone in the land died: The "damnation" of those who are in faith separate from charity.

From the Writings of Swedenborg

Arcana Coelestia, n. 7273: "*And I will multiply My signs and My wonders* (Exodus 7:3). That this signifies warnings of every kind, nor shall anything be wanting, is evident from the signification of 'signs and wonders,' as being confirmations of the truth . . . and also means of Divine power . . . here warnings; for thereby they both saw that they were in falsities, and saw the Divine power, and in this way were warned. The reason why it is said that to those who are in falsities warnings are given of every kind, nor shall anything be wanting, is that the condemnation of those who are in evils is not effected in a moment when they come into the other life, but after they have first been visited, that is, examined. The examinations are made in order that they themselves may take notice that they cannot but be condemned, because they have not lived differently, and also in order that spirits and angels may know that they have been of such a character; so that they can no longer be excused either by themselves or by others."

Arcana Coelestia, n. 7280: "*And the Egyptians shall know that I am Jehovah* (Exodus 7:5). That this signifies that they shall be in fear of the Divine, is evident from the signification of 'knowing that I am Jehovah,' as being to be in fear of the Divine (of which below); and from the signification of 'the Egyptians,' as being those who are in falsities and infest. As regards the fear of the Divine in which they who are in falsities and infest will be, be it known that fear is the only means of restraining the infernals and holding them in bonds. For fear is a common bond, both for those who are upright, and for those who are evil; but for those who are upright the fear is internal, which is fear for the sake of salvation, namely, lest they should perish as to their souls, and so lest they should do anything contrary to conscience, that is, contrary to the truth and good which are of conscience; consequently they have fear lest they should do anything contrary to what is just and fair, thus contrary to the neighbor; but this is holy fear in so far as it is conjoined with the affection of charity, and still more as it is conjoined with love to the Lord. . . . Such is the 'fear of God,' so frequently spoken of in the Word. But with those who are in evil there is no internal fear, namely, for the sake of salvation, and thence for the sake of conscience; for such fear they have utterly rejected in the world, both by their life, and by the principles of falsity favoring their life; but instead of internal fear they have external fear, namely lest they should be deprived of honors, of gain, or of reputation for the sake of these, lest they should be punished according to the laws, or be deprived of life. These are what are feared by men who are in evil, while they are in the world. As, when such men come into the other life, they cannot be restrained and held in bonds by internal fear, they are held by external fear, which is impressed on them by punishments. From this they are in fear of doing evil; and at last they are in fear of the Divine, but as before said external fear, which is devoid of any desire to desist from doing evil from the affection of good, but only from dread of the penalties, which they at last feel horror at."

Suggested Questions on the Lesson

P. What mistake did the children of Israel make after Joseph's death? *stayed in Egypt*
J. Why did the Egyptians become afraid of them? *multiplied*
P. What did the Pharaohs do to them? *made them slaves*
P. Whom did the Lord raise up to lead them out of Egypt? *Moses*
J. What power did the Lord give Moses? *to plague Egypt*
J. What sign did he give him to use to prove his power? *rod → serpent*
P. Who was chosen to help him? *Aaron*
P. What did Moses ask of Pharaoh? *let people go*
J. How did the Lord tell them to try to convince him? *threaten plagues*
P. How many plagues were there? *ten*
P. What was the first plague? *water → blood*

P. What was the second? *frogs*
J. What was the last one? *firstborn died*
J. How many of the plagues could the magicians imitate? *first two*
I. What does Egypt represent in our lives? *plane of worldly knowledge*
I. What is pictured by the captivity of the Israelites in Egypt? *our higher nature enslaved by worldliness*
S. What in general is represented by the ten plagues? *successive steps of degeneration of a stubbornly worldly person*

THE PASSOVER

Exodus 12

Discuss the change of state of the Israelites in Egypt and review briefly the birth and call of Moses. Do not try to go into detail about any of this or about the plagues, except for the final one, which is involved in the lesson for the day.

Doctrinal Points

We must always remember that it is the Lord who delivers us from evil.

The Passover is one of the events which, as it recurs again and again in the Word, helps us to see the whole Word as one book.

Everything we have learned can be made of spiritual use to us.

Our worship should always inspire us to put into immediate practice what we learn from the Word.

Notes for Parents

The word *exodus* means "a going out," and the book of Exodus is the story of how the children of Israel, after more than two hundred years in Egypt, were led out by Moses and back through the wilderness to their true home in the land of Canaan, the Holy Land.

The Israelites came into Egypt to be nourished and protected by Joseph through the years of famine. Egypt, because of its steady climate, was the great storehouse of the ancient world, to which people went to buy food when drought and famine struck other places. It pictures the world's store of knowledge, to which we must go when we realize that we do not know enough to take our next step in life. Sometimes it is knowledge of the natural world which we need, but there is another kind of knowledge in the storehouse: knowledge of the Bible and of the teachings of our church. Knowledge, however—all knowledge—is meant for use in the service of the Lord and the neighbor. When we forget this and become absorbed in learning for its own sake or for the sake of self-advancement, we are like the Israelites who stayed on in Egypt after Joseph died. Joseph pictures our higher spiritual perceptions. Without these we become slaves in Egypt just as the Israelites did. Life becomes hard and burdensome.

Moses was raised up to lead the children of Israel out of slavery. Moses, through whom a little later the ten commandments were given, represents divine law. This law shows up all of the false thoughts and the evil desires of selfish and worldly living but, if obeyed, it leads to heaven all who wish to be good people.

The Israelites were commanded to celebrate a great feast on the eve of their leaving Egypt. It was called the feast of the Passover because when the blood of the lamb killed for the feast was sprinkled on the doorposts and lintel of their houses, it became a sign which enabled the "angel of death" to pass over them when the firstborn of the Egyptians were killed. The Israelites were commanded for the future to keep this feast regularly as a memorial of their deliverance from Egypt. They keep it to this day.

It was at the feast of the Passover in Jerusalem just before the Lord was betrayed that He instituted the feast of the Holy Supper which takes the place of the Passover in the Christian Church. The Lord is called the "Paschal Lamb," and we celebrate the Holy Supper in remembrance of Him and in acknowledgment of the fact that He came into the world to save us and that, if we follow and obey Him, He will lead us out of bondage to sin, and on to our true home in heaven.

Primary

Be sure the children know the names of the first two books of the Bible and what the two words mean. After reading the lesson from the Word emphasize the feast of the Passover and why it was given that name. Go into the details of the Passover feast itself and stress the command to observe it always as a memorial of the deliverance from Egypt.

What is the second book in the Bible called?

Exodus means "a going out."
The book tells about how the children of Israel finally went out of Egypt and back to their true home in Canaan.

Nearly two hundred years had passed since Joseph's death, and the kings of Egypt had forgotten all about Joseph and how much they owed to him. So the children of Israel, although they still lived in the rich land of Goshen, were not safe and happy anymore. They had increased from the seventy who came with Jacob to six hundred thousand people, and the Egyptians were worried. So the king had made them slaves, and finally he even ordered that all the boy babies of the Hebrews should be killed.

Who was raised up by the Lord to free them?
The Lord gave Moses power to bring ten plagues, one after another, upon the Egyptians. What was the last plague?
How were the children of Israel told to save their own sons?
What feast were they to celebrate before they left?
How was the lamb to be prepared for eating?
What were they to eat with it?
How were they to be dressed when they ate it?
Why was this feast called the *Passover*?
What command was given regarding its later observance?
What were they to remember whenever they observed it?

Try to remember this feast of the Passover and why it was so named, for you will hear of it many times in the Bible story.

Junior

In covering the review and introduction be sure the Juniors have the answers to all the questions in their notes. The historical aspects of the lesson should be stressed—length of time in Egypt, increase in numbers, continuation of the Passover to the present day, etc.—and finally the connection between the Passover and the Holy Supper should be brought out and emphasized.

What is the name of the second book in the Bible?

Exodus means "a going out." The book tells the story of the fulfillment of Joseph's prediction (Genesis 50:24), which did not come for almost two hundred years after he died. Read Exodus 1:8. This is the key to all that followed. Let us see how much you remember of the story:

Why had the Egyptians become afraid of the Hebrews?
What had Pharaoh done to them?
How many plagues did Moses and Aaron bring upon the Egyptians?
What was the final plague?

The children of Israel had been saved from all the plagues. But from the tenth they were saved in a special way. They had to do something themselves.

What was it?
Why was the feast to be called the *Passover*?
What did it consist of?
How were they to eat it?

In verse 2 of our chapter we learn that this event was so important that the Lord told the Hebrews to change their calendar so that the month of the Passover should be the first month of their religious year. It was one of the spring months. Their months were governed by the phases of the moon and do not exactly coincide with any of our months. So this first Hebrew month sometimes begins in March and sometimes early in April, depending on the moon. Many years afterward the Lord was crucified during the Jewish Passover week; so our Easter still comes just after the Passover. This is why Easter does not always come on the same day of the month.

For the children of Israel the Passover marked their deliverance not only from the tenth plague but also from their bondage in Egypt, for they started on their journey that very night. The Egyptians were so glad to see them go that they willingly gave them jewels of silver and gold, and raiment. The word translated "borrow" (in KJV) really means "ask" (as it is translated in RSV). The things were presents—not merely loans. Many of them were later used in carrying out the Lord's instructions for the building of the tabernacle.

How many children of Israel were there when they left Egypt?

Look up Genesis 46:26-27. This shows us how the children of Israel had increased in Egypt. Verse 40 of our chapter says that they had been in Egypt for four hundred and thirty years, but this is counting from the time when Abraham first went down to Egypt because of the famine. It was actually about two hundred and fifteen years from the time when Jacob and his family came into Egypt to live until the time of the Passover.

We must study this story of the Passover with special care, for we shall be reminded of it many times in the Bible, even in the New Testament. The Jews still celebrate the Passover every year, although not in exactly the original way. Do you know why we Christians do not celebrate it? It is because the Lord, when He was on earth, gave us a new feast to take its place. That feast is the Lord's Supper or the Holy Communion. The Lord instituted it when He was partaking of the Passover feast with His disciples for the last time. In the book of Revelation the Lord is called "the Lamb that was slain." The Jews celebrate the Passover to commemorate their deliverance from Egypt. We celebrate the Lord's Supper to commemorate our deliverance from the power of the hells as a result of the Lord's life on earth.

Intermediate

The lesson for this class is the general meaning of the Passover and the correspondence of the details of the feast, and this should be carried over into a discussion of the Holy Supper.

We have studied the birth of Moses, his preparation and call by the Lord, and the ten plagues which he was permitted to bring upon the Egyptians in order to induce Pharaoh to let the children of Israel go back to the land of Canaan. They should have gone back as soon as the famine was over. A time of famine, you remember, pictures a crisis in our lives when we do not know what to do and realize that we need more knowledge; the land of Egypt pictures the plane of memory-knowledge. Egypt with Joseph as its ruler pictures the whole field of external truth as to both natural and spiritual things properly related to our true purpose in life. This means knowledge of the letter of the Word and in addition, for us in the New Church, knowledge of the writings of Swedenborg by means of which the Lord shows us the true doctrine to be drawn from the Word. We need this knowledge.

But we might spend all our lives studying the Bible and the writings and find the study very interesting and absorbing without ever trying to use what we learn to discover and correct our own evils or to help other people. This is what is pictured by the fact that the children of Israel did not go back to the Holy Land when the famine was over. They found themselves comfortable and prosperous in Egypt and forgot their true home and their duty to the Lord and finally even the name of their own God. The principle which had ruled them when they first came to Egypt had changed: "There arose up a new king over Egypt, which knew not Joseph." (Exodus 1:8) The Israelites gradually became slaves, just as we, if we do not use our knowledge in the Lord's service, become slaves to mere learning. Life becomes a burden and the Lord has to show us—sometimes by hard experiences—the way back to happiness.

For the Israelites, the deliverance from bondage in Egypt marked the great event which made possible the development of their nation and their religion. They were told to make the month in which they left Egypt the first month of their year, and the Passover was celebrated from the fourteenth to the twenty-first of that month. When the Lord came to Jerusalem the last week of His life on earth, it was to celebrate the Passover. So you can remember that the Passover is always celebrated by Jews during the week preceding our Easter.

The Passover was named from the fact that the houses of the Hebrews were passed over by the "angel of death" in the night when the firstborn son of everyone else in Egypt died, as well as the firstborn of all cattle. This was the tenth and last plague, and pictures the final result of a wholly worldly and selfish life, when there is no longer any possibility of the development of a living faith, which is represented by the firstborn. This is the state in which all those are who are in the hells; Swedenborg tells us that they reject any good or truth which is presented to them, just as

Pharaoh and the Egyptians finally were eager to drive out the Israelites, and even to give up with them their "jewels of silver and jewels of gold and raiment," which picture all the good and truth which remained in their possession.

The Passover feast was to become a memorial of deliverance. You may remember that in one of the visions of the book of Revelation the Lord is seen in the form of a lamb "as it had been slain." The lamb is the symbol of innocence. Swedenborg tells us that innocence is "to know, acknowledge, and believe, not with the mouth but with the heart, that nothing but evil is from one's self, and that all good is from the Lord." The word *innocence* means "harmlessness," and if we stop to think, we shall realize that it is always pride in ourselves which makes us say and do things which hurt other people. If we try to be honest and see ourselves as we really are deep down inside, the Lord can give us this quality of innocence. But we must really want to know the truth about ourselves. This quality of innocence must be sought from love—this is the symbolism of "being roast with fire." Unleavened bread pictures truth or goodness unmixed with any false ideas. Bitter herbs represent temptations—there will be some hardship and difficulty connected with our journey to heaven. And we are to be ready to start on this road at once, to put into immediate practice our good resolutions.

For the Jews the Passover was, and still is, celebrated as a memorial of the deliverance of their nation from bondage in Egypt. The Lord at His last Passover gave the Christian Church a new feast to celebrate in its place—the feast of the Holy Supper. For us the Lord is the paschal lamb who came on earth, took on our nature with all its temptations, and gave His life to us for our example. When we worship Him in the Holy Supper and accept Him as our example, we are "eating the paschal lamb," for He called the bread and wine His body and blood. The celebration of the Holy Supper—like the Passover in its deeper meaning—pictures our full realization of the evils to which a worldly and selfish life leads, and our determination with the Lord's help to turn our backs upon such a life and travel the long hard journey to the Holy Land, under the guidance of divine law—which is represented by Moses. We take with us all that is valuable of our worldly knowledge and accomplishments, and our characters just as they are up to the point of our new resolution. Verses 34 to 39 of our chapter picture this. We are not suddenly made over into good and wise people as some churches try to believe. Conversion is not salvation. Conversion is merely the resolution to change our ways. All the trials and temptations are still to come, and we shall make many mistakes and suffer many failures before we reach even the borders of the Holy Land itself.

Basic Correspondences

the firstborn	=	faith
a lamb	=	innocence
leaven (yeast)	=	falsity
bitter herbs	=	temptations

Senior

The meaning of the change in the condition of the Israelites because they prolonged their stay in Egypt is important for the Senior age, as well as the necessity for the plagues and the meaning of the details of the Passover feast, especially as carried over into our celebration of the Holy Supper.

Today our lesson is again from the second book in the Bible. The word *exodus* means "a going out," and the book of Exodus is the story of how the prediction made by Joseph in Genesis 50:24 was finally fulfilled some two hundred years later. Verse 40 of our chapter says the "sojourning of the children of Israel" in Egypt was four hundred and thirty years, but this is counting from the time when Abraham first came down into Egypt because of the famine.

The picture has changed. We are told in Genesis 46:26-27 that the number of souls belonging to Jacob at the time of his coming into Egypt was seventy, and verse 37 of our chapter for today says that six hundred thousand men went out on the night of the

Passover, besides children. This great increase had frightened the Egyptians into making slaves of the Hebrews so that their life in Egypt was no longer a happy one.

In the Bible narrative, any stay in Egypt represents a period of acquiring memory-knowledges. To save our spiritual lives we have to acquire memory-knowledges of the letter of the Word and of the doctrines drawn from its internal sense. But all knowledge is meant for use in the service of the Lord and the neighbor. As fast as we acquire new knowledge, we should try to put it to use. The Israelites should have gone back to their own home in Canaan as soon as the famine was over. When we continue to study and learn without applying our knowledge to its proper use, we become "slaves in Egypt." We are no longer protected by Joseph—our spiritual perceptions—and, like the Israelites, we have forgotten the name of our God—the qualities which the Lord exemplified in His life on earth.

Then the Lord has to arouse us by showing us the terrible results of worldliness and godlessness. These are the plagues brought upon the Egyptians, culminating in the destruction of the firstborn.

The firstborn is the symbol of faith. When anyone, like Pharaoh, stubbornly persists in a worldly and evil course, in spite of repeated experiences of the bad effects of such a course, he finally comes into a state in which the very possibility of faith is destroyed. Then all the things of spiritual life—represented by the Israelites—are driven out, taking with them everything that is of value in the learning which has been acquired. This is the plague from the point of view of Pharaoh.

But we are going with the Israelites. They had been spared all the plagues, but they had seen the terrible havoc they had wrought in the lives of the Egyptians, and were ready now to follow Moses out of Egypt. Moses represents divine law. To escape the last plague they had to do something themselves, both as a sign of their willingness to obey the Lord and in recognition of their deliverance.

The lamb of the Passover represents the affection of innocence.

What this is you will see from the first quotation at the end of this lesson. The blood of the lamb symbolizes the true thoughts which spring from that affection. The doorposts of the house stand for the portals of the mind. The sprinkling of the blood there pictures the safeguarding of the mind from falsity by means of true thoughts springing from pure affection. When the lamb was eaten, it was to be "roast with fire," not raw or "sodden with water" (boiled), because good must be loved, not merely acknowledged without interest or enjoyed as a mental concept. The unleavened bread pictures principles of goodness unmixed with the old false ideas, for leaven (yeast) in those days was a bit of sour dough from former bakings. The bitter herbs typify temptations which we must be willing to meet and overcome if we are to attain spiritual life. Finally, we are to eat the feast with our loins girded ready for the journey: we must be prepared to start out actively to carry the new principles we have accepted into our daily living—we cannot put off "turning over a new leaf" from day to day. We are also to take with us into the new life all that is of value from the Egyptian state, all our knowledges of worldly as well as of spiritual things, the jewels of silver and gold, and the raiment. Recall that Abraham also came up out of Egypt "rich in cattle, in silver, and in gold."

Just before the Lord's crucifixion He celebrated the Passover with His disciples—the Last Supper, as it is called. At that feast He instituted a new feast to take the place of the Passover for all His disciples, and thus for the Christian Church. This is the Lord's Supper or Holy Communion. In the Lord's Supper the bread and wine take the place of the unleavened bread and the flesh of the lamb, and the Holy Supper commemorates our deliverance by the Lord from bondage to the hells. So in this particular case, as in all others, the Lord came to "fulfill" the Law and the Prophets.

Adult

It has been thought best to center the lesson in the Adult notes on two or three major themes. Other points may come up, however, and the teacher should be thoroughly prepared. Further very interesting discussion material may be found especially in AC 7984, 7995, and 8005.

It is important to remember that the Israelites in the first place came down into Egypt to be nourished—under Joseph's protection—during the years of famine. They should have returned to their own country when the famine was over. But their home in Egypt seemed to promise more ease and prosperity than they had ever had. Joseph died, and his body was embalmed and put in a coffin in Egypt. If we should forget that the study of the letter of the Word and of the doctrines of our church is enjoined only for the purpose of enabling us to make spiritual progress, to serve the neighbor better, and so to draw closer to heaven and to the Lord, we may find that there are worldly rewards even for this study which may seem to us more real and desirable than heaven. But if we succumb to this appeal, gradually the plane of our daily life will come to be ruled by a principle which looks to self-interest rather than to the Lord's truth for direction. As Exodus 1:8 puts it, "There arose up a new king over Egypt, which knew not Joseph."

Then the Lord has to let us learn "the hard way." The Israelites became slaves in Egypt. Life in this state is full of worldly cares and anxieties and becomes a burden. When Moses was called to lead his people out of Egypt, they had not only become slaves to Pharaoh but they were worshiping the golden calf* and had forgotten even the name of the true God. They had to be taught by bitter experience the ruin in which they had permitted themselves to become involved. The ten plagues represent the gradual uncovering by divine law—represented by Moses—of the falsities and evils to which a purely worldly life leads. Not only did the Egyptians suffer, but Pharaoh imposed harder and harder conditions on the Hebrews as the plagues progressed. Only the final plague pro-

*Or so Swedenborg implies in AC 9391[7]. There is no biblical statement to this effect. —*Ed.*

cured their release.

We are born natural, and the purpose of our life here is that we may become regenerate. "Except a man be born of water and of the Spirit, he cannot enter into the kingdom of God." In the writings, faith is called the firstborn because it is the means by which falsity and evil are overcome and we become children of the first resurrection. The firstborn of Israel were saved. But when faith is destroyed, there can be no salvation. Spiritually the firstborn of Pharaoh is the faith of obedience from fear, without any love for doing what is right. This faith does not stand in the face of severe temptation. The firstborn of Egypt dies. This is the final judgment on the evil; all memory-knowledge of good and truth finally perishes, and with it the means of amendment.

But the possessions of the Egyptians are not in themselves evil. Egypt represents the natural plane of life, not only our life in the world but the most outward state of the church—its rituals, forms, and ceremonies. As a church declines in spirituality, it tends to make its rituals more elaborate, its buildings more impressive, and to amass wealth in silver and gold. Yet these are all good and necessary things. They are a defense to spiritual life. Regular external worship, instruction, hymns and prayers, the recitation of one's faith, teaching about religion and the letter of the Word are necessary. The more we know of the letter of the Word the better we are prepared to understand its spirit. We acquire memory-knowledge of many important and useful things, and these can serve us in our spiritual life. So the Hebrews were commanded to "borrow" of the Egyptians, and they took with them into their new life the treasures so acquired. We need to "borrow" of the Egyptians "vessels of gold and silver," the letter of the Word and the forms of worship which contain and protect the real treasure of the church, love to the Lord and the neighbor. And we also need to borrow "raiment," the commandments in their letter, the moral truths and principles of life kept as laws of man and of earthly success. We should appropriate from what our memories receive everything that serves and supports spiritual life.

Following the last plague the Passover was instituted. It was to become the most important of the Jewish feasts, and was to be observed annually as a memorial of their deliverance from Egypt. And this festival has been kept by the Jewish Church down the ages to the present day.

We are probably familiar with the thought that lambs represent innocence, and that eating lamb represents appropriating this quality of innocence. But just what is innocence? We associate the quality with little children, and think of their simplicity and trust and their ignorance of any real evil. This is the "innocence of ignorance" of which Swedenborg speaks. But when the Lord says, "Except ye be converted, and become as little children, ye shall not enter the kingdom of heaven," He is not asking us to return to a state of ignorance. Swedenborg speaks of another kind of innocence, which he calls the "innocence of wisdom." The word *innocent* means "not harming," and we need to recognize that all desires we may have to injure others—whether these desires are impulsive and fleeting or deep-seated and rankling—are from the love of self. In AC 3994, in interpreting Jacob's choice of black lambs as his wages in Haran, Swedenborg says that black signifies what is man's own, and continues, "An own [*proprium*] that is innocent is to know, acknowledge, and believe, not with the mouth but with the heart, that nothing but evil is from one's self and that all good is from the Lord; and therefore that what is man's own is nothing but blackness; that is to say, not only the own of his will, which is evil, but also the own of his understanding, which is falsity. When man is in this confession and belief from the heart, the Lord flows in with good and truth." This is the innocence of wisdom, which the Passover lamb signifies.

To sprinkle the blood of this lamb on the doorposts and lintel of the house is to write this truth on every thought we permit to enter the mind and on every desire also. To eat the lamb "roast with fire" instead of raw or "sodden with water" is to receive it from love, not without love nor yet from the mere enjoyment of knowing it. Unleavened bread is truth purified from falsity and bitter herbs signify "by means of temptations." That all of it shall be used means that it shall be made part of us "from the inmost to the external." And verse 11 means that we should stand prepared to think and act in every respect from this deep conviction with regard to self and the Lord.

The journey from Egypt to Canaan was to be long and difficult, although the people were not aware of this. This journey is the symbol of our spiritual journey from natural to spiritual living, and the Passover was the preparation for it. At the Passover feast immediately preceding His betrayal and crucifixion the Lord said to the twelve, "With desire I have desired to eat this passover with you before I suffer." Then He instituted the Holy Supper, which for the Christian Chruch takes the place of the Passover and is given to strengthen and protect us in our journey of life. In this new Christian form the Passover will be celebrated forever.

The lamb that was sacrificed in the Passover represents the Lord. So John the Baptist declared, "Behold the Lamb of God, which taketh away the sins of the world." In its inmost meaning the lamb is the Lord as to His divine innocence, the offering up of every selfish and worldly impulse and the complete consecration to the divine will and guidance.

From the Writings of Swedenborg

Arcana Coelestia, n. 3994: "In all good there must be innocence in order that it may be good. Charity without innocence is not charity; and still less is love to the Lord possible without innocence. For this reason innocence is the very essential of love and charity, consequently of good. An own [*proprium*] that is innocent is to know, acknowledge, and believe, not with the mouth but with the heart, that nothing but evil is from one's self, and that all good is from the Lord; and therefore that what is man's own is nothing but blackness; that is to say, not only the own of his will, which is evil, but also the own of his understanding, which is falsity. When man is in this confession and belief from the heart, the Lord flows in with good and truth, and insinuates into him a heavenly own, which is white and lustrous. No one can ever be in true humility unless he is in this acknowledgment and belief from the heart; for he is then in annihilation of self, and thus in absence from self;

and in this manner he is then in a state capable of receiving the Divine of the Lord. It is by this means that the Lord flows in with good into a humble and contrite heart."

Arcana Coelestia, n. 7996: "In general, feasts, both dinners and suppers, in ancient times were made within the church in order that they might be consociated and conjoined as to love, and that they might instruct one another in those things which are of love and faith, thus in the things of heaven . . . Such at that time were the delights attending their banquets, and such was the end for the sake of which were their dinners and suppers. Thus the mind and the body also were nourished unanimously and correspondently; and from this they had health and long life, and from it they had intelligence and wisdom; and also from this they had communication with heaven, and some had open communication with angels. But as in the course of time all internal things vanish away and pass into external ones, so also did the purposes of the feasts and banquets, which at this day are not for the sake of any spiritual conjunction, but for the sake of worldly conjunctions, namely, for the sake of gain, for the sake of the pursuit of honors, and for the sake of pleasures, from which there is nourishment of the body, but none of the mind."

Suggested Questions on the Lesson

P. What happened to the Israelites in Egypt after Joseph died? *became slaves*

P. Who was raised up to lead them out of Egypt? *Moses*

P. How were the Egyptians persuaded to let them go? *plagues*

P. How many plagues were there? *ten*

P. What was the last one? *firstborn died*

J. How were the Israelites told to save their own firstborn? *blood of lamb on doorway*

J. What did the Egyptians let them have to take away with them? *gold, silver, clothing*

P. What feast did they observe just before they left Egypt? *Passover*

J. Why was it called the *Passover*? *"I will pass over you"*

P. How was the lamb which they ate cooked? *roasted*

P. What did they eat with it? *unleavened bread, bitter herbs*

P. How were they dressed for the feast? *loins girded, sandals on, staff in hand*

J. What were they to do with any of the lamb that was left over? *burn it*

J. How many Israelites were there when they left Egypt? *six hundred thousand plus children*

J. What were they to remember whenever they kept the Passover? *deliverance from slavery*

J. How often were they told to observe it? *annually forever*

I. What feast takes the place of the Passover for Christians? *Holy Supper*

I. When and by whom was it instituted? *Jesus, on Maundy Thursday*

S. What does the lamb represent? *innocence*

S. What is innocence? *harmlessness, willingness to be led by the Lord*

CROSSING THE RED SEA

Exodus 13:17-22; 14

In general with the younger classes the emphasis should be on the crossing of the Red Sea, the story of the Passover being retold chiefly for the sake of getting the word *Passover* fixed in the children's minds in connection with the deliverance from Egypt.

Doctrinal Points

The Lord always protects those who trust in Him.
Goodness must be loved–not merely thought about.

Notes for Parents

Whenever any one of us realizes that he has become a slave to things of the world, the Lord "calls Moses" to lead him out of Egypt; that is, the Lord brings to his mind things of the Word of God which he has learned in childhood to remind him that his true home is not this world but heaven, and that he must free himself from the bondage into which he has drifted and set his feet once more in the path in which he was started as a little child.

But we know that habits are hard to break. Worldly desires and reasonings try to hold us fast. The bonds can be broken only as we come to see more and more clearly the disaster which surely overtakes the souls of the worldly. Moses brought ten plagues, one after another, upon the Egyptians, until finally Pharaoh knew he must let the Israelites go. The Passover feast, which they celebrated on the eve of their departure, was a feast of thanksgiving to the Lord for their deliverance.

In some churches a great deal of stress is laid upon "conversion," and we are familiar with the programs of revivalists. *Conversion* means a "turning" in another direction–in religion a turning from self to the Lord. Conversion is necessary. We have to make up our minds to "leave Egypt." But this decision, which in our story is marked by the celebration of the Passover feast, is only the first step on the way to heaven. We all know how often those who have been converted by the emotional appeal of powerful preaching to a responsive crowd very soon "backslide."

The initial decision must be followed by immediate action and then by steady progress in a new way of life, under the leadership of the Word of God, which Moses represents. This is the journey of the Israelites—a long, hard journey—from Egypt to the Holy Land through the wilderness, with the pillar of cloud and fire at their head.

Our story for today is a picture of the first temptation met and overcome in this journey. Pharaoh changed his mind and with his army pursued the Israelites to bring them back to slavery. Have we not all had related experiences? We resolve to break from some bad way of life. We start out full of determination and enthusiasm, but very soon we find all the force of our past habit following and catching up with us. It seems that we cannot possibly escape its power, that we are defeated at the outset. This experience is symbolized by the Red Sea. But Moses, instructed by the Lord, stretched forth his hand over the sea and the waters were divided. If we look to the Lord for help, He will lead us safely through this temptation.

Then the Israelites looked back and saw the pursuing Egyptians swallowed up in the sea. We learn by experience—good experience in this case—that even a seemingly irresistible temptation can be overcome with the Lord's help. Every temptation overcome in His strength shows us the actual powerlessness of the evils we have been serving. The Lord will always open the way for us if we trust and obey Him.

Primary

These children should remember *Pharaoh*, *Moses*, the *Passover*, and the *Red Sea*. They can be told that the reason why the children of Israel became slaves in Egypt was that they did not go back to the land of Canaan as they should have done when the famine was over. Emphasis should be put on the pillar of cloud and fire and on the power the Lord exercised through the hand of Moses, and the Lord's wonderful protection of His people.

After Moses grew up, he sided with his own people against the Egyptians, and this made the Pharaoh angry. So Moses had to leave Egypt. He went to the land of Midian, and there he was helped by Jethro, the priest of Midian. Moses married Jethro's daughter, Zipporah.

One day when Moses was tending the flocks of Jethro near Mount Sinai, he saw a strange sight. A bush was on fire but did not seem to be burning up. When Moses went over to look at it, the Lord spoke to him out of the midst of the fire in the bush.

The Lord told Moses to go back and lead his people out of Egypt.

He gave Moses power to work miracles, and told him that his brother Aaron would help him.

Pharaoh did not want to let the Hebrews go; so Moses and Aaron brought ten plagues, one after another, upon the Egyptians, and finally Pharaoh said they could go.

The Egyptians were so glad to see them go that they gave them gold and jewels and clothing to take with them.

Just before they left, they celebrated a great feast, called the Passover.

Before they got out of Egypt, Pharaoh changed his mind and went after them.

Where did he catch up with them?

How did the Lord keep them safe from the Egyptians through the night?

This pillar of cloud and fire was to lead them for forty years.

Then what did the Lord tell Moses to do?

What happened?

How did the children of Israel cross the Red Sea?

What happened to the Egyptians when they tried to follow?

Junior

The Juniors will remember the stories of the call of Moses at the burning bush and of the plagues. Give them an opportunity to recount what they can of these stories. In this class a little more should be done with the story of the Passover, and the reason for its name should be made clear. Attention should also be called to the command to observe the Passover every year as a memorial. Have the children study a map to see the difference between the two possible routes from Egypt to the Holy Land. The emphasis in the lesson should be put on the need of our going forward courageously on any course we know to be right, trusting in the Lord to help and protect us.

The children of Israel had been saved from all the plagues brought upon the Egyptians. But from the tenth and last they were saved in a special way.

Why was the feast they celebrate called the *Passover*?
How often were they commanded to celebrate this feast?
What did it consist of?
How were they to eat it?

The Lord also told them to change their calendar so that the month of the Passover should be the first month of the year. It was one of the spring months. Their months were governed by the phases of the moon; so they do not exactly coincide with our months, but this first month begins some time in March or April. Many years afterward the Lord was crucified during Passover week. So our Easter is always celebrated just after the Jewish Passover instead of coming on one particular date.

The Lord gave the children of Israel something to lead them on their journey. It was a pillar, a pillar of cloud by day and of fire by night, and it led them for forty years. They were to stop when it stopped and move on when it moved.

Where were they going?

Look at a map of this area. See how much shorter the journey would have been if they could have gone along near the Mediterranean Sea and through the Philistine country. But the Philistines were a strong people with fortified cities, and the Lord knew that the Hebrews were not ready as yet to do any real fighting; so the pillar led them by the longer route. Read Exodus 13:17-18.

The Egyptian people were so glad to see them go that they gave them many things to take with them: gold, and silver, and jewels, and clothing. But Pharaoh was not glad to lose his slaves. After they had left, he changed his mind again.

What else did they take with them? (Exodus 12:37)

They also had many children with them and all their herds and flocks and baggage. You can imagine that they could not travel very fast.

How did Pharaoh pursue them?
Where did he catch up with them?

They seemed to be trapped between the Egyptians and the Red Sea, and of course they had no boats.

Whom did they blame?
What did Moses tell them?
How did the Lord protect them during the night?
What did He tell Moses to do?
What happened?
How did the Israelites cross the Red Sea?
What happened to the Egyptians?

If we trust in the Lord and obey His commandments, His power will always protect us. His truth stands between us and evil just as the pillar of cloud and fire stood between the children of Israel and the Egyptians. We sometimes come to points in our lives when we do not know what to do. Every way seems full of danger. Then we must remember this story of the Red Sea. We must trust in the Lord and obey His commandments and He will open the way before us.

Intermediate

Emphasize the meaning of the Passover to the Jews and to us and show why the Christian Church celebrates the Holy Supper in its place. These young people will soon be looking toward confirmation and should understand the nature of the decision we are all called upon to make if we wish to be true followers of the Lord. Another good lesson for this age group is the necessity of carrying a good resolution into immediate action and pushing boldly forward, no matter how hard the right course may seem.

For us the coming of the Lord into the world to deliver us from slavery to the hells was so great an event that the Christian world counts the years from it. and even non-Christian nations have followed suit. For the Jews the deliverance from bondage in Egypt is the great event which started the development of their nation and their religion. They were told to make the month in which they left Egypt the first month of their year, and they still count their religious calendar on this basis although they also have a secular calendar—still different from ours—according to which they celebrate their New Year in the early autumn. Passover is celebrated from the fourteenth to the twenty-first of the first month of their religious calendar. The Lord came to Jerusalem for the last time on the first day of that week for the purpose of celebrating the Passover. So you may always remember that the Jewish Passover is celebrated during our Holy Week, the week before Easter. And you of course know that the Lord on the night of that last Passover feast instituted the Holy Supper, which takes its place for the Christian Church.

The Passover took its name from the fact that the houses of the Hebrews were passed over by the "angel of death" on the night when the firstborn in Egypt were slain. This was the tenth and last plague, and pictures the final result of a wholly worldly and selfish life—the time when there is no longer any possibility of the development of a living faith. The Passover feast was to be a memorial of the deliverance of the Jews from bondage, and it pictures our acknowledgment of our deliverance from bondage to the world and self. The lamb is the symbol of innocence, and this quality is to be loved and made a part of our lives. The word *innocence* literally means "harmlessness," and the quality of life it refers to consists in complete dependence upon the Lord for guidance and strength, because we recognize that of ourselves we are constantly inclined to evil. The lamb was to be eaten roasted with fire because love must be the heart of innocence. The unleavened bread of the Passover pictures goodness unmixed with false ideas. The bitter herbs remind us that there will be hardship connected with our journey to heaven. And as the Hebrews were to eat the feast with their loins girded, their shoes on their feet, and their staves in their hands, so we are to be ready to start out actively on this journey to heaven, to put our good resolutions into immediate practice.

The journey of the children of Israel from Egypt to the Holy Land is quite generally recognized as picturing the journey which every person who reaches heaven must take, but the symbolism is seldom carried further than a vague general idea. We see the journey as the gradual renunciation of worldly and selfish standards. It is never an easy journey. Many trials and temptations have to be endured and many enemies overcome before we reach even the border of the promised land of heavenly character. These are pictured by the various experiences of the Israelites in leaving Egypt and in the wilderness. Throughout their whole journey, the Lord led them by means of a pillar of cloud by day and fire by night. Swedenborg tells us that this pillar was actually a company or "choir" of angels with the Lord in their midst. The Lord's angels are messengers of truth, and it is the truth which both guides and protects us on our journey. Thus, the pillar of cloud and fire pictures the Word in its letter with the Lord Himself within it, as it leads us in our spiritual days and nights: our states of confidence and trust (days), and our states of doubt and discouragement (nights).

On this journey we set out boldly. But we have not gone far before the whole weight of our past selfish life catches up with us and tries to drag us back. We are faced by a sea of doubt and disbelief and fear. Our temptation is to give up. The children of Israel said, "Because there were no graves in Egypt, hast thou taken us away to die in the wilderness?"

But the Lord speaks to us through Moses: "Fear not, stand still, and see the salvation of the Lord." Our first need is for steadfastness and trust. As the Israelites obeyed, the pillar of cloud and fire went around and stood behind them, between them and the Egyptians, giving light and protection to the one, blocking the path of the other with darkness. The Word is not only our guide in our spiritual journey, but is also our protection from our enemies. The evil cannot see the truth of the Word because, since their minds are turned toward self, it is darkness to them. Read John

3:19-21.

The Red Sea here pictures an accumulation of falsity and evil. Swedenborg says it pictures hell. The Lord by means of the hand of Moses—the power of divine law—will disperse the barrier if we go forward boldly. First we must stand fast to our purpose and then go forward as the Lord opens the way. And once we have come safely through this first great temptation, we can look back and see how helpless is the enemy which seemed so threatening.

Basic Correspondences

bread	=	goodness
leaven	=	falsity
fire	=	truth as it is in the Lord, coming from His divine love
cloud	=	truth in the form it takes on earth, or the letter of the Word
the Red Sea	=	an accumulation of falsity from evil—or hell

Senior

Make the distinction clearly between the first decision to follow the Lord instead of self, signalized by the Passover; the period of reformation of our external conduct, the wilderness journey; and the process of regeneration or opening our hearts to the influx of a new will from the Lord, the conquest of the Holy Land. The correspondence of the actual lesson for the day will carry its own moral.

We recall the meaning of the period of bondage in Egypt, which ended with the raising up of Moses to lead the people back to the Holy Land, and we all remember the story of the ten plagues and of Pharaoh's final capitulation when the firstborn were slain. The firstborn is the symbol of faith. When one, like Pharaoh, stubbornly persists in a worldly and evil course, he finally comes into a state in which the very possibility of faith is destroyed. Such a person simply cannot believe in the existence of anything above the material plane. Then the Israelites, who represent the things of spiritual life, are finally driven out, taking with them all that is of real value (Exodus 12:35-36). This is the story from the point of view of the Egyptians.

But we are going with the Israelites. They had been spared all the plagues, but they had seen the terrible havoc wrought by them in the lives of the Egyptians, and they were ready now to follow Moses out of Egypt. To escape the last plague they had to do something themselves as a sign of their willingness to obey the Lord. This was the celebration of the Passover and the sprinkling of the blood of the slain lamb on the sideposts and lintel of their doors.

Let us review the meaning of this feast. The lamb represents pure and innocent affection; and its blood, the true thoughts which spring from that affection. The doorposts and lintel of the house stand for the portals of the mind. The sprinkling of the blood there pictures the safeguarding of the mind from evil by means of true thoughts springing from pure affection. The lamb was to be "roasted with fire" rather than eaten raw or "sodden with water" (boiled), because good must be loved, not merely thought about. The unleavened bread pictures principles of goodness unmixed with old, false ideas, for leaven (yeast) in those days was a bit of old, sour dough saved from former bakings. The bitter herbs are the difficulties which we must be willing to encounter if we are to attain spiritual life. And we are to eat the feast girded for the journey; we must be prepared to start out actively to carry the new principles we have adopted into our daily living. We are also to take with us into the new life all our knowledges of worldly as well as of spiritual things, the jewels of silver and gold and the raiment of the Egyptians.

The Lord's leading of the children of Israel by means of a pillar of cloud by day and of fire by night has a beautiful symbolism. Throughout the Scriptures clouds picture the letter of the Word in which the Lord veils His truth and accommodates it to our feeble sight. We cannot see Him as He is, any more than the physical eye can gaze at the sun. During our states of clear thinking—the daytime—we are led by the Lord through our knowledge and understanding of the Word. At night, in our states of mental darkness, we are led by our faith in the Lord's love. We say, "I don't understand why these things should happen to me or to my loved ones, but I know that the Lord loves me and them; so there must be a good reason." And we try to remain loving and kind in spite of our disappointments, and gradually the night passes and we find that we have made progress. So the Lord leads us both by day and by night. The pillar represents support.

The dramatic incident of the crossing of the Red Sea pictures the overcoming of the first great temptation which one has to face when he makes up his mind to serve the Lord instead of self. It comes early in the journey. How many people, "converted" at revival meetings, succumb to this temptation and go back to their Egyptian bondage as soon as their natural desires "catch up" with them! The sea looks too deep to cross. And indeed we cannot cross it on our own strength. But the Lord's power, the hand of Moses, will make a path for us through the waters if we will but go forward, and after the temptation is past, we look back and wonder why we were so dismayed. We shall have many other trials and temptations, but we have left Egypt, we have tasted victory, and we shall never go back to the old bondage. "For the Egyptians whom ye have seen today, ye shall see them again no more forever."

Adult

The lesson to be stressed is that if we are genuinely trying to obey the Lord and are willing to trust in Him, He will always open the way before us. We should learn to recognize anxiety as a sign that we are trusting in self instead of in the Lord and to see the difference between foresight and worry.

Our thought about our lesson for today should be prefaced by refreshing our minds concerning the Passover and its significance. Let us first look up four references: Numbers 9:1-5, Joshua 5:10-12, II Kings 23:21-23, and Matthew 26:17-30. These tell us about the first anniversary of the Passover celebrated in the wilderness of Sinai, the celebration of the Passover at Gilgal immediately after the entrance into the Holy Land under Joshua, the celebration of the Passover under Josiah after he found the book of the law which had been lost, and the celebration of the Passover by the Lord on the evening before the crucifixion. These are enough to indicate how necessary it is to have the signification of the Passover clearly in mind if only that we may understand subsequent Bible history. The Passover in general may well be associated in our minds with our thought of "conversion." In some churches much stress is laid on this experience, every effort being made through revivals and other means to lead people to it. In the New Church we recognize the necessity of conversion—of making the decision to turn away from self and toward the Lord—but we do not feel that it must necessarily take some immediate striking outward manifestation. Conversion is only the first step toward regeneration. We are all born natural, and must sometime, if we are to become spiritual, determine of our own free will to break our bondage to natural thoughts and affections and start on our journey toward a heavenly character. The Passover symbolizes this decision. The slaying of the firstborn of the Egyptians pictures the fact that it is impossible that any spiritual life should spring from the natural itself. The passing over of the houses on which the blood of the paschal lamb was sprinkled symbolizes the possibility of spiritual life with those who determine to look to the Lord for knowledge and power instead of to themselves. This decision is indeed a momentous one and we should keep it fresh in our memories, recalling it at the beginning of new undertakings, renewing it after periods of waywardness, and confirming it as we grow older by coming reverently to the Lord's Supper.

The actual feast of the Passover was one of the acts enjoined upon the Jewish Church as part of its representative worship, relating men to the Lord through correspondences during the period when they were actually so far from Him that there could be no interior conjunction. The Lord, when He was upon earth, bridged this gap Himself and reestablished the connection, and by instituting the Holy Supper did away with the need of continuing to keep the Passover. It was after He had eaten of the Passover with His disciples that He took the cup, broke the bread, and bade His disciples "do this in remembrance of me." Swedenborg speaks of this as the last Jewish and the first Christian Passover. That is, the Passover commemorated the deliverance of the Jews from bondage in Egypt, and the Holy Supper commemorates the reality of which that was the shadow—the deliverance of man from bondage to hell by the Lord Himself. The bread of the Lord's Supper takes the place of the flesh of the paschal lamb and has the same significance as the blood of the lamb. The Lord speaks of the bread and wine as His body and blood, and He is called the Paschal Lamb.

The Hebrews by command ate the Passover feast with their loins girded, their shoes on their feet, and their staves in their hands ready to depart from Egypt. We have all experienced the first pleasure that comes with a new resolution, the eagerness to carry it out, and the ideas and plans which spring to the mind while it is in this first state. And we have all experienced the fact that this first enthusiasm does not last. For our resolution marks the beginning of a long period called the period of reformation. Before we can even enter the border of the Holy Land of spiritual living, we have the task of putting our external lives in order according to the Lord's laws. The journey of the Israelites to Canaan represents this period of reformation. The pillar of cloud and fire which led them throughout their forty-year journey represents the letter of the Word which leads and also protects us, both in our daytimes of clear understanding and in our nighttimes of doubt and uncertainty. Swedenborg tells us that the actual pillar was a "choir" of angels with the Lord in their midst. Clouds always picture the letter of the Word; a cloud with fire within it, divine truth from divine love. Moses represents divine law as it connects man with God.

The first great event of the journey of the Israelites was the crossing of the Red Sea. This represents the first practical test of our new determination, the first temptation to be overcome, confirming our decision. It is a vivid picture, and one which our own experience readily verifies. Here are the children of Israel hastening on their way, led by the wonderful pillar. They have left the land of Goshen in haste, but with rejoicing and eagerness and confidence. Suddenly they find the Red Sea blocking their path and at the same time realize that Pharaoh and his chariots and his horsemen are in close pursuit. They must either cross the apparently impassable sea or be captured and brought back to slavery. How often, in some moment of high thought, we make a decision to break the chains of a long-standing bad habit! Almost immediately we are tempted; we realize that the power of our past indulgence is pressing close upon us, that if we do not break this particular temptation now—immediately—we shall slip back into the same old ways; but it seems impossible to take the right way. The story says to us, "Trust in the Lord and go forward. The Lord is with you and will uphold you." The Red Sea pictures an accumulation of evils and falsities which bounds the worldly and selfish life—specifically hell—but when the hand of Moses—the power of divine law—is stretched forth over it, the threatening waters will roll back under the strong east wind of truth from the Lord, and we shall pass over on dry ground—the firm basis of good character.

And once we are across, the very temptation which has been overcome will prove to us that our former bad habit is powerless when we obey the Lord and trust in His help. Pharaoh's army and his horsemen are drowned in the Red Sea. The chariots of the Egyptians are the doctrines of falsity of the natural worldly man; and the chariot wheels, the power of advancing these doctrines against our spiritual purpose. We should remember this story. The conquering of the first temptation after a new good decision is very important. We recall that although the Israelites in the wilderness many times looked back with longing to the "good things" they had enjoyed in Egypt (Numbers 11:5), they never went back.

From the Writings of Swedenborg

Arcana Coelestia, n. 8192: "*And the angel of the Lord set out.* [Genesis 14:19] That this signifies a setting in order by Divine truth is evident from the signification of 'setting out' as being a setting in order. That 'to set out' denotes a setting in order is because the pillar of cloud—which was an angelic choir—that had previously advanced before the sons of Israel, now betook itself between the camp of the Egyptians and the camp of Israel, and thus brought darkness upon the Egyptians, and gave light to the sons of Israel; and because these things were thus set in order by the Lord, by means of the setting out of the angel of God, or the pillar, and by means of its interposition, therefore by 'to set out' is here signified a setting in order. . . . Be it known further, that in the Word 'an angel' is spoken of, when yet many are meant; as in the present case, where it is said 'the angel of God,' and there is meant the pillar which advanced before the sons of Israel, and which was constituted of many angels. Moreover, in the Word angels are mentioned by name, as 'Michael,' 'Raphael,' and others. They who do not know the internal sense of the Word believe that 'Michael' or 'Raphael' is some one angel who is supreme among his associates; but by these names in the Word is not signified some one angel, but the angelic function itself, thus also the Divine of the Lord in respect to that which belongs to the function."

Arcana Coelestia, n. 8215: "*And he took off the wheel of his chariots.* That this signifies the power of inflicting falsities taken away, is evident from the signification of 'to take off' as being to take away; from the signification of 'a wheel' as being the power of advancing . . . and from the signification of 'the chariots of Pharaoh' as being doctrinal things of falsity . . . Chariots were of two kinds: there were chariots for conveying merchandise, and chariots for war. By chariots for conveying merchandise were signified doctrinal things of falsity; and by chariots for war were also signified doctrinal things in both senses, but fighting ones, thus the truths themselves, and the falsities themselves, prepared for war. From this it can be seen what is meant by 'the wheel of a chariot,' namely, the power of advancing, here of inflicting falsities and of fighting against truths. As this power belongs to man's intellectual part, by a 'wheel' is also signified the intellectual part in respect to those things which are of doctrine. In the other life there frequently appear chariots . . . These things appear when the angels discourse in heaven about doctrines."

Suggested Questions on the Lesson

J. How did Moses and Aaron finally persuade Pharaoh to let the Hebrews go? *plagues*

J. What great feast did they celebrate on the eve of their departure? *Passover*

P. What did the Egyptians give them? *jewels of gold and silver, clothing*

P. How did the Lord lead them? *pillar of cloud/fire*

J. What did Pharaoh do after they left? *pursued*

P. Where did he catch up with them? *Red Sea*

J. How did the Lord protect them through the night? *pillar of cloud between*

P. How did they cross the Red Sea in the morning? *waters parted miraculously*

P. What happened to the Egyptians when they tried to follow? *drowned*

S. What is pictured by the children of Israel's leaving Egypt? *deciding to stop being merely worldly and to seek spiritual way of life*

I. What does the Red Sea represent? *accumulation of falsity from evil*

S. What is pictured by the destruction of the Egyptians? *permanent removal of slavery to worldliness*

MARAH AND ELIM

Exodus 15

Cover briefly the story of Moses' return to Egypt and the events of the Exodus through the crossing of the Red Sea. Point out that one would think that after witnessing so many miracles the Israelites would never have doubted or disobeyed again. Yet the sense of deliverance, changing so soon to discouragement and murmuring is one of the keynotes of the whole wilderness story, and with the older classes this may be stressed as an experience common to all of us when we embark upon the effort to reform our lives according to the teaching of the Word. We are familiar with the expression "the ups and downs of life." This can be applied not only to changes in our worldly circumstances but to changes in our spiritual states as well. Our chapter starts with an "up" which is followed by a "down," and it ends in another "up." This gives an outline for taking up the lesson.

Doctrinal Points

We can always rely on the Lord to protect us if we obey Him.

The pillar of cloud and fire represents the letter of the Word in which the Lord's love glows even though it is partly concealed.

Every difficulty we meet in life is an opportunity to increase our spiritual strength.

A genuine desire to do what is good can make all our experiences sweet.

Notes for Parents

The wonderful story of the ten plagues in Egypt, the Passover feast, and the crossing of the Red Sea are stories we have recently studied. The lesson for today begins with the song of victory sung by the Israelites after their miraculous delivery from Pharaoh's army at the Red Sea.

Have you ever had some remarkable escape and felt thankful and been sure you would never forget it? How soon did you forget? Most of us forget very soon. When the next trouble comes along, we are just as fearful and just as rebellious as ever. This was true of the children of Israel in the Bible story. As we read our Bibles, we wonder sometimes how the Jews could have witnessed so many miracles and still have been so easily turned to the worship of idols. But don't we do just the same thing? The Lord does many wonderful things for us and we mean to be good people, but somehow the ways of the other people around us and the desire for the good things of this world all too easily lead us astray. For a long time the good life seems dry and hard. It is like the wilderness through which the Israelites were traveling, where for three days they found no water. Water is the symbol of truth—we all speak of a "thirst for knowledge." The Lord will always give us truth when we ask for it, but sometimes we do not like it when we hear it. The desire to serve the Lord and other people is the only thing which can always make the truth sweet to us. This is the first part of the lesson for today.

The second part is the beautiful picture of the oasis at Elim, "where there were twelve springs of water, and seventy palm trees." If we are faithful, the Lord always provides that every so often when we are tired and discouraged, we shall come suddenly into a quiet, happy, peaceful state when we feel how good the Lord is to us and how surely He tells us the right way of life. We need these moments to prepare us for further progress. Perhaps they may come at a time when our children are being good and affectionate and we realize how much we love them and how sad it would be not to have them. They will come more often if we cultivate the habit of reading the Bible with the children at bedtime and talking with them about the Lord's teachings in it. You have probably known old people who find great joy in reading their Bibles. They did not just begin to read them. They started long ago, and learned gradually how much the habit could help them.

Primary

This class should be able to get the whole outline of the story from Moses' return to Egypt to the encampment at Elim. Stress the pillar of cloud and fire, and compare it to the teachings of the Bible in our lives.

When the Israelites left their homes in Egypt, the Lord led them in a wonderful way. They saw a pillar of cloud in front of them which at night turned into a pillar of fire, so that they could always see it. It moved along before them and they followed it wherever it went, and when it stopped, they knew they must also stop and wait for it to move on.

First it led them to the Red Sea, and the Lord divided the waters by a miracle so that they could go across on dry ground. By this time Pharaoh had changed his mind and was following them to bring them back, but when his horses and chariots started across the Red Sea, the water closed and drowned them.

Moses and the people sang a song of triumph in praise of the Lord.
Who led the women in singing?
On what instrument did she play?
A timbrel is a kind of tambourine.
The journey to the Holy Land was not to be a short or an easy one.
What was the first trouble they had after they crossed the Red Sea?
How did the Lord help them?
What was the name of the place where this happened?
Marah means "bitter."
What was their next stopping place?
What did they find there?
You can imagine how happy they must have been to be able to rest in this pleasant place.
Dates, which grow on palm trees, are one of the principal foods of the people of the eastern countries.

Junior

On a map point out that a much shorter way from Egypt to the Holy Land would have been along the shore of the Mediterranean; have them read Exodus 13:17-19 to see why the people were not led that way. Read also to them Exodus 12:37-38 to give them the impression of the multitude. Then continue with the lesson, following their notes.

When the children of Israel left Egypt, the Lord led them by means of a pillar of cloud which at night became a pillar of fire. They were to follow it wherever it led them and to stop wherever it stopped. It led them first to a certain point on the shore of the Red Sea. By the time they got there, Pharaoh had changed his mind and sent an army to pursue them and bring them back. But the Lord parted the waters of the Red Sea before them. The Israelites crossed safely, but when Pharaoh's army followed, the waters closed over them and they were drowned.

Our lesson for today begins with the song of praise and thanksgiving which Moses and his people sang after their enemies had been destroyed. We need to remember that in all this rejoicing over enemies, the Bible is really speaking of the enemies of our souls, our wrong feelings and thoughts which we should be fighting all the time. Read Matthew 5:43-48 to see what the Lord tells us about how we should look upon people who seem to be our enemies. He does not want us to rejoice at anyone's misfortunes. But when He has helped us to put away our wrong thoughts and feelings, we should rejoice and thank Him for the victory.

Who besides Moses sang a song of triumph?

Miriam was the sister of Moses and Aaron. A timbrel is something like a tambourine. After these songs of triumph they started on their journey.

How far did they go before they found water?
What was the matter with the water when they found it?
What did they name the place?
How did the Lord tell Moses to make the water sweet?
Water symbolizes truth. When you have been doing something wrong and someone tells you the truth about yourself, do you find the truth sweet?
Can you think what can make it sweet?

The children of Israel were starting on a new life. They had had a hard time in Egypt, but they had always had enough to eat and drink and a home to sleep in at night. Now they were out in the wilderness, sleeping in tents and not really knowing where their next meal was to come from. They often thought it might have been better to have stayed in Egypt. It is just the same when we start out to try to live as the Lord wants us to live instead of just pleasing ourselves. At first we miss some of the kinds of fun we had in being selfish and we find the new life "dry." We see that it is the right way to live, but we don't enjoy it. But if we will keep on trying, reminding ourselves that we want to please the Lord, presently we shall begin to enjoy our new ways of thinking and feeling. This desire to please the Lord, to be truly good, is the "tree" which Moses was told to put into the water. Anything we do from love for others brings us happiness.

What was the next place to which they came?
What did they find there?

In all desert regions there are places like this, which are called *oases*. Caravans which have to cross the desert are planned so that they go from one oasis to another, so that they can stop and rest in the shade of palm trees, gather dates for their supplies, and replenish their water. As we travel through life, we shall have many long, hard places to go through, but we know that the Lord will surely give us times of great happiness and peace which make us know that we are on the right road and help us to gather courage and strength to go on. These are the oases in our life journey. And this is what Elim pictures. The Lord kept the children of Israel at Elim for about a month, by means of the pillar of cloud and fire. Then He saw that they were rested and refreshed and ready to move on again.

Intermediate

The lesson to impress at this age is that the right way is sometimes hard, but that the Lord is always with us to help us, and that if we obey the commandments, we shall be saved from much disappointment and unhappiness and will eventually come into greater joy than the worldly life can know. The correspondence of the journey can be given in some detail.

You remember from the story of Abraham that the land of Egypt pictures "memory-knowledges." Egypt was the storehouse of the ancient world. They have little rain there, but every year the Nile River overflows its banks and covers the whole valley with a layer of fresh soil brought down from the mountains. Then for the rest of the year the people irrigate the valley from the river; so it is very unusual for a drought or famine to affect Egypt. When Pharaoh brought Joseph out of prison and made him ruler over his land, one of the things he did—because of the interpretation of Pharaoh's dream—was to prepare for a drought and a famine that were to come. We have to "go down into Egypt"—to seek new knowledge—every time we feel such a need, but this knowledge is meant to be brought back to our Holy Land of service to the Lord. Moses was to lead his people back.

This was not an easy task. He had to convince his people that the Lord had really sent him and that they should follow him, and he had to convince Pharaoh by means of the ten plagues that the Hebrews must be let go. The children of Israel, according to the Lord's direction, borrowed gold and silver and jewels from their Egyptian neighbors, celebrated the Passover feast, and started on their journey, led by the Lord by means of a pillar of cloud by day which became a pillar of fire by night. When they came to the Red Sea, they found that Pharaoh had changed his mind and was pursuing them; but the Lord parted the waters and let them pass through on dry ground, and then brought the waters together again and drowned their pursuers.

Our lesson today begins with the song of triumph which Moses sang, giving praise and thanksgiving to the Lord for saving them. And then in verses 20 and 21 we read that Moses' sister Miriam, and all the other women, sang a similar song of triumph. This is the first time that we read of singing in the Bible. The song was, of course, in the Hebrew language, and the music was in the form of a chant, something like the chants we sometimes sing in church. Indeed this is the only way in which words of the Bible can be sung without changing them a great deal. Such chants were natural to the Jews, and they are still a part of worship in Jewish synagogues. Singing is a natural form of expression for our feelings;

so it corresponds to such expression. We find many songs in the Bible. All of the Psalms are songs. The ancient Hebrews were famous for them. Read Psalm 137.

After these songs of praise (which represent our immediate feeling of thanksgiving to the Lord when we have been delivered from some great danger or temptation) the children of Israel started on their journey through the wilderness. Their leaving Egypt to go back to the Holy Land pictures a time when we see that our life has been wrong and we determine to begin a new life. Many things make this hard to do. We never decide to do right without being immediately tempted to do wrong; this is represented by coming to the Red Sea and finding that the Egyptians are following. The same old selfish thoughts try to catch up with us. Then, if we have courage enough to overcome this first temptation—to cross the Red Sea—we find that a new kind of tamptation is waiting for us.

We read that "they went out into the wilderness of Shur; and they went three days in the wilderness, and found no water." When we turn our backs on our old bad habits, we hardly know at first how to live any other kind of life. You know that water corresponds to truth. A wilderness is a place which is not cultivated and where few people have made homes for themselves. Swedenborg tells us that it corresponds to an "obscure state." That means a state of mind in which we do not see our way clearly: we have to "feel" our way, as we say. In such a state we need truth very much and do not seem able to find it. Moses himself was in the same state as the rest of the people. All they could do was to follow the pillar of cloud and fire. For us this pillar represents the letter or literal sense of the Word. Even before we really come to the point when we see clearly what we ought to do and what life is all about, we know enough of the commandments and of the teachings of the Lord when He was in the world to lead us in the right direction. In the Bible the letter of the Word is often described by the term "clouds"; you can see why if you think a little. Clouds hide the sun; yet the sun is there shining through them; also, rain which we need so regularly falls from the clouds. So the letter of the Word sometimes hides the full understanding of the Lord's love and wisdom (the sun); yet these are within it shining through, and the letter of the Word gives us the truth day by day as we need it.

Finally the children of Israel came to a place they called *Marah* because they could not at first drink the bitter water which they found there. *Marah* means "bitter." And Moses "cried unto the Lord; and the Lord shewed him a tree, which when he had cast into the waters, the waters were made sweet." Wood is one of the many symbols of goodness in the Word. Casting the wood of the tree into the water is to put good or the love of doing good into the truths we learn, and this always makes them pleasant. Often we find that something the Word tells us we ought to do is not just what we should like to do; the water is bitter. But if we think about how much we owe to the Lord and how willing we ought to be to do what He tells us is right, we shall soon find it easy and pleasant to obey. It is only selfishness which makes truth seem bitter.

Then the cloud led the people on further: "And they came to Elim, where there were twelve springs of water, and seventy palm trees: and they encamped there by the waters." Have you ever resisted some temptation which presented itself to you perhaps in school or on the playground, and gone home feeling that maybe you had been foolish and cheated yourself out of a lot of fun, and then suddenly found that being able to face your mother and father without anything bothering your conscience made you feel so free and happy that it was worth a good deal more than the temporary fun would have been? This happy, satisfied state is pictured by the twelve springs and seventy palm trees. Springs of water picture truth; palm trees are symbols of good—the kind of good which comes from recognizing that the Lord's saving power was on your side helping you to resist temptation. When you know that you have done right, you feel "good." When we resist temptation and refuse to do wrong, the Lord always gives us this happy feeling and lets us enjoy it for a little while before we go on to a new temptation.

Basic Correspondences

clouds	=	the letter of the Word
palm trees	=	good through the Lord's saving power
wilderness	=	a spiritual state in which the mind has no settled home

Senior

All the stories of this period are applicable to the life of young people of this age. They see the worldly life all about them and constantly feel its temptations. They know it is not easy to be good, but often young people are urged to take the step of "commitment to Christ" without being shown what to expect or how to meet the tests that will come to them. The wilderness journey in its internal sense is the part of the Bible which most clearly meets just this need.

We all know the story of how Moses, in the power given him by the Lord at the burning bush, went back to Egypt, persuaded his people to accept him as their leader, and (by means of the ten plagues) finally convinced Pharaoh that it would be wise to let the Hebrews go back to their own land. We know the story of the first Passover, and of the miraculous crossing of the Red Sea.

So long as the natural and worldly desires and thoughts in us rule over our spiritual inclinations and thoughts, we cannot be in a healthy and happy spiritual state. The ten plagues picture the progressive deterioration of such a life until finally the person is not capable of producing any genuine good affection or any true thought which can live and grow—the tenth plague was the slaying of the firstborn of everything in the land. When a person realizes that he has fallen into this state and determines to break away, the Lord is always there providing leadership and guidance and protection for his new way of life. But the change is not an easy one. Old habits soon try to catch up with us, as Pharaoh's armies pursued the children of Israel. At the Red Sea, they were right behind. The Red Sea pictures the first great temptation to stop and turn back. You remember that the Lord told Moses to lift up his rod over the sea, and the waters rolled back and allowed the people to pass through on dry ground. Moses pictures the letter of the law: and his rod, the power which is in that letter when it is obeyed. When temptation comes, we should repeat to ourselves one of the commandments which applies to the particular temptation we are facing, and then go straight forward in the power of the truth. The way will open before us, the enemy will be swallowed up behind us, and we shall find ourselves safe on the other side.

This is the point at which our lesson for today takes up the story. Our chapter opens with the song of triumph sung by Moses and the children of Israel, and by Miriam (the sister of Moses and Aaron) and the other women, as they stood on the eastern shore of the Red Sea and looked back at the waters rolling over the enemy. In the literal sense such a triumphal song may seem cruel, but if we think of the Egyptians as representing worldly and selfish desires and false ideas which have been threatening our spiritual growth, we realize that rejoicing and thanksgiving are right and proper. We might note that this is the first of the many songs which we find in the Bible. Singing is a natural expression of the feelings. Even those of us who do not have particularly good voices are apt to break into singing when we are happy. Often we make up the tune as we go along, without stopping to think how surprising it is that we can. The songs of the Hebrews were chants made up in this way, the melody being composed spontaneously as the words were inspired into their minds. Some very ancient ones are still used in synagogues today. The reason why in the New Church we sometimes sing chants is that the Bible words cannot be sung in any other way without changing them a great deal: and our worship should, so far as possible, be expressed in the words of the Bible because they are what connect us with the Lord and the heavens.

After this song of praise, the people turned toward the wilderness and resumed their journey. We can imagine that, after their first experience with the Lord's saving power, they started full of courage and hope. They were led, as they were to be led for the next forty years, by the pillar of cloud and fire. This again pictures the letter of the Word, which will lead us safely even though we do not at first "see through" it. You who are starting out on life's journey are, like the Israelites, looking forward with high hopes, and you mean to live good and useful lives and to accomplish a great deal in them. You may know that if you obey the teachings of the Word, if you follow the pillar of cloud and fire, you will surely reach the Holy Land. The story of the Israelites teaches this plainly. But it teaches other things which you also need to know. The way will not be short or easy. Many things will happen to you which you cannot possibly foresee now. You will have times of hardship and disappointment: you will have battles to fight: you will not always measure up to what you know you want to be, and then you will suffer. Sometimes your life will seem to be at a standstill—the children of Israel had to stop whenever the pillar of cloud and fire stopped, and stay encamped there until it moved on. But you may be quite sure that each of these difficulties will be something you particularly need, and that if you look to the Lord for help, He will bring you safely through them, and you will be all the stronger for them.

The first thing we have to find out is that we do not know as much as we think we know. The Israelites went three days' journey into the wilderness "and found no water." In the new way we have undertaken, there are no familiar landmarks and no well-marked road. It seems at first a wilderness, and a dry wilderness. We have left behind our satisfaction with the water of natural knowledge, and have not learned how to find and enjoy spiritual knowledge. When we have tasted this state to the full (the three days' journey) the Lord brings us to the truth we need: but often we do not like it very well. We find the truth bitter when it is against our natural inclinations. The tree, or wood, which Moses was told to cast into the water, represents a genuine desire for a good life. This desire can make truth sweet to us. We have an immediate reward, if we are faithful to the truth. The people came next to Elim "where there were twelve springs of water, and seventy palm trees." The palm tree corresponds to good—the good of the wisdom which comes from the experiencing of the saving power of the Lord. All through life a good person has these experiences of quiet happiness which serve to strengthen his good resolutions and to give him courage to continue his journey. So these first two steps in the journey of the Israelites through the wilderness have very deep and necessary lessons for you as you start your own life journey. The wilderness journey as a whole is a picture of the period of "reformation"—the period, long or short, when we are of our own accord trying to make our daily lives right according to the teaching of the Word.

Adult

There are many interesting points of discussion here. The adult can appreciate many of them from experiences of his own, and the younger members of the class will get help from hearing the older ones admit some of their earlier difficulties. Always, in discussions, have these younger members in mind. One of the troubles young adults have is that they so seldom feel free to talk about their inner feelings with anyone who can really help them. They are afraid of being smiled at and treated as children, and unfortunately this sometimes happens.

The story of the return of Moses to Egypt, the convincing of Pharaoh by means of the ten plagues, the first Passover feast, the appearance of the pillar of cloud and fire, the pursuit by the Egyptians, and the miraculous crossing of the Red Sea are familiar to all of us. It is enough for the purpose of this lesson that we recognize that they picture the first understanding of the spiritual destruction which results from a merely worldly life, the first determination to break the chains of worldliness and selfishness and to set forth under the leadership of the teachings of the Word upon a new course of reformation which will eventually lead to a heavenly character, and the first temptation to give up and turn back.

Our lesson for today opens with the song of triumph sung by the Israelites after they had safely reached the eastern shore of the Red Sea and had seen the pursuing Egyptians swallowed up in the returning waters. When we realize that we have miraculously passed safely through a tamptation which at first appeared an impossible barrier to our progress, we do right to give thanks to the Lord through whose power the victory has been given us. In the Word song and music in general represent the expression of emotions. Music corresponds to the affections, and both expresses and arouses them. Different kinds of musical instruments correspond to different kinds of affections. In general, wind instruments correspond to affections for goodness and stringed instruments to affections for truth. The timbrel, which Miriam used, is a type of tambourine. Swedenborg says of it (AC 8337): "As regards the timbrel specifically, it corresponds to spiritual good, that is, to the good of truth. The reason is that the timbrel is not a stringed instrument, neither is it a wind instrument, but as it is made with a skin, it is as it were a continuous stringed instrument, and moreover its sound is graver and deeper than is the sound of stringed instruments." Then he quotes several passages in the Word in which the timbrel is mentioned. The "good of truth" is the good which comes into our lives as a result of experience in the practice of particular truths—in this case the truth that if we obey the Word, the Lord has power to save us.

Being heartened by their miraculous escape, the Israelites no doubt turned toward the wilderness with confidence, expecting a short and triumphant journey: but they were soon disillusioned. The wilderness is called the "wilderness of Shur"—the same wilderness into which Hagar fled when Sarai was angry with her (Genesis 16:7). Swedenborg says of Shur, " 'Shur' denotes the memory knowledges of the church which have not yet attained to life, thus such things as must attain to life through temptations, for spiritual life is acquired through temptations (which are spiritual combats, or combats against evils and falsities) and through victories in these combats." (AC 8346) We all have many such "memory-knowledges of the church" which we have not made living through use against our evils.

Throughout the wilderness journey the children of Israel were led by the pillar of cloud and fire. Exodus 13:21 says: "And the Lord went before them by day in a pillar of cloud, to lead them the way: and by night in a pillar of fire, to give them light; to go by day and night." Swedenborg tells us that this signifies the continuous presence of the Lord. When we are in a state of enlightenment—by day—the Lord tempers His presence to our need; many times in the Word He is said to come "in the clouds," and we are told that clouds represent the letter of the Word which is according to our understanding and yet permits the light from the Lord to shine through as we are able to receive it. The pillar of fire by night pictures the fact that when we are in a state of obscurity, the Lord leads us by good (AC 8105-8110). The Israelites were told to follow wherever the pillar led them, to stop when it stopped and remain there as long as it stood still, and when it moved on—whether it was day or night—to break camp and follow it. We seem to lead ourselves, but we know that our plans are often cut short or diverted by unexpected obstacles, and also that often the way opens before us when we least expect it. The Lord permits such experiences to come to us as are most likely to lead us to see and to correct our faults and weaknesses and to develop the particular abilities and qualities which will make us most helpful to others and so increase our spiritual worth.

When like the Israelites we have conquered some temptation and are feeling most confident, we often need the type of experience through which they passed after they had crossed the Red Sea. "They went three days in the wilderness, and found no water. And when they came to Marah, they could not drink the waters of Marah, for they were bitter." Our first thought when we begin the period of reformation is likely to be that the decision itself has changed us and that since we have decided that we want to lead a good life, we shall instinctively know what is good: that is, that what we want to do thenceforth will necessarily be good.

This is not the case, however. All our old habits and desires persist, and we have to learn a whole new way of life and practice it patiently until it actually replaces the old in our affections and thoughts. This is a long, slow process. We find at once that we do not know what is really right. This is the three days' journey without finding water. Then when the truth does present itself to us, it is not pleasant to us. It cuts across our natural desires. This is the bitter water of Marah. The tree (Swedenborg translates it "a piece of wood") which the Lord showed Moses is a symbol of good. Nothing can make truth sweet except the entrance of good into the will.

It is at this point (verses 25 and 26) that the Lord solemnly points out to Moses and the people that obedience to the truth is essential for their new life, but also that if they will obey, they will suffer none of the misfortunes which they had so recently witnessed among the Egyptians. Even in the beginning of our journey, it is well that we should realize that although the new life may not prove to be easy, it will be free from all the unhappiness and frustration which worldliness and selfishness inevitably produce.

Then the Lord gives the people a taste of the happiness and peace which the new life will surely bring: "And they came to Elim, where there were twelve springs of water, and seventy palm trees: and they encamped there by the waters." "By the 'twelve springs of waters' are signified truths in all abundance" (AC 8368). ". . . *seventy palm trees.* That this signifies the goods of truth in like manner, that is, in all abundance, is evident from the signification of 'seventy,' as being all things in the complex, in like manner as 'twelve': and from the signification of 'palm-trees,' as being the goods of the spiritual church, which are the goods of truth" (AC 8369). Have we not all from time to time, after we have passed through some difficult situation in which we tried sincerely to do right, experienced this sudden relief, refreshment, and new understanding? Because we have found the Lord's way the right way and His guidance adequate to our needs, our whole outlook is readjusted and we can go on with new courage and strength. Knowledge is truth in the memory: intelligence is the rational understanding of this truth; but wisdom is the certainty of the truth which comes only from having used and proved it in life.

From the Writings of Swedenborg

Arcana Coelestia, n. 8356: "That a man is affected with truth, is from good; for good and truth have been conjoined as in a marriage, consequently the one loves the other as consort loves consort. From this also the conjunction of good and truth is compared in the Word to a 'marriage,' and the truths and goods which are born from it are called 'sons and daughters.' From all this it can be seen that the delight of the affection of truth has its cause in no other source than good. This is also evident from experience, for they who are in the good of life, that is, who love God and the neighbor, these also love the truths of faith. Hence it is that so long as good flows in and is received, so long truth appears to be delightful . . ."

Suggested Questions on the Lesson

J. What feast did the Hebrews observe before they left Egypt? *Passover*
P. How were they led on their journey? *pillar of cloud/fire*
P. What happened to them at the Red Sea? *waters parted*
P. How did they express their gratitude to the Lord? *sang song*
P. Who was the sister of Moses and Aaron? *Miriam*
P. What musical instrument did she use? *timbrel*
J. How long did they travel in the wilderness before they found water? *three days*
P. What was the matter with the water when they did find it? *bitter*
J. What was the name of this place? *Marah*
J. Where did they go next? *Elim*
P. What did they find there? *twelve springs, seventy palm trees*
I. What is the meaning of the flight from Egypt? *leaving slavery to worldliness and seeking true spirituality*
I. What does the pillar of cloud and fire represent? *literal sense of the Word*
S. What are meant by (1) the bitter water, and (2) the wood which made it sweet? *(1) that which opposes our natural inclinations*
(2) a genuine desire to live a good life

S. What are meant by (1) the twelve wells, and (2) the seventy palm trees?
(1) the truth of the saving power of the Lord
(2) the good which comes from knowing that truth

I. What does the wilderness journey picture? *reformation*

QUAILS AND MANNA

Exodus 16

In review, the institution of the Passover should be mentioned in all classes because of the frequent recurrence of this feast in the Old Testament story and its importance in the story of the Lord's life on earth in the Gospels. The crossing of the Red Sea should also be mentioned, and the pupils should be reminded how the children of Israel were led on their long journey.

Doctrinal Points

What reformation is.
The difficulty of getting rid of the unregenerate life.
Why we need to read the Word and pray every day.

Notes for Parents

If you have been studying these notes consecutively, you will have freshly in mind the wonderful stories of the Passover feast, the crossing of the Red Sea, the sweetening of the bitter waters of Marah, and the period of rest which was given to the children of Israel at the oasis of Elim.

The Lord had performed one miracle after another for the Israelites, and still in our lesson for today we find them complaining and looking back longingly at the "flesh pots" of Egypt. Have you ever known a woman who was very much dissatisfied with the house in which she was living and finally succeeded in moving to another house, only to begin complaining about new inconveniences and recalling only the things she had liked in the old house? Aren't we all pretty much like that? What is hard in our immediate present is apt to fill our minds and crowd out the acknowledgment of the Lord's constant goodness to us. "When you feel like complaining, count your blessings" is an old and wise saying. We are all less grateful to the Lord than we should be, and He deals gently with us, as He did with the Israelites.

The beautiful story of the quails and manna teaches us something we need always to remember. If we look to the Lord and trust Him, He will give us each day our daily bread—not just food for our bodies but food for our souls, the wisdom and strength to meet our daily problems and temptations. But we must gather this spiritual food each day by reading the Word and by prayer. We cannot gather enough of it in church on Sunday to last all week. We should go to church on Sunday to worship the Lord and to thank Him for the blessings we have received during the week. The church is the Lord's house, and there all our own immediate concerns, all our likes and dislikes, all our worldly cares and anxieties should be laid aside for a short time while we "rest in the Lord." It is this spirit of worship and thanksgiving which alone can make the sabbath a day of rest. The other days of the week are the days of trial and temptation when we need a fresh supply of strength from the Lord, and He has provided it for us in His Word. It is there for our gathering each day. As the Psalmist calls it (Psalm 78:25), it is truly "angels' food."*

Primary

The reading of the lesson from the Word should lead to a discussion of how the Lord feeds all of us, and the connection should be made with the petition in the Lord's Prayer. Discuss the nature of the manna, the reason for its name, the instructions for gathering it, and the length of time during which it was provided for the people.

When Pharaoh finally agreed to let the children of Israel leave Egypt, they gathered together all their possessions and their cattle and left as quickly as they could. Just before they left they had a feast which the Lord had commanded them to hold to celebrate their being set free by Him. They were told to have the same feast

*Swedenborg, following Schmidius, renders this "bread of the mighty" (AC 5490). Cf. Psalm 103:20, HH 229. —*Ed.*

every year on that same day always so that they would never forget their deliverance, just as we celebrate Thanksgiving Day every year. They called their feast the Passover because at the time of the last of the ten plagues the angel of death had passed over their homes without injuring any of them.

On their journey back to the Holy Land they were led by the Lord during the day by means of a pillar of cloud, which became a pillar of fire at night. As long as it moved ahead of them, they were to follow it; and when it stopped, they were to stop and camp. Moses was their leader.

When they came to the Red Sea, the Lord parted the waters for them so that they crossed on dry land, and when they could not find water that was good to drink, the Lord showed them how to make the water good.

Wouldn't you think that by this time the children of Israel would have been glad to trust the Lord and obey Him?

But people have a way of forgetting how good the Lord has been to them.
Instead of this goodness what did the people soon begin to remember?
How did the Lord satisfy their hunger for meat?
What did He give them for bread?
Manna means "what is it?"
How often did they find the manna?
At what time of day did they find it?
How much was each person to gather?
An omer is a Hebrew measure equal to three or four quarts.
What happened when they tried to keep the manna overnight?
There was one exception to this.
On the sixth morning of each week they were to gather enough for two days.
This lasted them over the sabbath.
Read verse 31 of our chapter to see what the manna tasted like.

You know that it is really the Lord who gives us our food. We pray, "Give us this day our daily bread," and the Lord feeds us just as truly as He fed the children of Israel in the wilderness.

Junior

With this class the connection should be made by means of the story of the

Passover feast, emphasizing the reason for its being called the *Passover.* Give the children an opportunity to tell what they remember about the crossing of the Red Sea, the bitter waters of Marah, and the oasis at Elim. In the lesson for today the general correspondence of the manna can be given them. Stress the connection with the Lord's Prayer.

What Christian sacrament did the Lord institute at His last Passover?

After the first Passover the people started in haste on their journey. Moses and Aaron were their leaders, but the Lord gave them another guide also—a pillar of cloud in the daytime and of fire at night—which they were to follow, stopping whenever it stopped and going on when it moved. You remember the story of how the Red Sea was parted by a miracle so that they could cross on foot, and how the Egyptians tried to pursue them and were drowned when the waters closed again.

Then the children of Israel began their journey through the "wilderness"—the Sinai Peninsula. In *The Sower* we read the following about the country through which they passed: "Sand hills were on their right between them and the sea, and higher rocky hills made a wall upon their left. There were few clouds to shade the sky, and the sun even in spring was very hot. There were also at this season scorching southeast winds full of stifling dust. Rain falls in that country in the winter, but it makes a sudden flood and soon the brook beds are almost dry again." So they found little water and no food, and soon they began again to complain and to blame Moses for taking them out of Egypt. Do you remember what the angels told Lot when they led him out of Sodom, and what happened to Lot's wife? If you do not remember this story, you may read it in Genesis 19:17-26. We all have a tendency, whenever we are called upon to bear any present trouble, to remember only the pleasures we used to have and to forget the difficulties and dangers.

Our lesson for today is about how the Lord fed the children of Israel on their journey.

What did they long for especially?
What kind of meat did the Lord give them?

We are also told in *The Sower* that quails do not normally live in that country, but that in the spring great flocks of them pass over, migrating from their winter home in Africa, and that since they are not strong fliers they go with the wind and often have to settle down to rest. You may be interested to read in Numbers 11:18-20, 31-34 of a time when the Lord again sent quails and what happened to the people because they ate too greedily.

But there was another food which they missed perhaps even more than meat. Bread, as you know, is made from flour of various kinds, and of course the people could not very well grow grain while they were traveling through the wilderness.

At what time of day were the quails sent?
What did they find in the morning?
What did Moses tell them this bread was?
What was it called? *Manna* means "what is it?"
How often were they to gather it?
How much were they to gather?
An omer is about three or four quarts.
When were they not to gather it?
How were they fed on the sabbath?
What happened to the manna which they tried to keep on other days?
What did the manna look like?
How did it taste?

Look up Numbers 11:7-8 and see how they prepared it for eating. In Psalm 78:25 the manna is called "angels' food." The children of Israel were fed with the manna all through the rest of their forty years of wandering in the wilderness. Read Joshua 5:10-12 to see how the manna stopped as soon as they reached the Holy Land and were able to find grain again. Although the giving of the manna was of course a miracle, we know that all our daily food really comes to us from the Lord. Men cultivate and prepare it, but they do not make the seeds or the fish and birds and animals.

And there is a deeper lesson in our story which you are old enough to understand. The manna is a picture of another kind of food which the Lord will always give us if we ask Him for it—food for our souls. And we have to gather this kind of manna day by day also and to use it while it is fresh. Can we eat enough at one meal or on one day to last us all week? Some people think that if they go to church on Sunday, they can forget the Lord and do as they please all the rest of the week. That is like trying to keep the manna over. We need to read a little from the Bible every day, to think about the Lord, and to pray for enough goodness to meet the temptations which will come to us on that day. That is what we really mean when we say, "Give us this day our daily bread."

Intermediate

The correspondence of the quail and especially of the manna and the directions for its gathering make a simple, practical lesson for this class. It should be covered briefly enough so that time may be left for at least the statement of the doctrine of repentance, reformation, and regeneration which is involved in the beginning of the wilderness journey.

You will remember the institution of the Passover feast at the time of the tenth plague, and how the children of Israel were commanded to eat it girded for their journey, and how the Lord put in the hearts of their Egyptian neighbors to give them "jewels of silver, and jewels of gold, and raiment" to help them on their way. You remember also the miraculous crossing of the Red Sea and the first two stops on the farther side, when at Marah they were taught how to make the bitter waters sweet, and were rested and refreshed at the oasis of Elim. And you remember that they were being led by the pillar of cloud and fire.

From Elim they were led southward parallel to the sea, with sandy hills between them and the sea and higher rocky hills to their left. It was a dry and desolate way, and they began to complain and look back longingly to the "flesh pots" of Egypt. It does not take very much hardship sometimes to make us forget our blessings and our trust in the Lord.

But the Lord is indeed "long-suffering and plenteous in mercy." He promised Moses that He would give the people "in the evening flesh to eat, and in the morning bread to the full." You may remember from the first chapter in Genesis that evening pictures a state of waning intelligence and love: and the morning, the dawning of a new understanding. The Lord stands ready to give us the food our souls need in both these states: the quail—the pleasure we get from being praised and thanked for doing right—in our evening states, and the manna—true inward happiness in doing right—with each new beginning of spiritual progress.

The whole story of the manna is a beautiful study in correspondence. The manna came with the dew in the morning. Genuine good from the Lord, which is our spiritual bread, comes as we try to learn and apply particular truths from the Word. In Psalm 78, verse 25, the manna is called "angels' food," and Swedenborg tells us that it actually was angels' food given a material substance so that it might nourish the Israelites, just as divine good has to be embodied for us in concrete acts. The Israelites called it *manna*, which means "what is it?" People do not know what is meant by spiritual good until they have actually tasted it. Spiritual good—which Swedenborg calls the "good of truth"—is a heartfelt delight in practicing the truths we learn from the Word.

The manna had to be gathered every day and in quantity only sufficient for that day's eating. In the Lord's Prayer we say, "Give us this day our daily bread." We cannot absorb enough goodness on Sunday to last us all week any more than we can eat enough at one meal to support our bodies all week. Our spiritual strength must be maintained by daily reading of the Word and prayer, and anything we learn and do not use becomes worthless, just as the manna when kept over "bred worms, and stank." Yet the Lord also gives us our sabbaths, regularly recurring states of rest and peace in which we may enjoy what we have already gathered without the conscious effort to gain more.

The children of Israel were fed with the manna for the whole forty years of the wilderness journey, and it ceased when they entered the land of Canaan; for it pictures especially the spiritual food we need while we are struggling with temptations. We should keep in mind that the wilderness journey of the Israelites pictures the period of "reformation."

You know perhaps that some churches believe that one becomes a Christian and is "saved" by a single religious experience called *conversion*, in which he recognizes that his life has not been good, turns to the Lord and acknowledges Him as his Savior, and expresses his intention of being a Christian. This is not the New Church teaching. Conversion is necessary, but it is only the first step of the way. The word *convert* means to "turn with," in religion to turn in the direction of the Lord. We know that we are all born with strong tendencies to selfishness and that, if we are to be followers of the Lord, we must at some time—as early in our lives as possible—of our own free choice turn away from self and toward the Lord. In the Bible history of the Israelites, we recognize that their remaining in Egypt after Joseph's death was a yielding to self-indulgence. Their decision to obey the Lord and leave Egypt may be likened to conversion. It was the first necessary step on their way back to the Holy Land. But they had a long, long way to go before they reached their destination, and many trials and hardships to pass through.

In the teachings of our church we often hear this series of words: repentance, reformation, and regeneration. When we really see that we are selfish, are sorry, and determine to change our lives, we repent. When we persist in the effort to put selfishness aside and obey the Lord, we gradually "reform" our lives; that is, we make them over from the selfish pattern in which we have been living into the order in which the Lord would have us live. This is not done in a moment. We often become discouraged and rebellious and slip back. But if we ask the Lord's help and go on again, there comes a time when we find that living in the Lord's way gives us happiness; we have learned to love it. We have entered the Holy Land, which is a picture of regeneration. Regeneration means being *born again*. We have become new people, children of our heavenly Father.

Basic Correspondences

quails = natural satisfactions from "being good"

manna = spiritual good or the "good of truth"—genuine happiness in being good

Senior

The important lesson for this class is the difference between the New Church doctrine of salvation and that of other churches. The story for the day can then be presented to emphasize our need of looking to the Lord daily for the strength to meet the problems of the day and to overcome its temptations.

We are studying the meaning of the wilderness journey, that part of our spiritual development which lies between the state of living for self and the world and the state called "regeneration." Egypt under the Pharaoh of Moses' time represents, as we have seen, a state in which our higher possibilities are enslaved by selfishness and worldliness. Moses represents the law of the Lord, which should be our leader. The plagues were permitted not only to convince Pharaoh that he must let the children of Israel go, but also to convince the children of Israel that they must not stay in Egypt any longer and that Moses was actually the representative of the God of their fathers. If we are ever to get to heaven—represented by the Holy Land—we must come to a point where we see for ourselves that the merely worldly life is slavery.

The Passover feast, which the children of Israel celebrated on the eve of their departure from Egypt, symbolizes the decision to break off the bondage of natural and worldly desires and thoughts and be led by the Lord. This decision marks the beginning of the period called reformation, for before we can even enter the border of the Holy Land of spiritual living, we must put our external lives in order according to the Lord's laws. The journey of the Israelites from Egypt to Canaan represents this period of reformation. Its first great event was the crossing of the Red Sea, the first practical test of the new determination, the first temptation met and overcome, confirming the decision.

After this first victory the children of Israel were led by the pillar of cloud and fire down the east side of the sea on their way to Sinai. At Marah the Lord showed them how to make the bitter waters sweet for their drinking, and at Elim, "where there were twelve springs of water and seventy palm trees," He gave them a period of rest and refreshment.

The New Church does not teach—as some churches do—that a person can be "saved" by the single religious experience called *conversion*. One must indeed be converted, that is, turned from the way of self and toward the way of the Lord; but that is only the first step. The way to salvation is a lifelong spiritual journey in which we meet our problems and temptations one after another, sometimes enjoying victory and sometimes slipping back and being defeated, often discouraged and rebellious, but with the Lord's guidance and help, advancing little by little toward our true goal.

Between Elim and Sinai lay the wilderness of Sin—*Sin* or *Zin* being the Hebrew word meaning "clay." It was a dry, hot, dusty stretch of country, picturing the way a life of obedience to the Lord often appears to us in the early stages of our journey. It was at this point that the quails and manna were sent. The quails represent external satisfactions in doing good; an example of these would perhaps be our pleasure in the approbation of people whom we love and respect when they see us earnestly trying to overcome our bad habits. But this kind of satisfaction is only a temporary support; the quails were not sent regularly. We need something more, and the Lord gives it to us. The giving of the manna is a wonderful and beautiful story. No one can go on steadfastly through the temptations of this period of reformation unless he has more than external results to uphold him. The manna represents spiritual good. Swedenborg calls it "the good of truth, which is the life of the spiritual man." When the children of Israel first saw it, they said, "What is it?"

We all say this at first about spiritual thinking and living; they seem unreal and remote from any kind of pleasure we have experienced. Yet the manna sustained the children of Israel throughout their whole journey. It is a taste of genuine happiness in the effort to serve the Lord. We are to gather it daily, early in the morning.

The morning, of course, means at the beginning of each new state. At first the dew lay upon the ground. Each new state begins with the reception of some fresh truth. Then comes the manna, the inner satisfaction which nourishes and strengthens the soul. And "when the sun waxed hot, it melted." This fresh satisfaction disappears as the new state is put to the test through temptations; yet it has given strength to endure through them. We pray, "Give us this day our daily bread." It is the heavenly manna, the "angels' food" of the Psalmist (Psalm 78:25), for which we are really praying. We should literally look for this food every morning by reading the Word and praying if we wish to be sustained in the right way through the work of the day. We must gauge the amount of our reading according to our needs, for if we go on beyond the limit of eager and reverent interest, what we read will lose its power to feed us and will even give us a distaste for it, just as the manna which was kept over "bred worms, and stank." The fact that the children of Israel were not to gather the manna on the sabbath does not teach that we should not read the Word and look to the Lord on Sunday, but that in the holy states of peace and rest after victory, which the sabbath represents, we are sustained without conscious effort on our part. We advance in our reformation a step at a time; our spiritual food is given us "line upon line, precept upon precept, here a little and there a little," until we reach the promised land of spiritual abundance.

Adult

The most obvious topics for discussion are the relationship of reformation to regeneration and the progression from natural delight to spiritual good, as pictured by the quails and manna. The latter discussion will be helped by pointing out the contrast offered by the story of the second sending of the quails in Numbers 11. Note also the complaint of the people in Numbers 21:5 just before the plague of fiery serpents.

The wilderness journey of the Israelites pictures, as we know, the period of reformation. This, as the writings frequently tell us, is the state in which we make ourselves do what we know we should do, not because we love to do it but simply because it is commanded by the Lord. There is much of self in this obedience.

The final plague not only convinced Pharaoh that he must let the children of Israel go, but also convinced the Israelites that they must break their Egyptian bondage at all costs and start at once for their true home in Canaan. The Passover feast, celebrated then for the first time, was to be repeated annually to remind them of their deliverance, just as the Lord at His last Passover feast on earth instituted the Holy Supper and commanded His disciples, "This do in remembrance of me." When we take the Holy Supper, we pray that it may be to us "the sign and seal" that we are the Lord's children. The decision to leave Egypt represents the decision which everyone who is to be regenerated must make of his own free will sooner or later: the decision to turn his back on worldliness and self-indulgence and to set his face toward the achievement of spiritual life. This decision is the essential first step, but it is only the beginning.

We may remember from an earlier lesson on creation Swedenborg's statement in AC 13 in connection with men's progress toward regeneration: "The greatest part at this day attain only the first state; some only the second; others the third, fourth, or fifth; few the sixth; and scarcely anyone the seventh." Regeneration is a lifelong process. This should not discourage us. It should rather lead us to look upon each day we are granted in this world as an opportunity to grow a little further toward the angelic stature which is possible for us. We know that the process of growth is not continuous. The wilderness story is a picture of the temptations, failures, hardships, and rebellions which attend our efforts to bring even our outward lives into order. And after the children of Israel reached the Holy Land there were still wars, backslidings, and defeats. But the story is also a picture of the wonderful way in which the Lord leads and supports us, accommodating His providence to our changing states, and giving us victories and times of rest and refreshment for our encouragement all along the way.

Our story for today illustrates this constant presence and providence of the Lord. The children of Israel had come into a state in which they were looking back with longing at the external enjoyments which they had left behind, and forgetting the hardships of the bondage from which they had escaped. The Lord did not permit this state to lead to an actual turning back. He sent a new type of food to satisfy their craving for the "flesh pots" of Egypt.

Again we are reminded of the Creation story in which each day is described as advancing from evening to morning. In giving us the correspondence of the quail and manna in AC 8426[2] Swedenborg writes:

> That "in the evening" denotes the end of a former state, is because the changes of state in the other life are circumstanced as are the times of day in the world, namely, morning, noon, evening, and night, or twilight, and again morning. Be it known that in the spiritual world there are perpetual changes of state, and that all who are there pass through them. The reason is that they may be continually succeeding one another in order like the times of the day and the times of the year, never return quite the same, but are varied. The beginning of every state corresponds to morning on the earth, and also in the Word is sometimes meant by "morning"; but the end of every state corresponds to evening, and is likewise sometimes called "evening" in the Word. When it is morning they are in love; when it is noon, they are in light or in truth; but when it is evening they are in obscurity as to truths, and are in the delight of natural love. This delight is what is signified by the quail which they received in the evening, and the good is what is signified by the manna which they received every morning.

In our story the quail represent "natural delight through which is good." When we are not yet in states in which we can feel unselfish happiness in truth and goodness, we are permitted to feel satisfaction of a natural kind—that is, satisfaction in which there is a sense of self-merit—in doing right, because this encourages us to continue in the right path. We should compare this story, however, with the story in Numbers 11:10-23, 31-34, in which the quail were again sent and the result was disastrous because the people ate too greedily. We cannot safely remain long in any delight which smacks of self-righteousness. So our story shows us how divine providence leads us day by day, meeting our changing states with the kind of spiritual food which we can receive, and strengthening us to continue. We see immediately the connection between the instructions for gathering the manna and our daily petition, "Give us this day our daily bread." We cannot gather enough spiritual food on Sunday morning to last us all week. We need to go to the Word and pray daily, because we change from day to day and the problems of each day are different from those of the day before.

The manna which came down with the dew in the morning represents "the good of truth in its first formation." A helpful discussion of this is found in AC 8462 with reference to the people's calling the new gift from the Lord "manna": "That this signifies amazement at what was not known, is evident from the fact that the word 'manna' in its own tongue means *What?* thus, that which is not known. That from this the bread that was given to the sons of Israel in the wilderness was called 'manna,' is because this bread signifies the good of charity that is begotten through the truth of faith. Before regeneration this good is quite unknown to man, and it is not even known that it exists."

In an addition to the memorable relation in TCR 695, which we find in *Posthumous Theological Works*, Vol. 1, p. 152 (also in Document 302 of Tafel's *Documents Concerning Swedenborg*), we read: "I told them further that they should know that the miracles which are recorded in the Word likewise took place by an influx out of the prior into the posterior world, and that they were produced by an introduction of such things as are in the spiritual world in corresponding things in the natural world; e.g. that the manna which every morning descended upon the camp of the children of Israel, was produced by bread from heaven being introduced into the recipient vessels of nature; that in like manner bread and fishes were thus introduced into the baskets of the apostles, which they distributed to so many thousands of men; again, that wine out of heaven was instilled into the water in the pots at the wedding where the Lord was present; further, that the fig-tree withered, because there was no longer any influx into it of spiritual nutriment, by which it was fed from the roots." So we see that the manna was actually, as it is called in Psalm 78:25, "angels' food."

From the Writings of Swedenborg

Arcana Coelestia, n. 8452: "*That the quail came up*. That this signifies natural delight through which is good, is evident from the signification of 'quail,' as being natural delight. That the 'quail' denotes natural delight is because it was a bird of the sea, and by a bird of the sea is signified what is natural, and by its flesh, which was longed for, is signified delight . . . That it also denotes through which is good, is because it was given in the evening. For when in the other life there is a state which corresponds to evening, then good spirits, and also angels, are remitted into the state of the natural affections in which they had been when in the world, consequently into the delights of their natural man. The reason is that good may come out of it, that is, that they may thereby be perfected. All are perfected by the implantation of faith and charity in the external or natural man; for unless these are implanted, good and truth cannot flow in from the internal or spiritual man, that is, from the Lord through this man, because there is no reception; and if there is no reception, the influx is stopped and perishes, nay, the internal man also is closed. From this it is plain that the natural must be brought into a state of accommodation, in order that it may be a receptacle. This is effected by means of delights; for the goods that belong to the natural man are called delights, because they are felt."

Suggested Questions on the Lesson

J. What feast did the Israelites hold just before they left Egypt? *Passover*
P. How were they to be led on their journey? *pillar of cloud/fire*
J. How did the Lord help them at the Red Sea? *parted water*
P. What complaint did they make when they reached the wilderness of Sin? *no meat*
P. What did the Lord send them in the evening? *quails*
P. What did they find on the ground in the morning? *morsels of "bread"*
P. What did they call it? *manna*
J. What does *manna* mean? *"what is it?"*
J. What directions did the Lord give them for gathering it? *one omer each daily*

J. What happened when some of the people disobeyed? *it spoiled*
J. How were they fed on the sabbath? *double amount on sixth day*
P. How long did the Lord feed the children of Israel with the manna? *forty years*
P. Of what petition in the Lord's Prayer does this lesson remind us? *. . . our daily bread*
I. What does the journey of the Israelites through the wilderness picture? *reformation*
S. What do the quails represent? *external satisfaction from doing good*
S. What does the manna represent? *spiritual goodness which comes from the Lord as we try to learn and live truths from the Word*

AT REPHIDIM

Exodus 17

Several familiar stories—the crossing of the Red Sea, the sweetening of the bitter waters of Marah, the rest at Elim, and the giving of the quails and manna—form the background for this lesson. Each teacher will have to judge how much of the class time may safely be spent on the review of these stories without slighting the lesson for the day. The Lord's care and protection of the children of Israel is the unifying thought.

Doctrinal Points

We can overcome our temptations only by constantly looking to the Lord for help.

When we study the Word in order to find out how to live rightly, the Lord can show us what it means.

We do not really believe in the Lord if we do not trust Him.

It is evil deep within us which makes us subject to discouragement. Discouragement is really selfish.

Notes for Parents

On the very night on which the children of Israel celebrated the Passover feast, they started on their journey out of Egypt. The Lord showed them the way they were to go. All through their journey, which was to take a much longer time than they thought, He went before them in a pillar of cloud by day and of fire by night.

We all know the story of how Pharaoh changed his mind and sent an army after them which caught up with them at the Red Sea, and how the Red Sea parted before them and, after they had crossed, closed in upon the Egyptians who tried to follow. Then the pillar led the Israelites into the wilderness.

We start on our journey from Egypt to the Holy Land when we realize that living for self and the world is slavery, and determine to obey the Lord and find our way to the kind of living which the Lord calls "blessed." In the beginning of our journey we are eager and enthusiastic, and the way opens before us. But it is not long before we meet difficulties which discourage us, for there are many bad things in us which have to be recognized and overcome one by one. The wilderness journey, with all its trials and disappointments, is still before us.

Our chapter for today tells of two of these trials. The children of Israel are on their way to Sinai and are being led through a dry valley called Rephidim, and they are very thirsty. At the well in Samaria our Lord said, "Whosoever drinketh of this water shall thirst again: but whosoever drinketh of the water that I shall give him shall never thirst: but the water that I shall give him shall be in him a well of water springing up into everlasting life." The water which gushed from the rock of Horeb when Moses struck it with his rod is this same living water, truth for our daily use coming from the Word of God. You remember that the Lord is called in the Bible both the *Rock* and the *Word*.

Immediately after their thirst was satisfied, the Israelites had to fight their first battle. When we learn some new truth, it is not really ours until we have used it to overcome some evil within ourselves. But in order to win we must lift our minds above the low valley in which we are and look steadily to the Lord for help; and just as Aaron and Hur held up Moses' hands, so all our good resolutions and principles must be used to steady and support us.

Primary

Spend most of the class time on the two incidents at Rephidim. Be sure the children understand that Moses, when he stood on top of the hill and held up his hands, was asking for the Lord's help. They will remember about the crossing of the Red Sea, and they should remember the giving of the manna. In the lesson for today impress upon them the name and function of Joshua, as this is the first time he appears in the Bible story. The Lord's constant presence and help is the principal lesson.

You remember that when the children of Israel ate the feast of the Passover, they were dressed all ready for their journey out of Egypt. They left in great haste and traveled as fast as they could. It was fortunate that they did, because after they had gone, Pharaoh changed his mind and sent an army after them to bring them back. The army caught up with them just as they reached the shore of the Red Sea, and they thought their effort had failed.

But the Lord saved them in a wonderful way. First He caused the pillar of cloud and fire, which He had given to lead them on their journey, to move around behind the Israelites and hide them so that the Egyptians could neither see nor reach them. Then He rolled back the waters of the Red Sea so that they could cross on dry ground. And finally, when the Egyptian army tried to follow them, He made the waters come back again so that the Egyptians were all drowned.

To reach the Holy Land the people had to travel a long way.

What was the country like through which they were to travel?
How did the Lord feed them?
In our lesson for today, to what place had they come?
What were they complaining about?
How did the Lord give them water?
What enemy attacked them?
Who led the army of Israel in the battle?
What did Moses do to help?
What happened when he held up his hands?
What happened when he let them down?
When he grew tired, what did Aaron and Hur do?
What did Moses build at Rephidim after the battle?

Junior

This is a good opportunity to study with the Juniors a map of the wilderness journey and especially to point out Sinai in its geographical relation to Egypt and to the Holy Land. In both the incidents of our chapter the lesson to emphasize is the Lord's readiness to help us whenever we turn to Him. Call special attention to Joshua.

Look at a map and follow the course of the Israelites after they crossed the Red Sea. In chapter 14 of Exodus we read of their stop at Marah, where the Lord showed Moses how to make the bitter water sweet, and of the period of rest at Elim, "where there were twelve springs of water, and seventy palm trees." Chapter 16 tells of the giving of quails and the miraculous bread called "manna" with which they were to be fed every day throughout their whole forty years in the wilderness.

Then comes our chapter for today. The Israelites have left the seacoast and are traveling toward Sinai. They are going through a narrow valley between mountains. In flood time these valleys carry down torrents of water, but now they are dry.

What did the people demand of Moses?
To whom did Moses turn for help?
What did the Lord tell him to do?
What happened?
What was the name of the place to which they had come?
What is the mountain called in which the rock was?

This range of mountains is called in the Bible sometimes Horeb and sometimes Sinai, although we usually think of Sinai as the particular peak from which the commandments were given.

Also at Rephidim the Israelites had to fight their first battle. The people called *Amalek* or the *Amalekites* are often mentioned as enemies of Israel. The word *Amalek* means "valley dweller." They had a particularly troublesome method of attack. Read Deuteronomy 25:17-18 to see what it was.

Who was the leader of the fighting men of Israel?
Who went up on the hill with Moses?
What happened when Moses help up his hands to the Lord?
What happened when he let them down?
When Moses became tired, what did Aaron and Hur do?

The Amalekites were defeated, and Moses built an altar at Rephidim as a memorial of the fact that the Lord would always help the Israelites against Amalek. They had to fight them again under Gideon, and later under Saul and under David.

Intermediate

The lesson to stress with this class is the importance of using in our daily life and our daily thinking all the truth we learn and understand in Sunday school and church. This is the only way in which we can make spiritual progress.

The Israelites were to have a long, hard journey before they reached their home in Canaan, and this means that our reformation and regeneration—our journey to our heavenly home—is a long, slow process. The whole book of Exodus, from chapter 12 on, is in its spiritual sense a description of the period of reformation in us, the period in which we recognize and try to correct our faults, one by one. In this wilderness journey the children of Israel were led by Moses, who stands for divine law, and by a pillar of cloud by day and fire by night, which moved before them or stood still when the Lord wished them to stop. The pillar represented the presence of the Lord with them, and Swedenborg tells us that it was actually an angelic company through whom the Lord made His presence evident.

The Lord leads us in the same way, for we know that there are angels with us all the time reminding us of the truths we have learned and prompting us to obey them. It is these angels through whom the Lord shows us the truth in the Word when we read it with a desire to learn how to live rightly. For when we read the letter of the Word, the angels who are with us are reading its internal sense.

You remember the story of the miraculous crossing of the Red Sea and the drowning of the pursuing Egyptian army. This pictures our first real temptation after we make up our minds to obey the Lord. When it comes, we always think it is too strong for us, but if we trust in the Lord instead of in ourselves and go forward, we not only come through the temptation safely, but looking back we can see how weak our enemy really was.

We have also studied the stories of the first few weeks in the wilderness—how the Lord made the bitter water sweet at Marah, how He gave the people rest at Elim, and how He brought them quails when they begged for meat and supplied the manna for their daily bread.

Now we are studying two things that happened at Rephidim, in a narrow valley between mountains on the way to Sinai. First, the people were without water. Moses, at the command of the Lord, struck the rock with his rod and the water gushed out. Water and rock are both symbols of truth, but they are truth in different forms. Rock represents the fundamental truths on which a good life is to be built. We must learn and acknowledge these. But they sometimes seem to us hard and "dry." It is only as we try with all our might to use them—which is represented by Moses striking the rock with his rod—that we suddenly find how satisfying and helpful they can be in our daily living.

Then we are given opportunities to put our new truth into practice. We begin to see that there are faults in ourselves, wrong ideas which have been lurking within our minds because of our selfishness and worldliness. These are the Amalekites. Read Deuteronomy 25:17-18. These wrong thoughts come up in our minds when we are "tired of trying" and attack us where we are weakest. We do not overcome them at one stroke or in our own strength. We must go at them systematically. Joshua is our leader in this battle. He represents "the truth fighting," and he is to be the leader later in the conquest of the Holy Land. Moses went up on the hill and lifted up his hands to the Lord. This means that in our battle we must always remember that it is the Lord's law we are trying to obey and that He will help us if we ask Him.

Aaron and Hur went up with Moses and helped to hold up his hands. Aaron was Moses' brother, the one the Lord assigned to be his spokesman to Pharaoh and to the people (Exodus 4:10-16). He represented divine law as it has come to us in the teachings of the church; and Hur, who was one of the leaders of the people (Exodus 24:14), represents the particular things our teachers and parents have been able to give us from these teachings. That is, everything we have been taught can help us to meet our inner temptations in the right way and to overcome them with the Lord's help.

Then after the victory Moses built an altar of remembrance at Rephidim. When we say that we all have to learn some things by experience, we are usually thinking of our mistakes and failures. But victories are experience, too, and we need to remember them and especially to remember that it was the Lord who gave us the victory. The altar at Rephidim was named *Jehovah-nissi*, which means "the Lord my banner." Moses said that "the Lord will have war with Amalek from generation to generation." Remember this whenever wrong thoughts come up in your mind; then ask the Lord's help, and drive them out.

Basic Correspondences

rock	=	fundamental truth
water	=	truth in a form adapted to our daily use
Moses	=	divine law
Joshua	=	truth fighting
Amalek	=	falsity from interior evil

Senior

The Seniors are on the verge of adult life and are about to leave Egypt and begin the wilderness journey. All the stories of the wilderness wandering have, therefore, a very practical value in preparing them for the temptations they should recognize, and showing them the technique to be followed in fighting them.

We sometimes think that if we had been in the place of the Israelites—had seen the pillar of cloud and fire continually before us, had seen the Red Sea part for our passage and then close in over our enemies, had tasted the water of Marah before and after its miraculous sweetening, had eaten the quails and gathered the daily manna—we could never have complained or doubted again. Yet all these stories are symbolic pictures of our own common experience. The Word is our pillar of cloud and fire, always before us to lead us in the right way. The Lord has protected us and fed us throughout our lives. And yet, when hardship or temptation comes, time after time we complain and falter and doubt.

In our lesson for today the children of Israel, who have been traveling southward along the Red Sea, have turned inland on their way to Sinai and are going up a narrow, dry valley, or *wadi*, called Rephidim. And again they are complaining of thirst. We recognize thirst as picturing a lack of truth. Have you ever heard a good church member—perhaps you yourself—say in the face of some impending trouble, "I just don't know what to do; why should I have this hardship?" This is the Israelites complaining to Moses almost to the point of stoning him. And the Lord answers, "Take with thee of the elders of Israel; and thy rod, wherewith thou smotest the river, take in thine hand, and go." This means: take some of the principles to which you have been assenting in church, and your knowledge of all that the Lord has done for you in the past, and apply it to your present problem. Go to the rock in Horeb—to the truth as you find it in the Word—and strike the rock with your rod. Go to the Word with the real intention of using what you find there, and you will be given the truth you need in the present—the water of life.

The Lord knows the enemy which is lurking in ambush when a person is in this state. And He knows that we shall not make any further progress until we recognize and fight this enemy. The enemy is Amalek. Amalek, whose name means "valley dweller," was a grandson of Esau, one of those degenerate offshoots of the line of Abraham which represent in us the persistent effects of our early self-will and self-interest. As we learn from Deuteronomy 25:17-18, Amalek waited in ambush and attacked Israel from behind, falling on the weak stragglers. So when we are tired and discouraged, it often seems that all our old bad habits spring out to attack us.

Joshua, first mentioned here as the leader in the battle, was later to take the place of Moses. He represents the truth fighting. The Israelites are not yet well enough organized, however, to conquer by his leadership alone. For example, in our early battles, when we try to use the truth in argument—whether with other people or with our own selfish feelings—we are often overcome because we are not yet experienced in its use. But the Lord shows us in this story how we can conquer even the most insidious temptations. We still have Moses, the principle of simple obedience to the commandments. This obedience brings the Lord's power into our lives. Moses went up on a hill and lifted up his hands to the Lord. We must persist in our obedience to the commandments, lift up our minds above the low state in which we are fighting, and look to the Lord for power to overcome. We should always remember that we do not really believe in the Lord if we do not trust in Him.

When Moses grew tired, he sat down on a rock, just as we must "rest in the Lord," and Aaron and Hur held up his hands. Moses, Aaron, and Hur in the story picture the three means by which the Lord sustains us through the temptations which attack us when we are tired and discouraged. Moses stands for truth directly from the Word: Aaron, the doctrines of the church; and Hur, all the things we have learned in church and Sunday school which help us to understand and apply the truth. A little later (Exodus 24:13-14) when Moses was about to go up into the mount to receive the commandments, he told the people to go to Aaron and Hur if they needed guidance while he was gone. Steadfast reliance upon the truth as it has come to us in all these three ways will enable us to hold out until the temptation is over—until the "sun" of our immediate selfish desire goes down.

And when we conquer, we should not take the credit to ourselves but should, like Moses, build an altar to the Lord to mark the place of victory so that we may remember that the Lord will always be at hand to give us strength if we look to Him.

Adult

The right approach to the Word and the importance of steady reliance upon the Lord in times of temptation, doubt, and discouragement are two lessons we all need. Often we think we believe in the Lord and His power to direct and save us, and we think we believe in the Word, but we do not fully use His help in the emergencies of our daily life.

The children of Israel ate the first Passover feast with their loins girded, their shoes on their feet, and their staves in their hands, and immediately started on their journey, and they reached the Red Sea before their first great impetus suffered a setback. But the setback came. It was inevitable. We cannot go through life on the strength of one good resolution. At the Red Sea the Egyptian army caught up with the Israelites. All our former habits of thought and feeling are still with us in full strength. We need to recognize this and also to feel our inability to overcome them in our own strength. It is only the Lord, present with us in the form of our guardian angels, who stands between us and destruction. The writings tell us that the pillar of cloud and fire which led the Israelites throughout their journey and which stood behind them through the night at the Red Sea to hide them from the pursuing enemy, was actually a company of angels with the Lord in their midst. We read in the twenty-seventh Psalm: "For in the time of trouble he shall hide me in his pavilion." And before we can really be free of our bondage to the world, we must have the further experience of seeing our way opened before us by the Lord and must be made to acknowledge the powerlessness of our enemies to follow us if we go forward. This is our "crossing of the Red Sea."

We have studied the stories of the sweetening of the bitter water at Marah, the welcome period of rest at Elim, and the giving of the quails and manna. These early experiences in the wilderness picture the first benefits we receive from the Lord in our efforts to reform our lives. For we recall that the whole wilderness journey describes the period of "reformation" through which we must pass before actual regeneration begins.

"Blessed are they that do hunger and thirst after righteousness." The hunger of the Israelites pictures our realization that of ourselves we have no goodness. The story of the giving of the manna is the promise that the Lord will give us of His goodness day by day to strengthen us on our way. Thirst represents our sense of need for truth. How often we say, "I wish I knew"! After the manna comes the giving of water from the rock of Horeb.

Moses was commanded: "Go on before the people, and take with thee of the elders of Israel; and thy rod, wherewith thou smotest the river, take in thine hand, and go. Behold, I will stand before thee there upon the rock in Horeb; and thou shalt smite the rock, and there shall come water out of it, that the people may drink." This is our pattern for finding the truth which we need for our daily living—a pattern to follow every time we say, "I wish I knew." Here is how we may understand it: Moses as our leader represents our acknowledgment that we must obey the divine law. The rock in Horeb is the Word as the basis of our faith. The Lord always stands before us on the rock in Horeb. We are to go to the Word for the truth we need. But there are other specific directions. We are to take with us some of the elders of Israel—the principles given us in our doctrines—and the rod or power of the Lord as we have experienced it in past crises. We are to take the rod in our hand and smite the rock—that is, to go to the Word with the conviction that we shall be given the power to understand and use its truth. The Word does not yield the water of life to those who read it as a product of men or to those who go to it to find confirmation for their own ideas. This is one of the lessons we must learn early in our journey.

Our chapter today also contains another lesson which we all need many times in our lives. So far in the story there has been little for Israel to do but to follow the pillar of cloud and fire. Even when they crossed the Red Sea, the Israelites had only to go steadily forward. The Lord opened the way for them and destroyed their enemies. And in the experiences which followed, they had only to ask and the Lord provided their needs. But now they are permitted to encounter an enemy whom they have to fight. As soon as we have gone a little way on our journey toward the promised land and have gained a little confidence and strength, this strength must be tried.

The Israelites were at Rephidim, passing through a narrow valley leading inland, when they were attacked by the Amalekites.

Amalek means "valley dweller." Amalek was a grandson of Esau. He pictures an evil in the will, or a "low" state of the will. In Deuteronomy 25:17-18 we learn that it was the strategy of the Amalekites to spring out from ambush on the rear of the line of their enemy and attack the stragglers and the weary. How often when we are physically or mentally tired, we find it harder to resist the temptation to indulge in doubt and discouragement, and in hasty judgment or speech! Our will power is at a low point, and our individual weaknesses manifest themselves suddenly and are hard to control. It is these times which show us most clearly what our own real nature is—what we would be without the Lord's protection and help. We need this revelation.

Moses offered to take the rod of God in his hand and go up to the top of the nearest hill. This is a picture of the immediate attempt we should make to lift our thoughts to the Lord and, remembering His help in the past, to look confidently to Him for strength. Moses—symbol of the law as we find it in the Word—is our first reliance. As long as Moses' hands were lifted up, Israel prevailed.

But Moses' hands grew weary. We grow tired of fighting with only the stern "Thou shalt not" to support us. Swedenborg tells us that in this story Moses, Aaron, and Hur represent divine truth in three stages of its mediation to us. Moses represents truth received immediately from the Lord; that is, our knowledge of the Word itself. Aaron, who was presently to be appointed high priest and who had been Moses' spokesman from the beginning, represents the truth from the Word as it is explained in the doctrines of the church. Hur, who was one of the leaders of the people, represents this mediate truth again mediated, as, perhaps, it comes to us from our pastors and teachers and in our own meditation and experience. Aaron and Hur held up Moses' hands. When we are tired and discouraged and tempted to give in to our weaknesses, we should recall all that we have learned of the Lord's guidance and saving power from the Word, from the church, and from our own thought and experience. Moses sat on a rock and

Aaron and Hur held up his hands until the sun went down and Israel prevailed. We must rest on our faith in the Lord, our Rock, and make use of all we know of His love for us and His power to save and strengthen us, until the sun of our self-love goes down and we are victorious.

Then we should give thanks to the Lord for His help. Moses built an altar of remembrance and called it *Jehovah-nissi*, which means "the Lord my banner." We have added one more experience to strengthen us for the next conflict.

From the Writings of Swedenborg

Arcana Coelestia, nn. 8554-8555: "In the preceding chapter, in the internal sense, the third temptation was treated of—that there was a lack of good. This having been given them, in the internal sense in this chapter the fourth temptation is treated of—that there was a lack of truth. This temptation is signified by 'the murmuring of the sons of Israel because they had no water,' and therefore the truth of faith was given them by the Lord, which is signified by 'the water out of the rock of Horeb.' Then follows the combat of the falsity that is from evil against the truth and good of faith, which combat is represented by the fighting of Amalek against Israel. That they who are in the truth and good of faith conquer when they look upward to the Lord, and that they yield when they look downward, is represented by the sons of Israel conquering so long as Moses kept his hands raised, and by their yielding when he let them down."

Suggested Questions on the Lesson

J. How did the Israelites cross the Red Sea? *miraculous parting*

J. How were they led in their journey? *pillar of cloud/fire*

J. To what place have they come in our lesson for today? *Rephidim*

P. What are they complaining about? *no water*

P. What does the Lord tell Moses to do? *strike rock*

P. What happened when Moses struck the rock? *water came out*

J. After this what enemy attacked Israel? *Amalek*

P. What leader was appointed for the battle? *Joshua*

P. What did Moses do? *went up on hill*

J. Who went up on the hill with him? *Aaron and Hur*

P. How was Moses able to control the course of the battle? *holding hands up*

P. How was he helped when he grew tired? *Aaron, Hur, rock*

J. What did he build as a memorial of the victory? *altar*

I. What is represented by getting water out of the rock? *making effort to use "dry" truths*

I. What is pictured by Amalek? *discouragement, based on hereditary self-will*

S. What is pictured by the Israelites' being victorious as long as Moses held up his hands? *lifting thoughts to God, remembering His past help*

S. What do (1) Aaron, and (2) Hur, represent in this story?
(1) doctrines of church
(2) thoughts learned in Sunday school, church, from parents, etc.

THE TEN COMMANDMENTS

Exodus 19:16-25; 20:1-21

First see how much the children can tell about the crossing of the Red Sea. Then remind them that when the people found other difficulties and dangers as they traveled through the wilderness, the Lord saved them each time. They reached Sinai in the third month after they left Egypt. The teacher in preparation should read carefully chapters 15-19, especially all of the nineteenth chapter, and begin the story for today with the events of that chapter.

Doctrinal Points

The ten commandments are divine laws—not man-made ones.

Notes for Parents

The journey of the children of Israel through the wilderness was to last for forty years, although the Israelites had no idea of this when they started out. They were a great multitude of people—some six hundred thousand—with flocks and herds which had to feed along the way. But their delay was caused by their own complainings and rebellions and cowardice, not by the length or difficulty of the journey. So it is with us. The wilderness journey pictures the period in our lives when, after we have determined to break off the fetters of worldly and selfish living, we are trying to make our lives over, to break our bad habits and learn good ones. We, too, often complain and rebel and waste time and strength looking back instead of pressing forward.

You know the many wonderful ways in which the Lord met the needs of the people one after another as they arose. He also meets ours. When we find new truth bitter, as the Israelites found the water at Marah, He shows us the "tree" which will make it sweet—

the principle of loving service. He gives us our periods of rest and content—our "oases" of Elim. When we become too unhappy, He brings us some wholesome pleasure, like the flocks of quail which came over the camp in the evening. And in every new state, if we look for it, we find our daily bit of spiritual bread provided. He brings us living water from the apparently hard rock of the letter of His Word, and when doubts and discouragements, like the Amalekites, attack us, He teaches us to lift up our hands to Him and let His strength bring us victory.

Then we begin to see the orderly purpose behind all the Lord's laws, and we are ready for a better organization of our thoughts and for more detailed instruction. The Israelites spent nearly a year camped at the foot of Mount Sinai. During that time the Lord gave them through Moses a complete code of laws to govern their civil, moral, and religious life. From an unorganized horde of people they became a nation, with the tabernacle as the center of their life.

In the inmost room of the tabernacle was the ark containing the two tables of stone on which the ten commandments had been written by the finger of God. The first commandments, relating to duties to God, constitute the first table; and the rest, relating to duties to the neighbor, constitute the second table. We recall that in the Gospels the Lord says that love to God is the first and great commandment and love to the neighbor is the second.

Our chapter tells us, however, that the commandments were first given to the Israelites by the living voice of God. This is because they are God's laws, the fundamental laws of the universe. They had been known always, but men had forgotten—as some have forgotten today—that they were not man-made. Your older children should now be learning the ten commandments. We should all know them and repeat them often to ourselves, for keeping them is the only way to happiness and peace.

Primary

This class should be able to recall that the Israelites are on their way from

Egypt to the Holy Land, how they are being led, and who is their human leader. Now they should learn the name *Sinai* and the fact that it was a great mountain and that from its top the Lord spoke the ten commandments. Dwell on the verse, "And God spake all these words, saying." Then go through the commandments rapidly, being sure the children get the literal meaning of each one. Some will be familiar and easy for them to understand. Others will not. The commandment about coveting is a good one to emphasize with children of this age. Others may be suggested by their questions.

You can imagine how happy the children of Israel were when they found themselves on the other side of the Red Sea and saw how the Lord had saved them from the Egyptians. Moses sang a song of victory and praise of the Lord, and his sister Miriam and the other women sang and danced for joy.

Then the people set out into the wilderness, led by the pillar of cloud and fire. There were a great many of them, as many people as there are in a large city today, and they had flocks and herds with them which had to stop and feed; so they could not travel fast. They slept in tents. Whenever the pillar of cloud and fire stopped, they stopped and set up their tents: and when it moved on, they broke camp and followed it.

Once the Lord brought great flocks of quails for them to eat, and because they could not stop to raise grain for bread, He gave them something they called *manna*, which they gathered every morning and made into cakes. It tasted like honey. And He helped them to conquer an enemy who attacked them.

Their way was not easy and they often complained.
But the Lord always took care of them.
In the third month the pillar of cloud and fire stopped near a great mountain, and the people camped at its foot.
What was the name of this mountain?
The Lord told Moses that He would speak to them from the mountain.
On the third day there were "thunders and lightnings, and a thick cloud upon the mount, and the voice of the trumpet exceeding loud; so that all the people in the camp trembled."
Then the people all heard the voice of the Lord speaking.
What did He say first?
Then what did He give them?

We must all learn and keep the ten commandments because they are God's laws.
No one who breaks them can be happy.
So the Lord gave them for our good, to keep us from unhappiness.

Junior

The Juniors should all learn the commandments thoroughly. This is the age at which memorizing comes most easily. Impress the children with the fact that the Lord Himself gave the commandments to us so that we might go through life in the right way and be able to live in heaven when we die. All the unhappiness in the world comes from people's not obeying the commandments as the laws of God. Point out also that in addition to their literal meaning, each one has inner meanings which the children will understand as they grow older.

At what mountain did the Israelites arrive in the third month?
What wonderful thing happened there?
What famous laws were given there?

The commandments are the Lord's laws and are universal. They had always been known by men, but people had forgotten that they came from God and were not man-made laws. So God Himself spoke the commandments with a living voice from the top of Mount Sinai.

We should all know the commandments by heart and say them to ourselves often, for it is only by keeping them that we can be safe and happy. They were afterwards written on two tables, or tablets, of stone; the first three [four]* (Exodus 20:1-11) we think of as those of the first tablet, the last six [five] (verses 13-17) as those of the second, and the fourth [fifth] (verse 12) as belonging to both. This is because the first three [four] teach us our duty to God, the last six [five] our duty to our neighbor, and the

*The bracketed numbers reflect the most common way of numbering the commandments. Swedenborg, however, follows the Catholic-Lutheran numbering system which includes the injunction against graven images as part of No. 1. This in turn requires the illogical subdivision of the mandate against coveting into Nos. 9 and 10. The more usual numbering will be used in the following pages. —*Ed.*

fourth [fifth] ties the two duties together. For father and mother mean not only our earthly parents, but our heavenly Father and our spiritual mother, the Church. Read Matthew 22:34-40.

Many people nowadays complain of the commandments because most of them are *don't*'s. But this is necessary. For we all naturally do many wrong things, and we cannot be good until we stop doing wrong. For example, as long as one insists on telling lies, he cannot be truthful. Isaiah says (1:16-17), "Cease to do evil; learn to do well." If we wish to do right, the first thing necessary is to stop doing wrong.

We should keep the commandments literally. But, as we grow older, we shall find that there are deeper ways of keeping them, too. For example, take the commandment "Thou shalt not steal." We think first of stealing as taking someone's money or belongings. But when we say bad things about a person, we steal his reputation; when we make fun of a companion for doing right, calling him names, we are trying to steal his character; when we are proud of our own good deeds, we are stealing from the Lord, for all our power to do good comes from Him.

The commandments are our protection against wrongdoing, and they are all necessary. Many people acknowledge and try to keep those of the second table, but forget those of the first which command love and worship of the Lord. But we cannot be good without the Lord's help. When we imagine we do not need the Lord, we become self-satisfied, and that closes our minds against learning anything we do not want to learn about what is right and wrong. The first commandment comes first because it is necessary to keeping all the others.

See if you remember these important points:

How were the ten commandments first given at Sinai?
On what were they afterwards written?
Which commandments were written on the first table?
What do they teach?
Which were written on the second table?
What do these teach?
How was the fifth written? Why?

Intermediate

Note the fact that during the first two months of their journey the Israelites were an unorganized horde of people held together only by their recognition of Moses as their leader. They followed the pillar of cloud and fire with no real understanding of how they were to live—even physically—and no internal order or direction. They reached Sinai during the third month and remained there about eleven months. During that time, through the giving of the commandments and the great body of lesser laws and the establishment of the tabernacle and forms of worship, they were formed into an orderly nation and prepared for their further journeys and for the conquest of the Holy Land. If you have a copy of William Worcester's booklet *An Adventure with Children*, you will find it helpful in preparing this lesson.

The crossing of the Red Sea and the destruction of the Egyptians represent our victory over the first temptation which follows a good resolution, and the realization that our selfish habits are powerless if we obey the Lord and look to Him for help. As we read the story in the Word, we imagine that witnessing so great a miracle would surely have made the Israelites so convinced of the Lord's presence and help that they would have had no further difficulties. But the story goes on to tell how they traveled three days into the wilderness and found no water and then came to Marah where there was water; but the water was bitter so that they could not drink it, and again they were completely discouraged, and complained. The new life on which we set out often seems dry and bitter at first. We miss the old selfish indulgences and feel lost without the old selfish thoughts. The Lord made the waters of Marah sweet by showing Moses a particular tree—which represents the principle of loving service—which he was to cast into the water to make it sweet, and the next stopping-place was an oasis where they found ample shade and water. The Lord always gives us these needed intervals of peace and satisfaction.

After this the people hungered, and longed for the fleshpots of Egypt, and the Lord sent quails and manna and also showed Moses how to bring water out of a rock. Finally the Israelites met their first enemy, the Amalekites, and were given victory over them as Moses sat on the hilltop and Aaron and Hur kept his hands lifted toward the Lord. The Amalekites, whose method of attack was to lie in ambush and fall upon the stragglers, picture our doubts and discouragements, which attack us unexpectedly when we are physically weary. All these experiences were behind the children of Israel when in the third month they came to the wilderness of Sinai and camped at the foot of the mountain.

We are so familiar with the ten commandments that we scarcely realize their importance in our lives. From our early childhood our parents have been trying to form our characters according to the ten commandments. Even people who have been brought up with no direct knowledge of the Bible have learned through school and through the law courts that stealing and killing and falsehood will get them into trouble. Because the substance of the commandments is found in codes of law which antedate the time of Moses some have called the Bible story of Sinai a myth. But we are told that the Lord gave the commandments in such an awesome way because it is necessary that we recognize them as divine and not man-made laws. The ten commandments are not long as compared, for example, to the statutes of any state or city; yet they contain all the fundamental principles necessary to safe and happy individual and social life.

There are, however, some things about the commandments which the world at large does not recognize. One is that the first four commandments are quite as essential to happiness as the rest of them. Some people think they can do their duty to their neighbor without worshiping the Lord. But this is not true. Without worship of the Lord we naturally take credit to ourselves for our good deeds, and this self-satisfaction poisons all that we do. The Lord says, "Without me ye can do nothing."

Another thing not generally recognized is that there are deeper things within the letter of the commandments. For example, the commandment "Honor thy father and thy mother" means much more than to obey and cherish our earthly parents. Our true father is our heavenly Father and our true mother is the Church, by means of which we find heavenly life. Unless we honor the Lord and the Church we cannot be happy in heaven, where our earthly ties no longer exist.

Also, the deepest and worst form of stealing is stealing from the Lord, taking to ourselves credit for the good we do instead of recognizing that all good is the Lord's. And to steal another person's character by gossip and slander is just as much a breaking of this commandment as to steal his purse. So we might go through each of the ten and find its deeper meanings.

Each of the commandments, kept literally, opens the way to some positive good, and as we grow older and our problems become more complex and critical, we shall see more and more deeply into the meaning of these "Ten Words," as they are called—the *Decalogue*. They are like a complete and strong foundation on which the house of our character is to be built, or like strong walls which surround a city, giving the inhabitants protection from the attacks of enemies. We need to know and keep the commandments and never to fall into the error of thinking that they can be broken at any time with impunity.

Basic Correspondences

thy father = the Lord
thy mother = the Church

Senior

With the Seniors the emphasis should be placed on the fact that the commandments are divine laws and cannot be transgressed even in their letter without an aftermath of suffering and a permanent loss of some good which might have been gained. They have always been and always will be the basic rules for a sane life. They are the laws of the heavens. And they require specific things. We should know them by heart, repeat them often, and meditate on both their literal and their spiritual meaning. They are our blueprint for the building of our house of character.

Church people often mention the commandments. The Lord in the Gospels mentions them several times and says, for example, "If thou wilt enter into life, keep the commandments." Yet if we went through the membership of any church, how many do you think we should find today who could repeat the commandments or even who knew just where they are to be found in the Bible? How can we keep what we do not know? There is a tendency even with very well intentioned people to feel that if one is regarded as a good person by his neighbors, he is keeping the commandments.

Even in the letter the commandments require specific things. They are not broad generalities. They are injunctions to be obeyed in our daily lives. If we ignore the Lord, if we put anything above service to Him as our supreme object in life, if we take His name in vain in our daily conversation, if we fail to observe Sunday as a day in which to think of Him and to worship Him, if we fail in respect and obedience to our parents, we are breaking the commandments just as much as if we kill, commit adultery, steal, lie, and covet—things for which our neighbors would condemn us. Indeed the first few commandments are of prime importance, for they are the ones summed up by the Lord as "the first and great commandment" (Matthew 22:38). It is only because the committing of sin against the neighbor brings external consequences that we are prone to think the last five commandments are more important. But in reality the consequences of breaking the first five are much more serious because they go deeper.

And indeed when we consider all the commandments in their deeper meanings, the keeping of them requires self-examination and self-discipline of every one of us, for they reach our thoughts and motives and demand much more than a mere outwardly orderly life:

1. To have no other gods before the Lord requires that our ruling motive in all things great or small shall be to do right in His sight, not to be like those who love "the praise of men more than the praise of God."

2. To make no graven image means not to rely on man-made ideas or feelings in preference to God's as standards for our thoughts and affections.

3. Not to take the name of the Lord in vain requires that we inwardly love and respect divine qualities and especially the Word

of God, never taking them lightly or being led away into thinking the Word is a mere human book.

4. To keep the sabbath holy requires that we welcome Sunday as an opportunity to put aside our weekday preoccupations and seek spiritual nourishment and strength.

5. To honor our father and mother demands open acknowledgment and worship of our heavenly Father and support of our spiritual mother, the Church.

6. "Thou shalt not kill" requires, as the Lord Himself taught, that we rid our hearts of all feelings of resentment, hatred, and revenge, which are the root of murder.

7. "Thou shalt not commit adultery" demands not only purity of thought, speech, and conduct but, in the deepest sense, the acceptance of the truths of the Word in their purity, unmixed with our own ideas.

8. "Thou shalt not steal" forbids also harmful gossip, belittling of our neighbor, and especially anything which shakes his faith or puts a stumbling block in his way, and inmostly self-satisfaction, taking credit to ourselves for goodness and wisdom, for this is stealing from the Lord Himself.

9. "Thou shalt not bear false witness" requires honesty with ourselves as well as with others. We must seek to recognize and support the good in our neighbor and not to misjudge him or exaggerate his evils. And we should remember Swedenborg's teaching concerning the larger neighbor, and exercise the same justice and restraint in our dealings with our community, our country, and the church.

10. "Thou shalt not covet" demands contentment with the talents and opportunities which the Lord has given us to use and with the environment which He has assigned to us as our field of service. (Swedenborg numbers the commandments differently, dividing the commandment concerning coveting instead of that concerning worship of the Lord.*)

*It was Augustine (354-430) who first included image-making in the first

Adult

Stress the reason why the commandments were given as they were, and the primary importance of those on the first table. Then run through the ten, suggesting the deeper meaning of each, based on the outline given in the Senior notes. Finally call for questions and let these determine the points for further discussion.

Egypt is behind, but an unknown land, barren and rocky, is now being entered. When we take as an example the breaking of a bad habit, we know that one victory does not finish the conflict: it merely shows us that with the Lord's help we can conquer, if we go forward bravely. The story of the first two months of the journey of the Israelites through the wilderness pictures some of the experiences which come to us in the earlier stages of our period of reformation. They had to be undergone before the people arrived at Mount Sinai, where their nation was to be organized and fully instructed. They reached Sinai in the third month of their journey and camped at the foot of the mount.

The external laws embodied in the ten commandments were known long before the time of Moses: they are the basis of the oldest code of laws known to history. People who think of the Bible as a merely human composition have argued from this that the story of the giving of the commandments from Sinai is not a true story but merely an adaptation of an old myth. Swedenborg, however, explains why the Lord found it necessary to give the commandments to the children of Israel in such an impressive way. It was not because men did not know them, but because men had forgotten that they were the laws of God and thought of them as man-made rules which might be set aside or outgrown. Some people think of them in this way today. Not too many years ago a book was written by a Christian minister to prove that some of the commandments are out-of-date. But they are not out-of-date and never will be, and the Lord wished us to be very sure of this.

---

commandment. Among Protestants only Luther followed this method of division. Judaism, ancient and modern, the Greek Church and most Protestants use the more logical divisions. *—Ed.*

So there were thunders and lightnings, and Mount Sinai was covered with smoke, and all the people heard the voice of the Lord when He gave the commandments. And then they were written by the finger of God on two tables of stone that they might be preserved. They are divine laws, the foundation of all right and happy living both for the individual and for the social group.

We are told that there were two tables of stone. The laws of the first table were those telling of our duty to the Lord, and those of the second table were those telling us our duty to our neighbor. Many of these laws are prohibitions. This makes them seem harsh to those who do not want to obey them. But they must be put in this form for just these very people, which means for all of us part of the time. We are all often in a state of not wanting to do what we ought to do. In the story the people were not ready to receive the truth as it first came from the Lord on tables of stone taken from the top of the mount. We ourselves are not always willing to take the loving suggestions of our family and friends or to obey the Lord from love of Him. We persist in doing wrong, and the same advice, prompted by the same love, must take the form of stern command and harsh prohibition in order to reach us and affect our conduct. The second set of tables was hewed by Moses from stone found at the foot of the mount, which pictures the putting of truth in a form which would reach men in low states of life. We all need it in this form before we are prepared to see divine love and mercy showing through the harsh letter. We must stop doing wrong before we can learn to do right (Isaiah 1:16-17).

The Lord wants us to be happy, but we cannot be happy if we do any of the things forbidden by the commandments or if we neglect to do any of the things required by them. They are the foundations of a happy life. When you are driving along the road in your car, you see a great many signs which tell you where the road leads and how to get where you want to go. Then—very often, it seems—you come to a sign which says *Stop*. You do not always want to stop; sometimes it is very inconvenient and sometimes you see no reason for the sign at that particular place. But you know that the signs are not put up to make trouble for motorists but to keep them out of trouble, and that if you are wise, you will obey them. The journey of the Israelites from Egypt to the land of Canaan, as we know, is a picture of our journey to the promised land of heavenly character. The commandments were given to the Israelites as their guide. They were told that so long as they obeyed them they would prosper, and that when they disobeyed, trouble would inevitably follow. They are given to us for the same purpose. If we recognize this, and write them firmly in our minds, we shall find that whenever we are tempted to do some wrong which will lead us into trouble and may even perhaps wreck our lives, the Lord will recall to us one of these commandments, just as a stop sign appears suddenly at a dangerous crossing. We often think we know better than the Lord what we can do without harm, but we do not. He tells us that these laws are absolutely essential to our welfare and happiness, and we may believe Him. The testimony of history, of reason, and of everyday experience shows that where the ten commandments are broken there is neither peace nor happiness. The twenty-fourth verse of the sixth chapter of Deuteronomy is a good verse to learn and remember: "And the Lord commanded us to do all these statutes, to fear the Lord our God, *for our good always*, that he might preserve us alive, as it is this day."

All this is true of the commandments even in their literal sense. But, like everything else in the Word, the commandments have depths of meaning within the letter. Suppose we take the third commandment as an illustration: "Thou shalt not take the name of the Lord thy God in vain." What does this mean? The first and obvious meaning is that we should not indulge in profanity. Most of us are brought up not only to know that this is wrong but to have an actual distaste for it. It is perhaps no temptation to us. Is this commandment therefore of no importance in our lives? A name is the symbol of the quality of a person or thing. The

Lord's name is more than just the appellations by which He is called. It signifies all His qualities and especially the Word, which is the expression of His love and wisdom. When we in any way belittle the Word, allowing ourselves to think of any part of it as the work of men, to use its stories in jokes or in careless conversation, or even to let our minds wander to worldly thoughts when we are hearing it read in church, we are breaking this commandment. And when we indulge in this deeper form of profanity, we injure ourselves and also influence others to their hurt. This is especially true of the New Church person, who knows better—who knows the holiness of the Word and its source and has the responsibility of leading others to understand and reverence it.

We might go through all the commandments. We find them explained not only in the *Arcana Coelestia* (nn. 8859-8912) where this chapter of Exodus is covered, but in TCR 283-331.* These are sections which we should all study seriously in order to understand the meaning and relevance of the commandments in our lives. The Lord says, "If ye love me, keep my commandments."

From the Writings of Swedenborg

True Christian Religion, nn. 412-416: "Those who do not know what the term neighbor means in its true sense, suppose that it means nothing else than the individual man, and that loving the neighbor means conferring benefits upon him. But the neighbor and love to him have a wider meaning and a higher meaning as individuals are multiplied . . . Thus, a community smaller or greater is the neighbor because it is a collective man; and from this it follows that he who loves a community loves those of whom the community consists; therefore he who wills and acts rightly towards a community consults the good of each individual . . . One's country is more a neighbor than

---

*Also in the *Doctrine of Life* and the interchapter articles in *Apocalypse Explained* (nn. 950-1028). (This latter material has been abstracted and printed separately as *The Spiritual Life and the Word of God* [Swedenborg Foundation] and *Religion and Life* [Swedenborg Society].) Note that in this latter work, Swedenborg curiously followed the order of the decalogue as found in the LXX version, which reverses the "kill" and "steal" commandments. —*Ed.*

a single community . . . Moreover, loving one's country is loving the public welfare . . . It should be known that those who love their country and render good service to it from good will, after death love the Lord's kingdom, for then that is their country, and those who love the Lord's kingdom love the Lord Himself, because the Lord is the all in all things of His kingdom . . . Since man was born for eternal life, and is introduced into it by the church, the church is to be loved as the neighbor in a higher degree . . . This does not mean that the priesthood should be loved in a higher degree . . . The priesthood merely serves, and is to be honored so far as it serves . . . The Lord's kingdom is the neighbor that is to be loved in the highest degree. . . . he who loves the Lord's kingdom loves all in the world who acknowledge the Lord and have faith in Him and charity towards the neighbor; and he loves also all in heaven. Those who love the Lord's kingdom love the Lord above all things . . . Therefore love towards the Lord's kingdom is love towards the neighbor in its fullness."

Suggested Questions on the Lesson

J. Through what kind of country did the Israelites have to travel to reach the Holy Land? *wilderness or desert*
J. What things did they miss which they had had in Egypt? *fresh food, water*
J. How did the Lord take care of them? *manna, quails, water from rock*
P. To what mountain did they come in the third month? *Sinai*
J. Were they allowed to go up on the mountain? *no*
J. On the third morning what happened which made the people tremble? *thunder, trumpets*
P. Whose voice did they hear? *God's*
P. What did the Lord first say about Himself? *"I am the Lord thy God"*
P. Then what did He give the people? *the ten commandments*
J. Into what two groups can the commandments be divided? *1-5, 6-10*
J. What does the first group teach? *duties to God*
J. What does the second group teach? *duties to man*
I. Had these commandments been known before? *yes*
I. Why did the Lord speak them from Sinai? *to show they were divine laws*
S. What does the wilderness journey picture? *reformation—the long period of preparation for spiritual living*

THE ARK OF THE COVENANT

Exodus 25:1-22

It is important that certain major events be mentioned briefly, because they prepared the minds of the Israelites to receive willingly the long series of instructions and laws which were given to them at Sinai. Note especially two things: they came to Sinai early in their journey—the third month—and during their eleven-month stay there they were formed into an organized nation with a government which lasted them throughout their history and still to some extent persists with some Jews of the present day. Also call attention to the fact that the materials for the tabernacle and its furnishings were free offerings of all the people, and remind them of where they got those materials (Exodus 12:35-36). Some commentators have ridiculed the idea that the tabernacle was actually so fine a production, calling the Israelites a nomadic people who could not possibly have possessed the materials required or been capable of receiving so complex a system of laws. It is hard to see how they could forget that the Israelites had not been nomads for several hundred years and that Moses had been brought up as a member of the royal household, to say nothing of the plain statement as to the source of their material wealth.

Doctrinal Points

Worship of the Lord should be at the heart of everything we do.

A study of the spiritual sense of the laws given at Sinai shows us how practical and important every detail of the letter of the Word is for us.

The plan of the tabernacle is the blueprint for a heavenly character.

The commandments must be written in our hearts—not just in our minds.

Notes for Parents

You have read the stories of the remarkable experiences the children of Israel had during their first two months in the wilderness. Through these experiences they were shown that the Lord was really with them, and they must have begun to realize that they had a special mission to perform, since they were so miraculously protected and provided for. For various reasons, the Lord had chosen them as the nation through whom the Word could best be written in order that it might reach men in all stages of spiritual development. They were a very literal-minded people and very much interested in their own prosperity. Through fear of punishment and hope of reward they could be led to carry out all the elaborate rituals and to observe all the detailed laws which the Lord wanted recorded in His Word. In their letter these laws were for their nation, which was to be a "theocracy," a nation governed by religious laws; but every one of the directions given to them has an inner meaning which applies to the spiritual life of every one of us, even though most of the outward rules are no longer necessary to our life. Even the ten commandments, which—unlike some of the other laws—will never be out-of-date in their letter, have also deep meanings within them, and the further we go in our efforts to lead a good life the more we see and keep of this inner meaning.

The Lord gave the nation their laws while they were camped on the plain at the foot of Mount Sinai. Moses was called up into the mountain to receive them. The most important of them, aside from the ten commandments, were the directions for the construction, furnishing, and care of the tabernacle, their tent of worship. And the most important article of furniture in the tabernacle was the ark, in which the two tables of stone inscribed with the ten commandments were to be kept. Several times in the Bible we read that the commandments are to be written on our hearts. This means that if we keep them faithfully, we shall in time come to love to keep them. The state of loving to keep the commandments is heaven. We can easily see this if we think what a wonderful place the world would be if none of us ever wanted to hurt anyone else in any way. There would be no poverty, no hunger, no crime, no war. We know that the world is not like that now. What we do not always realize is that each one of us could help to bring heaven on earth by trying to feel and think and act every day in the spirit of love to the Lord and the neighbor. This is what we mean when we say in the Lord's Prayer, "Thy kingdom come, thy will be done, on earth as it is in heaven."

Primary

The description of the ark and its contents will make a sufficient lesson for this class. Read the story from the Word. Emphasize the importance of the commandments and their place in the tabernacle. These children can get the idea of the meaning of the ark and its position in our lives. They should be able to describe the ark in detail.

This is another story about Moses and what happened when he was leading his people from Egypt to the Holy Land. Do you remember about how the Lord spoke to Moses out of the burning bush? That was at a place near some mountains called Horeb. One of these mountains was *Mount Sinai.* Try to remember this name because you will hear it many times. The Lord had promised Moses at the burning bush that after they escaped from Egypt they would worship the Lord at this same place.

After three months they came to a great mountain called Mount Sinai, near the place where the Lord had talked with Moses from the burning bush.

They camped in the plain at the foot of this mountain.

From the top of the mountain the Lord spoke to them the ten commandments.

You will learn these commandments someday. They are the Lord's laws, which we must obey if we want to be safe and happy.

Then he called Moses to go up into the mountain and gave him many laws to govern the people.

And He told him how to build and furnish a tabernacle in which they were to worship.

The thing of most importance in the tabernacle was the ark, a box or chest in which they were to keep the two tables of stone on which the Lord had written the commandments after He spoke them.

What was the ark to be made of?
With what was it overlaid?
How was it to be carried?
What was on top of the ark?

After the ark was finished and the two tables of stone put into it, it was placed in the inmost room of the tabernacle, which was called the Holy of Holies. After that the Lord always spoke to Moses and Aaron from between the cherubim on the ark.

Junior

The plan and furnishings of the tabernacle should be reviewed with this class before taking up the ark and its meaning. See if any of the children can repeat any of the commandments. This is the time to begin to memorize them, and the teacher should have this project in mind and talk over with the superintendent some plan for carrying it out—perhaps call for one commandment a week and offer a suitable reward for the final ability to repeat all ten perfectly.

In the third month the Israelites came to Sinai, and they stayed there about eleven months. The ten commandments were given by the Lord from the top of Mount Sinai. They are found in chapter 20 of Exodus. If you haven't already memorized them, you should begin now and see how soon you can learn them all, for they are our directions for a good life. We cannot break any of the commandments without suffering for it and bringing suffering on other people, too. The laws of every nation in the world are founded on the ten commandments, for they were made known to people from the very beginning of the human race. The Israelites knew them in a general way; but they, as well as everybody else, had forgotten that they were laws of God and not just man-made laws.

In addition to the commandments, the Lord gave the people many other laws about all sorts of things in their lives. There are many of them in these chapters of Exodus, and the Book of Leviticus is full of them. We should know that, although most of them in their letter applied only to the ancient Hebrews, in their inner meaning every one of them applies to us. They are a wonderful study, but we have not time to take them up in Sunday school.

Along with the laws, the Lord gave the people through Moses directions for making and furnishing their place of worship. This was a tent, or tabernacle, which could be taken down and carried with them wherever they went. When they stopped, it was immediately set up in the middle of the camp. You are old enough to understand that this means that our worship of the Lord is to be at the very center of our lives and is to be taken with us wherever we go. Later we shall study the tabernacle and its furnishings, but in this lesson we are thinking especially of its most important piece of furniture, the ark of the covenant. You remember that an ark is a box or chest made to keep something safely.

What ark have we studied about?

There is another ark in the story of Moses. What was it?

The ark in our lesson today was not like either of these.

Of what was the ark of the covenant made?

Acacia wood is from a thorny desert tree.

How big was the ark?

A *cubit* is the length from a man's elbow to the tips of his fingers, about one and a half feet.

With what was the wood of the ark overlaid?

How was the ark to be carried?

What was to be placed on top of the ark?

The mercy seat was a covering the same length and width as the ark. The two cherubim on the mercy seat were symbolic figures, and they are usually thought of as angel figures. No one knows just what these figures on the ark were really like. How do you suppose the Israelites knew how to make them? Read Exodus 31:1-7.

What was to be kept in the ark?

The "testimony," or covenant, means the two tables of stone on which the ten commandments were written.

In verse 22 we read that the Lord promised to speak with the high priest from between the two cherubim on the mercy seat, and this happened many times afterward. Whenever Moses and Aaron were in doubt about what they should do, they consulted the Lord in front of the ark and received His answers. The ark was the only article of furniture that was in the inmost room or Holy of Holies of the tabernacle. The Holy of Holies pictures our hearts, and this means that the commandments should be "written in our hearts" or obeyed from love to the Lord and the neighbor. Read Psalm 37:31; 40:8; and Isaiah 51:7.

We should note one other point in our lesson. How was Moses told to get the materials for the tabernacle? Do you remember where the people got these things?

Intermediate

The correspondence of the details of the ark and the reason for its position in the tabernacle are the proper lessons for this class.

In the third month the people came to Sinai. We remember this as part of the range called Horeb near which Moses received his call at the burning bush. Sinai was a rugged mountain rising steeply from the plain. The people were told to camp in the plain and not come near the mount. Moses was called up into the mountain to receive from the Lord laws and directions which were to govern the people not only throughout their journey to the Holy Land, but always. Even today orthodox Jews observe many of them. Many of these laws (not, of course, the ten commandments) are not meant for us to obey in their letter, but in their inner meaning they apply to us and to all people at all times. When you are older, you will want to study some of them, and you will sometimes hear sermons preached on one or another of them. They go very deep into our experience and teach us a great deal.

You know, of course, that the ten commandments were given from Mount Sinai. This was not because people had never known them before. Men had been told them from the very beginning, and all people have them as the basis of their law. But people had forgotten—as people today sometimes forget—that they are laws of God and cannot be broken without causing suffering. So the giving

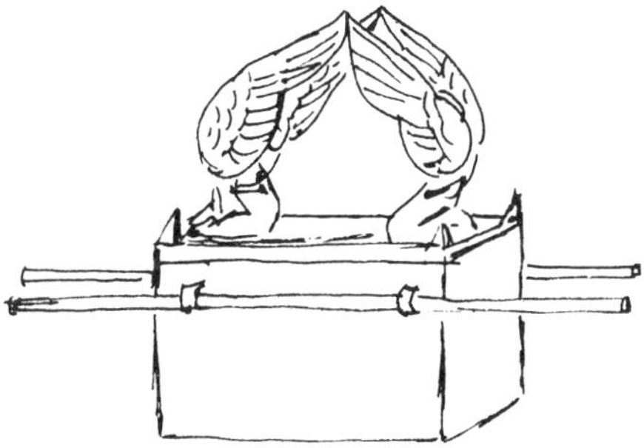

In the Holy of Holies:
The Ark

The Seven-Branched Candlestick

In the Holy Place:
The Altar of Incense

The Table of Shewbread

In the Outer Court:

The Altar of Burnt Offering

The Laver

(see following page for plan of the tabernacle)

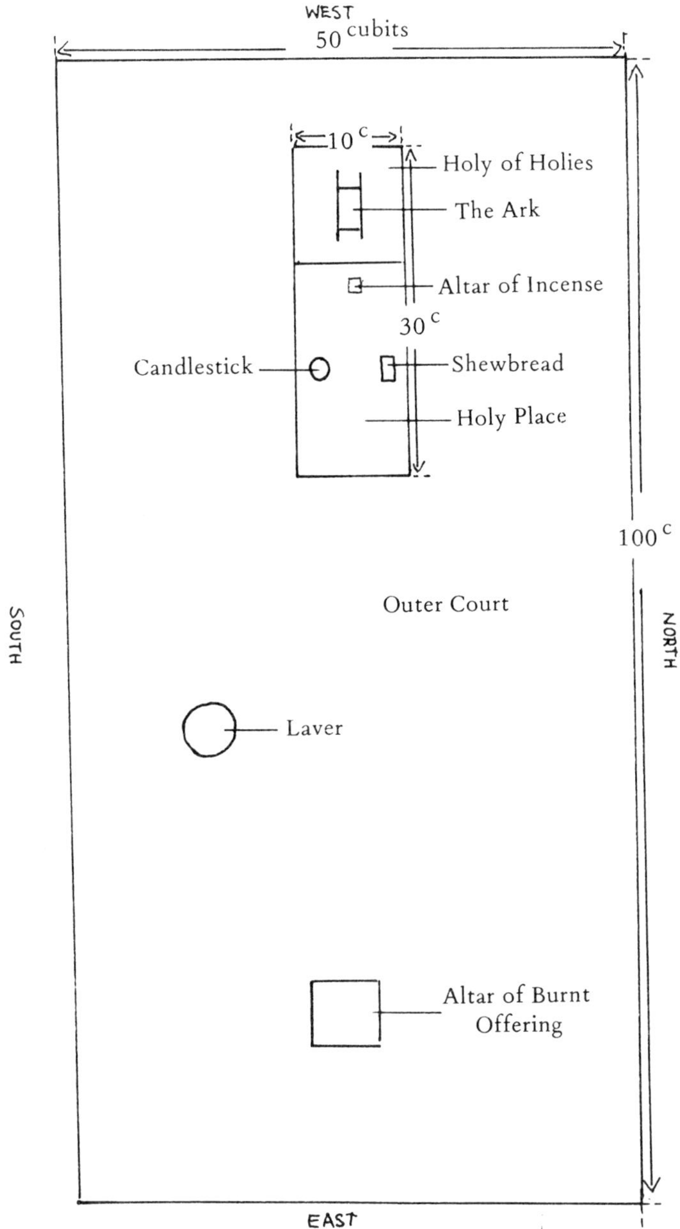

PLAN OF THE TABERNACLE

of them from Sinai was recorded in the Word so that we might always remember their source and importance.

The commandments were first spoken by the voice of the Lord from the top of the mountain, all the people hearing them—the only time when all the people heard the Lord speak. Then Moses was called up into the top of the mountain and the Lord wrote them on two tables of stone. When Moses brought the two tables down, he found that the people had already gone back to idolatry, and he broke the tables in his anger. Then the Lord told him to cut two more tables from stone at the foot of the mount and bring them up, and the same commandments were written again. The two tables from the foot of the mount were the ones which were placed in the ark and which traveled with the Israelites wherever they went. They were the holiest thing they possessed.

Among the things which the Lord gave Moses on the mount were directions for the construction and furnishing of the tabernacle, or tent, in which they were to worship throughout their journey. It was so constructed that it could be taken down and carried with them; and very careful instructions were given for its care, including directions as to which tribes should march in front of it, and which after it, and just how the tribes were to be aranged around it when they camped. It was to be the center of their camp and the center of their marching line. It is easy to see that this means that our worship is to be the center of our life whatever we do and wherever we go.

The first and most important article of furniture to be made for the tabernacle was the ark in which the two tables of stone inscribed with the ten commandments were to be kept. The ark was to be the only article of furniture in the Holy of Holies, or inmost room of the tabernacle. Our lesson tells us that it was a chest made of acacia wood overlaid with pure gold inside and out. The three divisions of the tabernacle represent the three planes of our lives on which we should serve the Lord: our hearts or wills, our minds, and our outward lives. The Holy of Holies pictures the heart. Several times in the Word we read that the commandments should be in the heart (Psalm 37:31; 40:8, and Isaiah 51:7). This means that we should love them and cherish them as the center of our life, and the ark is a picture of the way in which we make a place for them there. Acacia wood, Swedenborg tells us, represents "the good of righteousness," which is the good which we develop in our lives when we obey the Lord because we see that all good comes from Him. The gold with which it was overlaid is pure, unselfish love. This, too, comes into our hearts from the Lord as we form the habit of obedience in a spirit of humility. The golden mercy seat, or covering, on top of the ark pictures the cleansing from sins which follows our obedience, and the golden cherubs picture the Lord's providence protecting us against taking credit to ourselves for our obedience and goodness.

The last verse of our lesson tells us that the Lord promised to meet with the children of Israel and to commune with them "from above the mercy seat, and from between the cherubims." When we have a decision to make in our lives, how do we find out what the Lord wants us to do? First we think of the commandments and ask ourselves, "Is there anything in the ways I might choose which is contrary to the commandments?" If there is, our decision is easy. But suppose all possibilities square with the commandments; then we must ask, "Which one will do the most good to others?" And when we ask this, we are led to make the right decision. If we hold the commandments in our hearts and try to live from the principle of service to the Lord and the neighbor, being grateful to the Lord for everything we can do and not proud of ourselves, we may be sure that the Lord will form in us a heavenly character.

The ark of the covenant had a long history. The Israelites carried it faithfully all through their forty years in the wilderness and set it up in the tabernacle when they reached their homes in the Holy Land. Then, because they had reached their goal and were prosperous, they neglected it. Once they even tried to use it selfishly as a sort of good-luck piece, and they lost it for a while. It was finally carried to Jerusalem by David, and when Solomon built the temple, the ark was placed in the inmost chamber there. But after the temple was destroyed and the people were carried captive to Babylon, there is no further mention of the ark. Many stories have been written about its later history, but they are purely imaginary.

Basic Correspondences

acacia wood	=	the good of righteousness
cherubim [cherubs]	=	the Lord's providence protecting us from profaning holy things

Senior

Perhaps the most important lesson for the Seniors is the fact that the ten commandments are binding upon all men for all time and are the only basis for the development of a heavenly character. There is so much attempt in the world today to compromise with the commandments that young people should be led to realize that they cannot be broken with impunity now or at any time.

It may be helpful to us to look for a moment at the wilderness journey as a whole. It lasted in all about forty years. This seems a long time for a short journey, and a later lesson will tell us why it was prolonged. But most of its outstanding events were crowded into the first year, and all but the first two months of this year were spent at Sinai. What does this picture in our lives? We have said that the wilderness journey represents the period in which we are trying to bring our outward lives into order. Most of us are brought up in orderly homes and are taught what is right and wrong, and made to form good habits. But often when we leave home for work or college, we shed some of these habits and experiment with things we have been forbidden to do at home. We want to see what it is like to "do as others do." It is not until we have seen the dangers and unhappiness of this worldly life that we break away from Egypt and start back to the Holy Land. Our journey, like that of the Israelites, follows certain stages. There is the first real temptation (crossing the Red Sea); there is the period of discouragement when we do not find immediate satisfaction in the new life (the experience at Marah); the glimpse of a new kind of happiness (the rest at Elim). Then in the Bible story follow the giving of the quails and manna (the realization that the Lord does actually give us enough goodness to meet each day as it comes, if we are faithful); the bringing of water out of the rock at Rephidim (picturing our ability, with the Lord's help, to find satisfying truth even in the hard facts of life); the battle with Amalek (the overcoming of discouragement); and finally the arrival at Sinai "in the third month." We all have these experiences when we set out to correct our lives and bring them back into order.

Up to the time of their arrival at Sinai, the people had been a mere unorganized horde under Moses' leadership, following the pillar of cloud and fire. We fumble along in the same way at first. We are on our way and it is not altogether true that we don't know where we are going, but we haven't developed any very clear plan of action. After a few experiences, however, we know that the Lord really is helping us, and we sit down to think things through and organize our life. This is just what happened to the children of Israel at Sinai. They stayed there eleven months, and in that time—through the laws and statutes given to them by the Lord from the mount, they were organized into a nation. The twelve tribes were told their proper relation to each other; leaders were chosen not only for each tribe, but for the various divisions within the tribes; rules were laid down for the conduct of all their daily affairs; punishments were named for infractions of the laws; and, above all, the commandments were given and full instructions for maintaining worship. As we read the chapters concerning this stay at Sinai, and the book of Leviticus in which most of the laws are gathered together, it may seem that they received just a long series of minute directions, some of them quite strange and some hard for us today to understand. It is not surprising that without a knowledge of the internal sense of these laws, men have often decided they were not worth reading and completely out-of-date. But we know—and it takes only a little study of the internal sense to illustrate—that each one has an important meaning and application for us and for men and women of all times, and that they all bear relation to one another and, taken together, give us a complete blueprint for orderly living. Today blueprints are very important in engineering, architecture, city planning, and many other fields. It may help us to think of these laws given at Sinai as our blueprint for a good life; we may at first see only its general outlines, but as we begin to build, we find that each little detail is very necessary to the whole.

Today we are thinking of one detail: the ark. It was a chest approximately four feet long, two feet high, and two feet wide, made of acacia wood overlaid within and without with pure gold, and with a crown or edge of gold around the top, and upon it the golden mercy seat, or cover, on which stood the two golden cherubim, usually thought of as angel figures, with their wings meeting above the ark. In the box were kept the two tables of stone on which the ten commandments had been inscribed, and it was to be the only piece of furniture in the Holy of Holies or inmost room of the tabernacle. It was thus the central point of the whole religious organization, for the tabernacle was to be set up in the midst of the camp wherever they stopped, carried at the center of their line of march, and set up in the center of the Holy Land when they arrived there. The people recognized it as the Lord's presence with them and as their most important possession.

We think of the tabernacle as embodying all our thought about worship. Swedenborg says it represents heaven and that every good man or woman is a heaven in the least form. There would be no heaven anywhere if there were not heavenly men and women. And the thing that makes a man or woman heavenly is the Lord's presence in the life. This presence is given as we put selfishness away and learn and obey the Lord's laws from the desire to serve Him. The Holy of Holies of the tabernacle represents our hearts, and that is where we should keep the commandments, obeying the Lord from love. Acacia wood represents righteousness; the gold with which it was covered, love; the mercy seat, the cleansing of our evils as we hear and receive the Lord's Word from love; and the cherubim, the Lord's providence which constantly protects us against the evil of ascribing our goodness to ourselves. We all know how easy it is to fall into that evil and how much we need this protection. Whenever we catch ourselves counting up our accomplishments and our good deeds, and thinking we are better than someone else, we know the Lord is speaking a warning to us from between the cherubim. Obedience to the commandments from love to the Lord and the neighbor is the center of a heavenly life.

Adult

There are many important discussion topics in this lesson: the importance of the commandments, the different motives for obedience to them, the necessity for humility, the persistence of our selfish inheritance, the way in which divine providence protects us from ourselves, the time element in the journey and its relation to our experience.

As a background for this lesson, recall the stories of the giving of quails and manna, the bringing of water out of a rock at Rephidim, and the battle with Amalek, in which Joshua led the army and Moses went up to the top of the mountain and Aaron and Hur held up his hands to the Lord. We need to have them in mind, for the experiences confirmed in the children of Israel the certainty that the Lord was able and willing to provide for them and to give them victory over their enemies. They all belong, in their spiritual sense, to the very beginning of the period of reformation, for we are told in chapter 19 that the people came to Sinai in the third month. Their first experiences were the necessary preparation for their reception of the laws and instructions to be given at Sinai.

Another preparation is found in the story of the visit of Jethro to Moses (chapter 18). Jethro the Midianite, the father-in-law of Moses, represents a simple, childlike state of worship. Yet Jethro was very wise, as good children are often wiser than grown-ups. He found Moses overburdened with the tasks he had assumed in his leadership of the people, sitting all day hearing complaints and settling differences. Are we not likely, in the early stages of our journey heavenward, to think that we must stop to look into each little thought and act, and to become bogged down in the complexities of our nature? Jethro's advice to Moses was that wise judges be chosen from the tribes to hear and decide the ordinary cases, and that only the really difficult matters should be brought to Moses. We should set up principles in our lives to govern us in the small affairs of daily life, and put our real thought upon our deeper problems.

We all know the story of the giving of the commandments from Sinai and that, in addition to the commandments, the many detailed laws recorded in Exodus and especially in Leviticus were given during the eleven months in which the people were camped on the plain at the foot of Mount Sinai. In fact, the whole system of laws by which the Israelites were to be governed throughout their history as a representative nation was given there. When they studied and obeyed these laws, they prospered; when they neglected to study them and disobeyed them, disasters came upon them. Their most pressing motive in keeping them was apparently the desire for worldly prosperity, not unlike the way a child often tries to do things he thinks will please adults without understanding any deeper reasons for his actions. In their letter the minor laws were for the people of that day, instructions by which the chosen judges might be guided in their decisions. They were abrogated—in their letter—when that era came to its end. But we know that in their inner meaning every one of them is a directive to us and can help us in setting our lives in order and keeping them in order. And the ten commandments, for which Moses himself stands in the story, are both in their letter and in their spiritual meaning divine laws for all people for all time.

Next to the commandments the instructions for making and furnishing the tabernacle and for its use are the most important. As the tabernacle was the center of the nation's worship, we think of it as representative of worship in our lives—primarily a place, but a state of life, a state so ordered that the love and wisdom of the Lord can be received. The three divisions of the tabernacle represent the three planes of our lives: will, thought, and act.

The furnishings of each division picture the essential things which must be in these divisions if the life is to be heavenly.

We are concerned today with the ark. We know that each of us is kept alive from moment to moment by the influx of the Lord's life into the inmost of our being. This inmost presence of the Lord in our lives is pictured by the ark. Swedenborg says it represents the "inmost heaven." It was made of acacia wood, which pictures "the good of merit" which is in the Lord alone. It was overlaid within and without with pure gold, picturing the Lord's unselfish love. Its crown of pure gold and the golden rings by which it was carried are the encircling and support of the heavenly life by the Lord's love. The mercy seat—or, as Swedenborg renders it, the "propitiatorium"—is our cleansing from evil by the reception of that love. The golden cherubim picture divine providence protecting the good person from profaning that which he receives by attributing it to himself.

Swedenborg tells us many times that "the Divine of the Lord makes heaven." That is, no one can come into a heavenly state except as he puts self aside and so opens the way for the influx of the Lord's unselfish love. Obedience to the commandments is the essential at the heart of the heavenly life, but this heavenly life is not our first obedience through a sense of fear of consequences or the desire to be thought good; nor is it the second obedience from a sense of duty. It is obedience practiced until it has become willing and joyous, until it is so covered by our sense of the Lord's goodness and mercy that our natural self-righteousness disappears. The wood of the ark, the gold which overlaid it, and the golden crown around the top edge all picture the willing acknowledgment that all goodness and truth are the Lord's and not our own. The translation "mercy seat" was probably suggested by the fact that the Lord was to speak to Moses from between the cherubim, but it is not an accurate one. The Hebrew word is *koppar*, meaning merely a "covering," although the word "propitiatory" and the connotations of the Hebrew root indicate that it suggest the covering of our evils by divine mercy. The root is the same which comes out in "Yom Kippur," the day of atonement. We are told that even angels, when from time to time they begin to lose their lively consciousness that they have no real life except from the Lord, are "let down" into their own states briefly until they realize again what is their own and what is the Lord's in them. So the mercy seat or propitiatory pictures exactly the way in which the Lord in His mercy hides our evils from our sight and so cleanses us when we have learned to obey the commandments from love.

Cherubim are frequently mentioned in the Word. They are symbolic figures representing the care and protection which divine providence exercises over us, especially protection against "profaning" the truth and good which we have accepted. Genesis records that when Adam and Eve were driven out of the Garden of Eden, the Lord placed cherubim at the entrance to prevent their return; this means that when self-love began to occupy the human heart, the Lord closed the inner way of communication with heaven which had been open in the first people so that this "perception" should not be used for selfish ends. We are also told that whenever the Lord sees that we are no longer willing to live according to a given truth which we have previously acknowledged, He takes from us the belief that it is the truth. Swedenborg says that in this way one may gradually kill his conscience. This by no means leads toward heaven; it merely prevents one from going deeper into hell. Read here verses 23 through 31 of the thirty-seventh Psalm. These words express very beautifully the state of the "good" person, who has set up the tabernacle in the midst of his life and the ark in the Holy of Holies of the tabernacle. "The law of his God is in his heart; none of his steps shall slide."

From the Writings of Swedenborg

Arcana Coelestia, n. 9509: "*And thou shalt make two cherubs.* That this signifies no admission and approach to the Lord except through the good of love, is evident from the signification of 'cherubs,' as being guard and providence lest the Lord should be approached except through the good of love.

As this was signified by the 'cherubs,' they were placed over the propitiatory* that was upon the ark, and therefore they were made of solid gold; for by the 'ark' is signified heaven where the Lord is, and by 'gold,' the good of love. That there is no approach to the Lord except through the good of love, is because love is spiritual conjunction, and all good is of love. Therefore those who are in the good of love to the Lord are brought in to Him in heaven, because they are conjoined with Him, and so are those who are in the good of love toward the neighbor."

Suggested Questions on the Lesson

P. What did the Lord give all the people from the mountain top? *ten commandments*

J. What else did He tell Moses? *many minor laws*

P. What was their place of worship to be? *tabernacle (tent)*

J. What was the inmost room called? *Holy of Holies*

P. What piece of furniture was in it? *ark of covenant*

P. What was the ark to be made of? *acacia wood*

P. What was on top of the ark? *cover (mercy seat, propitiatory)*

P. What was inside of it? *two stone tablets (commandments)*

J. How did the Lord tell Moses He would use the ark? *to speak to them*

I. What does the ark represent? *our inner being, where the Lord can speak to us*

S. What does the "mercy seat" represent? *our cleansing from evil*

S. What does Swedenborg call the mercy seat? *propitiatory*

S. What are pictured by the cherubim? *protection of divine providence*

I. Why does the ark represent heaven? *heaven must be in our "hearts"*

---

*translated "mercy seat" in the King James Version. (Both the Vulgate and Schmidius [Latin] use "propitiatory." The New American Version, following the Vulgate, is the only English edition I am aware of which uses "propitiatory." *–Ed.*

THE TABERNACLE

Exodus 26-27

The children of Israel reached Sinai three months after they left Egypt, and they remained there almost a year. The departure does not come until Numbers 10:11. The pupils should get a clear idea of this year at Sinai and what it accomplished. The giving of the laws and especially the establishment of the external forms of worship welded the people into a nation.

Doctrinal Points

What the orderly life is.
Every individual is a church in least form.
The uses of formal worship.
The ancient Jewish Church in the historical series.

Notes for Parents

When they left Egypt under the leadership of Moses and the pillar of cloud and fire, the Israelites were just an unorganized horde of people bent on escaping from a bondage which had become unbearable. After three months in the wilderness they came to the great mountain called Sinai, which stands up abruptly out of the plain. There the pillar of cloud and fire stopped and they camped in the plain, and there they stayed for nearly a year.

During that time the Lord formed them into a nation by giving them an extensive code of laws to govern everything they did. The difference between this code and the codes which govern nations today was that religion was its center. The first thing given to them was the ten commandments. These commandments were not new. Most of them are found in codes of laws which existed before the time of Moses. And that is just what we should expect, for they are not man-made laws but the laws which are the very foundation of human society, laws given to mankind by God from the very beginning. It was to establish this very fact that they were again spoken by the living voice of the Lord Himself to the children of Israel from amidst the fire and smoke on the top of Mount Sinai.

Afterward the Lord gave Moses the plan on which the tabernacle was to be built and all the directions for its furnishings and for the worship that was to be carried on in it. The tabernacle was to be erected in the center of their encampment and carried at the center of their line of march. The tabernacle, like our churches today, was the "house of God," His dwelling place among men. It was to be the center of their life, just as worship of God should be the center of our lives, reaching out into and directing everything we do. Did you ever stop to think that if we do not look to the Lord for guidance in our daily lives, we are really setting ourselves up in place of God?

The tabernacle in the center of the camp of Israel is a picture of the Lord's unselfish love and His truth at the center of our life. The older children are studying the meaning of the three divisions of the tabernacle and of some of the other details of its construction and furnishing. Such a study will help them to see how they can build their own characters into a house of the Lord. Recall what the Apostle Paul wrote to the Corinthians (I Cor. 3:16): "Know ye not that ye are the temple of God, and that the Spirit of God dwelleth in you?"

Primary

The description of the tabernacle will interest the younger children. Emphasize the colors and the embroidery. This is a good lesson in which to present the thought of the church as the Lord's house and to discuss why we go to church. Working on the basis of the plan of the tabernacle, describe as many as possible of the details of its construction and furnishings. Stress especially the three parts, and the use of the three metals.

You know, don't you, that the church is called the Lord's house? The Lord is near to us all the time, although we can't see Him, but He is especially near in church because there we are thinking and talking about Him and trying to learn what He wants us to do.

When the children of Israel stayed on in Egypt for so many years, they forgot all about the Lord and how to worship Him. So before they had been in the wilderness very long, He brought them to the foot of a great mountain called Mount Sinai and had them camp there. Then He called Moses up to the top of the mountain and told him that He was going to give the people the laws by which they were to live and all the directions for their worship. Then the Lord came down upon the mountain in fire and spoke the ten commandments so that all the people heard them.

Afterwards He told Moses just how to build the tabernacle, the house in which they were to worship Him. You know that the children of Israel were traveling through the wilderness; so they could not have houses and churches like ours. They had to live in tents, and their church had to be a tent, too.

The tabernacle was about forty-five feet long and fifteen feet wide.
What were the walls made of?
What was it covered with?
What was the entrance?
Another curtain, called the *veil*, divided the tabernacle into two parts.
The inner part was called the Most Holy Place or the Holy of Holies, and the other part was called the Holy Place.
Outside was an open court surrounded by curtains hung on posts.
All the wood in the tabernacle was covered with gold.
The bases on which the boards were set were of silver.
The posts for the outer fence and their bases were of bronze.
Your teacher will show you a plan of the tabernacle and help you to understand it.

Junior

The Juniors can be given an idea of the meaning of the three parts of the tabernacle in our lives, and if they grasp this readily the teacher may go on to speak simply of the meaning of the furnishings in each part. The literal facts, however, are of first importance with this age group.

What is a tabernacle?
Why was the first church of the Israelites a tent?

The tabernacle itself was about fifteen feet wide and forty-five feet long, and the court which surrounded it was about seventy-five feet wide and a hundred and fifty feet long. A cubit is the length from the elbow to the tips of the fingers, or about a foot and a half. All the materials for the tabernacle and its furnishings were brought to Moses by the people as free-will offerings, and we read in Exodus 36:1-2 that the Lord put wisdom in the hearts of certain men to do the work properly.

The tabernacle proper was divided into two parts by a beautiful curtain called the *veil*. The inner division was a cube and was called the Most Holy Place or the Holy of Holies. The other division was called the Holy Place.

What were the walls of the tabernacle made of?
What were the bases for these walls made of?

The boards were so made that they would fit together when they were placed upright in the bases, and they were held together by long bars which ran through rings of gold. So the tabernacle could be set up and taken down very quickly. When they camped it was always to be set up in the center, and when they marched it was carried in the center of the line of march. Only the Levites, the descendants of Jacob's third son Levi, could handle the tabernacle.

What three coverings were made for the top of the tabernacle?
What was the fence around the outer court made of?
What was used to cover all the wood of the tabernacle?
What were the bases for the boards made of?
What were the posts on which the curtains of the outer court were hung and their bases made of?

Notice that the couplings of the inner covering of the tabernacle were of gold, but those of the outer covering were of brass or bronze. Try to remember the three metals used in the tabernacle and where they were used, because when you are older you will learn that there was a very deep reason in this. The wood used is thought to have been the wood of the thorny acacia tree. Study the chart with the last lesson to see what the furniture of the tabernacle was and where each piece was placed.

Now look up John 2:18-22. The tabernacle, like the temple which followed it, was built to be the dwelling place of the Lord with men. When the Lord Himself was on earth, the human body in which He lived was His dwelling place, and so He called it the temple also. But we can have a dwelling place of the Lord in us, too, and this is a heavenly character which is also a temple of the Lord. Look up I Corinthians 3:16. This temple in us is also divided into three parts. Our "Holy of Holies" is our inmost heart, where the Lord reaches us and speaks to us. Our "Holy Place" is our mind, where we think about the Lord and about what we ought to do. And our "outer court" is our behavior, which is open for everyone to see. You notice that the only piece of furniture in the Holy of Holies was the ark, and you will remember that the ark was a chest made to hold the two tables of stone on which the ten commandments had been written by the finger of God. Now look up Deuteronomy 6:6, Psalms 40:8 and 119:98, Isaiah 51:7, and Jeremiah 31:33. Can you see how clearly we are taught what is meant in our lives by the ark's being in the Holy of Holies of the tabernacle?

Intermediate

The correspondence of the tabernacle as a whole, of its three divisions, and of the three metals used and the place of each in the structure makes a well-ordered and on the whole simple lesson. The teacher, however, should also familiarize himself with the meaning of the articles of furniture and may add these if he has time.

After about three months in the wilderness, the Israelites came to Mount Sinai and camped on the plain at the foot of the mountain. There they remained nearly a year. You may easily see that after hundreds of years in Egypt, the latter part of which was spent in slavery, they were not a very well-organized people. Since they had forgotten even the name of their God, they must also have forgotten all that had been told Abraham, Isaac, and Jacob about how their God wanted them to live and to worship. At Sinai, therefore, the Lord gave them first the ten commandments.

These all the people heard, for they were given by the living voice of the Lord from the top of the mountain from the midst of fire and smoke. Then Moses was called up into the mountain and given detailed laws for their conduct and worship. These laws are found in the books of Exodus, Numbers, Deuteronomy, and especially in the book of Leviticus. They are often called the Levitical laws, because the members of the tribe of Levi were set apart to have charge of the worship.

Among the instructions given Moses at Sinai were those for the construction and furnishing of the tabernacle. The tabernacle, as well as the temple which followed it, was to be the dwelling place of the Lord among the Israelites. From the mercy seat above the ark in the Holy of Holies the Lord spoke to the high priest. The pillar of cloud and fire stood over the tabernacle throughout the times when they were camped. The tabernacle pictures the dwelling place of the Lord in each one of us, and in its inmost sense it pictures the divine humanity of the Lord in which He dwells forever with men. So the pattern of the tabernacle becomes the pattern of life by which we ought to form our characters, and its every detail is full of meaning for us.

We cannot study all these details in a single lesson; so let us think of the three divisions and of the three metals used. The three divisions were the Most Holy Place or Holy of Holies, the Holy Place, and the outer court. These correspond to will, thought, and outward act in us. The Holy of Holies was concealed by a veil which was never withdrawn. The people never saw within it. In the same way, our inmost heart is concealed from view; even we ourselves seldom see what is really there. The Holy place was also veiled, but by curtains which were moved frequently as the priests went in and out in the service of the tabernacle. In the same way, our thoughts are in general concealed, but people are constantly getting glimpses of them in our conversation and in the expressions of our faces. The outer court was open to all, as is our outward life. The chart found with the last lesson will show you what furniture was in each division of the tabernacle. Each piece, of course, has its correspondence.

Now think of the metals used. All the wood—which corresponds to what Swedenborg calls "corporeal [physical, bodily]" good, the kind of natural impulse which makes us hate to pass a beggar on the street without giving him something—had to be overlaid with gold, which pictures genuine love coming from the recognition that the Lord alone is good. The inner covering was joined with fastenings of gold, to picture the power of true love to unify the whole life. The bases which supported the walls of the tabernacle proper were of silver, the symbol of truth which must support our emotional as well as our intellectual life. But the fastenings of the third covering—the one of rams' skins—were made of brass or bronze, and so were the pillars and their bases on which the curtains of the outer court were hung. Brass or bronze pictures natural good, the kind of good which tries to make conditions in the world better. This kind of good is the foundation of the outward life and its unifying element.

We must note also the fact that everything used in the building and furnishing of the tabernacle was a free-will offering from the people, which pictures the fact that nothing really becomes a part of our character which we do not freely choose. The whole development of a spiritual character in us comes as we freely give ourselves to the service of the Lord and the neighbor. We should note, too, that the Lord "put it in the heart" of certain chosen ones of the people to do the work and gave them wisdom for their task. If we really want to serve the Lord, He will show us how from day to day.

Basic Correspondences

the tabernacle	=	the life planned and lived according to the Lord's directions
the Holy of Holies	=	the inmost heart
the Holy Place	=	the thoughts
the outer court	=	the outward life
gold	=	love to the Lord
silver	=	truth

brass or bronze = natural goodness
wood = corporeal good
[physical good, good of the body]

Senior

The lesson to be impressed at this age is that of the well-ordered life in which religion is at the center. We know that young people frequently drift away from the church when they leave home and their early associations. They need to think of the church as their own individual responsibility wherever they are, to be carried with them as the directive and organizer of all their plans and activities.

We are told specifically several times in the Word that the tabernacle and everything in it was made according to the pattern shown to Moses "in the mount" by the Lord Himself. And it is evident from several statements in the Epistles that the Lord showed His disciples that this was also the pattern of a heavenly character (see, e.g., Hebrews 8:5).

The three divisions—the Holy of Holies, the Holy Place, and the outer court—refer to the heart, the mind, and the outward life. Every detail of the structure and its furnishings pictures some essential detail of a heavenly character. The three metals—gold, silver, and brass or bronze—for example, were used in exactly the places where their correspondents—love, truth, and natural good—must be used to consecrate, unify, and support the character. The curtains of "fine twined linen" are interpreted for us in the letter of the Word itself, "for the fine linen is the righteousness of saints" (Revelation 19:8).

Swedenborg tells us that this fine twined linen is truth from a celestial origin, that blue signifies the celestial love of truth, purple the celestial love of good, and scarlet spiritual good or the good of truth. And the cherubim, like those on the mercy seat and those set to guard the gates of the Garden of Eden, picture the guard set by divine providence "lest heaven be approached and injured by the hells." The curtains of goats' hair signify the external of heaven, or truths from external celestial good; the rams' skins, external truths: and the badgers' skins, external goods. Perhaps these terms seem obscure and the distinctions between them hard to draw, but they are of profound meaning. We can think of the coverings of the tabernacle as the degrees of truth which clothe and protect our inner motives and thoughts, and can get some idea of their complexity by trying to analyze our efforts to express some deep feeling or some beautiful flash of inspiration which has come to us.

The fact that all the wood used had to be overlaid with gold reminds us that our natural kindly impulses must always be glorified by genuine love to the Lord if they are to serve in the building of true character. Otherwise they serve only to build up our self-satisfaction. And the careful description of the necessary bases and pillars and of the many loops and clasps and bars which joined the whole together emphasizes the fact that true character must be founded on sure truth and built into a consistent whole. We are reminded of the house founded on a rock and of Jerusalem "builded as a city that is compact together." A heavenly character which can make us a dwelling place of the Lord is not formed by wandering through life governed by the impulses of the moment or by what other people will think of us. It is not formed by merely "meaning well." It is formed only by studying and conforming to the "pattern showed at the mount."

Adult

The effort has been made in the notes for the Adults to outline the construction and furnishings of the tabernacle and merely to suggest their meaning. The teacher will use his judgment as to the points which his particular group will be most interested in discussing.

The commandments were given to the children of Israel from Mount Sinai as the essential basis of their life, and they are equally for us the only foundations for a good and happy life. We recall that after the giving of the manna the Bible story tells of the Israelites' thirsting and being given water out of a rock at Rephidim;

of the attack of their first enemy, the Amelekites, which they met successfully because Moses, with the help of Aaron and Hur, kept his hands uplifted to the Lord: and of the visit of Jethro, Moses' father-in-law, under whose advice Moses appointed various leading men to handle the lesser complaints and problems of the people. They reached Sinai after about three months' journey and camped there, and all the people heard the giving of the commandments. These commandments were not new. They had been known and recognized as essential from the beginning of the church on earth. They appear in the laws of pagan as well as of Jewish and Christian peoples, having come to them through traditions handed down from the Ancient Church. They were given again from Sinai with so many signs and wonders to impress upon us that they are the laws of God and not man-made laws. In our lesson today we find that they are to be given a permanent place at the very center of our life. Other things besides the commandments were also given to Moses by the Lord at Sinai: many laws and rites, and especially the plans for the tabernacle and its furnishings and for the worship to be carried on in it. The Israelites remained about eleven months at Sinai, and during this time they were to serve the world for all time as a picture of a life organized according to true order, with worship of the Lord at its center and reaching to every activity of the daily life. The tabernacle was the center and symbol of their national life. It was the center of their encampment and was carried in the center of their line of march, and in both cases every tribe had its appointed station with reference to it. And we recall that from the time when it was first set up, the pillar of cloud and fire rested upon the tabernacle.

All the details of the tabernacle cannot be taken up in any one lesson, or even kept in mind; but all, to the very least, have a meaning which may become clear and helpful to us at some point in our lives. We are all familiar with Paul's statement: "Know ye not that ye are the temple of God?" As the tabernacle and its ceremonies were the center of the whole life of Israel, so the worship of the Lord—our religion—should be the center of our whole life, reaching out into every least thing we do. The plan of the tabernacle is the plan according to which our lives should be built. We see the outward act, but within that is the thought which taught us how to perform it, and within the thought is the desire that inspired the thought. We may take a simple example from a familiar sport such as tennis. First there must be the desire to play tennis, then knowledge of the game and of how to go about playing it, then the practice. We sometimes think of practice as the all-important thing, that if we play often we shall inevitably come to play well. But this is not true. Much practice may confirm bad playing habits as readily as good ones, making it impossible for one to be a really good player. Furthermore, even given accurate knowledge of technique and much practice, if the impelling motive is not sound, failure may result. If we go into the game from a desire to make ourselves conspicuous, or if our desire to win is stronger than our love of fair play and willingness to recognize excellence in our opponent, we may easily spoil our game by playing to the gallery or by losing our temper. This is true in everything we do. Right action can come only from true thought, and true thought can come only from pure motive. This brings us back to the tabernacle.

The Most Holy Place stands for our inmost heart. Only the commandments of the Lord should be found there. Our inmost desire in all things should be to obey and serve the Lord. His laws should be "written upon our hearts." If they are, He will speak to us from the mercy seat of our conscience, from between the cherubim which represent the protecting power of the Lord. Here all should be gold—pure love—except that the foundations must be truths learned and obeyed, as the sockets or bases of the tabernacle wall throughout were of silver. Only occasionally did the high priest enter the Most Holy Place. In the same way, we are seldom able to penetrate our inner motives, but we are permitted to do so occasionally when we need to hear the voice of the Lord in a special way.

The Holy Place was not public either, though the priests entered morning and evening to burn incense and to tend the light. Here, too, the analogy holds true: our thoughts of the Lord are not open for everyone to see, yet they must never be neglected. In our minds there must always be an "altar of incense" (an attitude of prayer and humility), a "candlestick" (recognition that all our light comes from the Lord), and a "table of shewbread" (acknowledgment of the Lord as the giver of all good). Gold is the metal here, too: our thoughts must be loving thoughts.

The people could see all that went on in the outer court. Our external lives are open to view. The metal here is brass or bronze—natural good—but the curtains which form the wall are fastened together with silver—particular truths which make our outward life a consistent whole. Here, too, the priests minister continually with washings and sacrifices. The necessity of the laver is easily seen: the need for constant cleansing of the outward acts according to truth. The great altar stands for the principle that we are to do good not because it pays, nor with the idea of self-exaltation, but from love to the Lord and a desire to advance His kingdom. We usually think of sacrifice as meaning "giving up" something. It often does involve giving up things which seem desirable to us, but this is incidental. The real meaning of sacrifice is "to make sacred." All that we do in our external lives should be made sacred by being offered to the Lord through the acknowledgment that whatever good we may seem to do is really done by Him through us, and is not in any sense our own.

Thus the tabernacle becomes for us a picture of what our lives should be: the commandments of the Lord in our hearts, working out through our thoughts into our daily lives, cleansing and setting everything in order so that we shall be in very truth temples of the living God. The tabernacle in its highest sense is a picture of the Lord's perfect divine human life. It is this life which is the real "pattern shown in the mount," and without this pattern we cannot form our lives wisely.

From the Writings of Swedenborg

Arcana Coelestia, n. 9643: "The reason why the bases were of 'silver,' and the planks were overlaid with 'gold,' was that by the 'planks' is signified good, and by the 'bases' truth, and good has power and thus support through truth . . . also that 'gold' signifies good, and 'silver' truth . . . That good has power through truth, is because truth is the form of good . . . for where there is quality, there is form."

Suggested Questions on the Lesson

J. Where were the ten commandments given? *Mount Sinai*

J. What other laws did the Lord give Moses at Mount Sinai? *conduct and worship*

P. What was the tabernacle? *tent church*

J. What were its walls made of? *boards covered with gold*

J. What was used to cover the top? *animal skins*

P. Into how many parts was it divided? *three*

J. What were they called? *Holy of Holies, Holy Place, outer court*

P. What was in the Holy of Holies? *ark*

P. What were in the Holy Place? *table, incense altar, lamp*

J. What formed the wall of the outer court? *curtains*

J. What two things were in the outer court? *laver, altar*

J. What three metals were used in the construction of the tabernacle? *gold, silver, bronze*

J. How and where was each of them used? *gold covered wood, silver fastenings, bronze sockets*

J. What was the veil? *inner curtain*

P. Why did the Israelites have to worship in a tent? *nomads*

I. What does the tabernacle represent? *orderly human life or character*

I. What do the three divisions represent? *will, thought, actions*

S. What is pictured by the ark's being in the Holy of Holies? *God's law written in our hearts*

THE GOLDEN CALF

Exodus 32:1-24

The teachers should review chapters 19, 20, and 24 in order to have clearly in mind the sequence of events from the time of the arrival at Sinai to the incidents of our lesson for today. Moses has been up and down the mountain more than once. Note especially 24:18, which introduces the situation in chapter 32. In all the classes stress the fact that all the people had heard the commandments given by the voice of the Lord from the mount, and that they had several times promised to obey.

Doctrinal Points

We must guard against setting up anything as our supreme object in life except service of the Lord.

The Lord uses the weaknesses of the people in the Bible story to show us our weaknesses.

We are just as liable as the Israelites were to believe only what we can experience with our physical senses.

Love to the Lord and the neighbor are the only feelings which can be trusted to keep us straight.

Notes for Parents

All through their forty years of wandering in the wilderness the children of Israel were led by a miraculous pillar—of cloud by day and of fire by night. They knew it was the presence of the Lord with them, and they were to go wherever it led them, to camp where it stopped, and not to move on until it moved. The Lord is always with us, leading us from one experience to another. Everything which comes to us is something the Lord sees we need—sometimes for our encouragement, sometimes for a warning, and sometimes for a test. The important thing in life is not what happens to us but what we do about it.

From Rephidim the pillar led the children of Israel to Sinai. This was a steep and high mountain with a great plain at its foot, on which the whole people could camp. They were kept there for eleven months, and in that time the Lord gave them through Moses all the laws for their life,and for their worship, laws which changed them from a mere horde of people into an organized nation, and established the Israelitish Church.

The first thing given them was the ten commandments, which all the people heard spoken by the voice of the Lord from the top of the mountain, amid thunder and lightning. These laws had always been known, but the people had to be shown—and we have to see today—that they are not man-made laws but divine laws on which all happy life must be based. They can never be changed or broken without harm resulting.

To receive the other laws and instructions, Moses was several times called by the Lord to the top of the mountain. The last time he remained up there hidden in the cloud for forty days and forty nights, and the people decided he was not coming back. We all tend to have more faith in the things we can see and touch than in unseen things, although we know that even in nature it is unseen forces—like gravity and electricity—which have greatest power. The golden calf of our story for today is a picture of the successes and pleasures of this world when we set them up as the supreme object of life. Read the story with this in mind and you will find in it a wonderful lesson the Lord is teaching us.

Primary

The story is simple and dramatic. Tie it in with the giving of the commandments. Tell the children that one of the principal idols of the Egyptians was the calf.

You remember that the children of Israel were led out of Egypt in a wonderful way. The Lord went before them in a pillar of cloud by day and a pillar of fire by night. They were told to follow the pillar wherever it went, whether it moved by day or by night: and when it stopped, they were to stop and camp, and not to go on again until the pillar moved on.

When they left Rephidim the pillar led them to the wilderness of Sinai, a great plain at the foot of a steep mountain. They had been on their journey about three months. The pillar stopped in front of Mount Sinai and the people camped, and they remained there for nearly a year.

What did all the people hear the voice of the Lord speak from the mountain top?

Moses was called to come up to the top to receive the commandments and many other laws and instructions for the life and worship of Israel.

Some of the elders, including Joshua, went part way up with him, but not to the top.

Moses was gone forty days and forty nights.

The people had promised to obey the Lord in everything.

Did they keep their promise?

When they thought Moses was not coming back, what did they ask Aaron to do?

What idol did he make for them?

What did he use to make it?

What did Moses have in his hands when he came down from the mount?

When he found the people worshiping the golden calf, what did he do with the tables?

What did he do with the golden calf?

Junior

The teacher should have a picture of Mount Sinai to show to the class, and should be sure all the pupils know how the commandments were given, why the first tables were broken, and that the second tables were hewn from the foot of the mount. Discuss with them the reason why the people wanted a visible idol to worship, and our likeness in this to the Israelites.

Mount Sinai is a wedge-shaped mass of rock rising steeply out of a large plain. Its top is between eight and nine thousand feet above sea level. The mountain mass is two miles long and one mile broad, and the plain at the foot is about two miles long and half a mile broad—some four hundred acres in extent. The air in that region is wonderfully clear both for seeing and for hearing.

The ten commandments were spoken by the voice of the Lord Himself from the top of Mount Sinai amid thunder and lightning and smoke, and all the people heard them. Read Deuteronomy 5:22-24. Then Moses was called up into the mountain to receive these same laws written by the finger of the Lord upon two tables of stone cut from the top of the mountain, and to be instructed in all the laws which the people were to obey, particularly as to their worship. He was given also the directions for the construction of the tabernacle and its furnishings. As we read all these instructions in the chapters of Exodus, we find that they were not all given at once. Moses came down several times to instruct the people, and each time they all agreed to obey all that the Lord had commanded. When Moses went up, Joshua was his attendant and was allowed to go part way with him, and waited for him on the mountainside. This shows us that Joshua was closer to the Lord than most of the people, which is something we want to remember. Aaron and Hur were left in charge of the people down on the plain.

But the last time Moses was called up, he stayed in the cloud on the mountaintop for forty days and forty nights, and the people decided that he was gone for good. They forgot all the wonders the Lord had showed them and all that they had promised. Does this seem strange? Did you ever learn something new in Sunday school which made you feel very enthusiastic about being good? How long did you stay good? Perhaps you forgot even more quickly than the Israelites did.

What did they ask Aaron to do?

They were used to seeing idols worshiped in Egypt, and one of the principal Egyptian idols was the calf. They wanted a god they could see and touch. It seemed more real to them. It is hard for many people to believe that anything they cannot see and touch is real, even though they know that the most powerful things in nature itself are invisible forces.

What did Aaron take to make the idol?
In what other story have we heard of earrings?
How did Aaron make the calf?

Read verse 4 of our chapter and then verse 24. When Moses rebuked Aaron, Aaron tried to make it seem as though he had had no real part in making the idol. Do we ever try to "get out" of something in this way?

What was Moses carrying when he came down from the mountain?
What did he do with them?
What did he do with the golden calf?
How did he punish the people?

Moses was very angry, but still he prayed to the Lord to forgive the people.

After this the Lord had Moses hew out two tables of stone from the foot of the mountain and bring them up to the top, and then the Lord wrote the commandments again on these new tables and Moses took them down to the people. These were the two tables of stone which were afterward kept in the ark.

Then the Lord made a covenant or agreement with the children of Israel. They were to worship the Lord alone and to destroy idols wherever they found them. They were not to intermarry with the people of the countries through which they passed or in which they lived. They were to offer to the Lord the first fruits of all their cattle and crops. And they were to observe each year three great feasts: the Passover, the "feast of weeks" at the time of the early wheat harvest, and the feast of the ingathering at the end of the year when all their crops were safely gathered in. So the Lord tried to help them not to forget Him again, and He promised that if they would do these things faithfully, He would bless them. All the Lord's commands are given for our good, so that He will be enabled to bless us and make us happy.

Intermediate

The correspondence of idol worship and of the golden calf in particular should be made the central emphasis of the lesson. Point out also why the first tables had to be broken, and why the second tables were hewn from rock found at the foot of the mount.

The ten commandments were given by the voice of the Lord amid thunders and lightnings, and all the people heard the Lord speak them. They were not new laws. People had always had them and they are embodied in the laws of every nation in the world, but they are laws which we should recognize as God-made, not man-made. They cannot be broken anywhere or at any time without spiritual as well as natural harm resulting. This is why they were spoken by the Lord from Sinai.

Then the Lord called Moses up to the top of the mountain and gave him many other laws to give to the people. If you will read over the chapter headings of chapters 21 to 23, you will see what they were like, and they are given in still more detail in the book of Leviticus. They were for the most part what we call civil laws. In their letter they apply to the Israelites, but in their spiritual sense they are for all men for all time.

Then Moses went up again to receive the directions for their worship—the plan and furnishings of the tabernacle, the clothing of the priests, and the required offerings—and finally he was given two tables of stone on which the ten commandments were written "with the finger of God." During this last period of instruction, Moses withdrew into the thick cloud which covered the top of the mount, and was there for forty days and forty nights. Forty pictures a full period of temptation. When any temptation persists, we are likely to reach a state in which we feel we cannot resist it any longer. The Israelites, imagining themselves deserted by Moses, finally wavered in their allegiance to the unseen God and wanted something tangible to worship. In much the same way, we may come to feel that spiritual virtues are shadowy, and that worldly success is the only real aim in life.

Cattle were favorite idols in Egypt. This was because the Egyptians loved the good things of this world and worldly learning, and cattle represent external or natural goodness and its affections. When cattle cease to perform the uses for which they are intended and are instead set up as objects of worship, their correspondence becomes evil. So the idol which Aaron made represents the fact that the Israelites cared more for the things of the world than they did for the Lord and His service.

We often read in the Bible: "He that hath ears to hear, let him hear." Hearing represents obedience, and these words really mean, "If your mind is open to the Lord's teaching, obey it." Golden earrings represent the happiness which results from obedience to the Lord. But when we become worldly and selfish, this happiness is lost. So when the golden earrings were separated from the ears of the people, they became a golden calf. Do you remember where we have heard about earrings before? It was in the lesson about Jacob's return, when he had the people take off the earrings they had worn in Haran, and buried them under an oak in Shechem before they could worship the Lord truly at Bethel. The earrings worn in Haran represented the former natural state of their motives.

The two tables which Moses first brought down were of stone from the top of the mountain. They picture the commandments in the high spiritual form in which the Lord would like to give them to us. But the Israelites were in no state to understand or appreciate spiritual things, and so the first tables were broken. The second tables were hewn by Moses from the foot of the mount and carried up to be inscribed. These picture the present hard, external form of the commandments, the only form in which they could make any impression on people in low worldly states.

After Moses broke the first tables, he destroyed the golden calf, but the powder to which he reduced it was sprinkled on water and given to the Israelites to drink. This is a picture of the fact that, although the people of the Church from that time on observed in their external form all the laws given them through Moses, the spiritual truth which was within them was falsified by worldly and selfish loves.

Basic Correspondences

forty = a full state of temptation
the calf = the love of external good

Senior

The worldly and selfish state of the Israelites and our own liability to drift into this same state are the points to be brought out clearly in this class. As the Seniors go out into the world, "Moses" is very likely to seem to "vanish into the cloud on top of the mount." If they get a clear picture now of the temptation involved, they will be more likely to recognize and resist it when it comes.

The children of Israel had been in the wilderness about three months when they came to Sinai and camped in the great plain before the mount. Historians point out that the ten commandments were embodied in the laws of ancient peoples before the time of Moses, and so some people discredit the story of the giving of the commandments by the Lord from Sinai. But this is not a logical conclusion. If the commandments are the laws of God, they are basic laws which must always have been known and followed in every orderly social group. The Israelites were a people who had been living in slavery without any government of their own, and who had forgotten even the name of the true God. They were also a people who had lost all desire for any but earthly satisfactions. So the Lord could direct their history without interfering with their spiritual freedom. Because their interest was centered in externals, He could lead them through fear of punishment and hope of reward to establish an external pattern of worship in which by its correspondence He could maintain His connection with mankind until the time came for His own Advent into the world.

Our story for today tells this fact in symbolic form. And it shows us also how the Lord deals with us when we are in worldly states. Moses, we remember, represents divine law, the truth as it comes to us in the Word. Moses had been called up into the mount to receive instructions for the building and care of the tabernacle. Joshua was allowed to go part way with him, and Aaron and Hur were left in charge of the people. Moses disappeared into the cloud on the top of the mount and was gone forty days and forty nights. In much the same way, sometimes our sense of the direct leadership and power of the Lord seems to vanish, and we are left to the guidance of our religious training and our habitual moral code. In these times, when our spiritual life seems at a low ebb, we are liable to go astray and to fall into worldly thoughts and loves. Forty pictures a full state of temptation.

Cattle represent our affections for worldly uses—business, professions, art, music, scholarship, science—all of which are good so long as they are made to serve the Lord and the neighbor, and not set on a pedestal to be worshiped for themselves. The calf pictures the love of learning about such worldly uses. So here the worship of the calf is the setting up of worldly success as the all-important things in life. Anyone who is too busy pursuing his profession or his art or his business or his pleasure to read the Word or to go to church is a worshiper of the golden calf.

Then Moses comes down from the mountain. Our state is suddenly exposed to the judgment of divine law. Moses has in his hand the two tables of stone on which the commandments had been written by the finger of God. These picture the divine laws as they come to us from the Lord, the basic laws of a happy life. But the Israelites have become incapable of recognizing any values except earthly ones. The first tables must be broken. The idolatry which has been set up must be destroyed, but the truth can be given only in a defiled form, falsified by the selfish loves which the people have allowed to take possession of their lives. The golden calf, burnt and ground to powder, is sprinkled on the water which the people will drink.

After the destruction of the first tables and of the calf and the punishment of the people, described in the last part of chapter 32, Moses was again called up to the mount. He was told to hew two new tables of stone from the foot of the mount and bring them up with him that the same commandments might be written on them. This is told in chapter 34. People often ask why the Word of God is given in such a harsh form instead of in a high, spiritual way. This story is the answer. The first tables were cut by the Lord from the top of the mount. This pictures the truth in the high and spiritual form in which it proceeds from the Lord. But the people had turned from the worship of the Lord, as people do today, and were not in a state to receive spiritual instruction. So the first tables had to be broken and new ones hewn from the stone at the foot of the mount. The same commandments were to be given, but they had to be given in terms adapted to the low, worldly states of the people. So, too, at the end of chapter 34 it is recorded that when Moses finally came down from the mount, his face was shining, and that he had to veil his face before the people would come near him. In our selfish and worldly states we will not listen to the truth in its higher and beautiful forms, but must be kept in order by harsh commands and threats: we cannot bear to look upon the truth in its purity.

Adult

After reviewing very briefly chapters 19-31, it may be well to read aloud Exodus 24:12-18, as it forms a good basis for the introduction of the principal points in our story for the day. The important lesson is the insidious effect of neglecting the study of the Word and the writings and assuming that we can live good lives without such study.

We think of Sinai as the place where the ten commandments were given. The Word tells us that the mountain was covered with smoke, that there were thunder and lightning, and that all the people heard the living voice of the Lord speaking the commandments from the top of the mount. The objection which historians sometimes offer—that the commandments were not new with the Israelites but have been found embodied in codes of law existing before the time of Moses—in no way invalidates the account given in the Word. The commandments are the basic laws of order on which society has been founded from the beginning. They were known through perception by the people of the Most Ancient Church and through revelation by the people of the Ancient Church. They were embodied in the Egyptian code. But by the time of the Exodus men had forgotten that they were divine, not man-made laws, and what is regarded as man-made is subject to change by man. We have plenty of evidence of this in the attitude of our modern world toward the ten commandments. Every one of us needs spiritually to hear the voice of the Lord speaking the commandments. They are divine laws. They are not only laws of outward order, but spiritual laws which cannot be broken without spiritual harm, whatever popular sanctions may do to weaken their outward observance and effect.

In considering our story for today, we should note that the commandments have been given, that Moses has been up and down the mountain more than once, receiving instruction from the Lord and bringing it to the people, and that each time the people have pledged themselves to obey the Lord in all things. But now Moses and Joshua have both been in the mount a long time. We should read verses 12 to 18 of chapter 24 to get the background of our lesson, recalling that Moses represents divine law as it is given us in the Word, Joshua "the truth fighting," Aaron the law as it comes to us through the church, and Hur the religious principles which we have confirmed by our own meditation and experience.

If ever we say to ourselves, "I really don't need to read the Word regularly myself; I was brought up on it and I hear it in church, and after all I can't understand it very well," Moses–spiritually understood–has withdrawn into the cloud on the top of the mount and we do not know what has become of him. Or if we say, "I haven't time to study my religion to see just how I should apply it; I know my principles are good and so I'm not likely to do anything really bad," Joshua has also left us and is somewhere up on the mountainside waiting for Moses to come down. Finally, if we say, "I'm a member of the church in good standing and respected in the community; that's enough for me," Aaron and Hur have been left in charge of us.

What had happened? Moses had told the people to go to Aaron and Hur if they had "a cause" (24:14) while he was gone. They went to Aaron, but not for direction or advice. They said to him,

"Up, make us gods, which shall go before us." And Aaron proceeded to make them a god out of their own earrings. We remember that when Jacob returned from Haran and was commanded to build an altar at Bethel, he prepared his people for worship by making them put away their strange gods. Genesis 35:4 tells us: "And they gave unto Jacob all the strange gods which were in their hand, and all their earrings which were in their ears; and Jacob hid them under the oak which was by Shechem." The ear signifies obedience, and earrings the delight of obedience. In the Jacob story and again in our story today, the obedience and its delight were those of external and worldly loves.

When Moses later rebuked Aaron, Aaron said (verse 24): "And I said unto them, Whosoever hath any gold, let them break it off. So they gave it me: then I cast it into the fire, and there came out this calf." So Aaron disclaimed responsibility. But the fact was different, for verse 4 tells us concerning Aaron and the earrings: "And he received it at their hand and fashioned it with a graving tool, after he had made it a molten calf." Swedenborg says (AC 10406) that this forming with a graving tool, when said concerning an idol, is "to prepare false doctrine from one's own intelligence, which is effected by the application of the sense of the letter of the Word in favor of the loves of self and the world; for when these loves reign, the man is not in any enlightenment from heaven, but takes all things from his own intelligence, and confirms them from the sense of the letter of the Word, which he falsifies by a wrong application and a perverted interpretation, and afterwards favors such things because they are from himself."

The golden calf is what results from this process. The calf represents "external or natural good," and the calf as an idol represents the setting up of "natural or sensuous delight" as the supreme object of life. That is, when we no longer depend upon the Word as our constant guide, and cease to make use of divine truth to expose and overcome the evils within us, these evils inevitably take possession not only of our hearts but of our minds; our worship is performed from motives of self-love, and our minds seek and accept only such things as agree with that love.

Then Moses and Joshua returned. We are suddenly confronted with divine truth and its judgment. How often this happens to all of us! We go along smoothly in our accustomed ways and build up a pleasing image of ourselves; then some story or quotation from the Word strikes home and brings us face to face with our real selves.

In our story two things happened. In the hand of Moses were the tables of stone hewn by the Lord from the top of the mount and inscribed by "the finger of God" with the ten commandments. Moses broke these tables. The Lord would prefer that we receive the commandments as laws of love, in their high spiritual form. But our minds are functioning on a low plane. The tables on which the commandments were later written—the ones which were placed in the ark—were hewn out by Moses from the foot of the mount. The letter of the law had finally to be given in the harsh form in which alone it would be listened to by the Israelites and by all in selfish and worldly states. And, although the golden calf was destroyed, the powder to which it was reduced was mixed with the water which the people drank. We may be brought to recognize and reject the principle of worldliness and self-interest, but the falsities which have come from it, like the dust of the golden calf, continue to mingle with the truth which enters our minds. So long as we are in this world we should see and acknowledge that there is an element of self in everything we think and do.

From the Writings of Swedenborg

Arcana Coelestia, n. 10407: "The ancients, who were in representative worship, knew what was signified by the various kinds of animals; for each animal has its signification, and according to this they appear in heaven, consequently according to this they are mentioned in the Word, and also according to this they were employed in burnt-offerings and sacrifices. By a 'calf' is signified the good of innocence and of charity in the external or natural man (nn. 9391, 9990, 10132); but when there is no good of innocence and of charity, as is the case with those who are in externals without what is internal, then by a 'calf' is signified natural and sensuous delight, which is the delight of pleasures, of cupidities, and of the loves of self and of the world. It is this delight in which are those who are in externals without an internal, and which they worship, for a man worships that which he loves above all things. They do indeed say that they worship the God of the universe, but they say this with the mouth and not with the heart. Such persons are meant by those who worship a molten calf. The Egyptians were such above all others, and they, being in the knowledge of correspondences and of representations above all other nations, consequently made for themselves various idols, as is evident from the Egyptian idols which remain to this day. But their chief idol was a calf, whereby they wished to signify their external good in worship. When however the knowledge of correspondence and of representations, wherein they were versed above others, was turned among them into magic, then a calf put on the opposite signification, which is the delight of external loves; and when a calf was placed in their temples and worshiped as a god, it signified such a delight in worship. As the Israelitish nation brought with it from Egypt this idolatrous thing, therefore as applied to that nation, when a calf was worshiped by them as a god, it signified the delight of the loves of that nation in worship."

Suggested Questions on the Lesson

J. How long did the Israelites camp at Sinai? *almost a year*
P. What did all the people hear the Lord speak from the top of Sinai? *commandments*
J. What other instructions did the Lord give Moses for the people? *laws of conduct, worship*
P. Where did Moses go to speak with the Lord? *top of mount*
P. In our lesson today, how long had he been gone? *forty days*
J. What did the people think? *gone forever*
J. What did they demand of Aaron? *gods*
P. What did Aaron tell them to give him? *gold earrings*
P. What did he make for them? *calf*
P. What did Moses have in his hands when he came down from the mount? *two tablets*
P. What did he do when he saw the people worshiping the golden calf? *broke them*
J. What did he do with the calf? *melted, ground, sprinkled on water*
J. How did Aaron try to excuse himself? *threw gold in fire, calf came out*
I. What is pictured by the golden calf? *love of worldly success and pleasure*

S. What is the difference between (1) the first tables of stone, and (2) those hewn our later from the bottom of the mount?

(1) high, spiritual form of law

(2) law adapted to state of worldly men

NADAB AND ABIHU

Leviticus 10

It is easy to pass to the story of Nadab and Abihu by reminding the children that while the people were at Sinai the Lord gave Moses, in addition to the commandments, careful directions for the priests and for the people especially in regard to their worship. Review a little about the tabernacle, its three divisions and their furnishings, with special emphasis on the two altars: then tell them the law for the offering of incense which Nadab and Abihu broke.

Doctrinal Points

Worship from selfish motives destroys instead of strengthens our spiritual life.

Notes for Parents

The book of Leviticus contains the Levitical laws, the regulations governing the life of the Levites—the tribe of Levi—and their conduct of the tabernacle worship, as well as many laws for all the people. The tribe of Levi had been set apart by the Lord for the services connected with worship in the tabernacle, and Aaron the brother of Moses had been named high priest. His four sons were to be assistant priests, and Aaron's office was to pass down in succession to his descendants.

The tabernacle was the center of the life of the people. Detailed instructions for its construction and furnishing were given Moses at Sinai. It had three parts: the inmost room or Holy of Holies, the outer room or Holy Place, and the outer court. The only article of furniture in the Holy of Holies was the ark, the chest which contained the two tables of stone on which the commandments had been written by the finger of God. In the Holy Place were the altar of incense, the table of shewbread, and the seven-branched golden candlestick. In the open outer court were the great altar of sacrifice and the bronze laver for washing.

Our lesson today is concerned with the two altars. Sacrifices were offered at so many times and for so many reasons that there was always fire on the great altar. In fact it was commanded (Leviticus 6:13) that the fire on this altar should never go out. To sacrifice really means "to make sacred," and the various sacrifices represent the offering of all our thoughts and affections to the Lord, the fire on the altar being genuine love for the Lord and for serving Him. This should be the motive in everything we do, as we learn from the first commandment. Every morning and every evening Aaron's sons were to take fire from this great altar and carry it in their censers into the tabernacle to the altar of incense and put sweet incense upon it. The burning of incense pictures the lifting up of our thoughts in prayer to the Lord. We should read here Revelation 5:8 and 8:3.

But Nadab and Abihu, Aaron's two older sons, "offered strange [unholy] fire before the Lord" and were forthwith devoured by fire from the Lord. Strange fire is a love other than love to the Lord, that is, it is the love of self. When we pray selfishly or go to church for any reason except to worship the Lord, we are "offering strange fire." Then the things we receive, instead of being blessings, are turned by us to selfish uses and our spiritual life is destroyed. It is in this sense that fire from the Lord becomes destructive.

Nadab and Abihu were carried out of the camp, and Aaron and his two younger sons were told not to mourn for them in the usual way because they themselves were serving in the tabernacle. But the people were told to "bewail the burning." When evil is done, the consequences are inevitable. Punishment is inherent in sin. We naturally bewail the punishment, but if we are serving the Lord truly, it is the sin and not the punishment that grieves us.

Primary

The class should learn the name Aaron, that he was Moses' brother, and that he was the high priest. They can understand that he had four sons and that two of them were obedient and two disobedient. Tell them about the censers and what they were for before going into the story proper. These children can be told why Nadab and Abihu had no excuse for what they did. We are to blame if we do what we know is wrong. This is a good lesson from which to teach young children how important it is to do right in the little things as well as in the big.

You remember how the Lord spoke the ten commandments from the top of Mount Sinai and how all the people, in their camp at the foot of the mountain, heard Him say them. Then the Lord called Moses to come up to the top of the mountain and wrote the ten commandments on two tables of stone so that they could always be kept. And then He gave Moses a great many other laws by which the children of Israel were to be governed and especially all the laws for their worship.

They were to make a special tent, called the *tabernacle*, which was to be their church, and the Lord told Moses just what furniture was to be in it.

Do you remember what articles of furniture were kept in the two rooms of the tabernacle?
In the outer court were the great bronze altar of sacrifice and the bronze laver—a bowl to hold water for washing.
Aaron, the brother of Moses, was made high priest.
His four sons—Nadab, Abihu, Eleazar, and Ithamar—were to be assistant priests.
Eleazar and Ithamar were faithful priests, but Nadab and Abihu were not.
What did Nadab and Abihu do that was wrong?
The censer was the bowl or dish to hold the fire on which the incense was burned.
The fire was to be taken from the great altar in the outer court.

There was also another altar: the altar of incense, which was one of the four pieces of furniture inside the tabernacle itself. It was made of wood covered with gold, and it had a crown of pure gold around the top. Every morning and every evening the priests were to burn incense on this altar. The incense was made of spices which had a sweet smell when they were burning. Each priest carried a censer in which to place the coals on which the incense was sprinkled to make it burn. The priests were to take the coals for their censers from the fire burning on the great altar of sacrifice.

Every act of worship was to be performed just as the Lord commanded it. Nadab and Abihu knew this, and knew that they were disobeying the Lord.

What did they do that was wrong?

What happened to them?

The Israelites were accustomed, when a relative died, to shave their heads and tear their clothing as a sign of mourning.

What did the Lord tell Aaron and his other two sons about this?

This was because they were serving in the tabernacle as the Lord's priests and must recognize and show the people that Nadab and Abihu deserved their punishment.

Junior

The Juniors can understand why the details of ancient Hebrew worship had to be observed so carefully. They will be interested in the meaning of the fire from the great altar and the "strange" or unholy fire. Have them look up all the Bible references in their notes. Review the names of the five books of Moses, and tell them as much as you can about the book of Leviticus.

At Sinai the Lord also gave Moses a whole code of laws to govern the personal, civil, and religious life of the people. He gave special directions for the making of the tabernacle and its furnishings. The Levites—the tribe of Levi—were set aside to have charge of this tabernacle and the worship there, and Aaron, the brother of Moses, was named as high priest. His sons were to be his assistants. Their names were Nadab, Abihu, Eleazar, and Ithamar. Many of the laws given at Sinai are preserved in the book of Leviticus.

Every detail of worship in the tabernacle had been prescribed. We shall find the law for burning incense in Exodus 30:1, 7, 8 and Leviticus 16:12.

Where was the priest to get the fire on which to burn the incense?

The censer was the bowl made to hold this fire and carry it. In those days there were no matches or even flint and steel. When people went on a journey, they had to carry fire with them from place to place. The fire on the great altar was kept burning all the time, whether they were making sacrifices or not. Read Leviticus

6:13. Fire is a symbol of love and this ever-burning fire on the great altar pictures love for the Lord, which should be our motive in everything we do.

What did Nadab and Abihu do?

This means that they used fire taken from somewhere else than from the great altar. Incense stands for our prayers of gratitude to the Lord. Read Revelation 5:8. Do people ever go to church and take part in worship for other reasons than because they love the Lord and are grateful in Him? Sometimes they may go because they want to be thought well of, or because they want to get in with certain people, or because they think it will be good for their business. These are selfish reasons. Love of self is the opposite of love to the Lord. It is "strange" or unholy fire.

What happened to Nadab and Abihu?

Does this seem too great a punishment? We must remember that the ancient Hebrews liked to perform external acts of worship. It was because they thought mainly of external things that the Lord chose them for the writing of the Old Testament. Every detail of their worship had to be kept just as He gave it to them, or the inner meaning—which was for people of later times—would be destroyed. Those who would not preserve this external order could not continue to be useful. So a terrible thing did happen to Nadab and Abihu when they disobeyed. A terrible thing happens to us when we go to church from selfish motives. The love of the Lord is poured out to us as we listen to the reading of the Word and take part in the service, but our selfishness turns it into self-love, and our spiritual life is destroyed. It may seem to us that what Nadab and Abihu did was not very bad, but they knew that it was disobedience to the Lord. It is the things we do knowing that they are wrong in the Lord's sight which condemn us.

The ancient Hebrews were accustomed to shave their heads and tear their clothes as a sign of mourning when any of their relatives died. So the Lord told the people that they might mourn for the terrible burning of Nadab and Abihu; but Aaron and his sons were commanded not to mourn in this way because they were serving as priests and wearing the holy garments, and had been anointed with the holy oil. When we do wrong and are punished, it is natural for us to be unhappy about the punishment; but if we are really serving the Lord, we should not be sorry that we have been punished, but only that we have deserved punishment.

Wrongdoing always brings punishment of some kind even when we do not realize it. The harm it does to us in our hearts and minds is much more serious than any outward effects it may cause. It is not the Lord who punishes—evil brings its own consequences. We should learn from these, and avoid doing wrong the next time.

Intermediate

The meaning of "strange" or unholy fire as illustrated in our own lives and of the particular destruction which follows is the lesson to be stressed. Point out how brief a story this is and yet how deep and important its meaning. Call attention to the nature and value of the book of Leviticus. The sin of Nadab and Abihu comes into the experience of young people especially in the form of thinking they know better than the Lord—or better than their parents—how things should be done. Stress the importance of doing even little things in the right way and of obeying the Lord even if at the time we do not fully understand the reason for His commands.

The story of Nadab and Abihu is one of the stories in the Word to which people sometimes object because they think the punishment too severe for the crime. Even as to the literal story, however, we must remember that the externals of worship were all-important to the ancient Hebrews. For this reason the Lord chose this nation to receive and preserve these externals. To transgress them even in small ways was for them just as serious a crime as an interior sin would be for people today. Evil, in whatever degree, brings its own punishment, and it is right that it should be so. If we are thinking of eternal values, we shall not mourn because punishment follows our wrongdoings. Instead, because that is the only way we can see and check them, we shall mourn the wrongdoing itself. That is what is meant by verse 6.

The law for the burning of incense was given from Sinai among the many explicit laws and regulations which are recorded in the books of Exodus and Leviticus, laws which it was the special duty of the Levites to observe. Incense was to be burned on the altar of incense which stood in the Holy Place before the veil which covered the entrance to the Holy of Holies. It was to be burned night and morning. The very ingredients of the incense were specified: stacte, onycha, galbanum, and pure frankincense. The fire for the censers was to be taken from the ever-burning fire on the great altar in the outer court of the tabernacle.* This fire pictures love to the Lord, and all worship, to be pure, must be kindled from such a "fire."

But people sometimes worship from other motives, like the scribes and Pharisees who prayed standing on the street corners that they might be seen of men, and like people today who go to church because it may help their business. The motive in such cases is selfishness. This is the "strange" or unholy fire of our story. When this is the motive in worship, all the good things such people hear in church are turned into selfish channels and, instead of feeding the soul, their very worship helps to destroy their spiritual life. To use holy things for selfish purposes is profanation, which kills all good possibilities. So the fire from the Lord actually does destroy those who come before Him with strange fire in their censers.

Nadab and Abihu were carried "in their coats out of the camp." The "coat" (more properly the "tunic") was the inner garment, and the tunic of the priests represented the internal truths of the Word. The camp of Israel, which was always arranged according to the order prescribed on the mount, pictures a heavenly character, or heaven. So to be carried out of the camp is to be cast into hell.

---

*The sin of Hadab and Abihu is obscure. There is no clear regulation in the Pentateuch that fire to light incense must be taken from the main altar. Swedenborg, in AC 9965, presumes quite understandably–based on the correspondence of the fire from the great altar–that the infraction was that these men took fire from another source. –*Editor.*

Their being carried out in their tunics pictures the fact that in profaning their outward worship they had also profaned its internal.

Sometimes people excuse themselves for staying away from church and for condemning the church organization by saying that after all the organization is not the real church. But the fact is that the organization is the only body the church has in the world, and we are a part of it. In condemning the organization we are really only condemning ourselves, and by staying away from church we cut ourselves off from the spiritual life which is the soul of the external church.

Swedenborg writes in *Apocalypse Explained*, n. 324: "Nadab and Abihu, sons of Aaron, were consumed by fire from heaven because they burnt incense from other fire than the fire of the Altar of burnt offering, which is offering worship from a love other than love to the Lord."

Basic Correspondences

fire	=	love or hate
the fire on the great altar	=	love to the Lord
strange fire	=	the love of self
incense	=	prayer, especially public worship

Senior

After taking up the meaning of the story, it may be helpful to discuss some of the various ways in which we may spoil our lives by allowing selfish motives to control us. Stress the importance of humility and obedience.

The book of Leviticus contains very few incidents like that of our lesson today. For the most part it is composed of a long series of what often seem petty regulations concerning the conduct of the ancient Hebrews and particularly concerning their worship, with its offerings, sacrifices, and ceremonials. The book takes its name from the Levites, the tribe of Levi, who were set apart from the other tribes to have special charge of the tabernacle and its worship. Aaron, the brother of Moses, was appointed high priest by the Lord, and the office was to pass down through his descendants. His four sons—Nadab, Abihu, Eleazar, and Ithamar—were appointed his assistants. Eleazar was the one who actually succeeded Aaron when he died (Numbers 20:22-29).

We remember that the ancient Hebrew Church was a representative church. These people were "chosen" because they had lost all knowledge of true internal worship and cared only for externals and so could be led through fear of punishment and hope of reward to maintain external forms which by correspondence would keep the connection between man and the Lord until the time was ripe for the Lord Himself to come into the world to restore internal worship. So the all-important thing for the Jews was to observe the laws of their worship in every detail as the Lord had given them to Moses on the mount. A number of times in the Old Testament story, as in our lesson today, we read of sudden and violent death resulting from the breaking of what may seem to us a minor regulation. But we note that the people themselves accepted these punishments as just, because to them the small regulations were all essential—as they actually are for their correspondence.

Some of the deepest lessons in the Word are found within these Levitical laws. Leviticus 16:12-13* tells us that when incense was offered by the priests in the tabernacle, their censers were to be filled with burning coals taken from the great altar of sacrifice which stood in the outer court. The great altar represents our recognition that everything we have comes to us from the Lord and is to be used in His service. The fire on the great altar represents genuine love to the Lord. The offering of incense—which was sprinkled on the coals in the censers—represents our prayers, worship, and thanksgiving. We learn this from John's vision in Revelation 5:8 of the four beasts and the four and twenty elders who "fell down before the Lamb, having every one of them harps, and

*This records a special instruction to Aaron after the death of his two sons. There is a prohibition in Exodus 30:9 against offering "strange" or unholy *incense*, but no definite *general* instruction about the source of the coals. The sin, however, is clearly one of irreverence. —*Ed.*

golden vials full of odours, which are the prayers of saints." The law in regard to the offering of incense means that our prayers and thanksgivings are acceptable only when they are inspired by genuine love to the Lord kindled by our recognition of our own unworthiness and complete dependence upon Him.

The "strange" or unholy fire which Nadab and Abihu brought in their censers represents a selfish motive in worship. If we go to church because we like to be respected, or because it is "good business," or because it enables us to think of ourselves as good, if we pray for selfish indulgences or for the downfall of those we dislike, we are offering strange fire. And our punishment is just as immediate and dire as that of Nadab and Abihu, although we may not be conscious of it until we come into the other world. For the fire which goes forth from the altar, the Lord's love always going forth to those who seek Him, is turned in us to selfish ends, and our spiritual life perishes and we are carried "from before the sanctuary out of the camp." Read Matthew 8:10-12 and compare it with this story. The sin which the Lord condemned in the strongest language was the sin of hypocrisy. Read also Matthew 23:23-33. It is the urgent warning against hypocrisy in worship that is given us in this brief story of Nadab and Abihu. Aaron and his other two sons were commanded not to mourn for Nadab and Abihu, but the people were allowed to mourn. It is natural for us to feel sorry for the wrongdoer when he suffers the penalty of his deeds—especially if the wrongdoer is oneself—but our higher understanding should recognize the justice and necessity of this result of evil. Divine laws are fundamental laws, and if they could be broken with impunity there would be no order in the universe and no possibility of any sure hope for happiness and peace.

Adult

This lesson offers a good opportunity for discussion of our public worship and the spirit in which we should come to it. Another good discussion topic is the proper attitude toward a sinner and his punishment—whether the sinner be oneself or someone else.

In *Our Heavenly Father's Book*, part of the Bible series published for our Sunday School Association many years ago [1884], the Rev. Wm. B. Hayden writes concerning the book of Leviticus: "The Hebrews call this book *Vayyikra* meaning 'And [God] called,' from its first word 'And Jehovah called unto Moses, and spake unto him out of the tabernacle of the congregation, saying, Speak unto the children of Israel, and say unto them, etc.' This is indeed the keynote of the book. It is everywhere the 'call' of the voice of God speaking to the church. This Divine formula is repeated at the head of every distinct section or enactment, thus of nearly every chapter; while the closing sentence of the book contains this averment: 'These are the commandments which Jehovah commanded Moses for the children of Israel in Mount Sinai.' Thus nothing is left in doubt as to the Divine origin of the book.

"Our name *Leviticus* is simply the Latin derived from the Greek Leuitikon, meaning *Levitical*, or that which *pertains to the Levites*; in reference to the fact that its contents are so largely occupied with the duties of the Levites, in which body are included all the priests. It consists principally of laws, having historical matter only in chapters viii to x, relating to the dedication of Aaron and his sons to the priesthood, and the death of Nadab and Abihu for offering strange fire before the Lord. These laws relate to the offerings and sacrifices; to purity and impurity; to the priests, with the holy-days and festivals; and the regulations intended to mark the separation between Israel and the heathen nations. To which are added the blessings connected with obedience, and the evil consequences of disobedience, chapter xxvi, with the regulations concerning vows, xxvii." [pp. 62-63]

We recall that when the Lord called Moses at the burning bush, one of Moses' objections to his task was that he was not eloquent but "slow of speech, and of a slow tongue." Moses represents divine law. The law does not immediately appeal to the heart or emotions of men. The Lord told Moses that his brother Aaron should speak for him. He said (Exodus 4:14-16): "Is not Aaron the Levite thy brother? I know that he can speak well. And also, behold, he cometh forth to meet thee: and when he seeth thee, he will be glad in his heart. And thou shalt speak unto him, and put words in his mouth; and I will be with thy mouth, and with his mouth, and will teach you what he shall do. And he shall be thy spokesman unto the people; and he shall be, even he shall be to thee instead of a mouth, and thou shalt be to him instead of God." From that time Moses and Aaron were always together, and when the directions for the tabernacle and its worship were given Moses from Sinai, Aaron was appointed high priest, with his four sons as his assistants, and all the tribe of Levi were set apart for the service of the tabernacle and its worship. The high priesthood was to pass down in the line of Aaron. Nadab and Abihu were his two older sons, Eleazar and Ithamar the two younger. With the death of Nadab and Abihu, Eleazar became next in line and did become high priest upon Aaron's death.

Aaron, because he was high priest, in the inmost sense represents the Lord as to divine good, but in the spiritual sense he represents "what is outward of the Spiritual Church" while Moses represents "what is inward." Aaron's sons represent the doctrines of good and truth from the Word. The function of the priesthood is to lead in worship and to teach according to the pattern showed in the mount and under the direction of divine law. We recall that the ancient Hebrew Church was merely the representative of a church, maintaining—during the interval between the total loss of internal worship by men and the Lord's coming into the world to restore that worship—the connection between the Lord and man by means of the correspondence of their external worship. It was therefore essential that every detail of their worship be maintained exactly as commanded, and dire punishments were decreed and meted out for neglect of these details. We note in the literal story that Aaron and his two remaining sons accepted without question the justice of the punishment of Nadab and Abihu and the command not to observe mourning for them. This command and the permission to the people to mourn picture the fact that we are permitted in our natural and external states to feel horror and regret at the terrible consequences of evil, but that our higher spiritual understanding should recognize these as inevitable and right and as necessary to the preservation of the possibility of man's free reception of the Lord's love.

Nadab and Abihu broke the statute which required that when incense was offered in the tabernacle, the coals on which it was burned in the censers should be taken from the fire on the great altar of burnt offering in the outer court.* This altar represents our humble acknowledgment that of ourselves we are evil and ignorant and powerless to do good, that all goodness and truth are the Lord's, and that to Him we owe all our powers. The fire on this altar is genuine love to the Lord arising from this acknowledgment. The offering of incense represents our prayers and praises, especially those offered in public worship. The law means that our worship is acceptable only when it comes from genuine love to the Lord springing from recognition of our unworthiness and need of Him. "Strange" or unholy fire is a selfish motive prompting our worship. If, for example, we go to church "to be seen of men," to increase our self-esteem, to help our business, to establish desirable social contacts, or for any other reason which has self at its center instead of the Lord, we are taking strange fire in our censers. And such worship, by ministering to and increasing our self-love, destroys our spiritual life, just as the fire from the altar consumed Nadab and Abihu.

The camp of Israel, always arranged in the order given from Sinai, represents heaven or a heavenly character. When we offer worship from impure motives, we—like Nadab and Abihu—are carried "out of the camp." And we are carried out in our "coats." The coat—more properly "tunic"—was the inner, not the outer, garment of the priest, and represents the internal sense of the Word, or internal worship. When we profane external worship, all possibility of coming into internal worship is also destroyed.

In the letter the rest of the chapter seems to have no connection

---

*See notes on Intermediate and Senior pages.

with the story of Nadab and Abihu. But in the internal sense there is a wonderful continuity and order. For example, in verse 9 the command to drink no wine or strong drink when they entered the tabernacle signifies that "worship of the Lord should not be from truths either spiritual or celestial, but entirely from good." And the rest of the chapter carries further the explanation of what true worship is and of the states which profane and destroy it. Indeed the whole book of Leviticus, which by many today is laid aside as outdated and irrelevant to our modern life and its needs, offers us in its internal sense teaching of the deepest and most essential and practical nature.* We take up so little of it in our Sunday school lessons only because any adequate treatment of it would require many lessons. In the story of Nadab and Abihu, however, we at least touch the heart of the teaching of this book in a form which, like the Lord's parables, is easily grasped in its letter, and will stay in the mind.

From the Writings of Swedenborg

Arcana Coelestia, n. 9965: "*Lest they bear iniquity, and die* (Exodus 28:43). That this signifies the annihilation of the whole of worship, is evident from the signification of 'bearing iniquity,' when said of the priesthood of Aaron and his sons, as being the removal of falsities and evils with those who are in good from the Lord . . . But when they are said 'to bear iniquity and die,' it signifies the annihilation of all worship . . . for representative worship died, because nothing of it appeared any longer in the heavens . . . Moreover that they died when they did not act in accordance with the statutes, is plain from Aaron's sons, Nadab and Abihu, who were consumed by fire from heaven when they burned incense, not from the fire of the altar, but from strange fire . . . The fire of the altar represented love Divine, thus love from the Lord, whereas the strange fire represented love from hell. The annihilation of worship was signified by the burning of incense from this latter fire, which resulted in their death. It is said in many passages in the Word that 'they would bear iniquity' when they did not act according to the statutes, and by this was

*A helpful source of information on these deeper lessons is the New Church Commentary on Leviticus by Henry Maclagan published by James Speirs, London, 1912. —*Ed.*

signified damnation, because their sins were not removed; not that they were damned on this account, but that they thereby annihilated the representative worship, and thus represented the damned who remain in their sins. For no one is damned on account of the omission of external rites; but on account of evils of the heart, thus on account of the omission of them from evil of heart."

Suggested Questions on the Lesson

J. What was the tabernacle? *portable church*
P. Who was the high priest? *Aaron*
P. Who were his assistants? *his four sons*
J. What two altars are involved in our lesson for today? *great bronze, incense*
J. In what division of the tabernacle was the great altar? *outer court*
J. What was it used for? *sacrifices*
J. In what division of the tabernacle was the altar of incense? *Holy Place*
J. How often was incense to be burned upon it? *morning and evening*
P. What were the coals to burn the incense carried in? *a censer*
P. Where were these coals to be obtained? *great altar*
J. Who were the two oldest sons of Aaron? *Nadab and Abihu*
P. What did they do which was wrong? *offered "strange" or unholy fire*
P. What is meant by the fire's being "strange"? *not proper*
P. What happened to Nadab and Abihu? *fire killed them*
P. Where were their bodies taken? *outside camp*
J. What command did Moses give to Aaron and his two younger sons? *don't mourn*
J. What did he tell the people to do? *bewail the burning*
I. What does incense represent? *prayers*
S. What does the fire on the great altar represent? *genuine love to the Lord*
I. Spiritually, what is "strange" or unholy fire? *acting religious for selfish reasons*

THE TWELVE SPIES

Numbers 13; 14

It is suggested that in all classes the teacher read Exodus 31:1-7, then say that everything was made according to the Lord's directions, and that the tabernacle was finally set up in the midst of the encampment. Then read Exodus 40:33-38. Mention again the contents of the book of Leviticus and the reason for the name of the book of Numbers. Then read Numbers 10:33-36 as the beginning of the further journeyings of the Israelites, and tell the class briefly the story of the almost immediate murmurings and rebellion culminating in the rebellion of Aaron and Miriam. This shows the state of the Israelites at that time, and leads directly into the story of the spies.

Doctrinal Points

The Lord withholds us from temptations which we are not strong enough to meet.

The giants mentioned in the Old Testament were an evil remnant from the Most Ancient Church.

Our greatest enemies are the giants of selfishness and worldliness within our own hearts, which are there by heredity.

Notes for Parents

Before the children of Israel came to Sinai, they were a mere horde of men, women, and children, uprooted from the homes in which they had grown up, and facing a wild and strange life, with no one but Moses to tell them what to do, and no knowledge of the way before them except that they were to follow the pillar of cloud and fire. In the eleven months that they stayed encamped on the plain before Mount Sinai, they were organized into a nation, given laws by which they were to be governed—not only the ten commandments, but also laws for every little thing—provided with directions for their worship and a place in which to worship, told just how each tribe was to march and how to camp, and provided with a priesthood and with lesser judges to settle all their minor questions. This is a picture of the formation of an orderly life. If we understand our Bibles, we can see in each one of these strange laws something which applies to our spiritual life. The Lord had given the children of Israel everything they needed except the one thing he could not give them—the love of doing right. Isn't this true of us, too? We all have by gift of the Lord the means of knowing what we ought to do from day to day, but each one of us has to choose freely whether he will obey the Lord or not. The Israelites had not gone three days further on their wanderings before they were again murmuring against Moses and complaining of the kind of food given them to eat, and asking to go back to Egypt.

Then after a short time they came in sight of the Holy Land, the land their ancestors had possessed and which they had been promised by the Lord. Heaven is often called the *Promised Land*, and we know that it is where each one of us really belongs; but do we always keep steadily on the way to it? The Israelites were told to send twelve men, one from each tribe, to spy out the land and bring them back a report of it. That is just what we do when we think about heaven and try to find out what it is like. And the report is always that it is a beautiful land, a land "flowing with milk and honey." We are even allowed to taste little bits of heaven once in a while in our lives. But we also see the false ways of thinking we shall have to overcome, like the walled cities, and the giants of selfishness in our hearts which will stand in our way. So often, just like the Israelites, we say, "Oh, I never could really be good—it would be too hard work. I'll wait until some time when it looks easier." And, like the Israelites, we have to wander in the wilderness until all those weak, cowardly feelings and thoughts in us die out. We forget that the Lord will always help us if we really try. Now that the children have had this lesson, you can remind them of it whenever they complain that their lessons are too hard or that they are not able to do the things you ask them to help you with at home. Children need this lesson, but so do all of us.

Primary

The story of the spies is not hard to tell. The children will be interested in the fruits which they brought back and in the fact that they saw some giants in the land. Stress the fact that the Lord would have helped them if they had not been afraid to try to conquer the land. Discuss the point that the Lord cannot help us to do what we ought to do unless we are willing to try. Nothing good is ever accomplished if we think we can't do it. This applies to lessons in school, tasks at home, and to the overcoming of our faults as well.

The children of Israel stayed nearly a year at Mount Sinai. Then the pillar of cloud and fire led them on through the wilderness.

From there they were led to camp at a place called Kadesh.
Kadesh was close to the border of the Holy Land.
What did the Lord tell Moses to do?
How many were chosen to spy out the land?
How long were they gone?
What did they bring back?
Did they say the land was a good land?
What did they find there that was not good?
Which of the spies differed from all the others?
What did these two advise?
What did the others say?

But the people would not listen to Joshua and Caleb, and even tried to stone them. They believed the ten cowardly spies, and rebelled against Moses, and talked of going back to Egypt. So the Lord said that they should never enter the Holy Land. Only their children, the ones under twenty at the time of our lesson, who were not old enough to have a voice in the people's decision, and Joshua and Caleb would be allowed to enter the land.

What punishment came to the ten cowardly spies?
What was the people's punishment?
What reward was promised for Joshua and Caleb?

Junior

With this class review the wilderness journey by the use of a map. Be sure they get the general features of the journey clearly in mind, as well as the reason why they had to wander so long before they were ready to enter the Holy Land. Remind them that they could travel only when the pillar of cloud and fire was moving before them, and had to stop whenever it stopped. This class can easily see the general correspondence of the lesson.

In addition to the detailed instructions for building the tabernacle which the Lord gave to Moses in Mount Sinai, the Lord filled two men (Bezaleel and Aholiab) with wisdom and skill in workmanship, so that they would know just how to make the ark and the tabernacle. Read Exodus 35:30-35.

After the ark and the tabernacle had been made, the pillar of cloud led the people to a place called *Kadesh* near the northern edge of the wilderness. Here they were close to the southern border of the Promised Land, and at the Lord's command they sent spies to explore it and bring back a report of it.

How many spies were there?
How long were they gone?
What did they bring back?

The spies all agreed that the land of Canaan was a good land, "a land flowing with milk and honey." Yet they were not in agreement as to their advice.

Which two differed from the others?
What did these two advise?
Why did they think the people would be strong enough to overcome the giants and the great walled cities?
Whose advice did the children of Israel follow?
What was their punishment?
What happened to the ten cowardly spies?
What was the reward of Joshua and Caleb?

The journey which the children of Israel were making is a picture of the journey each one of us is making when we decide that we want to serve the Lord instead of ourselves. The land of Canaan—the "Promised Land"—is a picture of heaven or of the heavenly character we must have if we are to enjoy living in heaven when we die. Do we always move straight ahead toward this kind of character? No, we often act selfishly and weakly, and delay our progress.

The Israelites of old were very much like we are today. They murmured against Moses because they had no meat to eat, and wanted to go back to the flesh-pots of Egypt. They were not satisfied with the manna which the Lord gave them every day. The Lord satisfied their craving by sending quails again, but with them came a plague which killed many of those who had complained. At another time Aaron and Miriam, the brother and sister of Moses, became jealous of him and talked against him. Miriam was punished by becoming a leper, until Moses prayed to the Lord to heal her. We have to recognize the bad things in our characters and acknowledge them before we can make any real progress toward heaven.

The Lord wants us to choose the right way freely. He never asks us to go ahead blindly. So He commanded the children of Israel to send spies to bring a report of the Holy Land. They brought back wonderful reports of the land itself, but also frightening reports of its inhabitants. We can all see that heaven is a beautiful place where we should like to be. But we must also know that it is not easy to attain. There are giants in ourselves—love of having our own way, greediness, envy of those who have more than we have, laziness—which must be overcome before we can enjoy heaven. And there are walled cities—all the arguments which support and excuse our wrong desires. We cannot overcome these by ourselves, but the Lord can give us victory if we go forward trusting in Him.

Intermediate

The need of going forward courageously in the overcoming of our weaknesses and temptations is important for children of this age. They are willing enough to make great efforts in games and skills, but inclined to think their studies and their home chores too hard. We can do nothing unless we try. The correspondence of the fruits, of the walled cities, and of the giants should be discussed.

When the ark was actually made and placed in the finished tabernacle, the pillar of cloud and fire "rested" on the tabernacle. Aaron and his sons had been consecrated to the service of the tabernacle, and the people could begin to observe all the laws which had been given to them. These laws are recorded in the books of Exodus and Leviticus. Then Moses was told by the Lord to number the people. This numbering or census is the first thing recorded in the book of Numbers, and gives the book its name. After the numbering, each tribe brought an offering of silver according to its numbers. Moses was also told to make two trumpets of silver which were to be used to call the people together and to start them on the march. In Numbers 10:11-12 we are told: "And it came to pass on the twentieth day of the second month, in the second year, that the cloud was taken up from off the tabernacle of the testimony. And the children of Israel took their journeys out of the wilderness of Sinai: and the cloud rested in the wilderness of Paran."

Do you think that the children of Israel now went forward bravely and cheerfully? On the contrary: within a very few days they were complaining again and had to be punished to bring them to their senses. We read in chapter 11:4-6: "And the mixt multitude that was among them fell a lusting: and the children of Israel also wept again, and said, Who shall give us flesh to eat? We remember the fish, which we did eat in Egypt freely; the cucumbers, and the melons, and the leeks, and the onions, and the garlick: But now our soul is dried away; there is nothing at all, beside this manna, before our eyes." The rest of the chapter tells what came of their complaining, and chapter 12 tells how even Aaron and Miriam rebelled against Moses; and the Lord, in order to show the people their true leader, struck Miriam with leprosy and then cured her at Moses' request.

Then comes our lesson for today. The people reached a place called *Kadesh*, not far from the border of the Holy Land. When they camped here, the Lord told Moses to choose a man from each of the twelve tribes, and send the twelve to spy out the Holy Land to "see the land what it is; and the people that dwelleth therein, whether they be strong or weak, few or many; and what the land is that they dwell in, whether it be good or bad; and what cities they be that they dwell in, whether in tents or in strongholds; and what the land is, whether it be fat or lean, whether there be wood therein or not." And they were to bring back some of the fruit of the land.

This, too, is a picture of something that happens to us. However clearly the Lord shows us what we ought to do, our natural selfishness always hesitates and rebels. We can look back afterward and wonder how we could have been so foolish, but at the time, all we see is that we are not having just what we want at the moment. And we have to be reassured as to whether the heavenly life is really as happy a life as the Lord tells us it is. Our thoughts spy it out, just as the twelve chosen men did. And they bring back the same kind of report. They all recognize that the Holy Land is a beautiful country. And the Lord even permits us to taste the fruit of the land. When we have really done something good without thinking about ourselves at all, don't we usually feel very happy and lighthearted for a while? This is the taste of the fruit of heavenly living. It is said of the spies, "And they came unto the brook of Eshcol, and cut down from thence a branch with one cluster of grapes, and they bare it between two upon a staff; and they brought of the pomegranates, and of the figs." They all called it a "land flowing with milk and honey." Milk represents the truth in which there is goodness; and honey, the happiness which comes from such truth.

But our thoughts, like the spies, also bring back word that there are many enemies in the land, and strong walled cities, and even giants. When we think of really living a heavenly life, we immediately begin to see all our faults which we shall have to fight, the wrong ideas we shall have to correct, and the natural, selfish desires deep down in our hearts which will rise up like giants in our way. We should know that the giants mentioned several times in the Old Testament were an evil remnant of the Most Ancient Church and picture our deep inherited selfishness. The children of Israel were not particularly brave people. We, too, sometimes forget that the Lord has promised to help us, even though there is always something in us to remind us of this fact, just as Joshua and Caleb reminded the Israelites that "if the Lord delight in us, then he will bring us into this land." We draw back sometimes, just at the time when a little more effort would have given us the victory.

What happens to most of us is just what happened to the children of Israel. It takes a long, long time to get rid of our faults. Deuteronomy 2:14 tells us that it was thirty-eight years after the time of our lesson that the Israelites finally reached the point when all the men who had a part in the decision of our lesson—"all that were numbered of you, according to your whole number, from twenty years old and upward, which have murmured against me"—had died. All our weak, selfish thoughts and feelings must be given up before we can really enter the Holy Land. Those who were under twenty years of age at the time were not held responsible. They represent the new and more trusting thoughts which are gradually being developed in our minds as we learn more and more of the Lord's care and protection over us. They were the ones who entered the Holy Land under Joshua. Joshua and Caleb were the only ones of the older generation still living to see that day. Caleb represents the things in us which are fit for heaven, and Joshua—who was to be their leader after Moses—represents the truth fighting. We shall soon learn more about him.

Basic Correspondences

milk	=	truth in which there is goodness
honey	=	the happiness which comes from goodness and truth

Senior

A good discussion topic for this class is the origin and correspondence of the giants in the land, and also the mention of the walled cities in the same connection. Point out that our deep-seated selfishness always tries to justify itself and so builds up systems of falsity. It also turns truth into falsity.

The book of Numbers takes its name from the fact that the first incident recorded in it is the numbering or census of the people by Moses at the command of the Lord. We saw in our lesson on the Garden of Eden that to "name" a thing represented judging its quality. Swedenborg says that to "number" is always predicated of truth. So it was fitting that after all the laws had been given to the Israelites at Sinai, they should be numbered—that is, examined as to their possession of truths. The numbering was carried out by tribes, only the men fit for war being numbered; and afterward an offering of silver was brought by the heads of the tribes. This was in accordance with the law given in Exodus 30:12-13, which means that we are not to count up our knowledge and understanding without recognizing that we owe all we have to the Lord. In the Gospels we read, "Which of you, intending to build a tower, sitteth not down first, and counteth the cost, whether he have sufficient to finish it?" (Luke 14:28) That the mere giving of the laws did not make over the children of Israel was evidenced by the fact that at their first camping place, three days' journey from Sinai, it is recorded that they murmured again and were punished, and a little later even Aaron and Miriam rebelled against Moses and had to be taught a lesson of obedience all over again. It is after these incidents that they were led to camp at Kadesh, near the border of the Holy Land, and Moses was commanded to send out twelve spies to look through the Holy Land and bring back a report of it.

The story of the spies is a searching one in a very real sense. If the people had been willing to believe and trust the Lord, they might have entered the Holy Land at once and possessed it, but the Lord knows that trust and obedience are developed only through long experience: "For precept must be upon precept, precept upon precept; line upon line, line upon line; here a little, and there a little" (Isaiah 28:10). So it is always provided that we have opportunities to "search" the land before we try to enter it. We must see clearly the enemies which are in the land (the faults in ourselves which we will have to overcome) and we must also see clearly the advantages of heavenly living (we must have a taste of the fruits). Conquering our external bad habits is like overcoming the enemies in the wilderness, but the real work comes when we face the evils which lie deep within ourselves.

Our perceptions, like the spies, go on ahead of us to search the land. They bring back the report that it is a good land, a land "flowing with milk and honey," rich in spiritual instruction and the happiness which goes with it. They bring back one enormous bunch of grapes—one experience, perhaps, of what it means to be genuinely good—and also pomegranates and figs—knowledge of good and truth, and experiences of natural goodness. But they show us that we have to live in a world full of strongly entrenched false ideas (walled cities) and even that we shall have to overcome the giants of self-love and self-intelligence.

Then comes the choice. All that is good and wise in us, like Caleb and Joshua, prompts us to trust the Lord and go forward. But our baser impulses say, "I am not strong enough: I was born as I am: I cannot change: I would rather go back to Egypt." Read carefully verses 1 to 10 of chapter 14. The arguments with which we try to quiet the voice of conscience are the stones the congregation wanted to throw at Caleb and Joshua. Remember this when you are tempted to put off the effort to live a really good life. Every time we put it off, the journey becomes longer and harder.

What was true of the Israelites is true of us: We cannot enter the Holy Land until all our weak, cowardly, selfish thoughts have been put away. And when the Lord sees that we are not strong enough to do this, He makes us wait. We cannot rush ahead in our own strength, as some of the Israelites tried to do when they realized what was before them. If we are not willing to obey the Lord, the first enemy we meet will overcome us. But if we follow the pillar of cloud and fire patiently, the time will come when we find that all our foolish thoughts have one by one been left behind us.

Adult

The general lesson here is the reason for our slow progress in spiritual living.

To the end of our lives we have the tendency to say, "I can't help it; I was born that way," to see the beauty of the truly heavenly life but to balk at the effort necessary to attain it. Point out that we always lose when we put off the all-out effort. The topic suggested in the Adult notes is also a fruitful one: "What is the difference between the Church Universal and the Church Specific, and what is the function of the organized New Church in the world today?" Read *Heaven and Hell*, n. 308.

The book of Exodus ends with the setting up of the tabernacle and the descent of the pillar of cloud upon it. The book of Leviticus, with the exception of the account of the consecration of Aaron and his sons in chapters 8 and 9 and the brief incident of Nadab and Abihu in chapter 10:1-7, is entirely given over to laws of all kinds. With the book of Numbers the journey of the Israelites continues. The book takes its name from its first incident, the "numbering" or census of the people by Moses at the command of the Lord; but the name is also descriptive of the character of the book, since "numbering" is predicated of truth and the rest of the book of Numbers describes the testing of the Israelites as to their willingness to follow the truth which had been revealed to them. In our lives it pictures this same period of testing. In the New Church we are brought up to recognize the Word as our book of life. Theoretically we accept this fact. But we do not really "know" any truth until we have learned to practice it and proved it in practice. This is where our real testing begins.

When the cloud was lifted from the tabernacle, the Israelites resumed their march, and we read that after only three days' journey the people began to complain again. Note that this is the same period as the three days' march into the wilderness in the first place. The three days picture fullness of experience on the three planes of life: will, thought, and act. As soon as we bring new truth down into the plane of act, we meet temptation. This time the temptation reached even the higher thought and affection: Aaron and Miriam. We may remember the words of the serpent in the Garden of Eden: "Ye shall not surely die" if one ate of the fruit of the forbidden tree. We look about us and see people apparently blessed and happy who are not concerned about obedience to the commandments or worship of the Lord. In chapter 12 it is said that Miriam and Aaron spoke against Moses because he had married an Ethiopian* woman. What they said was: "Hath the Lord indeed spoken only by Moses? hath he not spoken also by us?" Ethiopia in a good sense represents interior knowledges of the Word. So this rebellion pictures unwillingness to look to the Word alone for leadership. Miriam's leprosy is a clear picture of the hypocrisy involved in such apparent liberalism or "broad-mindedness."

Finally—not long after this rebellion—the people arrived at Kadesh-barnea near the border of the Holy Land. The place has been almost certainly identified. It is only about forty miles south of Beersheba. In Numbers it is said that the Lord told Moses to send out twelve spies. The account of the same incident in Deuteronomy 1:19-46 says that the people asked that the spies be sent. Both are true. Our natural desire, before we embark on a new venture, is to look ahead and count the cost (Luke 14:28-32), and the Lord also wishes us to do so. But the Lord sees to it that in addition to our natural selfish affections and thoughts we have in us some good and true affections and thoughts represented by Joshua and Caleb. The perceptions which spring from our selfishness see the good qualities of the heavenly life—any rational person, as Swedenborg points out, can see the value of honesty and uprightness in moral and civil matters—but when it comes to a question of attempting the spiritual conquest which would give eternal value to these external virtues, they see only the difficulties in the way. They say, "Is it not enough to be a good moral person and a good citizen? No one can hope to stand against the world or to change his inherited nature." Walled cities represent false systems of thought which have been developed in defense of selfishness, and giants stand for that deep-seated selfishness itself. The giants, we are told, were evil remnants left over from the Most Ancient Church. Selfishness is always the power behind false reasoning. This is again

*Or Cushite (from Cush, son of Ham). —*Ed.*

illustrated by the fact that in the time of David, the Philistines—who represent an interest in the truth without a desire to live according to it—sent out one of these atavistic giants as their champion. The arguments stirred up in our minds by evil spirits in our times of temptation always rely on our inherent selfishness as their strongest ally. These arguments are also pictured by the stones with which the people sought to destroy Caleb and Joshua.

When the people realized that because of their cowardly choice they would not be allowed to enter the land but would die in the wilderness, some of them sought to rush forward in spite of the divine prohibition and were overcome by the Amalekites. This is a picture of trying to accomplish by one's own power something which only obedience to the Lord can attain. Such an attempt is ended by the first discouragement. We recall that the Amalekites picture the discouragement which results from distrust of the Lord—they attacked from ambush and chose the stragglers and the weary as their victims (Deuteronomy 25:17-18; Samuel 15:2). We can accomplish nothing spiritually in our own power alone.

The punishment of the people for refusing to take the advice of Caleb and Joshua seems severe. Does it mean that one wrong choice will cut a person off from the possibility of entering heaven? Certainly not. All the Israelites of our story represent things within each of us. Caleb and Joshua are there as the promptings of our higher nature. The children—those under twenty years—are there as the possibilities in us which are undeveloped at the time of any given choice. Moses is there as the principle of obedience to the commandments, which continues to lead us toward the Holy Land. The people who were refused admittance to the Holy Land as a result of their choice are all those thoughts and affections in us which lean toward self and refuse to obey the Lord. They must die one by one in the wilderness. Even Moses, although he was allowed to *see* the Holy Land from the height of Mount Nebo (Deuteronomy 34:1-4), was not allowed to enter it. We may read the story of the reason for this in Numbers 20:1-13. Literally, Moses at one time exalted himself instead of the Lord in his dealings with the people and so was refused admission to the Holy Land. Spiritually, Moses in us represents obedience to the commandments from a sense of duty, and this often has in it something of self-praise. We do not actually enter the Holy Land until external obedience to the commandments has become a habit of which we no longer think with pride.

In Deuteronomy 2:14 we read that thirty-eight years passed after the first sojourn in Kadesh-barnea before the children of Israel were again brought to the border of the Holy Land prepared to enter it. It sometimes seems to us that we shall never reach the free and happy state which is promised to those who patiently seek to obey. The Lord alone sees the heart and knows when we are ready. We are told that He never allows us to be tempted beyond our strength to resist, if we will, and that He withholds temptations altogether from those who are not willing to attempt the conquest. Our spiritual strength is developed and tested little by little. If we can believe that the Lord is leading us, and if we can look upon every such testing as an opportunity for spiritual development, our progress will be much more rapid and easy. The constant murmurings and complaints of the children of Israel in the wilderness are recorded in the Word to show us in concrete form the folly of our own discontents and rebellions. And the patience of the Lord through all their weaknesses should help us to see and acknowledge His patience with us.

From the Writings of Swedenborg

Arcana Coelestia, n. 1717: "He who supposes that the external man can be reduced into correspondence without combats and temptations is mistaken; for temptations are the means of dissipating evils and falsities, as also of introducing goods and truths, and of reducing the things which are of the external man into obedience, so that it may serve the interior or rational man, and through this the internal, that is, the Lord operating through the internal man. That these things are effected by temptations, no one can know but he who has been regenerated through temptations. But how this is done can scarcely be described even in the most general manner, since it is done without the man's knowing whence and how; for it is the Lord's Divine operation."

Arcana Coelestia, n. 1740: "That evils and falsities are conquered by the combats of temptations, and that goods and truths are thereby put on, comes from the fact that evils and falsities are thus dissipated; and when these have been dissipated goods and truths succeed in their place; and these are afterwards confirmed more and more, and are thus strengthened. For it is by evil spirits that evils and falsities are excited; and unless they are excited, the man scarcely knows that they are evils and falsities; but when excited they are manifest. And the longer the combats of temptations last, the more manifest do the evils and falsities become, until at last they are held in abhorrence."

Suggested Questions on the Lesson

J. When the Israelites left Sinai, to what place did they come which was near the Holy Land? *Kadesh*

J. Whom did they send out from there? *twelve spies*

P. What did the spies bring back from the Holy Land? *grapes, pomegranates, figs*

P. What did they report about the land? *land of milk and honey*

J. What did ten of the spies advise? *people too strong for us*

J. What two men reminded the people that the Lord would help them? *Caleb and Joshua*

P. Whose advice did the people take? *that of ten cowards*

J. What was their punishment? *forty years wandering*

P. Who were to be allowed to enter the Holy Land? *those then under twenty, Caleb and Joshua*

J. What happened to the ten spies who gave the bad advice? *died of plague*

J. How much longer did the people wander in the wilderness? *approx. 38 years*

I. What does the Holy Land picture? *heaven, or the regenerate life*

S. What is the meaning of the story of the spies? *our desire to be reassured that the heavenly way of life is really happy and worthwhile*

KORAH, DATHAN, AND ABIRAM

Numbers 16

The lesson of defeat at the hands of the Amalekites was not long-lived. Israel was far from ready to resign itself to the necessary unquestioning obedience to the Lord through Moses. So again we find a challenge to the leadership of Moses and Aaron, again with devastating results.

Doctrinal Points

The Lord is the source of all creation and sustains us from moment to moment.

The Word is given for our guidance, and we cannot safely set up our own judgment in place of its teachings.

True faith is not just saying we believe in God or even just going through the forms of worship.

Any good thing we do from selfish motives is not really good. Charity is love to the Lord and the neighbor in the heart.

Notes for Parents

The story for today is a strange one. Did these startling and terrible punishments actually overtake the people who rebelled against Moses and Aaron so long ago?

When men began to become absorbed in the study of the natural world, they found it so fascinating that many lost their balance and came to think that this world is all there is. They seemed to think that the natural world came into existence somehow all by itself and developed by its own power, and that man is just the highest of the animals and has somehow managed to improve his own condition and become civilized. Such people of course reject as impossible the miracles of both the Old and the New Testaments. The most unfortunate part of it is that their attitude has had a strong influence on others because they pose as the "thinkers" of the day. So even among people who see that nature could not have created itself and that there must be a God, an intelligent being behind all creation, there is an idea that we must explain the miracles in some natural way. In the case of our story for today, for instance, they would say that there just happened to be an earthquake and probably a bolt of lightning and the beginning of a plague at about the same time, and that Moses took advantage of them to strengthen his position.

But nothing in the world just happens. There are causes for everything, and behind the natural causes there are spiritual causes. Not only everything we do but everything we think and feel affects the world around us and helps or hinders the Lord in His effort to bless mankind. Sometimes men can be waked up out of their self-satisfaction and selfish ambitions only by being allowed to suffer the actual physical effects of their denial of God, and sometimes good people can be stirred to action only by being shown that these effects fall on the innocent as well as on the guilty. Korah, Dathan, and Abiram and those who supported them in their rebellion had to be made object lessons in order to prevent all the people from destroying themselves.

And the Lord included their story in the Bible as an object lesson for us. It is not hard to read the lesson. Those who pretend to worship the Lord in order to further selfish ambition are turning the unselfish love which comes to them from the Lord and from which they live from day to day into self-love, which ultimately "burns them up." Those who refuse to worship the Lord at all and insist on following their own will and understanding—staying in the door of their own tents instead of going to the tabernacle—are swallowed up by the earth: worldliness destroys their spiritual life. And everyone who lets either of these two foolish attitudes influence him is plagued by evils which may destroy him also.

Primary

The story from the Word is more impressive than any retelling of it could be.

Read to the children verses 1-7 and 18-35 of the chapter. The lessons to be drawn are the foolishness of jealousy and wanting always to be first, and especially of wanting our own way instead of the Lord's way. Some of these children are old enough to begin to think about obedience to the Lord as well as to their elders.

Do you remember how Moses was given power from the Lord to bring the plagues upon the Egyptians? And Moses by the same power had brought water out of the rock for the people at Rephidim, and he had been the one to whom the Lord at Sinai had given all the laws for the government of the people and the directions for building and furnishing the tabernacle. Wouldn't you think that all the people would have been quite sure that Moses was the one chosen by the Lord to govern them?

But you know sometimes we become jealous of anyone who has been made a leader. When you children are playing together, isn't each one of you likely to want to tell the others what to do?

There was a man named Korah who became jealous of Moses and of Moses' brother Aaron, whom the Lord had appointed to be high priest. Moses and Aaron were descendants of Jacob's son Levi, and the whole tribe of Levi had been set apart by the Lord to take care of the tabernacle; but only Aaron and his sons could be priests.

Of what tribe was Korah?
What two other men joined with him?
The fourth man, On, is mentioned only once.
How did Moses propose to settle the question of leadership?
What happened to Dathan and Abiram and their families?
What happened to Korah and the two hundred and fifty men who offered incense?
What happened to the people who still murmured?
How did Aaron stop the plague?
What did they do with the censers of the rebels?

The Lord gives us this story in the Bible to set us thinking about how foolish it is for us to imagine that we know better than the Lord how things should be done.

Junior

In addition to the lessons suggested for the Primary class, the Juniors may be given a little of the correspondence of the punishments which followed the rebellion.

After the book of Leviticus comes the book of Numbers. It is so named because it begins with a numbering or census of the people which Moses took at the command of the Lord. Then the pillar of cloud was taken up from the tabernacle and the children of Israel resumed their march through the wilderness.

We have seen how prone the Israelites were to forget all that the Lord had done for them and to be restless and dissatisfied. We must not think of the children of Israel as a mere handful of people who would all be well acquainted with each other and easy to instruct and lead. When they left Egypt, there were six hundred thousand of them who were grown up, besides the children. Among such a large number of people there are always some who find fault with everything and spend their time trying to stir others up to agree with them and make trouble. Even among the leaders there is sometimes jealousy and disagreement. So several times Moses had to deal with rebellion of one sort or another. Our story for today is about one of these rebellions.

Who was the principal leader of the revolt?
To what tribe did he belong?
Who plotted with him against Moses and Aaron?
What did they say about Moses and Aaron?
Who did Moses say would settle the question of leadership?
What did Moses tell Korah to do?
What happened to Dathan and Abiram and their families?
What happened to Korah and the two hundred and fifty princes who offered incense?
What was Moses told to do with their censers?

So the rebellion was stopped by the Lord Himself. But even such a terrible object lesson was not enough to silence the complaints of the people. Our chapter goes on to tell us that now they actually blamed Moses and Aaron for the death of their friends. And this brought upon them a plague which killed thousands of them and was stopped only by the intercession of Moses and Aaron themselves.

Why do you think the Lord gives us a story like this in the Bible? It is because the Lord used the history of the Israelites to teach us and other people in all times lessons which we need to learn. The Israelites, as we read often in the Word, were a "stubborn and rebellious" people and could be kept in order only by such startling punishments. And, although men have developed since that time and are better able to learn by reason, we still often need a vivid picture like this to make us stop to think. Korah, Dathan, and Abiram rebelled against Moses and Aaron primarily because they were jealous and wanted to be first themselves. Do we ever have these same feelings? When you see some other boy or girl given the position of honor and trust in school or in your club, are you never tempted to say, "Why should he be picked out instead of me? He's not so wonderful. Why should I have to do what he says?"

Sometimes, of course, it is true that the wrong person is picked for leadership, but not very often, and if we look at things honestly and unselfishly, we can usually see good reasons for the choice. The Israelites had had plenty of proof that Moses and Aaron were really the leaders chosen for them by the Lord.

Today we have the Lord Himself for our leader. When people had become so perverse that no human leaders could bring them back into order, the Lord came into the world Himself to save us and show us the right way to live. And what happens when we rebel against His leadership and want to have our own way instead? One of three things happens to us: Either the "earth"–our lower nature–swallows us up, or the "fire" of self-love destroys us, or we are "carried away" by various evils as the plague struck down the rebellious Israelites. The Lord's way is the only way to peace and happiness.

Intermediate

The correspondence of this story should make a clear and helpful lesson. The teacher may draw on the Adult notes for further points if he finds them of use.

Among the regulations for their worship given to the children of Israel at Sinai was the setting apart of the Levites—the descendants of Jacob's third son Levi—to have charge of the care and service of the tabernacle, whether in camp or on the march. At the same time it was commanded that Aaron should be the high priest and that no one but a descendant of Aaron might be a priest. The children of Israel had had abundant evidence of the fact that Moses, who was also a Levite of course, was the one appointed by the Lord to be their leader and governor—that the Lord spoke to them through Moses. The rebellion against Moses and Aaron of which our chapter for today tells was therefore actually a rebellion against the Lord, even though it was led by a Levite who pretended to wish to serve the Lord.

So the first lesson we may draw from this story is that a person may go through all the outward professions and forms of worship and inwardly be in opposition to the Lord. Isaiah said of the people of his time: "This people draw near me with their mouth, and with their lips do honor me, but have removed their heart far from me" (Isaiah 29:13), and the Lord said of the judgment: "Many will say unto me in that day, Lord, Lord, have we not prophesied in thy name? and in thy name have cast out devils? and in thy name done many wonderful works? And then will I profess unto them, I never knew you: depart from me, ye that work iniquity" (Matthew 7:22-23). This is one of the temptations of all those who are brought up in the habit of church-going—the temptation to let the habit be a substitute for real religion, which is love to the Lord and the neighbor in the heart, and obedience to the commandments in the outward life.

Dathan and Abiram were not Levites. They were descendants of Reuben, Jacob's first son. You remember that the twelve sons of Jacob picture all the different kinds of affections that enter into the development of a good character. Reuben, the firstborn, represents faith. If we do not believe there is a God, we cannot even begin to make spiritual progress. But people may say, "Oh yes, of course I believe in God," and never try to learn anything about Him or about how He wants them to live. They depend for direction on their own ideas and on the general standards of the community in which they live. You notice in the story that Dathan and Abiram would not come to the tabernacle when Moses summoned them, but stood in the door of their tents with all their families. This pictures that unless we are humble and willing to learn of the Lord, we are really looking only to ourselves for wisdom.

And what happened to Dathan and Abiram? "The ground clave asunder that was under them: and the earth opened her mouth, and swallowed them up." This really happened to Dathan and Abiram and their families, but it is in the Word because it pictures something that can happen to us spiritually. You remember the first verse in the Bible and that the heavens and the earth in us are the heavenly and the earthly part of us. If we refuse to learn of the Lord and obey Him and so fail to develop the heavenly part, then the earthly part actually swallows us up. Worldly ideas fill our minds and choke out the possibility of heavenly development. The Hebrew word which is translated *pit* in verse 33 is *Sheol*, which means "the place of the dead." When we shut the Lord out of our minds and hearts, the only life we have is selfish life, which is the equivalent of death spiritually.

Korah himself and the two hundred and fifty "princes of the assembly" who supported him did not remain in their tents, but gathered at the command of Moses before the tabernacle, each with his censer full of incense in his hand. Princes in the Word represent primary thoughts or precepts; so these princes picture the precepts which Korah had gathered to support him in his rebellion. One of these precepts we find in verse 3, where Korah says to Moses: "Ye take too much upon you, seeing *all the congregation are holy, every one of them, and the Lord is among them.*" This was a truth which Korah was using to set himself up as equal to Moses and Aaron (Exodus 19:6). When we are arguing in favor of getting our own way, we particularly try to find truths which can be twisted to support us. This is what Swedenborg calls the "falsification of truth." The censers represent worship; the fire in them, the kind of love which inspires the worship; and the incense, prayer. The censers in the tabernacle were of brass, which as we learned recently represents natural good.

What happened to Korah and the princes? Fire from the Lord came out and consumed them. Fire from the Lord is unselfish love, which goes out to all men constantly. It is the thing from which we all live. But when a selfish person receives this sacred fire, he turns it into self-love which destroys him. You notice, however, that the censers which the princes carried were not destroyed, but were beaten out and used to cover the great altar of sacrifice. For example, if we were to discover that some people who go to church are hypocrites, we should not stop going to church ourselves; instead, we should learn from our discovery that true worship is the recognition that any good we may do is really from the Lord and not from ourselves. Sacrifice, you know, means "to make sacred," and the great altar in the outer court of the tabernacle, on which all the sacrifices were offered, is the symbol of this acknowledgment that we can claim no goodness for ourselves. Only the Lord is good.

Even after these two terrible object lessons had been given, some of the people still murmured and actually blamed Moses and Aaron for causing the death of their leaders. This is the old constant temptation to shift the responsibility for our sins to someone else. It hangs on even after we have to acknowledge that we actually do have the sins. But until we honestly say, "This sin is my own fault and nobody else's," we cannot get rid of the sin. It continues to fester in us and to destroy our spiritual life, just as the plague began to destroy the people who murmured.

Now suppose this time you try to work out the rest of the story for yourselves. Read verses 46 to 50. Think of Moses as representing the Word; of Aaron, the high priest, as representing the Lord as to His divine goodness; and of the correspondence of the censer, the fire, and the incense. You will then have a sure recipe for getting rid of the evils in your own character which are plaguing you. (Following the "Suggested Questions on the Lesson" you will find an outline of the deeper meaning of verses 46-50 against which to check your results.)

Basic Correspondences

princes	=	primary truths or precepts
earth	=	the natural mind
censer	=	worship
incense	=	prayer
fire from the Lord	=	unselfish love

Senior

The lesson for this age should be the pervasive and devastating effect on the life and character of allowing self-seeking and self-intelligence to work in the heart and mind, and especially of allowing them to creep into our worship. Stress the fact that the rebellion began with the murmuring of the people and developed more or less under cover until it found a leader in Korah—that is, until it influenced the attitude toward worship.

Our story for today is a striking one in the literal account. We have noted how easily the Israelites in their journey through the wilderness became discouraged and dissatisfied. Even the complete organization of their civil and religious life which took place during their eleven months at Sinai could not prevent this. Is this so surprising? Think of our own country, founded on sound principles of freedom and democracy, more peaceful and prosperous than any other nation in the world, and yet never without its undercurrents of dissatisfaction and rebellion. And think how prone we all are to find fault with any restrictions which interfere with our ability to do as we please. Swedenborg tells us that the Israelites were strongly inclined to think only in terms of their immediate external condition. This was why they could be led by punishments or promises of reward, and why miracles could be wrought among them, without interfering with their freedom of choice. The Lord, when He was in the world, said to the people in some of the cities where He had wrought miracles: "If the mighty works which were done in you, had been done in Tyre and Sidon, they would have repented long ago in sackcloth and ashes" (Matthew 11:21). It would appear that the Israelites were such that miracles did not force their wills. So the Lord could direct their history in such a way that He could use its course and incidents to represent in the Word by correspondence the lessons He wants to teach us. The incidents of our chapter actually happened as they are recorded, but their value for us is in their internal meaning.

In general, the story pictures the consequences of rebellion against the Lord's established order and of setting up our own will against the Lord's and our own wisdom against the truths given us in the Word—that is, of claiming goodness and wisdom for ourselves. This rebellion, in the literal story, had been developing throughout the wilderness journey and gathering strength until it needed only leadership to bring it into the open. In very much the same way, the selfish elements in our own characters fester in our hearts and minds and gain strength until some particular issue brings them out into open rebellion.

Korah was a Levite. The tribe of Levi had been set apart by the Lord for the service of the tabernacle, but only Aaron and his descendants could minister as priests. This was the burden of Korah's complaint. As a Levite he felt himself as good as Aaron. In attacking Aaron's position he had to discredit Moses also, because it was through Moses that the Lord had given Aaron his commission. The Levites in general represent the affections and thoughts in us which lead us to worship the Lord and direct us in our worship. Aaron in his representative character as high priest symbolizes genuine goodness proceeding from the Lord, and Moses stands for genuine truth as we receive it through the Word. Korah represents a selfish motive entering into our worship. When we go to church because it is good policy or carry on our duties in the church with a feeling of self-righteousness or a desire to dominate over others, true worship is profaned and our whole character feels the effects.

In the rebellion there were four elements involved. (1) Korah himself is the selfish motive which leads all the others. (2) The two hundred and fifty "princes of the assembly" are the precepts which govern our reasoning. These princes had been appointed by Moses to govern under him. When Korah turns them against Moses, it is a picture of what Swedenborg calls the "falsification of truth." We find an example of it in verse 3 in Korah's statement, "seeing all the congregation are holy, every one of them, and the Lord is among them." This is a precept given to the children of Israel by the Lord (Exodus 19:6) but falsified by Korah through his use of it to justify himself in his rebellion.

When we are bent on getting something for ourselves or on proving something we want to believe, we try to find truths which can be used in such a way as to support us. The two hundred and fifty princes with Korah, presenting their censers full of incense before the tabernacle, were destroyed by fire proceeding from the Lord. When we profane our worship by entering into it with selfish motives, we turn the Lord's love—by which we all live—into self-love, which is spiritual death.

Then there were (3) Dathan and Abiram, and On who is mentioned only at the beginning of the story and must have thought better of his part in the rebellion because he is not said to have shared the punishment of the others. These three were of the tribe of Reuben. Reuben, Jacob's first son, represents "faith in the understanding." This is the first step in the development of our spiritual life. If we do not acknowledge with our minds that there is a God, we cannot even start on the road to a good life. But if we stop with this acknowledgment and do not go on to learn about the Lord and try to obey Him, the acknowledgment has no real force in our lives. Dathan and Abiram would not come to the tabernacle. They stood in the door of their own tents. A man who says, "I believe in God," but refuses to learn about Him or to worship Him, continues to live according to his own ideas and is presently "swallowed up" by worldly considerations and cut off from the light of heaven. Spiritually he goes down into "the pit" (*Sheol*) and the earth closes over him.

The last element in the rebellion was (4) "the people." The people in the Word represent the multitude of everyday thoughts in which our character expresses itself. When our worship is profaned by self-love and our ideas of right and wrong are self-directed, everything in our life is tainted. The scourge which destroyed so many of the people is a picture of the devastation which self-confidence and self-assertion cause in our minds and hearts. This plague can be stayed only by turning to the Lord with humility and praying for His help. The censer is the symbol of worship, the fire from the altar is unselfish love for the Lord and the neighbor, and the incense is prayer.

We should note that the censers carried by Korah and the princes were not destroyed. We do not abstain from public and private worship just because we find that our motives have not always been pure. Instead, we try to change ourselves and to make our worship a genuine offering of ourselves to the Lord, as the censers were beaten into plates to cover the great altar of sacrifice.

Adult

This story is one of many in the Bible given to shake us out of the easygoing self-satisfaction into which we all sometimes fall. The various elements which took part in the rebellion and the variety in their punishments make interesting discussion material.

We have seen that the wilderness journey of the Israelites pictures, in the life of the man or woman "who is to be regenerated," as Swedenborg frequently puts it, the period of reformation—that long, slow process of bringing the outward life into order from a principle of obedience to the commandments—which comes between the free decision to turn away from self toward the Lord and the real enjoyment of spiritual living which is regeneration. That period from its very beginning is punctuated by times of dissatisfaction, discouragement, and rebellion. The old selfish, worldly desires and reasonings persist, festering under the surface even as we plod forward, and from time to time breaking out, in spite of the constant evidences we have of the Lord's presence with us and power to save us and to supply all our needs. Sometimes these rebellious outbreaks are mere murmurings, quickly stilled by the Lord's merciful provision. But sometimes, as in our story today, they are the culmination of a long-unnoticed conspiracy of self-love and self-intelligence within us.

The rebellion which is the subject of our lesson came into the open when it found a leader in Korah. Korah was a Levite, a member of the tribe set apart by the Lord for the service of the tabernacle. But he was not of the house of Aaron, and only Aaron and his descendants could actually be priests. In the literal story Korah resents his subordinate position and tries to overthrow the authority of Moses and Aaron. The name Korah means "baldness"; conversely, hair represents outmost truth. Korah knew that Moses and Aaron had been specially appointed by the Lord, but his ambition prompted him to try to get around the acceptance of the literal fact. In order to do so he drew upon other statements of the Lord which he could interpret in support of his contention. His statement in verse 3 is taken from the Lord's words to Moses as recorded for us in Exodus 19:6. Isn't this something we church people are all prone to do? We profess to believe that the Word is inspired by the Lord and—in the New Church—that Swedenborg was the Lord's instrument in opening the Word and revealing its true doctrine; but when something in the Word or the writings runs counter to what we want to believe, we try to discount it and to find other statements more to our liking, instead of really examining what we read to find out the truth and applying it by changing our thought and conduct. The two hundred and fifty "princes of the assembly" who supported Korah in his rebellion represent just such precepts of the Word, given to govern us but taken out of their context and used to support us in doing what we like. This is what Swedenborg calls the "falsification of truth."

The punishment for such misuse of the truth is described in the punishment of the two hundred and fifty princes: "there came out a fire from the Lord, and consumed them." The "fire" which proceeds from the Lord is unselfish love. It is the very life of life which maintains us from moment to moment. When we profess to be seeking this life and then turn it into self-love, our souls perish. The brazen censers are a symbol of outward worship, the fire in them the motive which prompts it, and the incense the petitions we are offering in our minds. When we go to church professing to believe in the Lord and to be worshiping Him, and are really thinking about how good we are and hoping our worship will be properly credited to us and praying that we may be given the things we want, we are like Korah and the princes. We must note, however, that after these men were destroyed, the censers were preserved. People have been known to excuse themselves from going to church on the ground that there were "so many hypocrites in the churches." External worship is right and necessary. We cannot safely do without it. But our worship should be a humble offering of ourselves to the Lord and not an exaltation of self. This is what is meant by beating the censers into plates to cover the great altar of sacrifice.

There were two other groups concerned in the rebellion of Korah. One was the three Reubenites, Dathan, Abiram, and On. On is mentioned only in the first instance and apparently obeyed Moses and withdrew from the company of the others, as he was not included in their destruction. Reuben, Jacob's first son, represents faith—specifically faith in the understanding. This is the first step in the development of spiritual life; we must acknowledge divine truth with our minds before we do anything useful with it. But if we go no further than intellectual acknowledgment, divine truth has no real effect on our lives. Dathan and Abiram would not go to the tabernacle at the call of Moses. They stood in the door of their tents. Whenever we—any of us—fall into the idea that because we have joined the church and give lip service to the Lord we shall get to heaven without making any real effort to learn the truths of the Word and apply them in our daily lives, we are living in faith alone. When we do not try to learn of the Lord and to obey Him, we are led by our own ideas and the ideas of the world about us. We have cut ourselves off from the light of heaven. And eventually the earth opens her mouth and swallows us up and we go down alive into the pit (*Sheol*) just as really as Dathan and Abiram did. And all the affections and thoughts and deeds which we have produced and in which we take such pride are dragged down with us. Worldliness and self-interest are in all that we do.

The other group concerned in the rebellion were the people. "The people" are all our everyday thoughts and feelings. When Dathan and Abiram insisted on remaining by their own tents instead of coming to the tabernacle, Moses gave the people a solemn warning: "Depart, I pray you, from the tents of these wicked men, and touch nothing of theirs, lest ye be consumed in all their sins." We are told in AC 10130 that "by 'touching' is signified communication, transfer, and reception." Our minds touch other people's minds constantly in the course of our daily life in the world. How easily we fall into the habit of agreeing with our acquaintances without stopping to think whether we really should agree or not! It is so much easier to agree than to think, and the matter in question often seems unimportant. But in this way our own thinking is colored by the ideas of the world about us, and we sometimes wake up and realize that what we have been accepting as a matter of course is actually quite contrary to the principles we profess to hold. The Lord said, "Take heed how ye hear." In our story the people did withdraw from the tents of Dathan and Abiram, but many had been so tainted with the spirit of the rebellion that they still murmured, even after the terrible object lessons they received, and their murmuring took the form of the charge that Moses and Aaron were responsible for the death of their friends. This, too, strikes home to us. How often, when we can no longer deny that we have been wrong, our first impulse is to blame someone else for our condition! The plague which struck among the people who murmured is a picture of the spiritual consequences of refusing to acknowledge and repent of our own sins. Every time of rebellion and disobedience in our lives leaves its trail of consequences in our minds and hearts. The plague was stopped by Aaron by means of a censer full of fire from the altar and incense laid upon it. If we look to the Lord for help with sincere humility and a desire to be shown our weaknesses and evils and are led to serve Him truly, the effects of our rebellion can be checked.

From the Writings of Swedenborg

Apocalypse Explained, n. 324[6]: "Korah, Dathan, and Abiram, with their company, were swallowed up by the earth, although they took fire from the altar and burnt incense, because 'their murmuring against Moses and Aaron' signified profanation of the good of celestial love; for 'Moses' and 'Aaron' represented the Lord; and 'to murmur' (that is, to rebel) against the Lord and at the same time to perform holy offices, is profanation; but as they took the fire from the altar, that fire was cast out, and their censers were made into a covering for the altar."

Suggested Questions on the Lesson

P. Who led a rebellion against Moses and Aaron? *Korah*
P. What tribe was Korah from? *Levi*
J. What was the office of the Levites? *care of tabernacle and worship*
J. What was Aaron's office? *high priest*
J. Why was Korah dissatisfied? *jealous of Aaron*
P. What other men joined in the rebellion? *Dathan and Abiram*
J. What tribe were they from? *Reuben*
P. Where did they insist on staying? *in their own tents*
P. How were Dathan and Abiram and their families destroyed? *earth opened*
J. What other group of Korah's supporters went to the tabernacle with him? *250 princes of assembly*
P. What happened to them? *destroyed by fire*
J. What became of their censers? *made into plates to cover altar*
J. What happened to the people who still murmured? *plague*
J. How was the plague stopped? *Aaron with censer*
I. What is pictured by the punishment of Dathan and Abiram? *result of "faith alone"*
I. What does a censer represent? *worship*
S. What is pictured by the punishment of Korah and the princes with him? *result of twisting truth to support one's selfish desires*

S. Why were the censers not destroyed? *fault not with worship as such but with wrong attitude toward it*

[see Intermediate notes]

46. Make your worship real, removing evil of pretended worship.
47. Accept truth of this need and you will see that mere outward devotion is destructive.
48. Make a clear separation in your mind between dead and live worship, thus stopping further loss of spiritual values.
49. Soberly count the losses of your foolish behavior.
50. Then return to true worship of God.

AARON'S ROD

Numbers 17

The teacher should read Exodus 28:1-4, 40-43 concerning Aaron, and review Numbers 16 as a background for the current lesson. He should also look over the route of the Israelites as found in Numbers 33 and as marked on a Bible map of the wilderness journey, and he should refresh his memory of the story of the spies in Numbers 13 and 14, especially Numbers 14:26-35.

Doctrinal Points

The Lord knows what is best for us. We should recognize Him as wiser than we are.
The signs given the Israelites in the Word are signs for us, too.
Faith in the Lord is measured by obedience.
There is no genuine goodness in anything done from self.

Notes for Parents

In our lesson for today the children of Israel have left Sinai and have been traveling through the wilderness for some time. Once they even came almost in sight of the Holy Land; but when the spies they sent on ahead reported finding strong cities, powerful enemies, and even giants there, they refused to attempt the conquest, even though two of the spies—Joshua and Caleb—reminded them that the Lord was with them and would surely give them the victory. For this lack of trust in the Lord they were condemned to continue their wanderings in the wilderness for forty years, until all who were of age at the time of their cowardly decision, except Joshua and Caleb, should have died. In the same way, we ourselves all too often lose some great happiness because we refuse to "trust in the Lord and go forward."

And in another way we are very much like the children of Israel. When we are suffering from the results of some wrong we have done, we try to find someone else to blame instead of ourselves. The Israelites blamed Moses and Aaron and rebelled against their leadership. If you have read chapter 16, you will know the immediate result of the rebellion and the terrible lesson they were given.

Then the Lord gave them a different kind of lesson. At Sinai the Lord had appointed Aaron to be high priest, and only a descendant of his was ever to hold this office. Now the Lord confirms the choice in the eyes of all the people by the sign of the rods. When twelve rods—one for each tribe, each marked with the name of the leader of the tribe—were laid up overnight before the ark in the Holy of Holies of the tabernacle, Aaron's rod bore buds and blossoms and yielded almonds. The other eleven remained mere sticks. In the Gospels the Lord tells us, "By their fruits ye shall know them," and we all understand that fruits mean deeds. Almonds are delicious, nourishing, and long-lasting fruit, and the almond blossom is beautiful. The lesson is not hard to see. Only love to the Lord and obedience to Him can make us happy and good, with the kind of goodness which endures. We should take this lesson to heart, as Moses was afterward commanded to lay up Aaron's rod before the ark forever "to be kept for a token against the rebels."

Primary

Bring out especially Aaron's position with reference to Moses and the people. This class should learn the function of the Levites and that of Aaron and his sons, and should have the background story of Korah, Dathan, and Abiram refreshed in their minds. They are not too young to get the general lesson of the blossoming rod.

After the golden calf was destroyed, Moses set the people to work to build the tabernacle, a special tent in which they were to worship the Lord. The Lord had given Moses exact directions for making the tabernacle and the furniture that was to be in it. The holiest piece of furniture was the ark, a box or chest covered with gold, in which were kept the two tables of stone with the ten commandments written on them. You remember that Moses broke the first tables when he came down and found the people worshiping the golden calf. But afterward the Lord told Moses to hew out two new tables from the stone at the foot of the mountain and bring them up, and the Lord wrote the commandments on them again for the people.

Do you remember the name of Moses' brother who went everywhere with him? It was Aaron. The Lord told Moses that Aaron was to be the high priest of Israel and that Aaron's sons were also to be priests. The whole tribe of Levi, to which Moses and Aaron belonged, were to have charge of the tabernacle and its furnishings and of all the things connected with the people's worship, but only Aaron and his sons could perform the highest services.

After they left Sinai, the pillar of cloud and fire led them from place to place through the wilderness, and the people began to blame Moses and Aaron for their long journey and all their troubles.

They blamed them for all their troubles.
They thought someone else should be high priest.
What did the Lord tell Moses to do?
How many rods were brought to him?
How were they to know which was which?
Where were the rods placed?
Next morning what did Moses find had happened to Aaron's rod?
What did this mean?
What did the Lord tell Moses to do with Aaron's rod?

Junior

The historical and geographical sequences are important for this age group. The teacher should have a map to show them. The moral lesson is within their reach, and they can also get some idea of the correspondence of the seed-plant series, which will show them the reason for the Lord's choice of this particular sign.

Where did the children of Israel camp for eleven months?
What did they all hear the Lord speak from the mount?
What other instructions were given at Sinai?

Where did Moses have to go to speak with the Lord?
How long was he gone the last time?
What did the people ask Aaron to do?
What did he make for them?
What did he use to make it?
When Moses came down, what was he carrying?
What did he do with them?
What did he do with the golden calf?
Where did Moses cut two new tables of stone?
Who wrote the commandments on them?

During the rest of their stay at Sinai, the people were kept busy with the construction of the tabernacle and its furnishings and the dedication of it with sacrifices and offerings. This was the kind of thing they could see and enjoy. The tribe of Levi was set apart by the Lord to have charge of everything pertaining to worship. They were to set up the tabernacle when the people camped and to take it down and carry it when the march was resumed, and they were to assist in the offerings and ceremonies. But only Aaron and his sons could be priests. The Lord appointed Aaron to be high priest, and no one but a descendant of his was ever to hold this office.

Finally the pillar of cloud moved. The people were set on the march by the blowing of two special silver trumpets. They were led into the wilderness of Paran which forms a large part of the Arabian peninsula north of Sinai. The thirty-third chapter of Numbers lists the stopping places in their order. Finally they reached Kadesh-barnea, very near the southern border of the Holy Land. But they did not go forward then. They sent twelve men—one from each tribe—to spy out the land, and ten of them came back and said they found enemies there too strong for the Israelites to conquer. And although the other two spies—Joshua and Caleb—reminded them that the Lord was with them and urged them to go forward, they voted to take the advice of the other ten. And the Lord said that because of their lack of faith they would have to go on wandering about in the wilderness until all the men who had been old enough to vote at that time—except Joshua and Caleb—had died.

When we are being punished for some wrong thing we have done, we are never very happy, are we? We often forget that it was all our own fault and try to put the blame on innocent people, sometimes on the very ones who tried to keep us from doing wrong in the first place. Our story for today is really a continuation of the story of Korah, Dathan, and Abiram.

What did the Lord tell Moses to have brought for each tribe?
How many rods were there?
How were they to know which was which?
Whose name was written on the rod of the tribe of Levi?
What did Moses do with the rods?
In the morning what had happened to Aaron's rod?
What was Moses told to do with Aaron's rod?

You know what almonds are. They are nuts which keep well, have a fine flavor, and are nourishing. And the almond tree has lovely blossoms, too. The Lord made Aaron's rod blossom and bear almonds to show the people that only worship in obedience to the Lord could make them happy and good.

The people really knew that it was the Lord who had appointed Aaron, but people are not always ready to accept the Lord's will. We like to think we can be good in our own way. We have many good affections: love of our parents, love of study, love of making useful things, love of certain kinds of work, etc. All these lead us to do some good things. But sometimes none of these is strong enough to keep us from doing wrong, especially when we think no one will know what we have done. Only love of the Lord can always keep us in the right way, for we know that the Lord sees and knows everything we do, and even everything we think and feel. We must always remember this. That is why Aaron's rod was to be laid up beside the ark in the Holy of Holies of the tabernacle. You remember the first commandment. And the Lord says that the commandments should be written in our hearts. Our story for today is put in the Bible to help us see that only by obeying the Lord can we be happy.

Intermediate

A considerable part of the lesson time will need to be spent on background. The meaning of the lesson for the day itself is simple and should be given as a climax.

Our lesson today is from the book of Numbers. We have learned the meaning of the names *Genesis* and *Exodus* and why these two books are so called. The book of Leviticus is the detailed statement of the code of laws given to Moses at Sinai. These were called the "Levitical" laws because the tribe of Levi was set apart by the Lord to have charge of the Jewish worship and to teach and enforce the law. If we read the first four verses of the first chapter of the book of Numbers, we find the reason for its name. Before the people left Sinai, Moses was commanded by the Lord to number or count all the people by tribes, and there are many places in the book where numbers are prominent and where our attention is called to the twelve tribes, their leaders, and their individual functions. Our lesson for today is one of these.

In Exodus 28 we learn that among the Levites Aaron and his sons were given the priestly office by the Lord, and in Exodus 40 their solemn consecration to this office is described. Aaron himself was to be high priest, and only a descendant of his could hold that office.

The greater part of the wilderness journey came after the Israelites left Sinai. Chapter 33 of Numbers lists their stopping places. When they reached Kadesh near the southern border of the Holy Land, at the command of the Lord Moses sent twelve men—one from each tribe—to spy out the land. But the people let themselves be discouraged from attempting its conquest because ten of the spies said the enemies there were too strong for them. The other two spies, Joshua and Caleb, reminded them that the Lord was with them but they were not listened to, and so the Lord told them that they would have to wander in the wilderness until all who had been of age to vote at the time of the decision—except Joshua and Caleb—had died. So it was actually forty years before the entry into the Holy Land took place.

We know from experience how prone we are, when we are suffering from the effects of some wrongdoing of our own, to try to find someone else to blame. The Israelites blamed Moses and Aaron. The rule of Moses and Aaron pictures the rule of divine truth and love. When we turn against this, "the earth"–that is, worldliness–swallows us up and the love of our hearts is turned into consuming self-love. This is the negative side of the picture, detailed in the story of Korah, Dathan, and Abiram.

But the Lord, in the Word, follows this with a beautiful picture of the positive results of obedience to divine law. The twelve tribes picture all our good affections and thoughts, the tribe of Levi and especially Aaron as high priest portraying love of goodness from the Lord. The rods, one from each tribe, are symbols of power, the principles which put the various affections into practice.

We have many good affections: love of learning, love of useful service, etc. These are some of the things represented by the rods. But all these may fail under temptation. There is only one love which can carry us through everything, and that is love of the Lord–the power of which is symbolized by Aaron's rod.

The teachings of our church tell us that we are to shun evils as sins against God. This means that we are to judge our conduct by the standard of the Lord's laws instead of by any standards we make for ourselves or find in the world about us. Only in this way can we be sure of avoiding evil and doing good.

Aaron's rod, the power of love to the Lord, "brought forth buds, and bloomed blossoms, and yielded almonds." The buds stand for impulses toward good deeds; the blossoms, thoughts about how to do them; and the almonds, genuine good works, for nuts are both nourishing and lasting.

Moses was commanded to lay up Aaron's rod beside the ark in the Holy of Holies. In the same way, we must hold fast in our hearts to the one true guiding principle, which is love to the Lord.

Basic Correspondences

the twelve tribes	=	all our good affections and thoughts
Aaron as high priest	=	goodness from the Lord

a rod = power
the almond = goods of life

Senior

The principal lesson for this age is in the necessity of distinguishing between good works done from self and good works done from the desire to serve and obey the Lord. Even in the church there is a great deal of self-praise. There is no interior life in good works performed in this spirit.

It is not until the tenth chapter of the book of Numbers that we find the Israelites leaving Sinai. First the tabernacle and its furnishings had to be constructed, set up, and consecrated, and worship begun according to the prescribed rites. The Lord had named Aaron as high priest (Exodus 28) and his sons as priests under him, and the priesthood was to continue in his family. The book of Leviticus gives the detailed code of laws to be taught and administered by the tribe of Levi, to which both Moses and Aaron belonged. Then at the command of the Lord, all the people were numbered or counted by tribes, the event which gives the book of Numbers its name.

If you will look at a map of the wilderness journey, you will find that the Israelites traveled in a fairly steady line from Sinai to Kadesh-barnea near the southern border of the Holy Land. Their encampments along the way are given us in Numbers 33. At Kadesh they sent forward twelve men to spy out the Holy Land; but when the spies returned, the people allowed themselves to be discouraged from attempting the conquest. For their lack of trust in the Lord's power to give them victory—a power which Joshua and Caleb urged them to acknowledge—they were condemned to continue in the wilderness until all those over twenty years of age (voting age) at the time of their weak decision should have died. With the loss of their immediate hope and incentive, their natural selfishness inspired them to continual grumblings and to dissatisfaction with the leaders whom the Lord had given to them. The immediate background of our chapter is the rebellion of Korah,

Dathan, and Abiram and the two hundred and fifty "princes of the assembly" against Moses and Aaron. Their punishment is a vivid picture of the worldliness and self-love which overtake those who rebel against the Lord's direction while professing to worship Him.

But after this terrible lesson the Lord gave the people another sign, a beautiful one this time, of the fact that only love to the Lord is able to produce genuine and lasting fruit. We recognize the twelve tribes as standing for all our good affections and thoughts. A rod is a symbol of power. Aaron, as high priest and leader of the priestly tribe, represents the principle that life should be lived in recognition of the Lord and in the attempt to learn and do His will. This principle alone has power to make our lives truly happy and fruitful.

We can imagine that the rods, in the hands of their owners, all inspired respect among the people. We hear people say, even of a man who is an atheist, that he is a good man because he does things which benefit humanity. But we should realize that if such a man does recognize his duty to do good to others, it is from some early religious influence and training or from the acceptance of standards in the community which stemmed from a religious source, and that if he does not recognize God in what he does, he is ascribing goodness to himself. His goodness is then merely on the outside and is not genuine, for we read in the Gospels: "There is none good but one, that is, God." What the Lord shows us in this story is that He alone is the source of the power to do good, and that in His sight—when the rods are laid before the ark in the tabernacle—all principles except that of loving obedience to Him are unfruitful.

The almond was appropriate for several reasons. It is a noble and beautiful tree, blossoming profusely (see Jeremiah 1:11). The blossoms are lovely, and the fruit delicious, nourishing, and lasting. The blossoms of a plant or tree represent our thoughts about specific uses or good works; and the fruit, the good works themselves. If our lives are governed by the principle of love to the

Lord and desire to do His will, we shall find delight in thinking about His truth and its specific applications, and we shall find deep and lasting joy in serving Him from day to day. Our lives will not be sterile when laid before the judgment seat of the Lord.

There seems to have been enough power in this final demonstration of the leadership of Moses and Aaron to convince the people. The final proof to us of the rightness of the Lord's guidance is the joy that comes in doing His will. Until we see and taste this satisfaction we are constantly tempted to turn back toward self. And we, too, must "lay up the fruitful rod before the ark" as a constant reminder. That is, the Lord's laws must be written in our hearts. In times of trouble and temptation we must remind ourselves of the blessings that have come to us in the past through obedience, and so hold steadfast.

Adult

Discussion material is suggested in the Adult notes in the references to modern humanism and rejection of revelation. The lesson, however, should be directed toward self-examination rather than toward criticism of society.

We have studied the story of the destruction of two of Aaron's sons—Nadab and Abihu—because they offered "strange fire" in their censers (Leviticus 10:1-7); the story of the sending out of the twelve spies from Kadesh and the condemnation of all the adults who voted to follow the advice of the cowardly ten (Numbers 13, 14); and the story of the rebellion of Korah, Dathan, and Abiram (Numbers 16). All these stories show the steady disposition of the Israelites to set up their own will and their own intelligence in opposition to the Lord's commands and instructions. In these striking and dramatic stories it is easy for us to see and condemn the folly of the tendency in the Israelites to set up their own intelligence and their own will against the Lord, but we are slow to recognize this same tendency in ourselves and to acknowledge its foolishness. Yet it is an almost universal tendency. In national life it results in the belief in force rather than in righteousness, in social life in the struggle for money and power, in our individual lives in contempt for those who are different from ourselves and for anyone who disagrees with us. It appears most clearly of all in one modern theory that the Bible is the work of men—rather pretentiously described as "man's ascending search for God"—and in the tendency of churches, including our own, to measure themselves and their members in terms of external activities instead of in terms of justice and righteousness.

In our chapter for today the Lord gives the people a sign. The story is a simple one and we may wonder why the mere miraculous blossoming of a rod should have convinced the people. Yet the last two verses of the chapter indicate that, coming on top of the terrible events described in the preceding chapter, it did convince them, for the time at least.

What does this story mean for us? The Lord at Sinai had appointed Aaron to be high priest. His sons were also to be priests, and the high priesthood was to descend in his line. Aaron and Moses were descendants of Levi, who among the twelve sons of Jacob represents charity. In AC 342 Swedenborg says: "The church conceives and brings forth nothing else than faith and charity. The same is signified by the first children of Leah from Jacob; 'Reuben' denoting faith; 'Simeon' faith in act; and 'Levi' charity, wherefore also the tribe of Levi received the priesthood, and represented the 'shepherd of the flock.'" He says elsewhere that charity is love to the neighbor in the heart, springing from love to the Lord, and that recognition of the Lord and charity are the essentials of the church.

But among the Levites Aaron was singled out to be high priest. Aaron, like other individuals in the Bible story, has his basic correspondence, but it takes on various colorings according to the context in which he appears. Basically he represents "the Lord as to Divine good or the priesthood." But before he became high priest, when he was assigned to Moses "for a mouth," he represents "the doctrine of what is good and true." We saw this representation in our lesson on the battle with Amalek. Whenever Moses and Aaron are named together, Moses represents the divine law as it is in its inward sense, and Aaron the same law in its literal sense. In our present chapter it is Aaron as high priest whose authority has been called into question. Since in that office he represents the Lord as to good, to question his authority is to refuse to recognize that "there is none good but one, that is, God." Whenever we find ourselves thinking of ourselves as good, finding fault with others because they are not doing what we do, assuming that our own motives are above reproach and that what we think the Bible ought to mean is what it must mean, we are rebelling against the high priesthood of Aaron. It is a sad commentary on our inherited nature that it is so hard for us to learn the lesson of humility which is taught throughout the Word and emphasized again and again in the writings. Swedenborg tells us that without innocence there can be no charity and, as we saw in our lesson on the Passover, he defines innocence as "to know, acknowledge, and believe, not with the mouth but with the heart, that nothing but evil is from one's self and that all good is from the Lord."

The rod is a symbol of power, specifically of the power exercised by truth. The twelve tribes represent all the goods and truths of the church in a complex. The rods of the tribes are symbols of the power exercised by these. We need them all, but each has its specific place and use, and their immediate importance varies with the circumstances in which we are from time to time. We learn this, for example, as we study the shifting order in which the tribes are named in different stories in the Word. But the office of the tribe of Levi remains constant. Levi is given no separate lot in the Holy Land but is established in cities in every part of it. When the rods of the twelve tribes were laid before the ark in the Holy of Holies, only the rod of Aaron for the tribe of Levi blossomed and bore fruit.

We are familiar with the correspondence of the seed-plant series. The seed is truth from the Word, the tree itself represents a certain principle, the leaves thoughts from that principle, the blossoms particular thoughts leading to uses, the fruit the uses themselves.

Nuts, because they last a long time, represent lasting goods. Of the almond Swedenborg says in AC 5622: "This tree itself signifies in the spiritual sense a perception of interior truth which is from good, its 'blossom' interior truth which is from good, and its 'fruit' good of life thence derived." So the sign of Aaron's rod means that only the acknowledgment—from the heart—that the Lord alone is good can produce genuine good in the life. The laying of the twelve rods before the ark shows us that it is the Lord's judgment and not man's which counts.

The later laying up of Aaron's rod before the ark, "to be kept as a token against the rebels," tells us that the principle pictured by the fruitful rod should be taken to heart and never forgotten, so that we may not be guilty of setting ourselves up in judgment upon the Lord, the sin which caused the earth to open and swallow up Dathan and Abiram and fire from the Lord to consume Korah and the two hundred and fifty "princes of the assembly" who supported him in his rebellion. This is a lesson which is much needed today when some people are making a cult of the worship of humanity, claiming the innate goodness of human nature, attempting to build up a moral code without belief in revelation, and making external benefactions the test of goodness. The second of the two great commandments cannot be obeyed independently of the first; and the Lord's "new commandment"—"as I have loved you, that ye also love one another"—points with equal positiveness to the necessity of looking to the Lord for the understanding of what love to the neighbor involves and for the power to develop and exercise this love.

From the Writings of Swedenborg

Arcana Coelestia, n. 5622[2-3]: " 'Almonds' signify goods of life corresponding to the truths of good of the interior natural . . . This tree itself signifies in the spiritual sense a perception of interior truth which is from good, its 'blossom' interior truth which is from good, and its 'fruit' good of life thence derived. In this sense the 'almond tree' is spoken of in Jeremiah (1:11-12) . . . By the 'almonds which budded from the rod of Aaron for the tribe of Levi,' are also signified goods of charity or goods of life."

Suggested Questions on the Lesson

J. What set of laws did the Lord first give the children of Israel at Sinai? *ten commandments*

J. What other instructions did He give them there? *many tribal laws*

J. Why did the people at one time think that Moses was gone for good? *gone forty days*

J. What did they demand of Aaron? *"make us gods"*

P. What did Aaron make for them? *calf*

P. What did he use to make it? *gold earrings*

P. What did Moses do when he returned with the first tables of the law? *broke them*

J. What did he do with the golden calf? *destroyed it*

P. Whom did the Lord appoint to be high priest of Israel? *Aaron*

J. Why were the people kept wandering in the wilderness for forty years? *lack of faith*

P. Whom did they blame for their troubles? *Moses and Aaron*

J. What happened to the men who rebelled against Moses and Aaron? *destroyed*

P. In this lesson, what did the Lord tell Moses to have the leader of each tribe bring? *rod*

P. How were the twelve rods distinguished from one another? *names put on them*

P. Whose name was written on the rod of the tribe of Levi? *Aaron's*

P. Where did Moses put the rods? *in front of ark*

P. What did they find the next morning? *Aaron's rod bore almonds*

J. What did this show? *Aaron to remain priest*

J. Where did the Lord tell Moses to keep Aaron's rod? *near ark*

I. What does Aaron represent? *love of obeying the Lord*

S. What spiritual quality do almonds represent? *lasting goodness based on perception of spiritual truth*

BALAAM

Numbers 22; 23; 24

For review it is enough for the children now to recall that the Israelites wandered in the wilderness for forty years in all and had many adventures and trials, and that the events of our lesson for today took place close to the end of the forty years and constitute the last of their trials before they entered the Holy Land. In all classes stress the prophecy of the Star and point out that Balaam and the Wise Men came from the same country and possessed knowledge handed down from the Ancient Word.

Doctrinal Points

In the Ancient Church the knowledge of correspondences was turned by the evil into magic.

Even common sense tells us that we ought to obey the Lord's laws.

If we recognize and obey them, the Lord can protect us.

Notes for Parents

The book of Numbers gets its name from the fact that the Lord commanded Moses to number the people before they started on their journey from Mount Sinai, and the first few chapters of the book are concerned with this numbering. It is not until chapter 10 that the pillar of cloud and fire is taken up from the tabernacle, giving them their command to break camp and take up their march. The rest of the book treats of their journeyings. Because of their complainings and rebellion and their lack of trust in the Lord, it was nearly forty years before they finally reached the site of our lesson for today and made their last camp "in the plains of Moab on this side Jordan by Jericho."

They had conquered a number of enemies but had been commanded by the Lord not to disturb the nations of Moab, Ammon, and Edom because these three peoples were their own kin. However, the king of Moab, knowing their success against other nations, was afraid of them.

Everyone knows something of the story of Balaam and his ass, but few have read it carefully enough to realize the deep lessons it is given to teach us. Balaam came from Aram, or Syria, the "land of the east," the same land from which the Wise Men later came with their gifts to worship the infant Jesus. It was a land in which knowledge from the Ancient Word had been preserved, the Word from which the first eleven chapters of our Bible were taken. In our lesson (chapter 24:17) we find Balaam speaking the prophecy of the Star, and you remember that the Wise Men came to seek the Lord because they had "seen his star in the east." The Wise Men cherished the knowledges from the Ancient Word with a desire to serve the Lord, but Balaam used them for selfish purposes. In the same way, some people today use their knowledge of truth from the Bible to advance themselves to positions of honor and influence instead of for its true purpose.

Balaam wanted the rewards which Balak offered him, but he knew that he had no power except from the Lord. Read these chapters carefully, realizing that they picture the Lord's dealings with us when we are bent on seeking our own advantage. The Lord does not force us to do right—He always leaves us free to make our own choice—but He tells us first plainly what we should or should not do; then, if we choose the wrong way, He warns us, He puts obstacles in our way to make us stop and think, and in the end He turns our selfish efforts as far as possible into blessings for those whom we sought to injure.

Perhaps you remember from our lesson on Ishmael and Isaac that the ass represents our natural reason—our common sense. How often mere common sense will show us the folly of our selfish ways, if we will but listen! The ass, of course, did not actually speak, but because of this correspondence of the ass, the voice of the Lord seemed to come to Balaam through the ass's mouth.

Primary

The story of the ass and the angel is the part of the lesson which will most interest this class, but they should be told the highlights of the rest of the story. Even the youngest may remember pictures of the Wise Men and the Star, and they should learn Balaam's prophecy as a preparation for the Christmas lesson. They should be shown the reason why Balaam could not curse Israel when he saw them encamped around the tabernacle, which contained the ark with the ten commandments. They can be told that this means that if we believe in the Lord and keep the commandments, nothing can hurt our souls.

After the Lord had given Moses all the laws for the government of the people and for their worship, the pillar of cloud and fire finally moved on. The people took down their tents and the Levites took down the tabernacle and they all followed the pillar. For forty long years it led them from place to place in the wilderness before it finally brought them near to the Jordan River and the Holy Land.

They had conquered several enemies, but there were three nations which the Lord told them not to fight because they were their own relatives. These nations were Moab, Ammon, and Edom. But you know there are people who are never willing to trust anyone. The king of Moab was such a person. His name was Balak. When he saw the great encampment of the children of Israel so near the border of his land, he was frightened and sent for a famous wizard named Balaam and offered him great rewards if he would come and curse Israel for him.

Balaam lived in Aram, or Syria, the country between the Tigris and Euphrates rivers.
He was a diviner—that is, a man who has magic powers.
What did Balak, king of Moab, ask Balaam to do?
What did the Lord tell Balaam?
Balaam knew that he would have no power unless the Lord gave it to him.
Why was Balaam so anxious to do what Balak wanted?
Who stopped Balaam on the way?
How many times was he stopped?
This was to show Balaam that he must speak only what the Lord told him to speak.

Where did Balak take Balaam to see the camp of Israel?

What did Balaam have Balak do there?

How many times did Balaam try to curse Israel?

What happened each time?

Balaam could not do what Balak wanted, but we learn in the book of Revelation that he did give Balak advice which helped him to injure some of the Israelites.

Balaam was finally killed while fighting with the Midianites against Israel.

The Wise Men who followed the star to Bethlehem so long afterward came from and knew the same prophecy.

Junior

Balaam's background and connection with the Ancient Word and with the Wise Men will interest the Juniors, and also Balaam's character. Have them look up the Bible references to learn of the harm that Balaam actually did, and of his death. The meaning of the encampment of Israel is a good lesson to develop and illustrate.

In our lesson for today the children of Israel have nearly reached the end of their journey. The pillar of cloud and fire has been leading them about in the wilderness for almost forty years. In Numbers 33 you will find a list of all the places where they had camped during this journey. Now they are in their last encampment in the valley on the east side of the Jordan River not far from the head of the Dead Sea and just across the river from Jericho. They are in a country which had belonged to Moab, but which the Amorites had taken from Moab. The Israelites had overcome the Amorites, but they had been commanded not to fight with the nations of Moab, Ammon, and Edom because they were their relatives. You remember that Edom is another name for Esau. Moab and Ammon were the two sons of Abraham's nephew Lot. In spite of Israel's peaceful intentions, the people of Moab were afraid of the Israelites.

What did the king of Moab decide to do?

Balaam lived in Aram or Syria, a country also called Mesopotamia, which means "between the rivers"—the rivers being the Tigris and the Euphrates. In that country the people had had the Ancient Word and had understood the knowledge of correspondences, according to which it was written. The remains of this knowledge made it possible for them to receive enlightenment from the Lord, but it also made it possible for some of them to use this enlightenment for selfish purposes.

Balaam, as we learn from other statements in the Bible, was an evil man. When Balak, the king of Moab, asked him to come and curse Israel, he wanted very much to obey because of the great reward offered. But he knew that the power by which he worked magic came from the Lord and that he could not exercise it if the Lord was against him. All the incidents of his journey were meant to keep him reminded of this.

How many times did Balak send messengers to Balaam?
What stopped Balaam on the way?
How often was he stopped before he saw the angel?

The story says that Balaam's ass saw the angel when Balaam did not. The ass, which pictures our natural intelligence, is a very sure-footed animal—just as our natural intelligence enables us to make our way safely in the world. Balaam was blind to the angel because he was so bent on having his own way, even though he possessed enough natural intelligence to know that it was not the way the Lord wanted him to take. The Lord put obstacles in his way three times to make him stop and think, but he did not want to listen to reason. When we are bent on doing something which even our common sense shows us is wrong, don't we often try to force our reasoning into the way we want to go, just as Balaam tried to drive his ass? Finally the Lord spoke to Balaam through the mouth of the ass—the ass of course did not really speak—and showed him how foolish he was, and then he saw the angel in the way.

The Lord does not make us do what He wants us to do. If He did, we should be like slaves and could have no happiness. But He tries always to show us what we ought to do, and He continually puts obstacles in the way of our evil courses to make us stop and think. When this happens, we should not try to "ride over" the obstacles, but should ask ourselves if what we are trying to do is really right. The Lord also gives us parents and friends who, like the angel, help us to see the difference between right and wrong. And then if we persist in doing wrong, the Lord turns the things we do into blessings for others, although we ourselves must suffer.

From the heights overlooking the valley Balaam and Balak could see the whole encampment of the Israelites.

What did Balaam tell Balak to do?

You see, Balaam knew the correspondence of numbers and animals and sacrifices. So his arrangements established a connection with the spiritual world through which he could receive power from the Lord.

How many times did Balaam try to do what Balak wanted?
What happened each time?

The thing which saved Israel was the order of its encampment, with the tabernacle at its center. It pictured the true order of heaven or of a heavenly character, with worship of the Lord at the center and all the other affections and thoughts taking their proper places with respect to that. If we live in this order, no evil can harm our souls.

Let us see if we can understand this. Take such a simple evil as the temptation to overeat. Our bodies are given to us to use in the service of the Lord and the neighbor. They need to be properly cared for and fed in order to be useful, and so one of our proper affections is the affection for good food. But this affection should not have a very large place in our whole life. So long as we keep in mind the true purpose of eating, our love of good food stays in its proper place and we cannot be tampted to overeat. So it is with all our other affections.

Balaam did not succeed in cursing Israel, but we learn elsewhere (Revelation 2:14) that he did give Balak some advice which enabled him to lead some of the Israelites into idolatry and other evils. For this reason, Balaam was afterward killed in a battle which Israel fought with the Midianites (Numbers 31:8).

Notice the prophecy in verse 17 of chapter 24. This reminds us, of course, of the star of Bethlehem. The Wise Men who followed the star so long afterward came from the same eastern country from which Balaam came. So they also had remains of knowledge from the Ancient Word, and knew the prophecy of the star and what it meant. They used their knowledge to find the Lord and worship him.

Intermediate

The correspondence of the ass should be stressed with this class. Call attention to the similarity of the meaning of Ishmael and the ass, and tell them that Ishmael was called a "wild-ass man." In Genesis 16:12 the word which the King James version translates "wild man" really means "wild ass." Balaam's ass was not a wild ass. It saw the angel. A wild ass would not.

The story of Balaam's efforts to curse Israel and of his words being turned into blessings is a wonderful picture of the inability of evil to harm those whose lives are centered in service to the Lord. It is the same lesson which in the New Testament is taught by the parable of the house on the rock and the house on the sand.

The plan of encampment of Israel was prescribed by the Lord at Sinai and pictures the true order of life, with worship of the Lord at its heart and all other pursuits and enjoyments taking their proper place with reference to that central aim. A life so ordered cannot be shaken by trial or temptation. Attacks made upon it turn to blessings because they are accepted as opportunities to exercise the virtues of forgiveness and charity, and thus strengthen instead of weaken the character.

Balaam tried to make use of his knowledge of correspondence to do evil. He knew that the number seven was a holy number and he knew the proper sacrifices to make in order to establish connection with the spiritual world. But when this connection was established, the evil spirits could not stand against the power expressed in the order of Israel's encampment.

Balaam pictures those who seek to use sacred things, the Bible and the church, for selfish purposes. The evil efforts of Balaam, instead of injuring Israel, returned upon his own head. So we read in Numbers 31:8 that he was later killed when Israel overcame the Midianites. He did, however, show Balak how to lead some of the Israelites astray, as we learn in Revelation 2:14. We are weakened when we allow any of our desires to stray from their true relation to the Lord's service.

We learned in an early lesson in this course that animals represent affections. The horse and the ass represent affections for reasoning. Swedenborg says that the horse represents the power to reason from inner and higher principles and the ass, the power to reason from external knowledges. Or, the ass represents the natural reason which we sometimes call "common sense." This is a useful power in its proper place, although we must not think it is our only guide. If we do, it becomes a "wild ass." Ishmael, who mocked at the baby Isaac, was called a "wild ass."

In the story of Balaam the ass was a trained beast who had served his master faithfully. He saw the angel in the way when Balaam did not, and it was through the mouth of the ass that the Lord finally induced Balaam to stop and think. Often when we are bent on doing something we know is wrong, our very common sense tells us that we are making a mistake. The Lord never forces us to do right, but He warns us and tries in every possible way to show us the folly of wrongdoing.

Balaam's prophecy in 24:17 reminds us, of course, of the star of Bethlehem, and of the fact that the Wise Men who saw the star and knew its meaning came from the same country which produced Balaam. This was the land called Aram or Syria, and also Mesopotamia—which means "between the rivers"—because it was watered by the two famous rivers, the Tigris and the Euphrates. The people of this country were remnants of the Ancient Church who derived their religion by tradition from the Ancient Word. The prophecy of the star was undoubtedly a part of that Word. The chief delight of the people of the Ancient Church was the study of correspondences. It is evident from Balaam's directions to Balak for his offerings that even hundreds of years after the breakup of the Ancient Church (described in the story of the

Tower of Babel) some of this knowledge of correspondences still remained in Mesopotamia. We may also assume that it lasted even to the Lord's time, since the Wise Men brought correspondential gifts to Him. Swedenborg tells us that the hieroglyphics of Egypt were a survival of this same knowledge, and that the magicians of Egypt, like Balaam, found their power in it. The Wise Men are examples of those remnants of the Ancient Church who cherished the knowledges which remained from a love of the truth and a desire to learn of the Lord. Balaam represents those who used the same knowledge for selfish ends.

Basic Correspondences

seven = holy things
the ass = the natural reason

Senior

(1) The origin and character of Balaam, (2) the working of divine providence in warning him, and (3) the meaning and power of the orderly encampment of Israel are all important for the Seniors. They are just at the age when they most need this last lesson especially. Also, if they can be impressed with the important teaching of this familiar story in its internal sense, it will guard them against the temptation to fall in with any casual or profane talk about the Word.

Swedenborg says of Balaam: "Balaam was a hypocrite and a wizard, for he spoke well concerning the sons of Israel from Jehovah, and yet in his heart he burned to destroy them, and also did destroy them through the advice he gave to Balak, from which it is evident that his works were hypocritical" (*Apocalypse Revealed*, n. 114). It is in Revelation 2:14 that we learn that Balaam did succeed in giving some help to Balak, for it is said "he taught Balak to cast a stumbling block before the children of Israel, to eat things sacrificed unto idols, and to commit fornication."

The first part of the story of Balaam, which is the part usually studied, teaches in the letter how the Lord impressed upon Balaam the fact that in his character of diviner he must speak only what the Lord gave him to say. In the spiritual sense this teaches us how the Lord makes use of even our natural reason, our common sense, pictured by the ass, to force us to stop and think when we are bent on a selfish course.

Two general lessons may be drawn from the story of Balaam. One is that if we order our lives according to the Word, our souls cannot be injured by the evil efforts of others. We recall that the encampment of Israel, with the tabernacle in the center and the tribes each in its allotted place around it, pictures the order of heaven and of a heavenly character in the individual, with service of the Lord as its inmost motive and all the affections and abilities kept in their proper relation to that service. When our lives are so motivated and so ordered, temptations are easily recognized and resisted. Take for example the temptation—to which we are all sometimes subject—to feel that others have a better chance in the world than we have. If we really have at heart the service of the Lord, we see at once that we have ample opportunity for this service whatever the conditions of our outward life may be. "He that is faithful in that which is least is faithful also in much."

The second general lesson is that it is quite possible to manifest great power and zeal in spiritual matters and still be a hypocrite, and that we need to guard against undoing by our example good which we may try to do by our words. A common instance of this is the man who goes to church regularly and gives to it generously, and at the same time in his business underpays his employees, "outsmarts" his competitors, and evades taxes. Here we should remember that we may be doing the same thing in our small affairs, and that the verse quoted above (Luke 16:10) continues "and he that is unjust in the least is unjust also in much." Balaam, when he spoke from the Lord, could speak only the Lord's words; but when he spoke from himself, the evils which were in his heart appeared.

The same lesson is drawn from the fact that, while the Israelites could not be harmed by Balaam when they were encamped, they could individually be led astray by the temptations which he taught

Balak to put in their way. For the encampment of the Israelites was representative, and did not reflect their actual state as individuals. Swedenborg says: "The reason Balaam was able to lead astray the people by guile, was because that people were at heart of such a character" (*Apocalypse Explained*, n. 140[5]).

It is significant that Balaam was killed by Israel (Numbers 31:8) in a battle they fought by the Lord's command against the Midianites. For the Midianites in a good sense—as when Jethro protected and advised Moses—represent "those who are in the truths of simple good"; but in a bad sense, when they are enemies of Israel, they represent "those who are in the knowledges of truth; but still not in life according to them."

Adult

Note that the events of our lesson took place when the Israelites were in their final encampment near the Jordan. Then perhaps begin with the point made in the final paragraph of the Adult notes. The most important discussion topics are the way in which divine providence warns us, and hinders but does not force us to discontinue a wrong course, and the safety which comes with the proper ordering of our lives around worship of the Lord and in accordance with the commandments of His Word.

The story of Balaam contains a great many things of interest. In popular thought the incident of the ass has come to seem the principal part of the story, but it is merely preparatory to the real lesson.

First we should note that Israel has completed the wilderness journey and is encamped "in the plains of Moab on this side Jordan by Jericho." Balak, king of Moab, is afraid of the consequences of their coming, but he knows that the Lord is with them and that he cannot hope to conquer them by force. So he turns to sorcery and sends far away to the east for the famous wizard Balaam to come and curse Israel for him. Moab in a good sense represents natural good, a kinsman of Israel, whom Israel was commanded not to injure. But this Moab, when it sets itself up against the higher things of the spirit, represents the adulteration of good. Many today exalt natural goodness, saying that it is not necessary to worship the Lord or even to acknowledge Him if only one lives a life of neighborly kindness, enters into reform movements, gives to charitable causes, etc. This thought is expressed frequently by the misleading half-truth: "There are better people outside the church than many in it." This points to another and more subtle form of the same general thought–religious hypocrisy. Of such people Swedenborg says: "They are, in general, those who are in external worship, which appears in some respects holy; but not in internal worship; and who seize upon as goods and truths the things which are of external worship, but reject and despise the things of internal worship" (AC 2468). Later in the same number he says: "They who are in such good, care for external things only, and despise, reject, and indeed spew out the internal things of worship and doctrine." It is fitting that Balak should send for Balaam, for Balaam is the symbol of hypocrisy.

It is not easy to see this hypocrisy at first in the story, for one is impressed with Balaam's frequent declaration that he can speak only what the Lord gives him to speak. But it appears clearly later in his persistent attempt to satisfy Balak and win the rewards offered, and it is also stated in Revelation 2:14 where Balaam is named as the one who taught Balak how to lead the children of Israel astray. In interpreting this verse (AR 114, AE 140), Swedenborg tells interesting things of Balaam. He came from Aram, or Syria, also called Mesopotamia, where there existed remains of knowledge from the Ancient Word, which included a considerable knowledge of correspondences. Among the good, this knowledge was cherished; it culminated in the visit of the Wise Men to Bethlehem to find the newborn King. Among the evil, it was turned to sorcery and magic, as with Balaam. Even the evil, however, recognized that they could accomplish nothing by their own power, but only by the Lord's power working through the correspondences which they knew. It was this knowledge or correspondence which taught Balaam to instruct Balak to build seven altars and to sacrifice a bullock and a ram on each. And it was this knowledge in Balaam's mind through which the Lord could speak to him even to the point of enabling him to prophesy. We should note especially the wonderful prophecy in Numbers 24:17, referring to the Lord's Advent. The Star stands for the Lord as truth and the Sceptre the Lord as King; the smiting of the corners of Moab and the destruction of the children of Sheth show the Lord's complete conquest of evil and falsity in the natural man.

In general, the attempt of Balak with Balaam's help to undermine and overthrow Israel after they had reached the very border of the Promised Land pictures the last stand of the rebellious natural man against the spiritual. Even when we have fulfilled the requirements of the period of external reformation, have set our lives in order from the principle of obedience to the Lord, and are all ready to take the final step which will establish the spiritual principle within us and make us "at home" in heavenly living, friends instead of mere servants of the Lord . . . even then all that is earthly and natural in our minds rises up and conspires to undermine our resolution, even attempting to draw arguments from the Word itself to confirm the superiority of external over internal living. Witness the cry for "practical" Christianity. The loaves and fishes were not the real blessings which the Lord sought to give to men.

The story of Balaam and the ass is a wonderful picture of the Lord's providence over us when we are intent on doing evil. There is first the voice of conscience telling us that what we purpose to do is not the Lord's will: "And God came unto Balaam, and said." There is the second warning: "And God came unto Balaam at night and said unto him." But if we still wish to do wrong, the Lord permits us to go our way. He follows us, however, and puts obstacles in our path which appeal to our lower minds, since we have closed our higher selves to His counsel. The ass represents the natural reason. From merely natural considerations it becomes increasingly evident to us that what we are planning to do will get us into difficulties; we even experience some of these difficulties, as Balaam's foot was crushed against the wall. Three times the angel appeared to the ass and checked Balaam's journey. The Lord leaves nothing undone which will show us the folly of pursuing our own way. The ass of course did not speak, but the Lord spoke to Balaam through the mouth of the ass as a symbol of the appeal of His truth to our natural reason. When Balaam finally listened to this voice, his spiritual eyes could be opened to see the angel in the way.

In spite of all warnings Balaam went his way and made his three attempts to curse Israel. But when he looked upon the encampment of Israel—in one case even upon a small portion of the camp—the curse which he intended was turned into a blessing. This was because the encampment of Israel—with the tabernacle in the center and each tribe in its assigned place with reference to it—was according to the order prescribed by the Lord. It represents a life organized according to heavenly order, with worship of the Lord at the center and all our affections and thoughts kept in their proper relation to this center. Balaam could not curse a people so encamped. If our lives are organized according to this divine pattern, no outside cause can prevent our entering the Holy Land of spiritual living in this world or the next. We may be severely tempted and may yield here and there (Revelation 2:14), but we shall be given light to see the evil and to stamp it out, as the Israelites finally destroyed Balaam (Numbers 31:8). A good man whose inmost desire is to know and serve the Lord may be deceived from time to time by false prophets and may fall here and there into external evils, but the Lord's power is with him and will eventually give him light to see and strength to overcome.

We need to be deeply impressed with the power and beauty of this story of Balaam in its internal sense, because it is one of the stories often held up to ridicule by those who choose to think of the Bible as a man-made book. If we can realize what a tragedy it is to stop in the letter of the story and thus make it a means of discrediting the Word and cutting oneself and others off from the possibility of being reached through it by the Lord, we may be emboldened to speak out against such profanation and so help others to a truer appreciation of what the Lord has for them in the Word.

From the Writings of Swedenborg

Arcana Coelestia, n. 3762: "*And went to the land of the sons of the east.* That this signifies to the truths of love (that is, elevation thereto) is evident from the signification of the 'land of the sons of the east.' That Aram, or Syria, was called the 'land of the sons of the east,' is evident, because it was thither that Jacob betook himself. That by 'Syria' in general are signified the knowledges of good, was shown above; but specifically, by 'Aram-Naharaim' (that is, 'Syria of the rivers') are signified the knowledges of truth . . . These truths, that relate to charity toward the neighbor and to love to the Lord, must be learned before it is possible for a man to be regenerated; and must also be acknowledged and believed; and insofar as they are acknowledged, believed, and ingrafted in the life, so far the man is regenerated, and insofar they are at the same time implanted in the man's natural, in which they are as in their own ground . . . That the wise men from the east who came to Jesus at His birth were of those who were called 'the sons of the east,' is evident from the fact that they were in the knowledge that the Lord was to be born, and that they knew of His advent by a star which appeared to them in the east . . . That from ancient times such a prophetic knowledge had existed among the sons of the east, who were of Syria, is evident from Balaam's prophecy concerning the Lord's advent . . . (Numbers 24:17). That Balaam was from the land of the sons of the east, that is, from Syria, is evident from these words: 'Balaam uttered his enunciation and said, Balak hath brought me from Syria, out of the mountains of the east' (Numbers 23:7)."

Suggested Questions on the Lesson

P. Do you remember what led the children of Israel through the wilderness? *pillar of cloud/fire*

J. How long did it keep them wandering there? *forty years*

J. What was their last encampment in the wilderness? *plains of Moab*

P. What king was afraid of them? *Balak (king of Moab)*

P. To whom did he send for help? *Balaam*

P. What did he want Balaam to do? *curse Israel*

P. Where did Balaam get his power? *from God*

J. What did the Lord first tell Balaam? *not to go*

J. What did He tell him when Balak sent for him the second time? *speak only My word*

P. What happened to Balaam on the way? *angel frightened his ass*
J. What preparations did Balaam have Balak make? *seven altars, oxen, rams*
I. How did Balaam know what should be done? *knowledge of correspondences*
J. How many times did Balaam try to curse Israel? *three*
J. What happened each time? *became a blessing*
I. Why could he not curse Israel? *no real power in evil intentions*
P. What special prophecy did Balaam speak? *Star*
J. How was he able to injure Israel? *taught Balak how to tempt people*
J. What finally happened to Balaam? *killed in battle between Israel and Midian*
I. What does the ass represent? *natural or "common-sense" reasoning*
S. What does the encampment of Israel picture? *truly orderly life, with worship of the Lord at the center*

THE CALL OF JOSHUA

Joshua 1

The transition to this lesson can be made by reminding the children of a recent lesson where Joshua played a major part. This is a discussion lesson rather than a story. It can well be introduced by a brief review of the whole Bible story so far. An outline for such a review will be found with this lesson. This review is especially important for the Juniors and Intermediates.

Doctrinal Points

The Lord wants us to enjoy the things of this world, but not to put them first. He created the world for our happiness.

The difference between reformation and regeneration.

The best courage is the courage to say no in temptation.

Notes for Parents

The lesson the children have for today is an inspiring chapter. The children of Israel are encamped beside the Jordan River, not far from the northern end of the Dead Sea, about opposite the city of Jericho. They are looking across the river at the land of their fathers, the land toward which they have been traveling for forty years, the land which has been promised them by the Lord. Moses has died, but Joshua, who has led them in all their battles, has been appointed to take his place. They know Joshua and trust him. All the people who refused to take Joshua's advice thirty-eight years before have died in the wilderness.

The charge to Joshua, "Be strong and of good courage," is one which we all should learn, for we all need it again and again in our lives. The right way is not always the easy way, and it takes courage to do right. This is a lesson which parents should help the church to impress upon children, for they will often be tempted by others to do wrong and be called "sissies" if they refuse. If they can be brought to feel that it takes more courage to face ridicule than to do something wrong, it will be a help to them and to you. Children like to feel that they are brave. Bravery in a good cause is true bravery, and a virtue.

There is another part of the charge to Joshua which we must not forget. He was to obey the law of Moses and to "meditate therein day and night." This was the condition on which the Lord could help him and give him success. The Lord wants to help all of us to succeed, but because He loves us, He cannot help us when what we want to do is contrary to His laws. For His laws are the only laws which lead to happiness, and He wants us to be happy. This is also something the children especially need to understand. The Lord sees farther than we do. He sees the final result of anything we undertake to do, and many times He sees that the thing we think will make us happy will have just the opposite result in the end. Because we are naturally selfish, the Lord's laws seem hard to us, but obedience to them is actually much easier than suffering the consequences of breaking them will be. When the Lord was in the world He said, "Take my yoke upon you, and learn of me . . . For my yoke is easy, and my burden is light." (Matthew 11:29-30)

Primary

Build your story around Joshua, and talk about the necessity for being brave enough to do right. Even little children need this lesson. Something of the review should be given, especially with reference to the decision of the people when the spies returned, and its consequences. The children can see the connection between this and the charge to Joshua and can be shown how it applies to their own lives.

Do you remember the name of the man who led the children of Israel out of Egypt and in all their long journey through the wilderness? It was *Moses*. Now they have come to the time when they are to be allowed to enter the Holy Land. They are encamped on the banks of the Jordan River, looking across at the beautiful land that has been promised to them for their home.

What had the children of Israel done at Kadesh?
What report had the spies brought back?
What had the people decided to do?
What was their punishment?
Which two spies had given different advice?
What was their reward?

Now Moses is not to lead them across the river, for Moses is dead. Their new leader is *Joshua*. He was one of the two spies who trusted the Lord and told the people they could take the Holy Land if they tried because the Lord would help them.

Joshua had been the leader of their army in all the battles they had fought in the wilderness; so the people trusted him.
What words from the Lord are repeated three times in our chapter?
We have to be brave and strong to do right.
It is really cowardly to do wrong when we know better.
But there was one thing the Lord told Joshua he must remember.
What was it?

This is something we must all remember to do all our lives, too.

Junior

Begin with a suggestion of the difference between living in one's own proper country and living in a "strange" or foreign land. Point out that heaven is the true home of everyone, and that the Holy Land pictures heaven, which begins in us with a heavenly character. Then take up the review to give the children the background necessary for recognizing the importance of crossing the Jordan and understanding the meaning of the charge to Joshua. A challenge to courage is very helpful at this age.

The children of Israel had come to Kadesh sometime during the second year of their journey in the wilderness.

What did they do at Kadesh?
What good things did the spies find in the Holy Land?
What did they find that discouraged them?
What did ten of the spies advise?
Who were the two who gave different advice?
Which advice did the people take?
What was their punishment?

The children of Israel had to wander in the wilderness for another thirty-eight years before all the people had died who were responsible for their cowardly choice. Even Moses had at one time been disobedient to the Lord; so he could not enter the Holy Land either. You will find this story in Numbers 20:1-13. The forty years in the wilderness are a long history of unwilling obedience to the law of the Lord. And unwilling obedience has no place in heaven. This is because unwilling obedience is always mostly selfish—we obey because we want some reward or are afraid of some punishment—and we are never in heavenly states when we are selfish.

Everyone recognizes that the Holy Land (the "Promised Land") pictures heaven. But the Lord told His followers that the kingdom of heaven was within them. That is, heaven must be within our hearts before we can live in heaven. The heavenly life is a happy life because everyone in heaven loves to do what the Lord wants him to do. We know we are not born loving to do right. First our parents have to make us do it. Then we begin to make ourselves do right because we see that we get along better that way. This is like the children of Israel going about in the wilderness obeying Moses because they were sure to get into trouble if they didn't. But this is not a heavenly state of life.

However, if we keep on doing right until it becomes a habit, the Lord can put into our hearts the love of doing right. Then we are ready to enter the Holy Land—not necessarily to leave this world for heaven, but to have heaven in our hearts and minds.

After Moses died, the new leader appointed by the Lord was Joshua. He had been the leader of Israel's fighting men from the beginning of the wilderness journey and had led them to victory several times. And of course he was one of the two spies who had urged them to go bravely ahead into the Holy Land years before. The people obeyed him because they knew and trusted his leadership. We have seen that all the stories in the Bible are given us by the Lord to teach us things we need to know about our own lives. All the leaders appointed by the Lord picture the leadership of the

Word of God as it comes to us in different stages of our development. So Moses pictures the Law as it appears to us when we are obeying it because we know we have to. But Joshua pictures the same Law when we accept it freely and willingly, and use it to help us conquer our inner enemies, our selfishness and laziness and general hatefulness—all the bad things that keep cropping up in our hearts and minds all our lives. These are the enemies which the children of Israel were to find waiting for them in the Holy Land itself.

It takes courage for us to recognize and fight these enemies. That is why three times in our chapter Joshua is told to be strong and of a good courage. But we must also always keep in mind that we still do not know enough by ourselves to do right: we must always go on learning more and more from the Word of God and thinking about it and about what it teaches. The Lord says to Joshua, "This book of the law shall not depart out of thy mouth; but thou shalt meditate therein day and night, that thou mayest observe to do according to all that is written therein: for then thou shalt make thy way prosperous, and then thou shalt have good success." And He says, "Observe to do according to all the law which Moses my servant commanded thee: turn not from it to the right hand or to the left." Sometimes we get to thinking that we are pretty good and so don't need to worry anymore about doing wrong; we say that our conscience will tell us what is right. But our conscience tells us only what we have already learned about right—if we have not always had the wisest teachers, our conscience may even tell us wrong things. You remember Abraham's conscience told him to sacrifice Isaac, and he was saved from doing so great a wrong only by the Lord's voice speaking to him. The Lord speaks to us in His Word, and we need to read it every day all our lives and listen for the Lord's voice in it.

There is one other incident in our chapter which we need to understand. Read Numbers 32:1-6, 16-22. As the Holy Land pictures heaven, the country just outside of it on the east side of the Jordan pictures earthly life and the kind of pleasure we get out of

REVIEW OUTLINE OF THE PENTATEUCH

BOOK	CHAPTER	SUBJECT	OUTLINE OF THE STORY	GEOGRAPHICAL LOCATIONS
Genesis	1; 2:1-17 2:18-25; 3 4 5	The Creation Adam and Eve Cain and Abel Genealogy	Genesis 1-5 describes the Most Ancient Church, or "Golden Age" of the human race, and its decline.	Archaeological as well as Biblical research indicates that the earliest people lived in the Bible lands. Swedenborg says they were led by the Lord to give symbolic names to their rivers, mountains, etc., in preparation for the writing of the Word. Genesis 1-11 is allegorical, however, and we cannot necessarily identify the places mentioned with actual historical sites.
	6-10 11	Noah and the Flood The Tower of Babel	The rise and fall of the Ancient Church, or "Silver Age." *Eber* (Heber) in Genesis 11:14-17 is the first person in the Bible who was a real person. The Hebrews took their name from him.	
	12-25	Abraham	Abraham's journey Abraham and Lot	Ur of Chaldea, Haran, Shechem, Bethel, Egypt, Bethel and Hai (Ai)
			Abraham and Abimelech	Gerar
	17; 21-27	Isaac	Birth of Isaac	Beersheba
			Sacrifice of Isaac	Mount Moriah, Beersheba
			Isaac and Rebekah	Haran, Beer-lahairoi
	25-36	Jacob	Jacob and Esau	Bethel, Haran, Hebron
	30; 37-50	Joseph	Joseph and his brothers Joseph in Egypt	Hebron, Shechem, Dothan, Egypt (Land of Goshen)
Exodus	1-4	Moses: first 80 years	Birth of Moses	Land of Goshen (Rameses area)
			Moses flees from Egypt	Land of Midian (Sinai Peninsula)
			The Burning Bush	Horeb range, near Mount Sinai
	5-40	The Exodus	Plagues, Passover, crossing the Red Sea	Rameses (Egypt) southward to the Red Sea
			The first two months: water and food	Marah, Elim, wilderness of Sin, Rephidim, Sinai
			Mount Sinai (for about one year): ten commandments, ark, tabernacle, priesthood, laws	Mount Sinai
Leviticus Numbers Deuteronomy	All	The Wilderness Wanderings	Many detailed laws. The spies: 38 more years of wandering. Rebellions, fiery serpents, Balaam, death of Moses.	Kadesh, Mt. Hor and its environs, lands of Edom and Moab, Bashan, Mount Nebo, encampment on Jordan River (across from Jericho)

this world. The Lord wants us to enjoy the good things of this world—food, clothing, beautiful possessions, music, art, entertainment, success—but there is one condition: we must first be sure the selfish things in our hearts and minds are seen and overcome. There is a right way and a wrong way to use the possessions of this world and to enjoy its pleasures. So long as we are selfish and greedy, the good things that are given to us do us more harm than good. You remember the dangers into which Lot fell when he chose to live in the fertile and attractive valley. The two and a half tribes spoken of in Numbers 32 and mentioned again in this lesson agreed not to make this mistake; they agreed to fight alongside their brethren until the enemies were conquered, before going back and settling in the land of their choice.

Intermediate

The meaning of the change from the period of reformation to that of regeneration is important here. The Intermediates have not reached this change, but they should look forward to it. For all young people we may hope that the decision to lead heavenly lives will be made early, and orderly progress will then follow.

We have learned that the Israelites were condemned to wander in the wilderness for thirty-eight years because they allowed the ten spies to frighten them out of the attempt to conquer the Holy Land which the Lord had promised them. Of all the men twenty years old and upward (that is, all the men old enough to have voted at the time) only Joshua and Caleb, the two spies who told them to trust in the Lord and go forward, would live beyond this period and cross the Jordan. Even Moses was not allowed to enter the Holy Land. He had been told by the Lord on one occasion when he used his power to glorify himself in the eyes of the people (Numbers 20:1-13) that he would be allowed to see the Promised Land but not to enter it. The last chapter of the book of Deuteronomy tells how, at the end of the wanderings, Moses went up on top of Mount Nebo, was shown by the Lord all the land into which the people were to enter, and died.

During the thirty-eight years, the children of Israel had many experiences of the Lord's protection and mercy. For they were constantly becoming discouraged and discontented and had to be taught how much safer and happier they were when they obeyed the Lord. Can you see that we have to be taught in just the same way? We know that we get along better when we are good, but our own way always looks so much easier and pleasanter at the moment that, like the people in the Bible, we keep putting off the real effort to change. So we get into one trouble after another until gradually, one by one, our weak and selfish feelings are killed off and we are ready to face ourselves as we really are. This is the time when we are finally prepared to enter the Holy Land. For no one can live in the Holy Land of heavenly character who is not willing to see and acknowledge his own faults and fight against them with the Lord's help. As long as we are doing right just for the sake of getting along better in the world or from a general "sense of duty," we stay in the wilderness.

When Moses died, Joshua was appointed by the Lord to take his place. In fact, Moses had told the people that Joshua was to succeed him. Joshua had been the leader of the fighting men of Israel from the very first battle in the wilderness. The people knew and trusted him. Swedenborg tells us that he represents "the truth fighting." When we really begin to use the truth we know to fight against the bad things in ourselves and in the world, we are going forward under Joshua. For example, suppose you have a tendency to blame other people for everything that happens to you. This is a common fault, because it seems the easiest way of getting out of taking the blame ourselves. Your parents see this fault in you and try to break you of the bad habit, and you gradually learn to control it outwardly so that you will get along better at home; but you still have the same feelings inside, and every once in a while they get too strong for you and you have to be corrected again. This is like the enemies rising up against Israel in the wilderness. When you get a little older, the Lord shows you that this is really a fault in yourself which you must recognize and fight, that you yourself are responsible for your troubles and not someone else; you begin to fight it because you see that He is telling you the truth; and then you go ahead and overcome it. This is the time when you are entering the Holy Land under Joshua.

The Lord's charge to Joshua was a twofold one: He told him to be "strong and of a good courage," and He told him to "observe to do according to all the law" of Moses—to "turn not from it to the right hand or to the left," and to "meditate therein day and night." We need to read the Word every day and to study it and think about it so that our knowledge of what is really right in the Lord's sight will always lead us forward. And we need to try to live up to every bit of truth we learn from the Word. If we are doing this, we may be sure that the Lord is with us and will help us. He will never help us to get our own way when our own way is selfish, because He loves us and wants us to be happy, and selfishness always leads to unhappiness. And we need to remember that it takes courage to do what is right in the face of temptation. If we can say "no" when someone tries to get us to do what we know is wrong, we are showing ourselves to be "strong and of a good courage." The people in any community who are trusted and respected are those who have developed this kind of courage.

There is something else in our chapter which we will not understand unless we go back and read Numbers 32:1-6, 16-22. You remember from the lesson on Abram and Lot that the low valley of the Jordan was very fertile and a fine grazing country, and that it pictures the *natural* plane of our lives—the work and pleasure we have in making a living in this world and enjoying its good things. Lot, you remember, got into trouble because he separated from Abram and was drawn into the wicked city of Sodom which was in the plain. But the tribes which settled in the valley east of the Jordan River in our chapter today did not make this mistake. They had agreed that their fighting men would go on into the Holy Land with the others and not come back to settle down until they had helped overcome the enemies in the land. The fact that they left their wives and children and flocks and herds there means that they continued to love and think about the fertile valley, but they put doing right ahead of the enjoyment of the kind of life they had chosen. The Lord wants us to enjoy our life here in this world and to have its good things—food, entertainment, success—but He knows that there is only one way in which we can enjoy these things without their hurting us, and that is by obeying the divine laws and overcoming the selfishness which is natural to us. The Holy Land must be conquered before we can safely enjoy worldly things. Think, for example, of the possession of money. Naturally we all imagine we should like to have plenty of it. We think people who have money ought to be happy. But you know, if you stop to think, that some wealthy people are happy and others are not. Some make their money without hurting other people and use it to make other people as well as themselves happy. Others make their money at the expense of other people and use it selfishly. They may be lonely misers or they may live an apparently gay social life with others like themselves, but they are not happy because they always want more than they can have and wear themselves out trying to get it. All through the Word the Lord shows us the proper relation of worldly things to spiritual things. Of the worldly things He says (Matthew 6:32-33): "Your heavenly Father knoweth that ye have need of all these things. But seek ye first the kingdom of God and his righteousness; and all these things shall be added unto you."

Basic Correspondences

Joshua = truth fighting
valley = the natural plane of our lives

Senior

The twofold charge to Joshua is the important lesson for this age group. Stress the necessity of reading and studying the Word and accepting its teaching instead of trying to lead ourselves.

Since the death of Moses marks the end of a particular point in our life's journey, it may be well to review briefly at this point.

In one sense we pass through the whole cycle of the Bible story again and again, and there is no part of the Word which does not have its application to something in our experience at almost any point in our life. However, the narrative in its general outline covers our life from conception to the finding of our final home in heaven or hell. In this larger view the stories of Creation, the Garden of Eden, the Flood and the Tower of Babel give us an understanding of what is in us by heredity from our whole ancestry in the human race; and the stories of Abraham, Isaac, and Jacob tell us about our progress—after we are born into this world—from infancy to early youth, to later youth. During this period we descend spiritually as we develop naturally. That is, in infancy (the Abraham state) we are close to the Lord in a celestial state of innocence and trust, but entirely ignorant and helpless from the point of view of our ability to take care of ourselves in the world. In the state of early childhood we learn a measure of control over our bodies and physical wants. Then comes the period covered by the stories of Ishmael and Isaac, when our reasoning powers are developed: first the natural reason (Ishmael) and a little later the higher or spiritual reason (Isaac). Then we are ready to begin to try our wings independently of our parents, and the life of Jacob pictures the period when we first try to regulate our own external conduct, making a good many mistakes, but learning all the time and developing our various faculties as Jacob produced his twelve sons. We can see that this is an advance so far as our life in this world is concerned, but a descent from a celestial to a natural state as to our inner life. When we reach maturity—or nearly reach it—we come to the period of the Egyptian bondage, when we are so occupied with finding our place in the worldly scheme of things that we are apt to forget our spiritual responsibilities altogether for a time. In our recent lessons we have seen that most people sooner or later realize this bondage and try to break away from it. Then our spiritual progress upward begins. Its first essential is the recognition that the law of God must be our leader and guide—Moses and the pillar of cloud and fire. We have to remake our external conduct under this guidance, and it is a long, hard journey. We obey first from a rational perception that the orderly, religious life is actually the most likely to lead to success; then we progress to obedience from a sense of duty—as the Israelites came to think of themselves as the "chosen people." This whole period is the period of reformation: it is not a heavenly state. Fairly early in this process of reformation we come into sight of the Holy Land of heavenly character, see its beauties and even taste its fruits, but we cannot actually enter it until our good habits have become so firmly established that the Lord can remove the things in us which have been resisting and retarding our progress. Moses does not enter the Holy Land. This does not mean that when we become heavenly people we cease to obey the Law. But it does mean that the Law is no longer a hard taskmaster, but a trusted leader. We go forward eagerly and willingly instead of under compulsion.

Joshua, Swedenborg says, represents "truth fighting." He had been the leader of the fighting men of Israel from the beginning of the wilderness journey. He was also one of the two spies who urged the people to go forward into the Holy Land and reminded them that the Lord would help them. The Holy Land represents heaven or a heavenly character, for we do not enter heaven unless heaven is first within us. It is the Lord's spirit of unselfish love which makes heaven, and we can receive this in our hearts from Him if and when we are prepared to recognize the evils which are in our hearts and to fight them with His help. This is what is meant by the conquest of the Holy Land, and it is called *regeneration* or a new birth. *Reformation* and *regeneration* are two different things*: reformation is the setting in order of the external life, and regeneration has to do primarily with the will. All the stories of the Israelites up to our lesson for today have had to do with our development and preparation for the beginning of regeneration. Swedenborg says no one begins to regenerate until he is grown up:

*Or, to put it another way, two consecutive stages in the process of becoming a spiritual person. —*Ed.*

that is, until the Lord sees that his choices are really his own and not dictated by his parents and teachers, or by his other associates. So regeneration begins in the will and works down into the thought and then into the act. Regeneration is not our work, but the Lord's work in us as we prepare the way. It is like the growth of a plant after we have prepared the ground and planted the seed in it.

There are two parts to the charge given to Joshua as the Israelites lay encamped by the Jordan. He is told to be "strong and of a good courage"; and he is to do according to all the law of Moses, not to depart from it "to the right hand or to the left," and to "meditate therein day and night." This is the way in which our regeneration must go forward, constantly seeking new truth from the Word of God, obeying it, and fighting bravely with full belief that the Lord is present and helping us.

For the meaning of verses 12 to 15 of our chapter, look up Numbers 32:1-6 and 13-22. Notice the difference between this occupation of the Jordan valley by the two and a half tribes, and Lot's settling there in the time of Abraham. In the new settlement the same country is chosen, but the fighting men first go forward with the rest and help to conquer the Holy Land. When we have recognized and overcome the evils which lie deep within us, we can safely enjoy the things of this world.

Adult

The charge to Joshua offers plenty of material for discussion. The difference between reformation and regeneration is also a fruitful subject. The personal attitude toward the place of religion in life enters into both and carries over into our attitude toward the Word, the doctrines, and the church. There is a good deal of superficial thinking in regard to the organized New Church today. We need to go more deeply into the subject and to face our responsibility to the organization.

After the decision to follow the advice of the ten fainthearted spies, the children of Israel wandered for thirty-eight more years in the wilderness. There are three accounts of these wanderings: the longer account (Exodus 15 through Numbers 32) and two summaries (Numbers 33 and Deuteronomy 1-3). Because many of the places named have not been identified, it is not easy to trace the wanderings on the map, but we know that they were in the general region of what is called the wilderness of Zin and the Arabah or Mount Seir, the country which lies between the Gulf of Aqabah and the Dead Sea. Some of the incidents of this period are studied in this course: the rebellion of Korah, Dathan, and Abiram; the blossoming of Aaron's rod; and the story of Balaam. There is also the story of the fiery serpents in Numbers 21 which we need to know because of later mentions of the serpent of brass which Moses set up at that time. The Israelites fought a number of battles and conquered such enemies as opposed them. Their leader in battle was Joshua, who had been chosen for this duty in their first battle against Amalek, before they reached Sinai. We recall that he was also one of the two spies who urged the people to go bravely forward and take possession of the Holy Land in spite of the apparent difficulties in the way.

All the leaders chosen by the Lord throughout the Bible story picture the Word of God in some aspect. Moses represents the Law as it appears to us when we obey it through hope of reward or fear of consequences. This type of obedience serves to set our outward lives in order and leads us to the border of the Holy Land, but it cannot cross the border. Moses had been told by the Lord that he would not be allowed to enter the Holy Land, although he would have an opportunity to see it before he died. Read Numbers 20:1-13. In the type of obedience represented by Moses there is a spirit of self-praise. In fact, Swedenborg points out (AC 2946) that in the first stage of reformation a man does not believe that he is being reformed by the Lord but by himself. This spirit cannot enter the Holy Land. However, if the person in this first state wants to become good—if he longs for a more spiritual state—even if he goes no further in this life, he can be introduced into further states after death (TCR 571). The wilderness, Swedenborg says, is predicated both of those who are afterward reformed and of those who cannot be reformed (AC 2708[5]). In the literal sense of the story of the wilderness wanderings, the great mass of the people did actually die in the wilderness and never reached the Holy Land. But the children–those in states of innocence and trust–along with Joshua and Caleb–who in this application would represent those who progress to the point of regeneration from mature choice of truth and good–did go on into the Holy Land. The crossing of the Jordan represents the end of the state of reformation and the beginning of regeneration. Reformation and regeneration are two different things*: reformation is the setting in order of the external life, and regeneration has to do primarily with the will. We may reform our conduct without making any effort to change our feelings.

We "leave the wilderness and cross the Jordan" when we are ready to face the evils and falsities in our hearts and minds and fight against them. Then we begin to use the truth willingly because we have proved it and found that it led us to where we really wanted to go all the time. Joshua represents "truth fighting." We still know that our "Holy Land" is full of enemies; that we have our severest temptations ahead of us, those evils within ourselves which we have not yet faced; but we are now eager to go forward and face them. The whole spirit is changed. Read the people's answer to Joshua in our chapter for today (verses 16-18) and compare it with their treatment of Joshua in Numbers 14:6-10.

The Lord's charge to Joshua was twofold. We always remember the first part of it because it is three times repeated in this first chapter and impresses itself on our memories: "Be strong and of a good courage." The children of Israel had learned by long and bitter experience that they got nowhere by trying to avoid conflict. Neither do we. When we refuse to recognize and fight evil and falsity, our character is weakened and with it our influence for good in the world. We get nowhere ourselves and we are of no real help to anyone else. We should be "of a good courage." The charge is important to us at every step of our regeneration. To see an evil in

*See footnote in Senior notes.

oneself and regret it but say, "I was born that way; I can't change" is to close the mind to the Lord's promises and make it impossible for Him to give us power to overcome. To see so many evils in ourselves that we give up without attacking any one of them is not only cowardly but irrational. If we recognize our evils and fight them one by one, sure of the Lord's help, we shall progress steadily toward the desired goal.

The charge is also especially important to us in the New Church today. We are a small body and many of our societies have been dwindling and even going out of existence. Many have lost confidence in the importance of our organization. When we show this lack of trust and faith, our children are not inspired with love for the church, they are not adequately instructed in it, and no one else is made aware of what the New Church has to give them. In every community there are individuals hungering for just what we alone can give. We do not find these people by hiding our light under a bushel. If we believe—as we should—that our doctrines have been given by the Lord to meet the spiritual needs of the people of this new age, then we must take the Lord's charge to Joshua as a charge to each one of us.

And the second part of the charge is equally pertinent: "Observe to do according to all the law, which Moses my servant commanded thee: turn not from it to the right hand or to the left." To turn to the right hand is to err on the side of what we imagine to be charity, to refuse to recognize that sin brings inevitable punishment, not from God but from its own corrupting nature, to explain away the rational statements in our doctrines on the ground that the Lord could not have meant them. To turn to the left hand is to err on the side of intellectualism, to look at the Word from human reason and self-intelligence rather than accepting it as it was given and seeing divine wisdom in it. The charge goes on: "This book of the law shall not depart out of thy mouth; but thou shalt meditate therein day and night, that thou mayest observe to do according to all that is written therein." The Word—as the Lord has given it to us, not as men would like to interpret and change it—is our bulwark and defense, our leader, the light on our path, the river which cleanses our lives and quenches our spiritual thirst. If we go forward obeying this charge and trusting in the Lord, we shall have good success.

To understand verses 12 to 15 we need to read Numbers 32. Just as Lot long before had seen the rich Jordan valley and chosen it for his dwelling place, so now some of the tribes preferred it to the Holy Land itself. Many people want to know what is right and to do it, yet their real enjoyment is in outward activity, "good works" in the natural sense. But they should be like the tribes in our story rather than like Lot. They should be willing to cross the Jordan with their brethren and help in the conquest of the land before settling down in the valley; that is, to recognize their inner evils and fight and overcome them as a means to innocent enjoyment. The whole life must be set in order, inward as well as outward. Read here Joshua 22, which tells of the final settlement of these tribes and the altar they set up east of the Jordan as a reminder of their duty to the Lord.

From the Writings of Swedenborg

True Christian Religion, n. 42: "It must be understood that there are three degrees of love and wisdom and consequently three degrees of life, and that the human mind is formed into regions, as it were, in accordance with these degrees; and that in the highest region life is in its highest degree, in the second region in a less degree, and in the outmost region in the lowest degree. These regions are opened in man successively—the outmost region, where there is life in the lowest degree, from infancy to childhood; and this is done by means of knowledges: the second region, where there is life in a larger degree, from childhood to youth; and this is done by means of thought from knowledges: and the highest region, where there is life in the highest degree, from youth to early manhood and onward; and this is done by means of perceptions of moral and spiritual truths."

Suggested Questions on the Lesson

P. What did the spies bring back from the Holy Land? *fruit*

P. What good things did they report about the land? *fertile, beautiful*
P. What bad things did they report? *giants, walled cities*
J. What did ten of the spies advise? *"We are not able . . ."*
J. What did the other two say? *"We are well able . . ."*
P. Who were the two spies who trusted in the Lord? *Caleb, Joshua*
J. Which advice did the people take? *that of the ten*
J. What was the result? *38 years more in desert*
J. How long altogether did they wander in the wilderness? *40 years*
J. What was their last encampment before they entered the Holy Land? *Plain of Moab*
P. When Moses died, who became the leader of the Israelites? *Joshua*
J. What do you remember about Joshua from earlier lessons? *good spy, army leader*
J. What was the Lord's charge to Joshua? *"Be strong and of a good courage"*
J. What tribes were given homes east of the Jordan? *Reuben, Gad, half Manasseh*
J. What were the men of these tribes to do before they settled down? *help others fight*
I. What does entering the Holy Land mean? *beginning regeneration*
S. What is the difference in correspondence between (1) Moses, and (2) Joshua?
(1) law obeyed
(2) truth fighting
S. What is the difference between (1) reformation, and (2) regeneration?
(1) putting outer life in order
(2) getting a new will from the Lord

CROSSING THE JORDAN

Joshua 3-4

The transition to this lesson is easily made through emphasis on the unwillingness of the Israelites to obey the Lord as the cause of their long stay in the wilderness. The lesson to be drawn from this is an obvious one for all classes. Then Joshua may be used as the actual connecting link, recalling his leadership of the fighting men throughout the wilderness journey and the story of the spies (Numbers 13-14), in which Joshua and Caleb alone trusted the Lord and gave wise counsel.

Doctrinal Points

The Lord can always give us power to go forward in the right way if we are not afraid to try.

The commandments are our guide and protection in every difficult decision.

Faith is essentially trust in the Lord.

A feeling of real enjoyment in doing right is the beginning of the regenerate state.

Notes for Parents

People have long seen that in the Bible the land of Canaan—the Holy Land or the Promised Land—is a picture of heaven, and that the Jordan River is a picture of the dividing line or boundary between this world and heaven. But we need to realize that heaven is not just a place where good people go when they die. It is a state in which truly good people live while they are in this world. In fact, if we have not reached this heavenly character before we die, we shall not be able to live in heaven after death.

There are stages in our spiritual journey in this life, just as there were stages in the journey of the children of Israel from Egypt to the Holy Land. We do not become heavenly people all at once.

And there are two dividing lines to be crossed in this journey. The first is the line between completely worldly living and the determination to obey the Lord. This is pictured in the Bible by the Red Sea. The second is the line between obeying the Lord because we know we ought to and obeying Him because we love to. This is the Jordan River. The wilderness journey of struggle and trials lies between.

Both the Red Sea and the Jordan River seemed impassable to the Israelites, but when they went forward boldly, the Lord opened the way for them. So it is with us. Our natural worldliness and selfishness make obedience to the Lord and especially any real enjoyment in obedience seem impossible. But we need to remember that "with the Lord all things are possible." If we obey the commandments faithfully, the time will surely come when we pass over Jordan into a state of willing and joyful obedience which is heaven in this world as well as in the next. As we have told the Juniors in their notes, "I can't" never gets us anywhere. Joshua was given two charges by the Lord and these charges are meant for every one of us. One was that he must always read and meditate upon the book of the law and do as it taught. The other was that he must be "strong and of a good courage."

Primary

Stress the foolishness of the Israelites in not trusting and obeying the Lord, and the lesson which its result teaches us. The children will enjoy the story of the crossing of the Jordan from the Word, and should learn the names *Joshua* and *Jordan*. Read also the Lord's charge to Joshua (Joshua 1:7-8). In covering today's story, stress the fact that it was the ark containing the commandments which opened the way and held back the flood while they crossed. Stress also the importance of not being afraid to go forward in the right way.

You remember how the people rebelled against Moses and Aaron, through whom the Lord was leading and teaching them. They were traveling toward the Holy Land, which is sometimes called the *Promised Land* because the Lord had promised Abraham that it should belong to his descendants. If they had been willing and obedient, they could have made the whole journey from Egypt to the Holy Land in a few months. But because they were so unwilling to obey, the Lord could not give them their promised land until all the people who were dissatisfied had died off. You know how often we lose things because we are foolish and will not mind our parents.

To what country were the Israelites traveling?
Do you know how long they were on the way altogether?
It was their constant murmuring and disobedience that held them back.
The Holy Land stands for a heavenly character.
We cannot have a heavenly character until we learn to trust and obey the Lord.
Even Moses and Aaron were not wholly obedient and died in the wilderness.
Whom did the Lord appoint to be leader after Moses died?
What was the eastern boundary of the Holy Land?

In order to enter the Holy Land they had to cross the River Jordan. They reached it just at the time of year when the water was very high and was overflowing the fields on both sides of the river. Here was this great army of people with their wives and children and all their tents and their household belongings and their cattle—and they had no boats. What were they to do?

Who led the way into the river?
What were they carrying?
What happened?
What did Joshua set up in the midst of the Jordan?
What did he set up on the other side after they had all crossed?
Why did he set up these stones?
What was the name of the place where they set up the stones and camped?
The Lord will always help us if we have courage to do right, even when it looks hard.

Junior

With this class a little more should be done with the reason for the long stay in the wilderness. The figure of Joshua may be made central in this introduction. The whole emphasis in the story should be on the necessity of trust in the Lord, obedience to the commandments, and the courage to do right. If children of this age can be given the thought that yielding to temptation is cowardly and that doing right is brave, it will help them in their daily decisions.

Now we come to the story of how the Israelites actually entered the Holy Land. The murmurings and rebellions of the people had kept them in the wilderness for forty years. We often make it hard for our parents to do all they would like to do for us by not obeying them. There is a right way to behave, and it is always the best way for us in the end. The Lord had promised Abraham and Isaac and Jacob that the land of Canaan should belong to their descendants—this is why it is often called the Promised Land—but they were to be sure always to obey Him. The Lord promises us that we shall live forever in heaven if we will only obey Him. The land of Canaan, or the Holy Land, is a symbol of heaven. But heaven is not only a place where good people go after they die; it is a heavenly character in this world. People who obey the Lord are really living in heaven here because they have His unselfish love in their hearts and are not always thinking about themselves and what they want that they do not happen to have. So in the story of the Israelites the people who were always dissatisfied and rebellious could not enter the Holy Land.

Perhaps you remember the story (Numbers 13-14) of how Moses, at the command of the Lord, sent twelve men, one from each tribe, to "spy out" the Holy Land and come back and tell the people about it. All the spies reported that it was a wonderful land, but ten of them said the enemies in the land were so strong that they could not be overcome. Only two of the spies, Joshua and Caleb, urged the people to go ahead and enter the land. They said that the Lord would be with them and give them the victory. But all the people listened to the ten and refused to try to take the land. So the Lord said all the people must stay in the wilderness until every one of the cowards was dead. Only Joshua and Caleb and the children and young people who had not been old enough at the time to have a vote in the matter should ever enter the Holy Land. Even Moses and Aaron were to die before they entered it. "I can't" never gets us anywhere.

Moses was allowed to see the Holy Land. The last chapter of Deuteronomy tells us how, when the Israelites at the end of their forty years of wandering reached their last encampment not far from the Jordan River, the Lord called Moses up to the top of Mount Nebo and showed him all the Holy Land spread out far below him. Then Moses died.

Joshua had been appointed by the Lord to lead the Israelites in their conquest of the Holy Land. Joshua was a fighting man. He had been the leader of the army all through the forty years in the wilderness. After the death of Moses the Lord gave Joshua a solemn charge. Read it in Joshua 1:6-9.

In the thirty-third chapter of Numbers you will find a list of all the encampments of the Israelites from the time they left Egypt to the time of our lesson for today. Verse 48 of that chapter gives their final stop in the wilderness: "And they departed from the mountains of Abarim, and pitched in the plains of Moab by Jordan near Jericho." From this encampment Joshua sent two men across the Jordan to spy out the immediate country and especially the walled city of Jericho, which would be the first obstacle in their way after they crossed the river. When the men came back, the people advanced to the edge of the Jordan and remained there until the third day looking at the river which barred their further progress, for they were a great host of people with many children and all their tents and household goods and cattle–and they had no boats. You notice, however, that this time there is no statement that they were doubtful or afraid.

What was the condition of the river at this time? (verse 15)
Who were to go first?
What were they to carry.
What was in the ark?
What happened when the foot of the first priest touched the brink of the river?
Where did the priests bearing the ark stop?
What did Joshua set up in the middle of the river bed?
What did he order one man from each tribe to do?
Who were the last people to come up out of the river?
What happened as soon as they had crossed?
What did Joshua do with the twelve stones the men carried?
Why did he do this?

This first encampment of the Israelites in the Holy Land, where the stones were set up for a memorial, was named Gilgal. *Gilgal* means "rolling." Read Joshua 5:9 to see why this name was given to the place. Like the Israelites we are sometimes very, very slow to make up our minds to be brave enough to shake off our selfish ways and go forward in the Lord's way. But when we finally do, the way opens before us—because the Lord can be with us when we follow the commandments. Now read Joshua 5:10-12 as the end of our story for today.

Intermediate

The difference between the states of reformation and regeneration should be stressed. This may be done through the correspondence of the change of leadership. The meaning of the Jordan and the central place of the ark in the story, and the need of having the "courage of our convictions" are important points. The teacher should keep in mind, however, that the Intermediates themselves are still "in Egypt" and that for them all this is necessary memory-knowledge—the "corn" (grain) being stored up in Egypt.

Deuteronomy means a "second naming" or repetition. The book of Deuteronomy is a summing up by Moses in his last days on earth of the dealings of the Lord with the Israelites from the time when they first encamped at Sinai to their arrival at the Jordan River, and a reiteration of the commandments and many other laws given them at Sinai. It closes with Moses' song of thanksgiving to the Lord, his solemn charge to the people to observe the law, his blessing of the twelve tribes, and finally his being called by the Lord up to the top of Mount Nebo, where he was permitted to view the Holy Land spread out far below, and then his death. For even Moses had on one occasion disobeyed the Lord (Numbers 20:7-13) and could not enter the Holy Land.

Joshua had been appointed by the Lord to succeed Moses as leader of the Israelites. We hear of Joshua first in Exodus 17 when, in the first battle Israel fought, he led the army against the Amelekites while Moses went up on top of the mountain and Aaron and Hur helped him keep his hands uplifted to the Lord until Amalek was defeated. Joshua continued to be the leader of Israel's army. In the story of the sending out of the spies (Numbers 13-14), Joshua and Caleb were the only ones of the twelve spies who, after searching out the land of Canaan, encouraged the people to go forward immediately and conquer it because the Lord would be with them and give them the victory. Because the people refused to trust the Lord and instead followed the advice of the other ten spies, the Lord told Moses that of all the men who at that time were twenty years of age and over—old enough to vote in the matter—only Joshua and Caleb should ever enter the Holy Land. The others would all die in the wilderness. That was why the pillar of cloud and fire kept them wandering from place to place for forty years before it finally brought them to Jordan. The people who follow Joshua into the Holy Land in our story for today—except for Caleb—are the young people and children who have grown up in the wilderness, and their children.

Nevertheless, it was a great host of people, with many little children and all their tents and household goods and their flocks and herds. Verse 15 of chapter 3 tells us that they reached the Jordan at harvest time and that the river at that time was always at flood. You remember that the wilderness journey represents the period of reformation, when we are obeying the truth because we know we ought to but against all our natural inclinations. If we keep trying, however, the time comes when our natural inclinations to rebel—like the people who had been brought up in Egypt—have died out, and we find that we are no longer unwilling to obey or afraid in the face of temptations and difficulties. This is the harvest of all our efforts, when we can begin to gather the good fruit, the real enjoyment of doing right. There is only one more river to cross, and when the Lord shows us how to cross it, we are no longer afraid to try. We have learned to trust our leader. Moses and Joshua both represent the Lord's truth, but whereas Moses represents the law of the Lord obeyed from a sense of duty, Joshua represents this same law obeyed willingly and eagerly. Joshua, Swedenborg says, represents "the truth fighting." The entrance into the Holy Land represents the beginning of real regeneration, when we have set our outer lives in order and begin to search out and overcome the evils which are within us. These evils are the strong enemies who lived within the Holy Land itself. We use the same law of the Lord to direct us, but we use it now by our own will, because the Lord has been able to give us a new will very different from our old selfish will. This change in our will is regeneration—being "born again."

The name *Jordan* means "the descender." In a little more than two hundred miles the Jordan descends from the mountains of Lebanon to the Dead Sea, the lowest spot on the face of the earth. This pictures the truth from the Lord flowing down to people in the very lowest possible spiritual states. The Jordan is also the boundary of the Holy Land on the east, and you remember that the east, where the sun rises, represents the Lord. So the truths pictured by the Jordan are those truths which introduce us into the land of heavenly living, the primary truths of the Word such as that the Lord is our Heavenly Father, that all good and truth are from Him, and that He can help us only as we are willing to obey Him. We all want to enter the Holy Land. What is it that makes these simple truths appear as a barrier just when we are ready to enter—at the time of harvest? It is the enemies in the land, the evils deep within us. When our "Holy Land" is full of evil tendencies, they make these introductory truths seem false.* Even after all our experience with the Lord's goodness to us, can we really believe that everything that happens to us is a sign of the Lord's love for us, and that the only right way of life is the way of obedience to the commandments?

At Joshua's command the priests bearing the ark stepped boldly forward into the river, and immediately the river parted. And so

---

*Cf. AE 700[12-13] where Swedenborg takes note of the *basic* correspondence of Jordan, but notes that *here* "its waters signify falsities of evil." Thus "they were parted and removed to give a passage to the sons of Israel, who were to represent the church." After the people had passed over, "the waters returned. Then these same waters signified truths that introduce."

long as the ark remained in the midst of the channel, the waters were held back and the people passed over safely. So long as we keep the commandments central in our thinking and go forward boldly, the Lord can keep the way open before us.

You remember that stones represent foundation truths. Joshua set up twelve stones in the midst of Jordan and twelve stones from Jordan at Gilgal, their first encampment in the Holy Land. These were to serve forever as reminders of what they had been enabled to do that day. Think of this and read the Lord's charge to Joshua (Joshua 1:6-9), which is a charge to everyone who wishes to achieve a heavenly character and so live in heaven both here and in the life after death.

Basic Correspondences

the Jordan	=	the truths which introduce us into heavenly life
the Jordan as a barrier to Israel	=	falsities of evil
stones	=	foundation truths

Senior

The important lesson for this age group is the difference between setting our outward conduct in order and actually beginning to search out and overcome our inward foes. The law of the Lord, as summed up in the commandments, is our guide and support in both efforts, but there is a change in our attitude toward it—a new will—when regeneration begins.

With this lesson we come to the end of the period of "reformation" pictured by the wilderness journey. What makes it seem so hard for us to remake our outward lives in the order prescribed by the Lord is the persistence of the worldly standards developed during our life of slavery in Egypt. The Israelites were not allowed to reach their final encampment near the Jordan until all these unwilling followers of Moses had died. Those who encamped by the Jordan had been only children in Egypt and had all done their growing up in the wilderness, except for two men, Joshua and Caleb. Even Moses, although he was allowed to view the Holy Land from the top of Mount Nebo, died on that mountain and never set foot in the land. Moses represents the law of the Lord followed from the mere principle of obedience.

Joshua, Swedenborg says, represents "the truth fighting." When outward obedience has finally become so habitual as to be willing obedience, actual regeneration begins. Then—and not until then—we are ready to search out and overcome our inner evils. It takes far more courage to conquer these inward foes than to do right outwardly. Joshua is given two great charges: "Be strong and of a good courage" and "This book of the law shall not depart out of thy mouth; but thou shalt meditate therein day and night, that thou mayest observe to do according to all that is written therein." These are both essential to regeneration.

Everything in the Scriptures may have both a good and a bad correspondence, depending upon whether at the moment it is a friend or a foe of the spiritual progress of man. This is only to say that goodness or badness is never in the outward expression or act, but is in the motive which is behind it. A man may keep all the commandments outwardly from the selfish desire to appear good and to receive honor and profit from his neighbors. The devil can quote Scripture, as we may remember from the story of the Lord's temptations in the wilderness.

So the Jordan River, which almost always represents the Lord's truth flowing down from its pure source through all the planes of life to the very lowest, pictures in our lesson today the opposite of this truth.

The Jordan is the boundary of the Holy Land, those simple truths without which no one can enter a heavenly state of life. But when the Holy Land is full of evil people and the Jordan bars the entrance of the Israelites, it represents the false ideas in the mind which must be overcome before one can enter upon the conquest of his deeper evils—ideas, perhaps, of one's own importance and wisdom. The priests bearing the ark are our religious principles which rally around the Lord's laws as their guide and protector. These are told to go forward boldly, and before them the apparent barrier draws back. As long as they stand firm, the people—all our other affections and thoughts—can pass through safely into the Holy Land. There are still many enemies to face, but the line has been crossed and we have gained a sure foothold in heavenly living.

We have said that the crossing of the Red Sea pictures our first decision to "be good," to follow the Lord instead of the world and our own desires. We have gone a long way since then, fighting our bad habits and bringing our outward conduct into order. Now we cross another barrier of water and begin to enjoy the good life and to face confidently the foes which will keep cropping up within our hearts and minds as long as we live in this world.

Joshua's first act in this new land was to set up twelve stones from the river as a memorial to be pointed out to future generations. These twelve stones are the fundamental truths of the Word which we are to set up in our minds in the very beginning of the regenerate life so that we may never forget the mercy and saving power of the Lord; so that, no matter how successful we may be in our efforts, we may never attribute our success to our own wisdom and goodness or imagine we have got beyond the necessity of keeping the commandments.

Adult

Good discussion topics are: the meaning of the change from Moses to Joshua; the correspondence—good and bad—of the Jordan; and the central place that the commandments must take in our lives in the regenerate state as well as in the period of reformation.

We note that we have left the books of Moses. Most of our lessons have been from Genesis, Exodus, and Numbers. This does not mean that Leviticus and Deuteronomy are of less value than the other three, but merely that the instruction contained in them is for the most part too detailed for the purpose of a rapid survey of the whole Word. Each one of the statutes in the book of Leviticus has an inner meaning which applies to our life and conduct. The book of Deuteronomy, called the second giving of the law, was all delivered after the Israelites had reached their final encampment near the Jordan, and is in itself a summary of all that had happened to them under Moses and of all the instruction given them through him. Much of it is in the first person, as spoken by Moses directly to the people. In the first four chapters he rehearses briefly the story of their wanderings, bringing to their remembrance the wonderful way in which the Lord has upheld them together with a picture of their own weakness and disobedience. Chapters 5 to 26 are a recapitulation of the laws and statutes previously given to them, with a constant exhortation to obedience. In the rest of the book these laws are delivered into the stewardship of the Levites, and Joshua and the people are solemnly urged to observe them faithfully in the years to come, particularly in times of safety and prosperity, when they will be tempted to forget their dependence upon the Lord.

The leadership of Moses represents the first stage of our journey out of Egypt, away from the dominion of purely natural and worldly feelings and thoughts. As we have seen, these worldly motives and ideas cling to us and are constantly cropping up. The Israelites in the wilderness were always looking back longingly toward the fleshpots of Egypt. Throughout the period of reformation we have a tendency to look upon the law of the Lord as a hard master, and to take considerable credit to ourselves when we obey it. The higher part of our mind recognizes that happiness and peace can come only through conquering self and wholly following the Lord, but the old self persists in intruding itself in everything we do. The type of obedience represented by Moses can bring us in sight of the Holy Land of truly spiritual living, but cannot take us across the border line into it.

Joshua, whose name means "whose help is the Lord," represents another type of leadership—the truth fighting. When we have obeyed the Lord's law until it has become so interwoven with our lives that we no longer struggle against it, but see it in a new spirit as an expression of the Lord's love and look to its leadership as a matter of course, the truth becomes ours to use and we are ready to pass over from merely external living to genuine spiritual living, to apply the test of the Lord's truth to our inner motives and thoughts and to fight from it against deeper enemies than mere evils of conduct.

The conquest of the Holy Land is the period of regeneration, and the Lord wants us to go as far in regeneration as we possibly can. He will be with us in this deeper conflict as he was in the more external battles. He says to Joshua, "As I was with Moses, so I will be with thee: I will not fail thee, nor forsake thee." But we must remember the charge. All our efforts must be founded upon the Word, and we must "meditate therein day and night." We never reach the state where we can discard the law or break the law with impunity, nor do we ever get so far that we cannot learn more about the Word and its meaning for us. Also, we must be "strong and of a good courage." The Christian life is an active, constructive, progressive life, in which we must always advance, never resting satisfied with what we have attained. It requires the highest form of courage, the courage to speak truth, to say "no" to temptation, to face our own evils squarely, often to go against popular opinion, to face ridicule, to love our enemies. And there is only one source of such courage: we must not look to ourselves as strong, but we must be strong and of a good courage "for the Lord thy God is with thee whithersoever thou goest." We must recognize that we have no strength except from the Lord, that our victories are the Lord's victories in us. This is a lesson which the Lord teaches over and over again throughout the Word: "Without me ye can do nothing."

The Israelites reached the Jordan at the time of harvest. The beginning of regeneration is the time of harvest for all the victories we have won in our wilderness journey. But the Israelites found one more barrier which must be overcome. The Jordan River stands for the Lord's truth coming down to the level of everyday life, the boundary of heavenly living. If we want to have eternal life, we must first of all keep the commandments. At the time when Israel camped before Jordan, the Holy Land was full of evil people who were ready to fight them. We all have selfishness deeply entrenched within us, and self-interest can turn even truth from the Lord into falsity. So Swedenborg tells us that the Jordan barring the way of entrance into the Holy Land represents falsity instead of truth (or, more precisely, truth falsified). Once it is passed it again becomes truth.

It was by the power of the ark that Israel passed safely through these waters. The commandments laid up in the ark in the Holy of Holies of the tabernacle represent the commandments "written on the heart." This is what enables us to enter the Holy Land of a regenerate life. When we examine ourselves to make sure that we have been doing right outwardly not just to avoid trouble or to seem "respectable" or even just to get to heaven, and when we determine to live from truly worthy motives, obeying the commandments from love to the Lord and the neighbor, keeping them written in our hearts and minds as well as in our outward conduct, then we really enter the Holy Land.

And even then we need reminders. We know that we all have a tendency to slip back, especially when things are going well with us, as Moses had warned the people before he died. We need something to bring frequently to our attention the remembrance of our past difficulties, of the Lord's saving power, and of our good resolutions. The twelve stones taken from the bed of Jordan and set up at Gilgal for a memorial picture this reminder. We need them for ourselves and we need them to help us in teaching our children the way of life and in teaching others. If the commandments are set up in our lives so that others see that they are of the utmost importance to us, we shall not belie our teaching by our practice. Read Joshua 4:20-24.

Other important events are connected with Gilgal. There the Israelites celebrated their first Passover in the Holy Land. This, as we know, was also ordained as a solemn reminder of the Lord's mercy and saving power. And at Gilgal the manna ceased and they began to eat the fruits of the land. When we reach the regenerate state, we know where our spiritual food comes from and how it is produced. We no longer have to say of spiritual nourishment,

"What is it?" It no longer melts in the heat of the day or spoils when we store it up. It was here, too, that the ritual of circumcision was restored as the sign of dedication to purity of life. The "reproach of Egypt" has been "rolled away" as we are told in Joshua 5:9 in explanation of the naming of Gilgal, which means either *rolling* or *a circle* [of stones].

From the Writings of Swedenborg

Apocalypse Explained, n. 700: "Here 'Jordan' and its waters signify falsities of evil . . . since the land of Canaan was then filled with idolatrous nations . . . Now as the Lord alone removes and scatters the falsities of evil that are from hell, and by His Divine truths brings the faithful into the church and into heaven, and as the ark and the law inclosed in it represented the Lord in relation to Divine truth, it was commanded that the ark should go before the people and thus lead them. This is why it came to pass that as soon as the priests bearing the ark dipped their feet in the waters of Jordan those waters were divided and went down, and the people passed over on dry land, and after this was done the waters returned. Then these same waters signify truths that bring in; for Jordan was the first boundary of the land of Canaan, and that land, when the sons of Israel had entered into it, represented the church, and that river introduction into it. As the waters of Jordan signified truths that bring in they were commanded to take up out of the midst of it twelve stones, and carry them over to the first place where they passed the night, and this because 'stones' signify truths, and 'twelve stones according to the number of the tribes of Israel' signified the truths of the church."

Suggested Questions on the Lesson

J. Where did Moses die? *Mount Nebo*
P. Who succeeded him as leader? *Joshua*
J. What charge was given to Joshua? *Be strong and of a good courage*
J. Where was the last encampment of the Israelites in the wilderness? *opposite Jericho*
J. At what time of year did they reach it? *harvest*
P. What barred their way into the Holy Land? *Jordan*
P. How was the river parted for them? *by a miracle*
J. What did Joshua set up in the middle of the river bed? *twelve stones*
J. What did he set up at their first camp in the Holy Land? *twelve stones*

I. Why did he set up these stones? *reminder of miracle*
J. What was this first camping place called? *Gilgal [rolling]*
J. Why? *reproach of Egypt "rolled away"*
J. What else happened there? *Passover, circumcision*
I. What does Joshua represent in us? *the truth fighting*
I. What does the Jordan represent? *introductory truths to spiritual living*
S. What is pictured by crossing the Jordan into the Holy Land? *beginning to change will and hence to live truly spiritual lives*

AT GILGAL

Joshua 5

This lesson may be begun without special introduction as the story of the final arrival of the Israelites at their destination. The death of Moses, the succession of Joshua, and the Lord's charge to Joshua (Joshua 1:7-9) will come in naturally. The story of the crossing of the Jordan and the setting up of the twelve stones at Gilgal tie in with the first verse of the chapter.

Doctrinal Points

The Lord alone can control our spiritual enemies.

Every place mentioned in the Word has a special meaning.

When we begin to regenerate, we must continue to study in order to make spiritual progress.

Circumcision corresponds to purification of the heart from self-love.

Notes for Parents

Finally, after forty years, the children of Israel were led to the brink of the Jordan River with the Holy Land before them. All the rebellious men had died—Moses last of all just before they reached Jordan. Only Joshua and Caleb were left. The young people had grown up and Joshua was now their leader. When we have followed the leadership of Moses—the law of the Lord—long enough so that the orderly outward life has become habitual with us and all our rebellious feelings and thoughts have died out, we are ready for a new state.

Everyone recognizes the Holy Land in the Bible story as a symbol of heaven. What they do not always recognize is that heaven begins in this world. If we do not, while we are in this world, develop the kind of character which is heavenly, we shall not choose to live in heaven after we die. The Lord, when He was in the world, said, "Ye must be born again." We are born children of the world. We must become children of God by learning about our heavenly Father and cultivating in our own hearts and minds the qualities of unselfish love and true wisdom which we find in Him. This is regeneration, for which the conquest of the Holy Land stands. The enemies in the Holy Land are the evils and falsities which are in our own hearts and minds.

The Lord parted the waters of Jordan, as He had parted those of the Red Sea, so that the Israelites could pass through. If we obey the Lord, He will always open the way before us. Their first encampment in the Holy Land was at Gilgal, a word which means "rolling," and verse 9 of our chapter tells us that it was so called because there the Lord "rolled away the reproach of Egypt" from them. In Egypt they were slaves. Now they were free men with a country of their own. In John 15:15 the Lord says to His disciples, "Henceforth I call you not servants; for the servant knoweth not what his lord doeth: but I have called you friends; for all things that I have heard of my Father I have made known unto you." When we enter the Holy Land of a regenerate state, we no longer look back with longing to our bad habits, obeying the Lord unwillingly and without understanding. We set out eagerly under a fighting leader to hunt down and destroy our inward foes.

But there are things we must remember, and our chapter is a reminder of these. We must continue to obey the commandments, which never change. Read Joshua 4:1-5, 20-24. We must keep our outward lives clean (verses 2-8). We must be grateful to the Lord for our deliverance (verse 10). We must plant in our minds the seed of truth from the Word, cultivate it, and harvest the good grain (verses 11-12). And we must remember that the regenerate life is a holy life, put off the worldly ideas in which we naturally walk, and use the truths of the Lord to fight our inner selfishness (verses 13-15).

Primary

For this age level we have included the last few verses of chapter 4 instead of the first part of chapter 5, as the setting up of the stones will interest the children and they are not old enough for the lesson on circumcision. They should learn the names Joshua and Gilgal and what Gilgal means. Something should be done to review the Passover lesson in connection with verses 9 and 10, and the teacher should be sure the children know about the manna.

In order to enter the Holy Land the people had to cross the Jordan River.
It was springtime, and the river was in flood.
Do you remember how they had crossed the Red Sea?
Now the Lord parted the waters of Jordan for them in the same wonderful way.

Before they crossed, the Lord had told Joshua to appoint one man from each of the twelve tribes, telling each of them to pick up a stone from the bed of the river as they went through it. Let us read what they did with these stones at their first camping place in the Holy Land, and then read some of the other things that happened there. [Read Joshua 4:19-24 and 5:9-16.]

What was the name of their first encampment in the Holy Land?
Why was it called this?
What feast did they celebrate there?
What can you tell about this feast?
How had the Lord fed them every day in the wilderness?
What happened at Gilgal with regard to the manna?
Who afterward appeared to Joshua at Gilgal?
What did Joshua ask him?
What did he answer?
What did he tell Joshua to do?

Junior

The Junior notes suggest an adequate approach to the lesson by way of a reminder of the story of the spies and an account of the death of Moses and the charge to Joshua. Have the children look up and read the Bible references in their notes. The order of events at Gilgal should be learned.

Why did the people not go into the Holy Land when they first came near its border?
What was their punishment for not trusting the Lord?
What two men were to be exempt from this punishment?

It was forty years before all these older people had died. Moses himself was the last to go. When finally the pillar of cloud and fire led them again to the southern border of Canaan, Moses was allowed to see the Promised Land from the top of Mount Nebo. Then he died, and we are told in Deuteronomy 34:6 that the Lord "buried him in a valley in the land of Moab, over against Bethpeor: but no man knoweth of his sepulchre unto this day." He was a hundred and twenty years old when he died, and it is said: "His eye was not dim, nor his natural force abated." *Deuteronomy*, the "repetition of the law," is the last of the five books of Moses, which are called the *Pentateuch*.

The book of Joshua, from which our lesson for today is taken, tells the story of the conquest, division, and settling of the Holy Land itself. In the very first chapter of Deuteronomy, verse 38, Moses has told the people that Joshua is to be his successor as their leader. The first chapter of Joshua, verses 7-9, tells of the Lord's charge to Joshua after the death of Moses, when He told him to "observe to do according to all the law," and to "meditate therein day and night," and ended: "For then thou shalt make thy way prosperous, and then thou shalt have good success. Have not I commanded thee? Be strong and of a good courage; be not afraid, neither be thou dismayed: for the Lord thy God is with thee, whithersoever thou goest." Joshua was a fighting leader. You remember we first heard of him when he led the fighting men of Israel in the battle with Amalek at Rephidim, and he and Caleb were the two spies who told the people at Kadesh that they ought to go ahead and conquer the land because, no matter how strong the enemies were there, the Lord was with them and would give them the victory.

There is one incident in the crossing which you may not remember, but which is important for our lesson today. Read Joshua 4:1-5, 19-24. You remember that Abraham, Isaac, and Jacob built altars to the Lord in various places, both for worship and to remind the people of all the Lord had done for them. And Moses built an altar at Rephidim after the victory over Amalek. And now one of the first things Joshua does in the Holy Land is to set up these twelve stones at Gilgal as a memorial of the miracle performed by the Lord at Jordan. Gratitude to the Lord for the many blessings He brings us should be in our hearts always.

Now read Genesis 17:9-12, which tells of the beginning of the rite of circumcision among the Jews back in the time of Abraham. The Israelites had continued to observe this rite throughout their history until they entered the wilderness. Then it was neglected, and Joshua knew that it must be resumed if he was to keep the law. Baptism takes the place of circumcision for the Christian Church.

What was the name of the first encampment of the Israelites in the Holy Land?
Gilgal means "rolling."
Why was it given this name?
What feast did the people observe at Gilgal?
What does verse 11 say they ate the day after the Passover?
What stopped on the same day?
Why do you think it stopped?

We want to remember these things which happened at Gilgal, for they were all a necessary preparation for the conquest; and we want to notice the beginning and end of our chapter, too. The protection and power of the Lord were clearly with Joshua from the beginning. In fact, the name *Joshua* means "savior" and its Greek form is *Jesus*.

Gilgal remained the headquarters of the Israelites for some time, for after the conquest of the cities of Jericho and Ai we find it said of the Gibeonites in Joshua 9:6: "And they went to Joshua unto the camp at Gilgal." The rolling away of the reproach of Egypt, from which Gilgal took its name, was the final firm establishment of the children of Israel as a free people in the land which had been promised to their fathers.

Intermediate

The difference in correspondence between the wilderness journey and the conquest of the Holy Land should be made clear and the difference in our own attitude during reformation and regeneration. The place of the law in each state and the manner of the Lord's dealing with us is an important lesson. The connection with the two Christian sacraments should be stressed. The teacher—knowing his pupils—should decide beforehand just how much to say about circumcision. He should be prepared with a simple answer to a possible question about it so that he will not be caught off guard and in doubt as to what to say.

The wilderness journey pictures the period of reformation, the time when we are trying to put our outward conduct in order in obedience to the law of the Lord. Moses represents the law as it appears to us at this time. It seems harsh and we do not like to obey it any more than the Israelites enjoyed obeying Moses. We stay in this state of reformation until doing right becomes a habit and all our rebellious thoughts and feelings die out, just as the Israelites had to stay in the wilderness until all those who chose to listen to the ten cowardly spies had died. Then Moses dies. This does not mean that we no longer need to obey the law of the Lord, but the law has ceased to appear harsh. We see it now as our friend and protector, something to be followed with confidence and courage. Joshua, the "truth fighting," has become our leader. Read the Lord's charge to Joshua in Joshua 1:7-9.

At the time of our lesson for today the Israelites have crossed the Jordan—which the Lord parted miraculously for them as He had at the Red Sea—and are finally in the Holy Land itself. The conquest of the Holy Land, of which the book of Joshua treats, pictures the process of regeneration, the time when we are trying to discover and overcome not just our outward bad habits but the evils and falsities which are in our hearts and minds. We do this not from fear of punishment or from hope of reward but because we have begun to love to serve the Lord and are eager to make ourselves all that He wants us to be.

The first encampment of the Israelites in the Holy Land was called Gilgal, a word which means "rolling," and verse 9 of our chapter tells us why it was so named. Egypt, we remember, pictures the plane of external knowledge and in a bad sense—when the Egyptians held the Israelites in slavery—it means worldliness. We are all naturally worldly—inclined to think of this world and success in it as the important thing in life—and this "reproach of Egypt" is not rolled away from us until we are ready of our own accord to follow the Lord's truth as leader.

Several interesting things happened at Gilgal. First Joshua set up there the twelve stones which had been picked up from the bed of the Jordan as the people crossed (Joshua 4:1-5, 20-24). The Jordan as the boundary of the Holy Land represents the introductory truths of the regenerate life. The setting up of the twelve stones from Jordan at Gilgal as a memorial emphasizes our need never to forget this part of the Lord's charge to Joshua: "This book of the law shall not depart out of thy mouth; but thou shalt meditate therein day and night, that thou mayest observe to do according to all that is written therein: for then thou shalt make thy way prosperous, and then thou shalt have good success." We never reach the point when we no longer need to read and study the Word and to keep the commandments.

Then Joshua was commanded to circumcise all the children of Israel. Circumcision signified to the Jews that a person was of their own church, and they had been told to circumcise every male child when he was eight days old. But they had neglected this rite all through the wilderness journey. Circumcision represents purification from selfish and worldly loves, and Swedenborg tells us that the sacrament of baptism takes the place of circumcision for the Christian Church.

After the circumcision at Gilgal the next they did was to celebrate the Passover. We remember that the Passover feast was to be celebrated on the fourteenth day of the first month of the Jewish year as a memorial of their deliverance from Egypt; so their arrival in the Holy Land had been timed by the Lord to coincide with the beginning of a new year. In the Word the time when a thing happens is always important; it is never accidental. For the Christian Church, the sacrament of the Lord's Supper takes the place of the Passover. So you see we learn from our chapter that baptism and the Holy Supper are the orderly basis on which we begin a regenerate life.

Then on the day after the Passover the manna ceased. The manna represents goodness from the Lord provided for our gathering day by day when we are trying to do right from a sense of duty. The people had been fed with it throughout their wilderness journey. At times they got very tired of it, as we learn from Numbers 21:5, but they could not live without it. When they entered the Holy Land, however, the barrenness of the wilderness was behind them. Now they could eat immediately "of the old corn [produce] of the land" and presently they would be sowing seed and raising their own grain. In the regenerate state there is goodness which is lasting, which does not–as the manna did–melt when the sun comes up or spoil if we try to keep it.

Finally Joshua has a vision of the Lord in the form of an angel with a drawn sword in his hand. Joshua was to be a fighting leader and was to have great success, but he was never to forget that it was the Lord who gave him all his power. Our chapter begins with the statement that the enemies of Israel in the Holy Land were brought into a state of weakness and fear not by the strength of the army of Israel but by the fact that the Lord had parted the Jordan for their passage. And in the end of the chapter Joshua is told to take off his shoes because the ground is holy. Our shoes, spiritually speaking, are our natural ideas in which we walk from day to day. If we are to regenerate–to be "born again"–we must see and acknowledge and never for a moment forget that it is from the Lord alone that we receive power to overcome our spiritual foes, and that a heavenly character is not mere morality and the kind of good works which bring us respect and praise in the world. Heaven is "holy ground," made so not by us but by the presence of the Lord.

Basic Correspondences

Jordan = introductory truths
circumcision = purification from selfish and worldly loves

shoes = natural ideas of goodness

Senior

The Seniors are nearing the age at which regeneration may begin, for regeneration is an adult process. They should learn from the events in this chapter just what the difference is between reformation and regeneration and what the essential basis of regeneration is. Stress the need for humility, for knowledge of the fundamental truths of the Word and of doctrine, for continual study of the Word, and for recognition of the importance of the sacraments.

Joshua and Caleb, the two spies who had stood out against the other ten and against the whole congregation when the people were afraid to trust the Lord and to undertake the conquest forty years before, were the only two men to enter the Holy Land out of all the adults who had crossed the Red Sea under Moses. It was a new generation for whom the Lord performed a similar miracle at Jordan.

So we can see immediately one explanation of verse 9 of our chapter for today (Gilgal means "rolling"). All through the wilderness journey the people had been looking back to Egypt, remembering the good things about their life there and forgetting the bad, because they were rebellious in the face of hardship and danger. This is a picture of our state when we are in the period of reformation, the time when we are trying to make our outward conduct over into the order required by divine law. We look back to certain pleasures we had before we decided to reform, forgetting the hard experiences which led us to the decision to reform, and we rebel against the principles which are leading us on. But if we persist our rebellion dies out a little at a time, until finally the law of the Lord is no longer a harsh taskmaster but a stirring leader. Moses is dead, and Joshua—the truth fighting—has taken his place.

The conquest of the Holy Land, which the book of Joshua tells us about, is the period of regeneration. We are born again. We feel ourselves to be really children of God going forward in His name and in His strength to overcome the deeper evils and falsities within ourselves which stand in the way of our possession of the Holy Land—a heavenly character. In the book of Joshua we find the people making occasional mistakes, one case of flagrant disobedience, and a falling short of the full conquest because of cowardice, but no more looking back to the purely worldly standards pictured by Egypt, and no more complaint and rebellion.

The crossing of the Jordan began a new life for the Israelites. The entrance upon regeneration begins a new life for us. But we should recall the Lord's charge to Joshua in Joshua 1:7-9, which shows what is required of us, and our whole chapter for today is a solemn reminder that we are to go forward in the Lord's strength, not in our own.

The first item in this reminder is found in verses 19 to 24 of the preceding chapter. Joshua had been told by the Lord to have one man from each of the twelve tribes pick up a stone from the bed of the Jordan as they crossed. These twelve stones were then set up at Gilgal, their first encampment in the Holy Land, as a memorial of the miraculous crossing. The Jordan represents the introductory truths of the Christian faith, which we must never forget. We need indeed to study them continually.

Our chapter begins with the statement that the enemies in the Holy Land became weak when they learned how the Jordan had been parted by the Lord for the passage of Israel. It is recognition of the Lord's power to save which shows us the actual weakness of our spiritual enemies.

Then Joshua was ordered to circumcise the people. Circumcision represents cleansing from selfish and worldly lusts. It is the recognition that our natural will is not good but evil, and that goodness comes from the Lord alone as we obey Him. Circumcision was a rite which was specifically enjoined upon the Jews but had been neglected throughout the wilderness journey. When we are in the rebellious state of reformation, we are not willing to admit that our natural desires are evil. You will see in the quotation at the end of this lesson why baptism takes the place of circumcision for the Christian Church.

After the circumcision the Passover was celebrated. This again was a reminder that it was the Lord who had delivered them from the Egyptian state of bondage. In the Christian Church the Lord's Supper takes the place of the Passover.

Then on the day after the Passover the manna ceased, because they could now eat "of the old corn [produce] of the land." When we are in the reformation period, the goodness which is represented by bread and which gives us the strength to go forward cannot in any way be produced or preserved by us, because we are still in the state in which our constant desire is not to obey but to turn back to self and the world. In that state the Lord has to supply us day by day with just enough goodness to carry us through the temptations of the day. We must gather this in the early morning of each work day by looking to the Lord for it, but we cannot store it up. We do not understand it. You remember that *manna* means "What is it?" But when our rebellious thoughts and desires have died and we have been "born again," we understand what genuine goodness is and where it comes from, and we can begin to plant the seed of truth, to develop and eat the good grain, and to store it up in our permanent character, although it still is the Lord's and not ours.

The last three verses of our chapter—Joshua's vision of the Lord as a man of war and his recognition that the ground on which he stood was holy—is the final summing up of all these reminders designed to keep us progressing spiritually by means of the Lord's truth toward the stature which He wishes us to attain.

Adult

This is a wonderful chapter in which to bring out the completeness of detail with which the Lord gives us our instruction in the Word. The basis of regenerate living is all here. Nothing is omitted and nothing given here can be neglected.

The entry of the children of Israel into the Holy Land pictures the beginning of the period of regeneration as distinguished from the period of reformation. If we continue to follow the pillar of cloud and fire—if we obey the commands of the Lord as they come to us in the Word—our regrets and rebellions will die away one by one and we shall actually reach the point at which the Lord can give us a new will which is good. This does not mean that the old selfish will is gone and that we have no more work to do. Swedenborg tells us (AC 3200) that our regeneration must go on throughout this life and to eternity in the other, for an individual "can never be perfected." But with the beginning of regeneration our rebellion is over. We are consciously and willingly on the Lord's side, and the Lord's power is so obvious to us that the promptings of the old selfish will and the falsities which linger in our minds—the enemies in the Holy Land—are weakened and can be controlled. As the first verse of our chapter says of these enemies, "their heart melted, neither was there spirit in them any more." This is true in this world and we are promised that in heaven, if we attain it, our inherited nature is held in complete check by the Lord so that we are never conscious of it unless we begin to become overconfident and need a momentary reminder that it is still there. The conquest of the Holy Land describes our progress in regeneration in this world rather than in heaven, however. In the book of Joshua, although we find no more looking back or rebellion, we do find mistakes in judgment, one outstanding case of disobedience, and in most places in the land a weakness in accomplishment. But, as verse 9 tells us, "the reproach of Egypt is rolled away" (*Gilgal* means "rolling"). We are no longer obeying Moses in fear, much as we formerly obeyed Pharaoh, but are free men. In the language of the Gospel: "Henceforth I call you not servants; for the servant knoweth not what his lord doeth: but I have called you friends; for all things that I have heard of my Father I have made known unto you."

It is significant that in the Bible the beginning of every new state is marked by the setting up of an altar of some sort as a "memorial," a reminder for future generations. It was an entirely new generation which entered the Holy Land under Joshua, and the first thing Joshua did was to set up at Gilgal the twelve stones which had been taken from the bed of the Jordan as they passed over. Read Joshua 4:1-5, 20-24.

Next Joshua was commanded to circumcise all the people. We are told in the writings that "circumcision is a sign of purification from filthy loves," and we read in AC 4462: "As the foreskin covers the genital, in the Most Ancient Church it corresponded to the obscuration of good and truth, but in the Ancient Church to their defilement. For with the man of the Most Ancient Church, who was an internal man, good and truth could be obscured but not defiled; whereas with the man of the Ancient Church, being a comparatively external man, good and truth could be defiled, because it is external things–that is, external loves–which defile. For this reason they who were of the Most Ancient Church knew nothing of circumcision, but only they who were of the Ancient Church. From this church circumcision spread to many nations; and it was not enjoined upon Abraham and his descendants as anything new, but merely as a discontinued rite that was to be restored; and it became to his posterity a sign that they were of the church." Circumcision had been neglected during the wilderness journey because in the period of reformation we are concerned with our outward conduct and unwilling to face the necessity of self-examination and inward change. But this is one of our first duties when regeneration begins.

Then after the circumcision at Gilgal the feast of the Passover was celebrated. From the beginning of regeneration we must recognize and acknowledge that it is the Lord who has delivered us from bondage to the world and the flesh. And we recall that in the Christian Church the Holy Supper takes the place of the Passover feast. So our chapter for today should bring home to us the fact that the two Christian sacraments were ordained by the Lord as the orderly beginning of the regenerate Christian life. We cannot omit or neglect them without interfering with our spiritual progress. Through them the Lord reaches us in inner ways, and even though we may not be conscious of this presence of the Lord, we know it is a fact. We should observe these two sacraments because they have been commanded by the Lord, if for no other reason. The Lord knows our needs better than we know them.

After this celebration of the Passover at Gilgal we read that the people ate the produce of the land and that the next day the manna ceased. When the Lord has been able to give each of us a new will, we can be given something of His goodness as our own, with a feeling that we have a part in developing and preserving it. Our desire to partake of His goodness is expressed when we eat the bread of the Holy Supper. The manna in the wilderness is the form in which alone the Lord's goodness can come to us before regeneration—a little at a time, just enough to give us strength for the immediate need, melting away when the sun of self-love grows hot, spoiling when it is not put to immediate use, and never understood. We recall that *manna* means "What is it?" The grain of the Holy Land is lasting goodness, developed with our willing and conscious cooperation from the seed of truth from the Word, and wholly satisfying.

Our chapter closes with the appearance to Joshua of an angel with a drawn sword who commands Joshua: "Loose thy shoe from off thy foot; for the place whereon thou standest is holy." Joshua represents "the truth fighting." If we are to make progress in regeneration, we must accept the challenge of the "captain of the host of the Lord." We must recognize that the regenerate life is a holy life and put off the materialistic ideas in which we are accustomed to walk and go forward to battle against our inward foes under the leadership of the sword of divine truth.

From the Writings of Swedenborg

Apocalypse Explained, n. 700[14]: "As the waters of Jordan signified truths that introduce they were commanded to take up out of the midst of it twelve stones, and carry them over to the first place where they passed the night, and this because 'stones' signify truths, and 'twelve stones according to the number of the tribes of Israel' signified the truths of the church. Joshua set up those stones in Gilgal to the east of Jericho, because 'Gilgal' signified the doctrine of natural truth, which is serviceable for introduction into the church."

True Christian Religion, n. 674: "When churches are viewed in the order of their succession from ancient times to the present, it will be seen that the former churches were external, that is, that their worship consisted of externals which represented the internals of the Christian church which was founded by the Lord when He was in the world, and which is now for the first time being built up by Him. That which primarily distinguished the Israelitish church from the other churches in Asia, and afterward from the Christian church, was circumcision. And because, as before said, all things of the Israelitish church, being external, prefigured all things in the Christian church, which are internal, so the especial sign of that church was interiorly like the sign of the Christian church; circumcision signifying the rejection of the lusts of the flesh, and thus purification from evils, and baptism having the same signification; from which it is clear that baptism was commanded in the place of circumcision, in order that the Christian church might not only be distinguished from the Jewish, but also might thus be more clearly recognized as an internal church."

Suggested Questions on the Lesson

J. How long did the Israelites wander in the wilderness? *forty years*
J. Where did Moses die? *Mount Nebo*
P. Who succeeded him as leader? *Joshua*
P. How did the Israelites cross the Jordan? *miracle*
P. What did they take from the bed of the river? *twelve stones*
P. What was done with these twelve stones? *made monument*
P. What was their first encampment in the Holy Land? *Gilgal*
J. What does *Gilgal* mean? *rolling*
J. Why was it called that? *"I have rolled away the reproach of Egypt"*
J. What rite was Joshua commanded to observe at Gilgal? *circumcision*
P. What feast did they celebrate there? *Passover*
P. What is said about the manna? *it stopped*
J. Why did they no longer need it? *ample food there*
J. What vision did Joshua see? *angel with sword*
J. What did the angel say of himself? *captain of God's army*
J. What did he tell Joshua to do? *take shoes off*
I. What is pictured by the wandering in the wilderness? *reformation (reordering life)*

I. What is pictured by the entrance into the Holy Land? *beginning of real spiritual living*

S. What is the difference in representation between (1) Moses, and (2) Joshua?
(1) truth obeyed through fear
(2) truth fighting in our lives

S. What two things were done at Gilgal which prefigure (1) baptism, and (2) the Holy Supper?
(1) circumcision (purification rite)
(2) Passover (memorial of salvation)

THE TAKING OF JERICHO

Joshua 6

The crossing of the Jordan should be briefly reviewed and compared with the crossing of the Red Sea; and the setting up of the stones at Gilgal, the celebration of the Passover, and the ceasing of the manna should be noted. Teachers should have read the first five chapters of Joshua in order to be sure of this background.

Doctrinal Points

All good and truth are in the Lord alone. To acknowledge this from the heart is the first essential of a regenerate life. It is always the Lord who conquers for us in temptation.

We must be persistent as well as sincere in our efforts to do right.

Notes for Parents

In our course we pass over the book of Deuteronomy, whose name means "the second law," or the repetition of the law. It is a summing up—through Moses shortly before his death—of the laws which had been given to him for the people, together with a reminder of all the Lord had done for them and a solemn charge to them to keep the law that they might live and prosper, blessed and protected by the Lord—a charge to choose life and good instead of death and evil.

Moses, as we read in the last chapter of Deuteronomy, was permitted to see the Promised Land toward which he had been leading the people, but not to enter it. He was led up to the top of Mount Nebo near their final camp, and there the Lord showed him the whole land spread out below him. Then he died.

He was succeeded by Joshua, who had been his aide throughout the wilderness journey and the leader of Israel's army whenever there was a battle. You have read with the children the Lord's solemn charge to Joshua when he was given command. Joshua fulfilled this charge, and under him the Israelites conquered the Holy Land, were assigned their places in it by lot, and settled in their new homes. This is the story covered by the book of Joshua.

The Jordan River was parted by the Lord for their crossing just as the Red Sea had been, the power of the Lord being this time manifested through the ark which contained the stone tables inscribed with the commandments by the finger of God. Then the people made their camp at Gilgal not far from the strong city of Jericho. There they celebrated the Passover in token of thanksgiving, and there the daily gift of the manna ceased, since they were now able to eat "the old corn of the land."

Then we have our story for today, the striking story of the fall of Jericho. This miracle was performed by the Lord to impress upon the people at the very beginning of their conquest the fact that all their power to conquer was from the Lord and not from themselves. If they obeyed Him, they would always be victorious. If they disobeyed, they would fail. This was later proved to them many times.

The lesson for us all is easy to see. We all hope to find our homes at last in the Promised Land—in heaven. This land is waiting within us to be conquered, but because of our inherited selfishness, it can be won only by a long struggle. The enemies in the land are our natural tendencies to evil. The walled cities are the wrong ideas built up to defend these evils. Of ourselves we could never break down the walls of falsity and overcome our temptations. But if we follow the ark—if we faithfully and persistently keep the commandments, looking to the Lord for strength and trusting in Him—He will give us the victory.

Primary

Remind the children of what the ark was and what was contained, and tell the story of Jericho with emphasis on the power of the ark. But be sure to give the children an opportunity to tell what they know about Moses, the Passover, the wilderness journey, the crossing of the Red Sea, the manna, and the ark with the commandments. It is a good lesson for review, and more will be obtained from the story of Jericho if it comes as a climax.

The people had camped near the river at a place called Gilgal and celebrated the feast of the Passover to mark their thanksgiving to the Lord for delivering them from slavery and bringing them back to the Promised Land. Then they prepared to attack the first city which stood in the way of their progress into the land. This was a strong city surrounded by a great wall.

What was the name of this city?
Did the Lord tell Joshua to attack the city of Jericho?
What were they to carry around the city each day for six days?
Who were to go ahead of the ark?
What were they to do on the seventh day?
When Joshua finally told the people to shout, what happened?
All the gold, silver, brass, and iron which they found in Jericho was to be devoted to the Lord.
Everything and everybody else was to be destroyed, except a woman named Rahab and her family.
They were spared because Rahab had saved some of Joshua's men when they were sent ahead to spy out the city.
Jericho was burned to the ground, and a curse placed upon it. Read verse 26.

It was really the Lord who conquered Jericho for the Israelites, wasn't it? When we do as the Lord tells us to do, He will always help us.

Junior

In this class review is important. The teacher will find it helpful to prepare in advance a list of Bible references bearing on the events which lead up to this miracle. If there is time, have the children look up those they do not easily recall.

When the Israelites arrived at Gilgal, they set up twelve stones from the Jordan for a memorial at this place where they made their first camp in the Holy Land. There they also celebrated the Passover feast.

What did this feast commemorate?

The name Gilgal means "a rolling." Read Joshua 5:9 to see why it was given this name. After this the manna, with which they had been fed for forty years in the wilderness, ceased; and they began to eat "the corn of the land."

The first city which stood in the way of their possession of the Holy Land was Jericho. In a book called *On Holy Ground* the Rev. William L. Worcester writes: "In the Gospel days Jericho was a city standing back in the edge of the plain just where the brook Kelt and the road from Jerusalem come out from the hills. But the old Jericho of the time of Joshua was a mile further north. The fine spring called Elisha's fountain is still there, coming out from the foot of a hill which is formed in part by the ruins of the old city. From this hill of ruins you look out over the broad plain; and behind it is a stern weather-beaten cliff with caves in which hermits live." Jericho was the first walled city the Israelites had ever had to attack, and the Lord used it to teach the Israelites that it would always be His power and not their own strength which would give them victory. He told them just what they were to do.

What were they to carry around the city?
Who were to go ahead of the ark?
What were they to carry?
How many times a day were they to march around it for the first six days?
How many times were they to march around it on the seventh day?
Do you remember where the number seven first appears in the Bible?

As the Lord, in the allegory of Creation, labored for six days and then rested on the seventh, so the number six stands for our struggles with temptation and the number seven for the peaceful, happy, and holy state which follows victory over temptation. In the Bible, whenever one is commanded to do a thing seven times, it pictures perseverance in doing right until we have come to love the right. See how many times the number seven is used in the story of the fall of Jericho. With the Jews, after the commandments were given at Sinai and the two tables of stone on which the Lord had written them were placed in the ark, the Lord's power was exercised through the ark, and you can easily see that this means for us that the Lord can always help us if we obey the commandments.

In chapter 2, which we have omitted, we are told that while the children of Israel were encamped at Shittim in the land of Moab, Joshua sent two men into the Holy Land to spy out Jericho. While they were in Jericho, these men became suspected and they would have been killed had not a woman named Rahab hidden them among the stalks of flax which she had piled up on her roof. Her house was built on the wall of the city, and after dark she let the two spies down by a rope through her window on the outside of the wall so that they could escape. They promised her that when Jericho was captured, she and all her family would be spared. Now we see that Joshua kept their promise. Tradition says that this Rahab was the Rachab mentioned in Matthew 1:5, who was an ancestress of David.

What was saved out of Jericho besides Rahab and her family?
What were these things to be used for?
What was done with everything else in the city?
What curse was put on the city?

Read I Kings 16:34 to see how this curse was fulfilled. There are two familiar stories in the New Testament in which Jericho also figures. Look up Luke 10:30 and 19:1-10. And read carefully verse 18 of our chapter for today, which you will want to remember when we come to our next lesson from the book of Joshua.

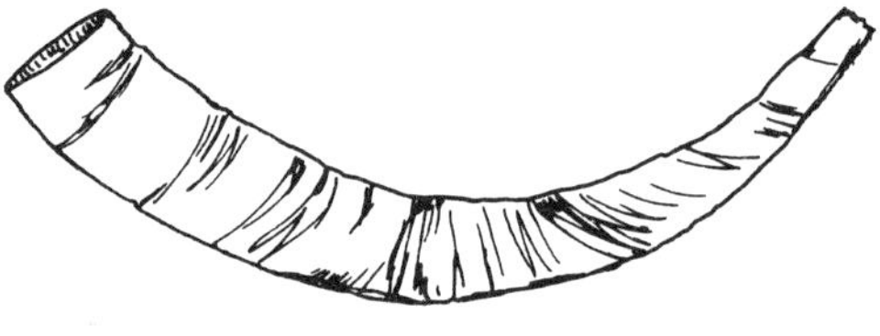

A Shofar, or Ram's Horn Trumpet

J. G. Wood in *Bible Animals* tells us: "The same instrument is used even at the present day in parts of the Jewish ritual. One of these instruments is now before me, and is shown in the accompanying illustration. In length it measures eighteen inches, i.e. a cubit, and it is formed entirely in one piece. As far as I can judge, it is made from the left horn of the broad-tailed sheep, which . . . is not spiral, but flattish, curved backwards, and forming nearly a circle . . . In order to bring it to the proper shape, the horn is softened by heat, and is then modelled into the very form which was used by the Jewish priests who blew the trumpet before the ark."

Intermediate

The correspondence of the story itself is important for this class, with emphasis on our constant need to guard against the thought that we of ourselves are able to win victories apart from obedience to the Lord and trust in Him.

In chapter 5 are described four important things connected with Gilgal, the first encampment of the Israelites in the Holy Land. First they set up the twelve stones taken from the bed of Jordan as memorial of their miraculous crossing. Then came the circumcision of all the males who entered the Holy Land. This, the Jewish equivalent of our baptism, represented purification and the dedication of their lives to the service of God. They had not observed this practice while they were wandering in the wilderness, and you perhaps remember that Joshua and Caleb were the only ones who had left Egypt as adults who were permitted to enter the Holy Land. Next the Passover was celebrated, to remind them at the very beginning of their conquest that they owed their freedom and success to the Lord. And finally the manna ceased to appear and they began to eat the fruits of the Holy Land itself—the "old corn of the land." The manna represents the day-by-day sustenance which the Lord gives us during our period of reformation without our knowing just how it comes or doing anything ourselves to help produce it. This cannot be stored up or provided in advance of our need. When we begin the period of regeneration, however, we experience a spiritual satisfaction which we can understand and in some measure cultivate.

Jericho was the first city in the Holy Land which Israel had to conquer. A city is the symbol of a system of doctrine or belief. This first city in the Holy Land, in the plain of Jordan, represents in its good sense the simplest understanding of genuine truth necessary to spiritual living. Jericho was called the "city of palm trees," and the palm tree pictures the principle that the Lord gives the victory. But Jericho in the hands of the enemy represents the denial of this principle, or our natural and strongly entrenched feeling that our power to understand and do right is in ourselves. Even after we enter the Holy Land we find clinging to us false ideas and points of view carried over from the time when we believed ourselves to be independent of the Lord. The recognition and overcoming of these remains of self-confidence and pride are pictured by the conquest of Jericho. Note that Jericho was to be utterly destroyed, only those things in it being saved which could be devoted to the service of the Lord.

The conquest of Jericho shows us the way in which our natural self-confidence is to be overcome. It is by persistently declaring to ourselves and confirming from the Word the truth that all our power comes from the Lord as we obey the commandments. The seven priests with the seven trumpets of ram's horn were to go before the ark around the city. A lamb represents innocence, or trust in the Lord. We associate the lamb with the kind of innocence which we find in little children before they begin to assert themselves. But if this quality is cherished and developed, it becomes a strong, beautiful trait of mature character which makes one want to protect and defend everything that is pure and good, and aid all people in the name of the Lord. The ram represents this strong kind of innocence, and his horns are the symbol of his power. When we "speak up" for the right against evil either in ourselves or in others, it is like blowing on a trumpet of ram's horn. Seven, the holy number, always pictures the fulfillment which comes after persistent struggle to do right. Only by steady determination to look to the Lord instead of to self can our natural selfish will be changed.

The curse on Jericho warns us against slipping back into former states. All through the Bible we are repeatedly taught that when we go back on any truth we have really acknowledged, we do ourselves lasting harm. This is what is called "profanation." The curse on Jericho was literally fulfilled (see I Kings 16:34).

Basic Correspondences

Joshua = truth fighting
a city = a system of doctrine
Jericho = the simplest understanding of the truth that everything is from

		the Lord; and in a bad sense the denial of this truth
the palm tree	=	the principle that victory over evil comes from the Lord
the ram	=	innocence which has developed and acquired strength
the trumpet of ram's horn	=	speaking up for the right

Senior

The whole sequence of events and their spiritual meaning should be carefully reviewed. The change from the period of reformation to that of regeneration is very important. Emphasis might also be placed on the command to preserve the gold and silver and other metals for the service of the Lord and to destroy everything else in the perverted city.

In chapter 2 of Joshua there is the incident of the spies sent by Joshua into Jericho before Israel crossed the Jordan. They were saved by Rahab the harlot, and they promised her that when Jericho fell, she and her family would be spared. We find in our chapter for today that Joshua fulfilled this promise. We note also that the silver and gold and the vessels of brass and iron which were found in Jericho were by the Lord's command saved and devoted to the Lord's service.

When we enter the Holy Land of spiritual living, the first enemy to be overcome is the false ideas about the Lord and spiritual things which we have in our minds. These cannot be overcome by our own power and intelligence, but only by looking to the Lord for direction and strength. This is pictured in the story of the fall of Jericho. We have probably been making preparation for this conquest ourselves, although we may not have recognized it as such. The story of the spies and the command in regard to the metals of Jericho describe part of this preparation. They teach us that the possibilities for good in our natural selfishness must be sought out and saved even when we fully surrender our wills to the Lord's guidance. Swedenborg tells us that there is a type of care for self and a type of self-controlled action and judgment which are good, that care which impels us to develop our capabilities for the purpose of more adequately serving the Lord and the neighbor and that we may study and understand better the Lord's teaching for the sake of obeying intelligently. The spies sent forward to explore Jericho, like those earlier sent by Moses to explore the Holy Land—of whom, we remember, Joshua himself was one—picture our thoughts which go forward and explore the possibilities of regeneration before regeneration actually takes place. The story of Rahab the harlot teaches us to remember that what seems outwardly bad may be inwardly good. We learn in our chapter that not only was Rahab saved but that she continued to dwell among the Israelites. Tradition says that she is the same person (Rachab or Rahab) mentioned in Matthew 1:5 as an ancestress of David. We should, of course, seek to live outwardly orderly lives, but the Lord looks on the heart.

Other preparations for the conquest were the setting up of the stones at Gilgal as a reminder of the Lord's aid (Joshua 4:1-3, 20) and the several incidents described in chapter 5. There we are told that at Gilgal all the males were circumcised, the Jewish symbol of purification and dedication to the Lord, corresponding to our baptism; the Passover was celebrated, the memorial of their deliverance from bondage in Egypt; and on the day after the Passover they began to eat the produce of the land and the manna ceased, picturing a new type of spiritual nourishment, in the production of which we cooperate with the Lord voluntarily. All the incidents inspire and strengthen the new willingness to trust in the Lord, and the conquest of Jericho itself completes the series.

This conquest was accomplished without a struggle on the part of Israel. The ark pictures obedience to the commandments; the trumpets of ram's horn, the voice of the Lord speaking with the power of unselfish love; and the reiteration of the number seven, perseverance in obedience until the holy state of willing service is reached. Then the people were told to shout with a great shout, and the walls of Jericho fell down flat. That is, by this persistent obedience we come into conjunction with the Lord and the walls built up within us by our natural self-esteem and self-love fall down flat, so that we can enter the city "every man straight before him." We are reminded of the fifth Psalm, so familiar to us as part of our morning service: "Lead me, O Lord, in thy righteousness because of mine enemies; make thy way straight before my face." A more detailed study of the fall of Jericho will be found in the quotation from the *Apocalypse Explained* below.

Adult

In this lesson the emphasis should be on the necessity of recognizing that all goodness and truth and all power to do right are from the Lord alone. This recognition is a constant factor in regenerate living, and without it there is no regeneration. No matter how orderly and benevolent and even religious the outward life may be, if we cling to feelings of self-esteem we have not even conquered Jericho.

The occupation of the Holy Land represents the achievement of truly spiritual living, in which the crossing of the Jordan and the taking of Jericho represent the first steps. It is hard for many people to see the difference between spiritual and natural living, especially if the natural living is charitable and orderly. Natural living is living for the pleasures and satisfactions of this life, even though these may not be merely physical enjoyments. There may even be recognition and worship of the Lord, but from a principle of obedience only, with hope of reward and fear of the consequences of evil as the principal motives in obeying. Spiritual living is living in conscious knowledge of the Lord and His purposes, substituting eternal for temporal values, trying to make and keep the mind and heart as well as the outward conduct pure in the sight of the Lord. For example, the natural man is likely to look upon his troubles in this world as sent by the Lord for his chastening, upon death as a calamity, upon success as measured in terms of the good things of this world, upon worship as a duty, upon those who injure him as his enemies and those who favor him as his friends. This is because he does not live in spiritual light. The spiritual man looks upon his troubles as opportunities for seeing and conquering his own evils, upon death as an orderly and happy step, upon success as measured in terms of the ability to help others, upon worship as a privilege, upon those who injure him and those who favor him alike as the Lord's children whom he should help to do right and, where possible, turn from wrongdoing. The natural man is content with general knowledge about the Lord, while the spiritual man loves to learn more and more. The natural man sets an orderly external life as his goal, but the spiritual man examines himself for deeper evils and tries to overcome them.

To become spiritual one must be born again, born of the spirit. Swedenborg says: "Before regeneration man acts from obedience; but after regeneration from affection." (AC 8505) A familiar hymn expresses this desire to become spiritual: "Give us to think as angels think, and feel as angels feel." A good test to apply to our thoughts and feelings is just that: Can I imagine an angel thinking and feeling as I do now? The Lord expressed the difference in this way: "Henceforth I call you not servants; for the servant knoweth not what his lord doeth: but I have called you friends; for all things that I have heard of my Father I have made known unto you." (John 15:15)

The Lord intends us all to live spiritual lives, to attain the Holy Land of heavenly character, to live within its borders. But we are born with all sorts of inherited tendencies to evil and falsity. These are the hostile peoples which occupied the Holy Land and the walled cities which had to be taken. For example, let anyone try genuinely to love his enemy and he will immediately become conscious of the foes which are settled within himself. It is comparatively easy to learn not to strike back—worldly prudence and even common politeness will teach us that—but it is not so easy to learn not to feel injured, not to allow the mind to dwell on the injury, but instead to think of the one who has injured us as someone needing our help. "A man's foes shall be they of his own household." (Matthew 10:36) We should accustom ourselves to thinking of all the evil peoples described in the Word as within ourselves—

not in somebody else. If we examine ourselves honestly, we shall soon pick out the "giants." Our "walled cities" are entrenchments of false reasonings by which we seek to defend these evils. This will light up for us the story of the taking of Jericho.

First we come to the Jordan as the means of entrance to the Holy Land. This wonderful river, whose name means "descender," rushing down from the snows of Hermon to lose itself finally in the Dead Sea, is in general a picture of the Lord's truth in the Word, coming down from Him through the heavens and then through the minds of men in various states until it touches the lowest possible state of life. As a border of the Holy Land it pictures especially the simple truths which introduce us to the spiritual life, and when the land is filled with evil people and the Jordan seems to oppose the entrance of the conquering host, it pictures the perversions of truth, the falsities which would keep us from engaging in battle against our inner foes—such falsities as "I can't help it; I was born that way," and, "You can't change human nature."

It should be noted that when the people entered the Holy Land, the manna ceased (Joshua 5:10-12). *The Sower* (Vol. 2, p. 24) puts very simply what is meant by this: "The manna represents the strength from the Lord in times of trial. It does not represent the full satisfaction of a life that has become altogether heavenly. That satisfaction is represented by the Passover in Canaan and by the old corn of the land, and when the people had eaten of this, the manna ceased." The occasional sense of spiritual satisfaction which we get during the process of reformation is merely a foretaste of the steady joy of heavenly living. People who live spiritually are happy with a deep, abiding happiness which no natural satisfaction can ever give. "These things have I spoken unto you, that my joy might remain in you, and that your joy might be full." (John 15:11)

There were three elements in the Lord's charge to Joshua (Joshua 1:6-9): (1) the cherishing of the law, (2) active, courageous attack upon the enemy, and (3) trust in the Lord's power to save. These are wonderfully carried out in the story of the crossing of Jordan and the conquest of Jericho. (1) It is the ark containing the commandments which leads the way across Jordan. The twelve stones from the Jordan, representing all the introductory truths, are set up for a memorial at Gilgal; the ark goes before the people as they compass the city of Jericho. (2) The priests bearing the ark are commanded to go forward straight into the river, and the river does not part until the feet of the priests have touched it. The sevenfold marching around Jericho represents a complete examination of the falsities which defend our inner evils. (3) The Jordan is parted by a miracle. The people are commanded to celebrate the Passover, the memorial of their miraculous deliverance from Egypt. Seven priests with seven trumpets of ram's horn, signifying the power of divine truth from divine good, are to go before the ark when they compass Jericho. Jericho is delivered to them by a miracle.

The conquest of Jericho in general represents the change from a feeling that we can indulge our evils with impunity to a sense that we are safe only in the care of the Lord. Jericho was called the "city of palm trees," and the palm is the symbol of the principle that salvation is from the Lord alone. This is the first lesson we must learn if we are to live spiritually. The sense of self-sufficiency, the tendency of self-esteem, the pride of self-intelligence—which are deeply entrenched within each one of us from our natural inheritance—must be recognized and overcome before we can go forward to face and root out our other evils and find our true homes in the heavenly land of promise. For the detailed correspondence of the story of the fall of Jericho, read the passage from *Apocalypse Explained* below.

From the Writings of Swedenborg

Apocalypse Explained, n. 700 d: "The 'city of Jericho' signifies instruction in the knowledges of good and truth, by which a man is brought into the church; for Jericho was a city not far from the Jordan, and that river signified introduction into the church. For all places in the land of Canaan were significative of things celestial and spiritual belonging to the church, and this from most ancient times; and as the sons of Israel were to represent the church, and among them the Word was written, in which those places were to be mentioned signifying such things as are of heaven and the church, the sons of Israel were brought into it, and their introduction was signified by 'the river Jordan,' and their instruction by 'Jericho.' And as 'Jericho' signified instruction it signified also good of life, because unless one is in good of life he cannot be instructed in truths of doctrine. But when the land of Canaan was held by idolatrous nations the signification of the places and cities in that land was changed into the opposite, Jericho then signifying the profanation of truth and good. From this it follows that the 'city' itself signified the doctrine of falsity and evil, which perverted and profaned the truths and goods of the church, its 'wall' signifying falsities of evil defending that doctrine, and the 'inhabitants' those who are profane; and as all profaneness is from infernal love after acknowledgment of truth and good, the city was burned with fire, the inhabitants given to the curse, and its wall overthrown, 'fire' signifying infernal love, 'curse' a total blotting out, and 'the overthrow of the wall' exposure to evil and falsity. The sounding of the trumpets by the priests signified the proclamation of Divine truth from Divine good; the shouting and acclamation of the people signified consent and confirmation; compassing of the city signified a survey of falsity and evil and their dispersion by an influx of Divine truth from the Lord; this influx was signified by carrying the ark about it. The priests were seven in number, and the city was compassed seven days, seven times on the seventh day, to signify what is holy, and the holy proclamation of Divine truth, 'seven' signifying holiness, and in the contrary sense profaneness, and as there was holiness on the one part and profaneness on the other, there were seven priests with seven trumpets, and the city was compassed seven times. The gold, the silver, and vessels of brass and iron, were put into the treasury of the house of Jehovah, because these signified knowledges of spiritual and natural truth and good, 'gold and silver' knowledges of spiritual truth and good, which with those who profane are changed into dreadful falsities and evils; but as they continue to be knowledges, although adapted to evils, they are serviceable to the good by application to what is good, and therefore these things were put into the treasury of the house of Jehovah."

Suggested Questions on the Lesson

P. What river separated the Israelites from the Holy Land? *Jordan*

J. How did they cross it? *miracle*

J. Where was their first camp in the Holy Land? *Gilgal*

P. What feast did they celebrate there? *Passover*

J. What change was made in their food? *manna ceased*

P. What was the first strong city they had to conquer? *Jericho*

P. What did the Lord tell them to carry around the city? *the ark*

P. How many priests were to go before the ark? *seven*

J. What were they to carry? *ram's horn trumpets*

P. How many times were they to march around the city each day for six days? *once*

P. How many times were they to march around it on the seventh day? *seven*

P. What happened when they finally blew the trumpets and shouted? *walls fell*

J. What did they save out of the city? *Rahab and family, all metals*

J. What did they do with everything else in it? *destroyed it*

J. What curse was pronounced against Jericho? *rebuilder will lose two sons*

I. What does entrance into the Holy Land represent? *beginning regenerate life*

S. What does Jericho represent? *natural self-confidence*

S. Why did the Lord overcome Jericho in this way? *to show that such tendencies can only be conquered by the Lord's power*

THE CAPTURE OF AI

Joshua 7; 8

The teacher will need to review carefully chapters 2-6 and prepare himself to tell briefly the story of the events contained in those chapters. The emphasis in this summary should be on the fact that the Lord was showing the people His power to give them victory, and warning them against trusting in themselves or allowing the thought to linger in their minds that their victories were in any sense theirs. Then make the transition to today's lesson by calling attention to the Lord's command as to the spoils of Jericho.

Doctrinal Points

The Lord wants us to enjoy the good things of this world, but not to put them first. He created the world for our happiness.

We must give up the thought that we can know the truth of ourselves without constantly learning it from the Lord through the Word.

We must examine our motives systematically according to the truth.

Notes for Parents

Most people know the story of the fall of Jericho, the first city which the Israelites took in the Holy Land—how they marched around the city led by the priests bearing the ark until, on the seventh day, the walls of the city fell without a blow having been struck. The victory was given to them in this way to teach them beyond a doubt that it was the Lord who gave them victory and that obedience to His commands would always result in success.

Not so many know the story of the capture of Ai, the next city, but it is given in the Bible to teach the same lesson from another point of view—the failure which results from disobedience and the need of being sure that we obey the Lord wholly and do not try to hold onto any of our favorite sins. This is a temptation we all have. We are willing to get rid of the faults in ourselves which are obvious and which we can see stand in the way of our success. But we cannot see just why the Lord tells us that some other things we do are wrong and must be given up; they "look good" to us, and we try to enjoy them in secret even if we give them up openly. This is like Achan's taking some of the forbidden spoils of Jericho.

People often cannot see why Achan's family should have been destroyed when only Achan was the offender. There are many places in the Bible where it says the Lord commanded the destruction of apparently innocent people just because they were connected with someone who was evil. People in those days were cruel, and we saw in the story of Abraham's sacrifice how the Lord's truth took on the forms of thought of the person to whom it came. We ourselves do not kill a criminal's family, but we sometimes are equally cruel to them in other ways. In the Bible the Lord used the things in people's minds to illustrate lessons. The family is a picture of all the things which spring from some desire or affection and its corresponding thought. For example, when we have an evil desire—perhaps the desire to hurt someone—all the thoughts and feelings which come from it are bad. So when we recognize that our desire is evil and decide to get rid of it, we must also try to get rid of all the thoughts and feelings which have come from it; this is symbolized by Achan's family in the story. We need to remember that everything in the Word is a picture of something in us, and that all the wars and battles and killings are pictures of the struggles which we have with the enemies within our own souls. We must not, as Joshua at first did, blame the Lord for our failures. Our real enemies are within ourselves. This is what the Lord means when he says, "A man's foes shall be they of his own household." (Matthew 10:36)

Primary

Center the story for this class around the figure of Achan rather than the attack on Ai. They can get the idea that when we come into difficulties, we should first of all look for what may have been wrong with us, rather than blaming someone else. Show the children why Achan's fault was so serious. They can see it as an illustration of two things they themselves might do: disobey, and hide their disobedience. Achan's sin was not immediately found out, but it led to trouble later which did uncover it, and his punishment was heavy. Disobedience always leads to trouble, and hiding it makes things worse.

Do you remember that the spies sent shortly after Israel left Egypt told the people that there were walled cities in the Holy Land which they would have to conquer?

Now Joshua and the people have crossed the Jordan River, which the Lord parted for them just as He had parted the waters of the Red Sea, and they are beginning to attack these walled cities. The first one they captured was Jericho. They did not have to fight to conquer that one. The Lord told them to march around the city, following the ark which the priests carried, once every day for seven days and seven times on the seventh day, and after they had done this, He made the walls of the city fall down flat. And they were told to destroy everything they found in Jericho except the gold and silver and the vessels of brass and iron, and all these they were to devote to the service of the Lord. They were to take nothing for themselves.

Did they all obey?
Who disobeyed?
What had Achan taken?
What defeat did they suffer because of this disobedience?
How did they find out who had done the wrong?
According to the law Achan and his whole family were destroyed.

After that Joshua made careful plans for capturing the city of Ai. He sent part of the fighting men to hide near the west side of the city—on the side toward Bethel. Do you remember anything about Bethel? Then in the morning he led the rest of the army to attack the city. When the men of Ai came out to meet them, they pretended to run away again, and the men of Ai chased them away from the city. Then the men who were hiding came out and took the city and set it on fire, and Joshua and his men turned on their pursuers and attacked and destroyed them.

What did they do at Shechem?

Read Deuteronomy 27:1-8 to see why they did this.

This story is one which we should remember because it teaches us that when things do not go as we want them to go, the first thing to do is not to blame other people or the Lord, but to see if we ourselves have done anything wrong.

Junior

After the summary of previous events, cover the story for the day briefly, and then have the children find on a map all the places mentioned; then look up all the references to previous stories concerning these places. This will help to fix important facts in their minds. They will be interested in the difference between the two attacks on Ai, and in what happened at Shechem. At this age they also need to have the killing of Achan's family explained.

When the Lord gave the directions for the taking of Jericho, He told the Israelites that they were to take none of the spoils of the city for themselves. Everybody and everything in Jericho was to be destroyed except the gold and silver and the vessels of brass and iron, and these were to be consecrated to the service of the Lord.

Who disobeyed this command?
What did he take?
What happened to the people because of Achan's disobedience?

There are two places mentioned in our story today of which we have read before: Shechem and Bethel. You remember that when Abraham first came down into the Holy Land, he stopped at Shechem and set up an altar there, and then went on and built another altar near Bethel, "having Bethel on the west, and Hai on the east" (Genesis 12:6-8). *Hai* (KJV) is the same as the *Ai* of our lesson today, and we want to remember that the ambush of which the second chapter of our lesson speaks was laid on the side of Ai toward Bethel. Bethel is also the place where Abraham and Lot separated, and where Jacob had his dream.

What does the word *Bethel* mean?

Why did the people think they could take Ai easily?
What did Joshua do when his men fled from Ai?
What did the Lord say to him?
How did they find out who was to blame?

Their casting lots made sure that the Lord would point out the true offender. To us it seems very cruel to kill the man's whole family because he had done wrong. People were cruel in those days, and the Lord used this fact to teach us something. When we get into trouble and ask the Lord sincerely to help us find out just what is the wrong thing in our hearts which caused the trouble, the Lord will always show us what it is, and then we must get rid of both it and all the wrong ideas which came from it. This is "Achan's family." Suppose, for example, we find that we have let ourselves become jealous of some friend. Jealousy produces a whole train of bad thoughts about the person. When we acknowledge our jealousy and put it away, we must hunt out the bad thoughts and put them away, too.

Joshua had been overconfident in his first attack on Ai, but he had learned a lesson. So he put his whole army into the second attack and used his head in the planning of it. All the enemies which the children of Israel found in the Holy Land picture bad things which lie hidden in us and have to be overcome one after another. Sometimes when we overcome one temptation, we begin to think we are pretty good, and often it takes a defeat to show us that we need to put all our mind and heart into the battle every time. And we need to look to the Lord for help, too. This is the ambush toward Bethel.

Read Deuteronomy 27:1-8 as a background for understanding the last part of our lesson. Shechem was the very center of the Holy Land. It lay between two mountains, Mount Ebal and Mount Gerizim. There is a natural amphitheater there which is one of the places—like the rotunda of our Capitol in Washington—where one can stand in the center and make even a whisper heard on the sides higher up. So the altar which Joshua set up there was just the place from which to read the law, because the tribes on the slopes of the two mountains on either side could hear.

Shechem was the place where they buried the bones of Joseph, which they had carried with them all through the wilderness journey. Read Genesis 50:25-26 and Joshua 24:32. Another very famous event took place at Shechem hundreds of years later. Read John 4:4-7 (Sychar is the same as Shechem). Shechem was also the center of a revolt in the time of King David.

Intermediate

The general correspondence of the whole story should be given, with emphasis on the meaning of Achan's trespass and the meaning of the ambush. Call attention to the setting up of the stones and celebration of the Passover at Gilgal and the setting up of the altar and reading of the law at Shechem.

Joshua obeyed the Lord. His obedience was immediately tested in the story of the crossing of the Jordan. The river was at flood, but the people were not to travel north to one of the fords. They were to go straight into the water. As soon as the foot of the first priest touched the brink of the river, the waters parted before them, just as the waters of the Red Sea had parted, and they went through on dry ground. The priests with the ark stood still in the middle of the river bed until all the people had passed over. Twelve men, one chosen from each tribe, picked up one stone each from the midst of the river bed, and when they reached the other side the stones were set up as a memorial of their crossing. They also celebrated the Passover at this time, and the manna ceased. They named the place *Gilgal*, which means "rolling," because the Lord told Joshua (Joshua 5:9) that on this day He had "rolled away the reproach of Egypt" from them. Then follows the familiar story of the taking of Jericho, when by simple and exact obedience to the Lord they were enabled to conquer without fighting at all, because the Lord caused the walls to fall down. The walled cities they found in the Holy Land represent false ideas which have grown up in our minds as the result of our natural selfishness. The Lord's truth is able to overcome those false ideas if we will obey it.

In the conquest of Jericho, however, one man disobeyed part of the Lord's command. The Israelites had been told (Joshua 6:18-19) not to take from the city anything for themselves. Everything was to be destroyed except the silver and gold and the vessels of brass and iron, and these were to be consecrated to the service of the Lord. It takes us a long time to realize that we must try to obey the Lord wholly. We can see that some of our faults are really bad and should be corrected, but there are always some that we feel are excusable—they bring us so much pleasure. Sometimes we are even proud of some fault. Perhaps you have heard someone say, "Oh, I have a terrible temper!" as if it made him important. In other words, we tend to keep the faults we really like, although we sometimes try to hide them. This is what Achan's sin pictures.

Jericho was down near the level of the river and pictures some evil in us which is obvious to us as soon as we begin to examine ourselves; so we are willing to accept the Lord's commands and try hard to get rid of it. But the next city in the way of the Israelites, Ai, was different. It was up in the hills near Bethel. You remember that Abram, when he first came into the Holy Land, built an altar at Shechem in the center of the land and then went on and built another altar near Bethel, between Bethel and Hai. (Hai [KJV] is the Ai of our story today.) Bethel, where Jacob had his dream of the way of steps leading to heaven, means "house of God." It pictures our knowledge of spiritual things; it is in this knowledge that the Lord dwells in our minds. Ai, its companion city, pictures our knowledge of natural things. In our story Ai is inhabited by the enemy, which means that we have been using our knowledge of natural things selfishly, so that instead of helping us on our way to Bethel it stands in our way. The spies whom Joshua sent out reported that Ai was not a strong city and that the whole army would not be needed to take it, and the small army that Joshua sent against it was promptly put to rout. When, with the Lord's help, we have won the first victory over our temptations, we sometimes become overconfident and imagine we are going straight ahead victoriously without any further thought or self-examination.

We think we know enough, not realizing that some of the things we know may be a hindrance to us instead of a help. When the next temptation comes, we form a "snap judgment" as to what we ought to do, and we are defeated. We are liable, like Joshua, to be discouraged by this setback, but the Lord tells us, just as He told Joshua, that the trouble is in ourselves and that we must not give up because of it. We must examine ourselves more deeply to see just where we have done wrong. The true process of self-examination is vividly described in the story of the finding of the sinner Achan by lot. To decide anything by lot is to let the Lord's truth be the judge; that is, to judge ourselves according to the truths of the Word. And we should do this systematically, first thinking of our general principles and gradually getting down to particular wrong things we may have been feeling and thinking, and rooting them out. Achan's hiding the forbidden things in the earth of his tent is a picture of how such secret evils may be hidden at the very center of our life. When they are destroyed, we can return to the attack. This time we shall put our whole strength into it and if we are wise we shall, like Joshua, plan to use some of our "men" as a reserve on the side toward Bethel; that is, we shall realize that our real power comes from our knowledge of spiritual things and try to apply this knowledge. We notice that the spoil of Ai could be taken; it did not have to be destroyed or devoted to the formal service of the Lord. This is because our natural knowledges in themselves are good and can be useful if we do not pride ourselves on them or use them selfishly.

The building of the altar at Shechem, Abraham's first stopping place in the Holy Land, and the rehearsing there of the law with its blessings and cursings remind us that no matter what victories we win we need over and over again to return to the "little child" state of humility and worship, and to keep the commandments always before us as the laws of life.

Basic Correspondences

walled cities	=	firmly entrenched truths or falsities
Bethel	=	knowledges of celestial things

Ai = natural knowledges
casting lots = letting the Lord's truth decide

Senior

Two common failings of young people of this age are too much self-confidence and the tendency to underestimate others. Both these failings are illustrated in this story. The necessity of trust in the Lord instead of in self, of occasional thorough self-examination in the light of the Lord's truth, and of trying with all one's might to overcome each fault with the help of the Lord should be stressed.

All rivers in the Bible represent moving or living truth of some sort. The Jordan, as a boundary of the Holy Land, represents those basic truths such as the commandments which define the limits of a religious life. At first they seem to be a barrier to the person seeking to lead a truly spiritual life—just as the Jordan stood in the way of the Israelites. But with faith in God and willingness to go forward and try to live according to basic Christian teachings, we find that the Lord opens a way for us—just as He parted the Jordan—and we enter the Canaan of heavenly living without harm. Then the Jordan returns to its normal flow and, spiritually, becomes a protecting force, forever defining for us "the steps of a good man" (Psalms 37:23). The truth will now lead us in battle against our inner foes, but there are certain lessons which need to be impressed upon us at the start. So the first stories in the period of the conquest are all stories warning us against self-confidence. First there is the setting up of the stones from the river bed at Gilgal and the celebration of the Passover there—both reminders of the fact that the Lord is our Savior. Then there is the conquest of Jericho entirely by the Lord's power. The walls fell not under the blows of the Israelites but through the power of the ark. Jericho in the hands of enemies pictures "the profanation of good and truth," and good and truth are profaned when we ascribe them to ourselves once we know better. The Israelites were warned not to take any of the spoils of Jericho for themselves, because we must not retain any of the thought or feeling that we are good or wise if we are to go further in the heavenly life.

Then comes the story of Ai. In this story all the Israelites were threatened with defeat because of the disobedience of one man. This seems hard, but when we study the inner meaning, we recognize it as inevitable. We have all had the experience of failing in some worthy attempt because of some one hasty word or action which revealed a hidden flaw in our motives.

Bethel, the "house of God," where Abraham set up his second altar and where Jacob had his dream, pictures a doctrine or philosophy of life based on knowledge of God and spiritual things. Ai, the twin city of Bethel, pictures a philosophy based on knowledges of the natural world. In *Apocalypse Explained*, n. 655[8] Swedenborg says that Ai signifies "the knowledges of good and in the contrary sense the confirmations of evil." We all know very well that our natural knowledges can be used either for selfish or for unselfish purposes. When Ai is occupied by the enemy and standing in the way of our approach to Bethel, it must be conquered and its evil inhabitants destroyed. The general meaning of our story is that the false philosophy built upon natural knowledges alone cannot be rooted out so long as we cherish—even in the recesses of our hearts, the "earth of the tent"—anything of the spoils of Jericho, any remnants of the belief that we can achieve the truth for ourselves. The "goodly Babylonish garment" suggests self-righteousness, the attitude which says, "I am wise; everyone who disagrees with me must be foolish or evil." The two hundred shekels of silver and the wedge of gold are the true thoughts and good desires we have for which we take credit to ourselves instead of attributing them to the Lord.

Achan means "troubler." The regenerating life easily discards what is obviously contrary to the commandments, but it is constantly tried and troubled by the pride and self-will which still lurk in the heart and are discovered only when they lead to outward calamity. And when we fail, we are all prone at first to blame the Lord instead of ourselves. "And Joshua rent his clothes, and fell to the earth upon his face . . . And Joshua said, Alas, O Lord God, wherefore hast thou at all brought this people over Jordan?"

But the Lord says to us, as to Joshua, "Get thee up; wherefore liest thou thus upon thy face? Israel hath sinned."

The searching out of the hidden sin by means of truth is pictured in the account of the discovery of the "troubler" by a succession of lots. We must examine first our general attitudes, then our attitudes toward more and more specific matters, until we get down to the particular thing which is wrong with us at the moment and destroy it. After Achan was destroyed, Ai was again attacked, but this time there was no self-confidence. The strategy was based on the placing of a large body of men in ambush on the side of the city toward Bethel. Then when the men of the city came out to attack and pursue the Israelites, those in ambush fell upon the city and set it afire, catching the men of Ai between two forces. The company placed in ambush toward Bethel pictures the hidden reserves of strength which come from spiritual knowledge. We by our own reasoning cannot meet the attack of worldly arguments; but reinforced by spiritual knowledge, whose power the worldly minded do not suspect, we can easily conquer. We note that the Israelites were allowed to keep the spoil of Ai. Natural knowledges are useful to us. It is only the principle that they are all-important which must be destroyed.

This victory is properly followed—before any further conquests are undertaken—by the setting up of the altar at Shechem in the center of the land and the proclamation of the law there, with the response of the people to the reading of the blessings and curses. We need again and again to remind ourselves that we stand or fall spiritually according to whether we obey or disobey the Word.

Adult

The way in which all the incidents of the first weeks of the conquest center about our need for humility and trust in the Lord offers a good opening for discussion. A brief quiz on the events connected with the cities of Jericho, Bethel, Ai, and Shechem may be rewarding. We often think we know our Bible story better than we do. The fate of Achan and his family and the meaning of the ambush toward Bethel are also fruitful topics.

We remind ourselves that the conquest of the Holy Land pictures the searching out and conquest of the evils and falsities within ourselves which stand in the way of our being truly heavenly people. There were, we recall, two elements in the Lord's charge to Joshua as found in Joshua 1:6-9: active, courageous attack upon the enemy, and the cherishing of the law. For the carrying out of these charges absolute trust in the Lord's power was essential, and the first incidents in the occupation of the Holy Land were designed to impress this upon the people. It was the ark containing the commandments which led them across Jordan, and the Jordan was parted by a miracle. The twelve stones from the Jordan, representing all the introductory truths, were set up for a memorial at Gilgal, and there they celebrated the Passover, the feast which commemorated their deliverance from bondage in Egypt. Then Jericho was delivered to them by a miracle, the ark again going before them, and they were commanded that none of the spoils of the city be taken for themselves, but that all should be destroyed except the gold and silver and vessels of brass and iron, which should be consecrated to the service of the Lord. We "conquer Jericho" when we see in ourselves and reject the feeling of self-sufficiency and security in wrongdoing which profanes the truth that the Lord alone saves and that we of ourselves are incapable of doing good–a general truth which we must recognize if we are to advance in spiritual living.

Ai, further up in the hills, is the next entrenchment of the enemy to which we come. In AC 1453, in connection with Abraham's stop between Bethel and Ai on his first passage through the Holy Land, Swedenborg says that Ai represents knowledges of worldly things; and in AE 655[8] he says that in the opposite sense Ai represents "confirmation of evil," and refers for proof to Jeremiah 49:3-4. The story of the defeat at Ai and its cause shows us a very common tendency, one to which we are all subject: that is, the tendency to rest satisfied with a general recognition of our weakness and sinfulness, and to feel that this general confession enables us to be safe in choosing our own way. Swedenborg tells us that we should indeed make this general confession sincerely, but that this is not enough. We must go on to search out specific evils in ourselves and look to the Lord for knowledge and strength to overcome them. This is what the Lord tells us in the story of Ai. When we secretly cherish some pet evil, as Achan took what appealed to him most in the spoil of Jericho and hid it in the earth in the midst of his tent, we are confirming that evil in ourselves, and so cannot conquer Ai—which represents just such confirmation of evil. How often children will offer to do anything except the one thing which their parents wish them to do. And grown-up children behave in the same way. They do not think much of the strength of Ai and so do not feel it necessary to fight it with all their might—"make not all the people to labor thither"—and so they fail. The command to keep none of the spoil of Jericho for ourselves means that we are to give up our own desires and thoughts whenever we see that they are not in accordance with the Lord's love and truth. The goodly Babylonish garment pictures the flattering thought that we ourselves are good—perhaps the thought that after all we are pretty good to have chosen to follow the Lord at all when some other people have not. The silver and gold are the truths and the good affections which we ascribe to ourselves.

When we find ourselves yielding to temptation and getting into difficulties, we are likely at first to blame everyone but ourselves—even to blame the Lord. Joshua said, "Alas, O Lord God, wherefore hast thou at all brought this people over Jordan, to deliver us into the hand of the Amorites, to destroy us?" But the Lord says to us, as to Joshua, "Get thee up; wherefore liest thou upon thy face? Israel hath sinned." And He tells us in plain language: "Thou canst not stand before thine enemies, until ye take away the accursed thing from among you." The method of discovering the offender is very suggestive. In the first place, it is by lot, the decision being left in the Lord's hands. This tells us that we must examine our lives according to the Lord's truth and not according to any imagined wisdom of our own or of other men. Then the people are brought first tribe by tribe, then family by family, household by household, man by man. This suggests an orderly and thorough self-examination, beginning with general affections and working down gradually to more specific ones until the particular evil which is being cherished is discovered. Swedenborg tells us that we should examine ourselves thus thoroughly before we come to the Lord's Supper. The evil must then be confessed, subjected to the judgment of the Lord's truth and good, and wholly rejected, together with all the evils and falsities which have come from it, as Achan and his whole family were stoned with stones and burned with fire. "And they raised over him a great heap of stones unto this day" suggests the clinching of the matter with truths from the Word, which will prevent that particular evil from rising within us again and keep us reminded of its consequences.

After the death of Achan, the Israelites went about the conquest of Ai in a very different spirit, looking to the Lord for help and making careful plans. The ambush toward Bethel reminds us of the secret strength from the Lord which is with us when we try to obey Him, just as the horses and chariots of fire were round about Elisha (II Kings 6:8-17). The apparent flight, as at first, is the humble recognition that we have no strength of our own. The drawing of the enemy out of their city and away from it is the separation of evils from the false reasonings which protect and defend them, so that they may be clearly seen and overcome. As Ai in a good sense represents "knowledge of worldly things," there are goods and truths connected with it, even in its perverted state, which may be singled out and appropriated; so Israel was allowed to take of the spoil of Ai. But the king, the ruling principle of evil, must be put to death, together with all the people.

The conclusion of chapter 8 is especially interesting in connection with the victory of Ai. Israel fulfills the command of Moses by going to the valley between Mount Ebal and Mount Gerizim and renewing the solemn covenant. In order to get the whole picture in the letter we need to read Deuteronomy 27:11-13. In William Worcester's book *On Holy Ground* there are interesting photographs of the natural amphitheater at this place, and he says of it: "It is a remarkable valley; all travelers who climb the mountain-sides are surprised at the distinctness with which sounds and voices from the city below are heard. At the highest part of the valley there is a recess in the mountain on either side which seems as if made by nature for the gathering of the tribes, six on each side of the valley. Here they listened to the law as Joshua read it, and answered, Amen, from the side of Ebal, to the curses, and from Gerizim, to the blessings." Shechem, which is associated with first instruction in heavenly life, is situated in this valley. There Abraham made his first stop when he came into the Holy Land from Haran. He built his first altar there. Jacob also built an altar there and bought a piece of ground which he afterward gave to Joseph (Genesis 33:18-20; 48:21-22; Joshua 24:32). The bones of Joseph were to be buried there. This is also the site of Jacob's well, on which the Lord sat when He talked with the woman of Samaria (John 4:4-7). The rehearsal of the law and renewal of the covenant, coming as they do between the first victories and the further campaigns, teach us our need of returning regularly to the childlike state of openness to instruction and in this spirit reading the Word, meditating upon it, and renewing our pledges to the Lord as we pass from state to state in regeneration.

From the Writings of Swedenborg

Arcana Coelestia, n. 8391: "He who leads a life of faith does repentance daily; for he reflects upon the evils that are in him; acknowledges them, guards himself against them, and supplicates the Lord for aid."

Arcana Coelestia, n. 8394: "After a man has examined himself, and has acknowledged his sins, and has done repentance, he must remain constant in good up to the end of life. If however he afterward falls back into his former life of evil, and embraces it, he commits profanation, for he then conjoins evil with good, and consequently his latter state becomes worse than his former one." (See Matthew 12:43-45.)

Suggested Questions on the Lesson

J. What was the first city the Israelites had to conquer? *Jericho*
P. How did the Lord help them to take it? *made walls fall*
P. What command did the Lord give them as to the spoils of Jericho? *not to take any for themselves*
P. What was the next city they had to take? *Ai*
J. How did Joshua at first try to take it? *small army*
J. What did he do when his army fled? *fell on face, tore clothes, blamed God*
P. What did the Lord tell him? *someone had sinned*
P. How did they find the offender? *drew lots*
P. Who was he? *Achan*
J. What had he done? *taken garment, gold, silver*
J. How was he punished? *stoned, burned*
J. How much of the army did Joshua use in the second attack on Ai? *all*
J. What did he do with part of his men? *hid as ambush*
J. What was done with the spoils of Ai? *people could take*
P. What did they do at Shechem? *built altar, wrote and read laws*
I. What does the sin of Achan picture? *feeling some of our faults are excusable*
I. What lesson does it teach? *don't blame God, or others, when you get into trouble*
S. What is the meaning of the ambush? *using reserve strength we have from our knowledge of spiritual things*

THE GIBEONITES

Joshua 9

The lesson should be introduced by emphasis on the fact that when the Israelites returned to the Holy Land from Egypt, they found the land full of enemies, but the Lord had promised them victory if they obeyed Him. The teacher should be prepared to tell briefly the story of the fall of Jericho and the capture of Ai. The older pupils may be able to tell these stories themselves.

Doctrinal Points

The Lord knows our weaknesses and takes them into account as He makes provision for us.

The Word teaches us the truth about ourselves.

Our obedience is the measure of our faith.

When we have made a mistake, we must take the consequences and make the best of them.

Notes for Parents

In the book of Revelation, chapter 21, we read how an angel was sent to John to show him the holy city. The angel had a golden reed to measure the city and found its length, breadth, and height to be equal, and its measurement is said to be "according to the measure of a man, that is, of the angel." People have always recognized the holy city in Revelation, like the Holy Land in the Old Testament, as a symbol of heaven. Heaven is possible for each one of us not only after we die but within our hearts and minds while we live here. There is a potential angel within each one of us whose measure is the measure of heaven. Our task in this world is to try to "measure up" to our spiritual possibilities.

Yet each one of us is different from every other. Each of us is born with certain inherited abilities and certain inherited limitations. Our Holy Land, like the land of Canaan which Joshua set out to conquer, is full of enemies trying to check our spiritual progress. The story of the Gibeonites is a picture of how the Lord takes into account our weaknesses and enables us to recognize and make use of them, if we try. Like Joshua with the Gibeonites we are sometimes deceived about our natural tendencies, thinking some of them to be friends which are really enemies. So we accept them as part of our character just as Joshua made a league with the Gibeonites.

Take, for example, the love of "knowing other people's business" which we all have to some extent. This seems to us often to be a desire which, being born in us—coming, like the Gibeonites from the far country of our ancestry—should be accepted as a proper faculty without question. We do not at first see it as a possible enemy. When we do realize that it is a weakness to be dealt with, the Lord will, if we ask His help, show us how to put it in its place, making it serve our heavenly purpose of being of use to our neighbors. We all know the difference between watching and studying others in a critical spirit or from idle curiosity and doing the same thing from a desire to find out their needs and see how we may help them.

The Lord knows the measure of the angel in each one of us; and if we look to Him with willingness to acknowledge our weaknesses, He will help us to grow day by day closer to our true heavenly stature.

Primary

Your introduction should be given as an explanation of why the Gibeonites were afraid of the Israelites and wanted to make peace with them. The lesson to be drawn from the story is that we are all easily deceived by the way things seem to us at first glance and that we should never make careless promises. Emphasize the need to stop and think whether a thing is right or not before promising to do it.

When the children of Israel crossed the Jordan River into the Holy Land, the land was full of enemies and there were many strong walled cities which they had to conquer. The city nearest the place where they crossed the river was Jericho, and perhaps you remember how the Lord told them to carry the ark around the city once a day for six days and then seven times on the seventh day, and how the Lord then made the walls fall down so that they could go in and take the city. After that the Lord showed Joshua how to take another city named Ai.

When these two cities fell, the inhabitants of the land were frightened.
What people decided to try to make peace with Israel?
How did they deceive Joshua?
Joshua had been told by the Lord to conquer all the people of the land.
When the Gibeonites came to him, what did he forget to do?
Joshua made a hasty and careless promise.
Do we ever do the same thing?
Before we make a promise, we should always stop to think and to be sure that what we are promising is right.
But Joshua knew that he could not break his promise once it was made.
He had to let the Gibeonites live.

Joshua had made a mistake. So Joshua had to make the best of what he had done. He let the Gibeonites live and did not destroy their cities, but he punished them for lying to him by making them servants of the Israelites forever—hewers of wood and drawers of water.

Junior

Deal in this class with the connecting material and also with the origin of the evil peoples in the land, especially the Hivites. Have the class look up the Bible references. This helps to give them a sense of the continuity of the Bible story and forms a basis for later instruction. The moral lesson in the story for today is one which the Juniors need.

Read in Joshua 8:30-35 how Joshua obeyed the command Moses had given in Deuteronomy 27:1-13 and set up an altar between Mount Ebal and Mount Gerizim and read the book of the law to the people there. This was the same place where Abraham set up his first altar when he came from Ur to the land of Canaan.

You remember that the children of Israel had been in Egypt for about two hundred and fifty years. During that time the idol-worshipers who lived in the land of Canaan had increased so that the land was full of enemies whom Joshua would have to conquer. The fall of Jericho and Ai filled all these people with fear because they trusted in their strong cities, and all through the land they were preparing to resist Joshua. But there was one nation in the land which preferred to make peace with the Israelites. These were the people who lived in four cities in the center of the land, one of them not far from Jerusalem, the cities of Gibeon, Chephirah, Beeroth, and Kirjathjearim. These people were Hivites. The Hivites are mentioned first in Genesis 10:17, where they are said to be descendants of Canaan, one of the sons of Ham the son of Noah. The Canaanites lived in the Holy Land and gave their name to it. There were a number of tribes of them and they were enemies of Israel, but the groups called the Hittites and the Hivites were more inclined than the rest to make peace. There are several stories in the Bible which show this.

Noah and his sons belonged to the second church on earth, the Ancient Church, and this church especially loved knowledge or truth. At first it loved the truth for the sake of living according to it, but the good motive gradually died out. You know some people like to learn a great many facts about everything without ever making use of them. The Hivites in our lesson were such people. The trick they played on Joshua was not honest, but it was better than it would have been for them to fight him.

What did they tell Joshua about themselves?
How did they make him believe it?

The wine "bottles" of the Holy Land were skins, usually of goats, not bottles as we think of them; so even these could be made to look old.

Joshua made a serious mistake. See if you can find what it was by reading verse 14. He formed his judgment in this case according to "appearances"; that is, he judged hastily by the way things looked on the outside. If he had taken counsel of the Lord, the Lord could have shown him the truth which was hidden under the appearances. Do we ever form hasty judgments in this way and then find out that we have been mistaken?

We all do make such mistakes, and when we do, we should acknowledge them and try to make the best of it. If we face them honestly, the Lord can use our mistakes to teach us our weaknesses and so to make us better. Can you see how Joshua's mistake was used? You know that water represents truth. Wood pictures external good deeds like feeding the hungry and helping people to be more healthy and comfortable in the world. We need knowledge of facts to help us perform good deeds and also to understand the truth about things. This was why the Gibeonites were made to serve the Israelites as hewers of wood and drawers of water.

But wrong things always have bad consequences also. In the very next chapter we find that because the Gibeonites had made peace with Joshua, the other people in the land made war on them, and because Joshua had made a league with them he had to go to their assistance. So when we act hastily, we often bring upon ourselves consequences which we did not expect.

Intermediate

The correspondence of the ruse of the Gibeonites is simple and is helpful in showing how a thing which in the letter is wrong may in its internal meaning be truth.

The Israelites retained their camp at Gilgal for some time, but not long after they celebrated the Passover there and had conquered the two strong cities of Jericho and Ai, they made a pilgrimage to Shechem to fulfill a command given by Moses. (You will find it in the twenty-seventh chapter of Deuteronomy.) You may remember that Shechem was the first place where Abraham stopped when he came into the Holy Land from Ur, and that he built an altar there. Now Joshua also builds an altar there (8:30) and reads the book of the law to the people. The place was a natural amphitheater between two mountains, Ebal and Gerizim, and the people divided, six tribes standing on the slopes of Ebal and six on the slopes of Gerizim, as Moses had decreed, and said "Amen" to the laws as they were read. Then they went back to Gilgal.

The nations which lived in the Holy Land at this time were all—except the giants—remnants of the Ancient Church. We remember that this was a spiritual church, whose principal delight was the study of correspondences, and that it perished because it perverted its knowledge by using it for self-exaltation. Its end is described in the story of the Tower of Babel. Swedenborg tells us that the people of the Ancient Church made images of things in nature and set them up as reminders of the spiritual things to which they correspond, and that when they became selfish and began to lose their spiritual knowledges, they fell into the worship of the images themselves, and so idolatry sprang up and with their dispersion was spread all over the earth. (See AC 1241, SS 23.)

But there are always among all nations people who sin because of ignorance rather than from evil desires and who are not opposed to the truth when it is presented to them. The Gibeonites did not join with the other nations in the Holy Land in resistance to Israel. Instead they sought to make peace with them. Their method was in the letter dishonest, but their intent was sincere—as their later conduct proved.

And in the internal meaning their statements were true. The "far country" they came from was the Ancient Church. The "bread" was the spiritual good which had been warm and fresh when they started, and had grown dry and moldy as they wandered from true worship. The "wine-skins" were their doctrines, which had been strong and true once but were now unfit to hold new truth (read Matthew 9:17). The "old patched garments and shoes" were their understanding of right ways of living, which had declined through the years.

The Gibeonites represent the desire for knowledge for its own sake without any particular thought of its use. This desire is in all of us as part of our heredity. Every child goes through a period when his every other word seems to be *Why?* and most of us never stop asking why, whether we have any conscious need of the answer or not. If this "mental curiosity" is taken as wholly a friend, and is not put in its proper place in our lives, it may be an enemy to our spiritual life because it can lead us to clutter our minds with a lot of unnecessary and even harmful information. But if it is understood, it can be brought into subjection and made useful to our spiritual progress. The Gibeonites were made "hewers of wood and drawers of water" for the congregation of Israel and for the tabernacle. Knowledges of all kinds are needed if we are to carry our good purposes into concrete action. Wood represents right action, and water, of course, truth. For example, every Christian feels that war should be abolished, but there will have to be much "hewing of wood and drawing of water"–i.e., many carefully worked out plans of action and much gathering of accurate information and formulation of principle–before the desired result is attained.

The wood and water for the tabernacle would be for the use of the great brazen altar in the outer court and for the brazen laver there, and the outer court of the tabernacle represents our outward conduct as we attempt to serve the Lord.

Joshua's part of the story is interesting, too. He acted hastily according to a judgment formed on the basis of appearances, without taking counsel of the Lord (verse 14) and, although he afterward made the Gibeonites useful, bound himself to them in a pact which presently involved him in battle on their account, as you may learn by reading chapter 10. All our lives we have to fight the temptation to judge by appearances, and every time we yield and act hastily, we bring upon ourselves unexpected and unwanted consequences. We need to take counsel of the Lord every step of the way.

Basic Correspondences

bread = spiritual good
wine-skins = doctrines
garments = truths clothing our affections

Senior

Use this lesson to show how the Lord can make use even of our weaknesses and mistakes and preserves everything in us which may be of service in our spiritual development.

When Israel reentered the Holy Land, the land was full of enemies. It is interesting to note that in the letter of the Word all the nations mentioned as occupying the Holy Land when Israel returned to it can be traced back to the prehistoric churches, the Most Ancient and Ancient, the giants to the Most Ancient and all the others to the Ancient Church, their names occurring first in the genealogies taken from the Ancient Word, notably Genesis 10:15-18. On the other hand, the ancestry of the nations outside of the Holy Land can be traced no further back than Abraham.* The nations outside the land picture evils which come to us through our external environment as we grow up, while those within the land represent the deep internal evils of our heredity. We never wholly destroy these nations; but if we look to the Lord, He can give us power to keep them in subjection and even in some cases to make them useful to our spiritual development.

The Gibeonites of our lesson today were the best remnant of the degenerated Ancient Church. They were, according to the letter, Hivites, descendants of Canaan, the son of Ham. They represent the love of knowledge for its own sake, without thought of its use. We all have this love, especially in our childhood. We like to find out about everything. Under the control of spiritual purposes this faculty can help us decide what we ought to do in our outward life, finding out for us the truth about the conditions we face

---

*There is at least one exception to this rule (there perhaps being others), namely "Amalek," the first enemy which attacked Israel in the wilderness (Exodus 17). This ancient nation is first mentioned in Genesis 14:7 as one of the nations attacked by Chedorlaomer shortly after Abram arrived in Canaan. This nation seems to have had branches both within and without the Holy Land. Dr. Bayley, in *From Egypt to Canaan*, notes: "Afterwards a portion of the family of Esau likewise took the name of Amalek [Genesis 36:12], perhaps from settling in the very same district that had been occupied by the Amalekites of old." –*Ed.*

and showing us the best ways of meeting them. This is why the Gibeonites were to be spared as long as they were willing to be hewers of wood and drawers of water for the altar and for the congregation.

The appearance of the Gibeonites when they came to Joshua, although it was assumed to deceive him, had genuine truth behind it. Suppose we think of an example. Here, let us say, is a scientist who has let his interest in the natural world wean him away from religious belief. He pursues his profession eagerly and works hard at it, but only for the purpose of finding out ever more and more about the natural world. What is to be done with his discoveries he leaves to other people, both good and bad. The innocent goodness which he had when he was a little child close to the Lord has deteriorated, like the bread which was hot from the oven at the start but had become dry and moldy. His unquestioning belief in God and his tender conscience, like the wine-skins, have become dry and cracked during the years. His ways of thinking and living have, like the garments, come to be full of holes instead of all of one piece, and patched, like the shoes, with worldly expedients. He has indeed come a long journey from that far country of his infancy when he was in his Father's house. Yet if we can see his shortcomings and put them in their place in our lives, the results of his labors can be made serviceable to the spiritual life in providing us with accurate knowledge by means of which we may benefit the world.

This dry scientist may actually be living right in our own mental country. Whenever our interest in worldly knowledge of any kind—whether it be of science, of art, of money-making, of social conventions, of sports, or even of the text of the Bible—comes to be a thing we pursue for its own sake apart from its use to the spiritual life of men, our spiritual bread begins to spoil in us, our religious principles are broken, our knowledge of how to live usefully declines. The fault is not in the knowledges we love to acquire but in the fact that we have come to regard them as ends in themselves and not in their true character as servants to our higher faculties.

The Lord did not require Joshua to break his promise to the Gibeonites. He let them live, but He required that they be put and kept in their proper place. In chapter 10 we find that the other nations, as soon as they found that Gibeon had made a league with Israel, banded together and attacked it. This forced Joshua to go to its aid. When we yield to our weaknesses, even though later we realize our mistake and get them under control, there are always the unlooked-for consequences which have to be faced.

Adult

An interesting study for the Adults is to trace the ancestry of the Canaanites and to identify them with the evil tendencies which we inherit from our earliest ancestry. The Lord's providence in making use of these tendencies to further our spiritual development is brought out by this story.

In the introduction to the story of Abraham, we learned that the origin of idolatry was in the perversion of the knowledge of correspondence possessed by the Ancient Church. The idolatrous remnants of that church were scattered all over the world, and the pagan religions are the descendants of those remnants. But there were also remnants which remained in the Holy Land itself. They were the several tribes grouped under the title of *Canaanites* from whom the country was called the *land of Canaan*. In the letter of the Word Canaan (Genesis 9:18) was the son of Ham, and Genesis 10:19 tells us that "the border of the Canaanites was from Sidon, as thou comest to Gerar, unto Gaza; as thou goest unto Sodom, and Gomorrah, and Admah, and Zeboim, even unto Lasha." Of the three sons of Noah, Ham represents "internal worship corrupted." Throughout the Word, therefore, the Canaanites represent those interior evils which by heredity lie deep within us and oppose the entrance of the Lord into our hearts and minds. In addition to the Canaanites there were in the land the giants, an evil remnant of the Most Ancient Church, who represent our common tendency to exalt self.

The Canaanites were in the land when Abraham first came from

Ur. We remember the wicked cities of Sodom and Gomorrah, and the kings who carried off Lot and were overcome by Abraham. These stories picture our first struggles against our inherited evils while we are in the tender and innocent states of little childhood. But the descendants of Abraham, as we have seen, did not remain continuously in the Holy Land to hold down these enemies. They went into Egypt and stayed there for two hundred and fifty years. And while they were away, the Canaanites increased and built themselves many strong, walled cities, and gained complete control of the land. So when the Israelites returned under Joshua, they faced a long struggle for possession of the country which had been promised to them. This is a true picture of our own experience. As little children, cared for and protected by our parents and trusting wholly in them, we have a taste of heavenly living. But then we go out from our homes into the world of school and work and begin to develop as independent individuals, and for a long time we are chiefly concerned with external things and with our outward conduct. Our battles during this period are on the external plane. When we return to the Holy Land to repossess it—that is, when we finally are prepared for the development of our minds and hearts—we find that the few inner enemies we had to fight when we were little children have gathered strength and have entrenched themselves in strongholds of worldly thought and argument.

The Lord gave Joshua victory over all these enemies and enabled the Israelites to possess the land. Yet it was never a final victory. From the rest of the Bible story we know how the enemies in the land persisted, how constantly the Jews were tempted to mingle with them and adopt their ways, how their enemies gathered strength whenever the Jews became self-confident, and how at times they gained the upper hand and put the Jews to tribute. This too we can see in our own experience. There is never a time in this world when we can take our ease and relax our vigilance against the evils within us, never a time when we are not in need of examining ourselves and turning to the Lord for help.

We are now taking as our lesson the incident concerning the Gibeonites. The Gibeonites were Hivites. Among the descendants of Canaan listed in Genesis 10:15-18 were Heth–the Hittites–and the Hivites. These two remnants of the Ancient Church all through the Bible story were more inclined to be friendly to the Jews than any of the other Canaanites. It was from the Hittites that Abraham bought the field and cave of Machpelah; Esau married two wives from the Hittites; and we have an occasional Hittite mentioned in the period of the kings as rendering good service–notably Uriah the Hittite, who was so faithful to his duty in David's army that David could not cover his sin with Bathsheba by deceit. We first encounter the Hivites in Genesis 34 when Shechem the son of Hamor wishes to marry Jacob's daughter Dinah, and his father offers Jacob any price for her.

Swedenborg tells us that the Hittites and the Hivites were the more upright of the Canaanites because they still cherished the knowledges which had come down from the Ancient Church: the Hittites, the external knowledges which regard life; and the Hivites, the interior knowledges in the rituals and representatives. In AC 3058 Swedenborg says that the Gibeonites of our lesson for today represent "those who continually desire to know truths, but for no other end than to know them, while caring nothing for the use."

The ruse by which the Gibeonites deceived Joshua was a falsehood on the surface, but truth interiorly. They had indeed come from a far country, the Ancient Church. The "bread" which they carried–spiritual good–had come hot for their provision out of their houses in the day they came forth, and the "wine-skins"–the doctrines of spiritual truth–had been new when the branch called the Hivites had first developed in the Ancient Church. Their "garments" and their "shoes"–their ideas of external life and their practical applications of these ideas–had been whole and new. Over the centuries they had all become dry and moldy and torn and patched. But the Gibeonites recognized that the Lord was on the side of Israel and they preferred to serve rather than to resist, knowing that if they resisted they would be destroyed.

And on Joshua's part, what in the letter was a weakness—he asked not counsel at the mouth of the Lord but made a league with them—expresses a truth interiorly. As Joseph told his brothers (Genesis 50:20): "Ye thought evil against me: but God meant it unto good, to bring to pass, as it is this day, to save much people alive." The Lord "knoweth our frame; he remembereth that we are dust." His providence over us in the matter of the inherited evils within us gives us a means of turning into useful channels those evils which we would not destroy.

In our own lives this law means that there are many things in us which in themselves are weaknesses—"strangers" to the angel in us—yet which, if recognized and properly subordinated, may be made to serve our higher goals. We all have that which the Gibeonites symbolize within us: that natural desire to seek all kinds of information regardless of whether it is good or bad, useful or potentially harmful. Our fondness for looking into things and acquiring information can be made to show us the best means of helping others in material ways, and can bring us truths which are useful in our daily life. The Gibeonites were to hew wood and draw water for the house of the Lord, and we recall that it was only in the outer court of the tabernacle that wood and water were regularly used.

From the Writings of Swedenborg

Arcana Coelestia, n. 4431: "Because the Hivites had from ancient time signified interior truth, and because they were one of the better disposed nations, with whom iniquity was not so far consummated (that is, the truth of the church was not so far extinguished as with others), the Gibeonite Hivites were of the Lord's providence preserved, by means of a covenant made with them by Joshua and the princes."

Arcana Coelestia, n. 1097: "Everything written in the Word concerning the Jewish Church was representative of the kingdom of the Lord. The kingdom of the Lord is such that every one in it, whosoever and whatsoever he may be, must perform some use. Nothing but use is regarded by the Lord in his kingdom. Even the infernals must perform some use."

Suggested Questions on the Lesson

P. What did Joshua set up at Gilgal? *twelve stones*

J. What feast did the Israelites celebrate there? *Passover*

J. What change in their diet was made there? *manna ceased*

P. Which one of the enemies in the Holy Land wanted to make peace with Joshua? *Gibeonites*

P. How did they deceive him? *pretended to be from far away*

J. In what way was Joshua careless? *failed to consult the Lord*

J. What promise did he make to the Gibeonites? *not to kill them*

P. When he found out that they had deceived him, did he break his promise? *no*

J. How did he decide they should be treated? *made to cut wood, haul water*

J. What does this story teach us about promises? *shouldn't make hasty ones*

I. What was the ancestry of the Gibeonites? *Hivites (from Ham, son of Noah*

S. What do they represent? *intellectual curiosity*

I. What is pictured by their (1) patched garments, and (2) moldy bread?
(1) ideas of conduct
(2) spirituality

S. What is pictured by their being made hewers of wood and drawers of water? *using intellectual curiosity to get accurate knowledge of ways to benefit the world*

THE DIVISION OF THE LAND

Joshua 18:1-10

This lesson should cover the conquest as well as the division of the land. With the younger classes the statement that the land was conquered will be enough. The Juniors should be told the fact that there were three campaigns, and their order. A little more should be done in the three older classes. Suggestions as to outstanding points will be found in the pupils' notes.

Doctrinal Points

Casting lots means that we leave the decision of a thing in the Lord's hands. There is no such thing as chance or accident. Everything is under the control of divine providence.

The Word is so closely knit together that the oftener we read it the more comes to us from it and the more we find we have to learn.

Our faith needs to be supported by an understanding of the whole plan and organization of life.

We have to drive out our spiritual foes in order to attain a heavenly character.

Notes for Parents

Joshua conquered the Holy Land in three campaigns. The first was in the center of the land. When we determine to make our character heavenly, we must first of all strike at the heart of all our evil feelings and false ideas: we must recognize and fight the love of self. Then we must fight the wrong desires which spring from self-love—the campaign in the south—and finally acknowledge and correct the false ideas which fill our minds—the campaign in the north. We never make a complete conquest. The Israelites left many enemies untouched. But we can gain a sufficient mastery with the Lord's help so that we become settled in a heavenly order.

This is the division of the land among the tribes, of which our chapter for today tells us.

The tabernacle with the ark in it was set up at Shiloh in the center of the land. The commandments must be "written on the heart" if we are to know peace. *Shiloh* means "peace." The Levites were given cities throughout the land. This means that the desire to serve the Lord must pervade everything we do, for you remember that the Levites were the tribe who had charge of the worship of Israel. Each of the other tribes was given its own special inheritance. All our powers and abilities must recognize and perform their proper functions in the interests of the whole character. Regeneration is not something which is accomplished for us by the Lord without any cooperation on our part, and our cooperation involves thought as well as action. The Lord gives us the power to conquer our inner foes; our place in heaven comes to us as an inheritance from Him. But we must never cease to learn from Him, to ask for His help, and to be on our guard against these evils within ourselves which are always lurking there and gain strength as we become careless and self-confident, and may even get control of us again before we realize what is happening.

Primary

The setting up of the tabernacle at Shiloh can be made the principal part of the lesson, and the children should learn the name *Shiloh* and what it means. They should learn what casting lots means, that the Lord governed the choice, and also where the various tribes settled, including the tribe of Levi.

From the camp at Gilgal, Joshua led the fighting men out to conquer the whole land of Canaan. It took them more than twenty years during the life of Joshua, and even then they never wholly overcame their enemies.

But after seven years they had gained enough control so that they could divide the land and settle in their homes.

Where did they set up the tabernacle?

Shiloh means "peace."

The tabernacle remained at Shiloh for three hundred years.

Do you remember what the tabernacle was? It was the tent for worship which was made at Mount Sinai according to the Lord's directions. The ark—the gold-covered chest in which they kept the two tables of stone on which the Lord had written the commandments—was always placed in the inner chamber or Holy of Holies of the tabernacle, just as we always keep a copy of the Word on the altar in our church.

The tabernacle had been carried by the Levites along with the children of Israel wherever they went throughout their wilderness journey. The Levites, you remember, were set apart to have charge of everything pertaining to the worship of the people. They set up the tabernacle in the midst of every camping place. But after the land was conquered, they did not have to take it down any more, but could have a permanent place for it.

How did the Israelites mark out the divisions of the land?

Where had the tribes of Judah and of Joseph been given lots?

In verse 5 "on the north" means north of the tribe of Judah, not the northern part of the land.

You remember that Joseph had become two tribes—Ephraim and Manasseh.

The Levites did not have any separate area, but they were given forty-eight cities, four in the land of each of the twelve tribes, so that they could teach the people how to worship the Lord and could receive the sacrifices and offerings which had been commanded all through the year. But the Passover and the other two great feasts which were celebrated once a year were centered at the tabernacle in Shiloh.

Where had Reuben and Gad and half the tribe of Manasseh been given their lots?

How was it determined which lot each of the remaining seven tribes was to have?

When lots are cast, it is the Lord who really makes the choice.

Two men were given special inheritances.

Joshua was given a city called Timnath-serah in the lot of Ephraim.

Caleb was given Hebron.

What do you remember about Hebron?

Junior

Map study is indicated for this class, as well as the reading of the Bible references in its notes. This will help the children develop a background for many of the Bible stories, as well as fixing names of persons and places in their memories.

From the camp at Gilgal, Joshua led the fighting men out to the conquest of the land. The conquest was carried out in three campaigns, the first in the central part of the land, the second in the south, and the third in the north. These three campaigns are described in chapters 6 to 11 of the book of Joshua, which are stirring chapters to read. Chapter 12 reminds us that Moses had conquered Sihon king of the Amorites and Og king of Basham, the two great kings on the west side of the Jordan. This whole effort, which took about seven years, gave the Israelites the mastery of the land and enabled them to divide it and settle in their homes, but there were still many cities which had not been taken, and most of the people in the land never ceased to be enemies.

Caleb had been promised by Moses—at the command of the Lord (Deuteronomy 1:36)—that he should have a certain place in the land for himself. Read Joshua 14:6-15 and 15:13-14 to see how this promise was kept.

Whose home had Hebron been?

Joshua also was given a city of his own in the allotment of Ephraim (Joshua 19:49-50). And before the final division described in our chapter for today, five of the tribes had been taken care of. The tribes of Reuben and Gad had asked for and received land in the south and center of the cross-Jordan country, and half of the tribe of Manasseh had been given land north of them. The other half of the tribe of Manasseh and the tribe of Ephraim—you remember Joseph's two sons were to be heads of tribes—had the center of the Holy Land proper, and Judah had already been given all the land south of them.

How did Joshua have the rest of the land divided?
How did they decide which property each tribe should have?
When lots are cast, who really decides the choice?

Now look at a map of the Holy Land as divided among the tribes. You will see that the southern part of the land went to the tribes of Simeon and Judah; the central part to the descendants of Joseph, to Benjamin, and to Dan; and the northern part to the other tribes. In chapter 19:47 we learn that Dan found its lot too small and went up to the north of the others and conquered more territory, taking the city of Leshem, elsewhere called Laish, and changing its name to Dan. This made Dan the northernmost city of the Holy Land, as Beersheba was the southernmost, and from this comes the expression "from Dan to Beersheba," meaning everywhere. In Joshua 19:9 we find that the inheritance of Simeon was taken out of the portion of Judah because it was found that too much land had been given to Judah. From this point on in the Bible story there is little mention of the tribe of Simeon.

Why did the tribe of Levi have no separate area?

In chapters 20 and 21 we are told of the establishment of six cities of refuge and forty-eight Levitical cities. The first fifteen verses of the thirty-fifth chapter of Numbers explain why these cities were commanded.

Now the tabernacle was moved from Gilgal, where it had been during the conquest, and set up at Shiloh. *Shiloh* means "peace." Find Shiloh on the map. You see it is near the center of the land. The tabernacle remained here for three hundred years. Worship was conducted in it, and the people came to it for the three great feasts of the Jewish year.

Intermediate

The meaning of regeneration should be stressed—the fact that it involves the rooting out of evil and falsity from our hearts and minds. Speak of the fixing of the commandments and service of the Lord as the center of our life—the tabernacle at Shiloh—and then as an outline follow the specific correspondences given at the end of the Intermediate notes.

Joshua conquered the Holy Land in three campaigns. The first gave him control of the center of the land. This campaign, described in chapters 6 through 9, includes the stories of the fall of Jericho and Ai and the league with the Gibeonites, which we have studied earlier. The second gave him control of all the southern part of the land and is told in chapter 10. The third, described in chapter 11, gave him all the northern part; and in chapter 12 we are reminded that Moses had conquered the country east of the Jordan. Chapter 13 tells us the boundaries of the two and a half tribes which had chosen this cross-Jordan country for their inheritance. Then in chapters 14 through 17 we are told of the settlement of the tribe of Judah in the southern part of the land, Caleb being given the city of Hebron, the home of Abraham, and of the assignment of the very center of the land to the tribes of Joseph–Ephraim and the other half of Manasseh.

The conquest in the north completed the task assigned to Joshua. Israel was now master of the whole land, although only the people who had actively resisted Joshua had been destroyed. Joshua 11:13 and 11:22 tell us that the cities "that stood still in their strength" were not destroyed, and that a few of the giants also were still left. These picture the falsities and evils within us which lie dormant during our early efforts at regeneration, to rise up later when we think the conquest is over.

Joshua's final work was the setting up of the tabernacle at Shiloh, where it remained for more than three hundred years–*Shiloh* means "peace"–and the division of the previously unassigned land among the remaining tribes. The rest of chapter 18 and chapter 19 describe the boundaries of the various tribes. We remember that the twelve tribes represent all our abilities and powers. The order in which the twelve sons of Jacob–or Israel–were born is the order in which these abilities and powers develop, beginning with the simple general ones we use in childhood, then followed by the faculties which enable us to take our places in the world, and finally by the higher spiritual faculties pictured by Jacob's two youngest sons, Joseph and Benjamin. In the distribution of the tribes in the Holy Land we find the oldest sons, Reuben, Simeon, and Judah are all in the south, which is the will part of our nature. (Levi, of course, is scattered throughout the land because he represents worship.) The next six sons are in the north, the thought part of us. And in the center of the land, where the higher land is and where the tabernacle is set up, are the tribe of Benjamin and the tribes of Ephraim and Manasseh, the sons of Joseph. On the map Dan is also near the center, but on the seacoast; later this tribe spread to the far north. This is because Dan represents the ability to judge, and specifically the acknowledgment of the truths of revelation which is necessary before any correct judgment can be formed and truth can enter the mind and will; so Dan is rightly a boundary tribe. Thus the map of the Holy Land becomes a wonderful picture of the way in which our various abilities, faculties, and powers are meant to be arranged in order to make up a heavenly character.*

Chapter 21 tells of the forty-eight cities with their pasture lands which were given to the Levites. Worship of the Lord must be within everything we think, feel, and do.

Chapter 22 tells us how Joshua dismissed with his blessing the two and a half tribes which had been given homes east of the Jordan, since they had now fully kept their promise to help their brethren conquer the land. Like Lot they had chosen to live in the fertile plain rather than in the mountains, and they picture that part of us which is most concerned with activities and enjoyments of the world. Joshua charged them solemnly to be faithful to the worship of the Lord if they wished to prosper. To keep this in remembrance they set up an altar near the Jordan, not for worship and sacrifice but as a witness of their promise. The Lord wants us to enjoy the good things of this world and its activities but always to make them serve the higher goals of our spiritual life. When the Lord prayed for His disciples, He said, "I pray not that thou shouldest take them out of the world, but that thou shouldest keep them from the evil." This should always be our guide in

---

*There is a map showing the correspondences of the twelve tribes on p. 80 of Hugo Odhner's *The Divine Allegory* (New York: Swedenborg Foundation, 1954). *–Ed.*

deciding what occupations we choose, how we conduct them, and what pleasures we may enjoy.

Basic Correspondences

the southern part of the land	=	the will or affection part of us
the cross-Jordan country	=	our natural or external life

Senior

The meaning of the twelve tribes and the reason for their particular allotments in the Holy Land is the general lesson, but stress the fact that we never succeed in conquering all our inner foes and that we need constantly to watch and to study so that we may recognize and resist them.

The taking of Jericho and Ai and the treaty with the Gibeonites were the beginning of the conquest and gave Joshua control of the central part of the land. The "divide and conquer" principle thus has a scriptural basis, for with the center of the land in his hands, Joshua was able to proceed to gain mastery over the rest in two campaigns, the first in the south and the second in the north. In all these stories of conquest we find an element of miracle. Joshua and the Israelites were not allowed to forget that it was the Lord who gave them the victory. The conquest under Joshua is a picture of the process of regeneration in its earlier states, when we are in an ardent and enthusiastic state and willing to attack our faults boldly.

Then comes our lesson for today. The land is conquered. The enemies in heart and mind have been recognized and brought into a state of subjection. But we should notice that although some have been altogether destroyed, others have merely been driven back into their cities. Nevertheless a time of temporary peace comes when we take stock of ourselves and make orderly plans for future accomplishment. The tribes are ready to take their allotted places and to settle down, each man under his own vine and fig tree (Micah 4:4).

First the tabernacle is set up in Shiloh ("peace") in the center of the land. We can see that this is as it should be. The two and a half tribes who chose the cross-Jordan country are allowed to go and take possession of it. Caleb, who with Joshua long before had trusted the Lord and urged the people to go forward and conquer the land in spite of its seeming strength, and who was at that time promised a special inheritance, is given Hebron, the former home of Abraham. The Levites are assigned their forty-eight cities throughout the land, so that there may be worship and remembrance of the Lord everywhere. And the land is divided by lot among the rest of the tribes.

This is a picture of an orderly life, each faculty in its proper place and serving the Lord in its appointed way. The highest faculties, the spiritual, are in the center. Joseph and Benjamin, Jacob's last-born sons, represent these faculties, which develop later in our lives than the so-called "practical" faculties. The tribes of Simeon and Judah are in the south, the affectional part of our life, where our childhood states—Hebron, the home of Abraham—persist. The other tribes, concerned with our intellectual life, are in the north. In the cross-Jordan country also, in the plane of our outer activities, all three types of faculty are needed.

The place of Dan in the Holy Land is interesting. He was given an inheritance along the seacoast near the center of the land, but finding it too "straight" or confined for him later went up and conquered territory north of all the other tribes. Dan was the son of Bilhah, Rachel's handmaid, the first indirect fruit of the spiritual love pictured by Rachel. *Dan* means "judging." Swedenborg tells us that he represents the affirmation or acknowledgment that we should believe in God and live a good life. And he says, "affirmation and also acknowledgment is the first general principle with the man who is being regenerated, but it is the last with the man who has been regenerated." This is the reason why Dan moved from the central seacoast to the northernmost border of the land.

There were still conquests to be made. Joshua commanded each tribe to continue the conquest in its own territory and to keep in subjection the enemies already overcome. We need this injunction.

One of our most subtle temptations is to become self-satisfied and think we have no more to do. We shall find in the book of Judges a picture of the results of such a mistake.

Adult

The whole subject of regeneration is presented in this lesson. We should note especially that it is no haphazard process accomplished in us by the Lord without constant cooperation on our part. It is the achievement of a well-ordered inner as well as outward life.

We have studied in Joshua 6 through 9 the three principal stories concerning Joshua's first campaign, which gave him control of the central part of the Holy Land: the conquest of Jericho, the conquest of Ai, and the treaty with the Gibeonites.

The conquest of the rest of the land was divided into two campaigns, the first in the south and the second in the north. In general the south represents states of affection and the north intellectual states, and these two campaigns thus represent the effort to recognize and overcome evils and falsities in our hearts and minds. We sometimes use the terms *evil* and *falsity* without stopping to think just what they mean. An example may help us here. Take dishonesty in business, for instance. The evil involved is the love of selfish gain; the falsity is the excuse we make for doing what we know to be wrong—as, for example, that our first duty is to take care of ourselves, that everyone does such things, that it is impossible to survive in the business world without such practices. The evil is the underlying desire; the falsity, the thoughts and reasonings which excuse and support it. Our hearts and minds are full of these evils and falsities, as the Holy Land was full of hostile peoples, and they band together against our efforts at regeneration, one evil drawing others to support it, and many falsities bearing each other up, so that in fighting against one we must fight against many. These are the general campaigns, first against the five kings in the south, the league of evil desires; and then against the kings of the north, the host of false ideas and reasonings. The campaign in the south comes first. We must recognize and overcome the underlying evil before we are prepared to see the true nature of the excuses we have been making and discard them. In the southern campaign the Lord sent hailstones against the enemy and also gave the Israelites light to pursue them into complete rout. Our evils are conquered not so much by our own efforts as by the power of the Lord's truth* and by the clear light of the Word. "Thou searchest the reins and the heart." In the northern campaign, the use of horses and chariots is noteworthy, as the affection for our own intellectual powers and the systems of thought through which we have made these powers effective. The Lord promised Joshua that they should "hough [hamstring] their horses and burn their chariots with fire"; our admiration for our own wisdom can be broken, and love will destroy the false ideas on which we have acted.

After these first campaigns the Israelites were masters of the Holy Land and ready to settle in their homes there. This does not mean that they had conquered all their enemies. The Lord permits us to begin to enjoy spiritual living while we have still many battles to fight. We never come to the end of our spiritual battles while we are in this world; yet we can know a measure of heavenly joy and peace even while here. The tabernacle was set up at Shiloh, the name of which means "peace." The Holy Land is always spoken of as the "inheritance" of the tribes. This is because they received it as a gift from the Lord. A place in the heavens, which means a heavenly character, is the inheritance of each one of us who will recognize the Lord as his Heavenly Father and try to do His will. And as each one of us is born with different qualities and gifts from those of any other, his place is a specific one, the place where he alone can serve, which no other could possibly fill, his particular inheritance. "Then shall the King say unto them on his right hand, Come, ye blessed of my Father, inherit the kingdom prepared for you from the foundation of the world." (Matt. 25:34)

---

*In this case it is turned into something coldly destructive by our negative attitudes. The truth hurts when we are evil. *–Ed.*

The twelve sons of Jacob represent the various good affections which make up a complete person. Each of these affections has its proper place in the perfect life; people governed by each of these affections have their proper place in the Grand Man. So the division of the Holy Land by lot among the tribes pictures the well-rounded spiritual life, and also the well-rounded spiritual society, in which good men and women of all types and gifts have their proper place and work together harmoniously in the Lord's service. And we should notice that the fundamental choice of place is not ours but the Lord's, for the casting of lots always pictures the acknowledgment that the decision is in the Lord's hands.

The tribes of Reuben, Gad, and half the tribe of Manasseh were permitted to settle east of the Jordan, after they had helped their brothers conquer the Holy Land. The cross-Jordan country represents the plane of natural living. It was a fertile land and good for cattle; that is, the plane of natural living is meant for the carrying out of the good affections for useful service of an external kind. Many people love such service who do not care to think very deeply. They are at home in useful, kindly, external living. Such people, if they are willing to recognize the necessity of the deeper things of worship and doctrine and to make due effort to examine themselves and to conquer selfishness and its supporting excuses, are permitted to spend their lives for the most part in the land of external service. They do not attain very deep or high states, but they are useful and happy. Part of the Lord's ministry was in this cross-Jordan country. It is interesting to note that the two tribes who asked for an inheritance in this country were Reuben, who represents the first faith of the natural man, and Gad, who represents good works of an external kind, and that half the tribe of Manasseh was assigned a lot to the north of them, although there is no record that Manasseh had asked for this assignment.* Manas-

*While this is correct (see Numbers 32:33, where the original assignment is recorded), one could, of course, *infer* that a request was made by the Manassites even though such request was not recorded in the letter. *—Ed.*

seh, the older son of Joseph, represents the good of the church; so we may understand that his being placed as a bulwark to the north of Reuben and Gad indicates that those who settle in the natural plane need to have their thinking guarded by the recognition that good comes from the Lord and not from themselves.

We should note also that the Levites received no particular part of the land as their inheritance. They were to be responsible for the worship and spiritual instruction of the people, as well as to carry on the service of the tabernacle. It is said of them that "the Lord God of Israel was their inheritance." Among the tribes, the Levites represent the element of worship. They are those affections in us which look directly to the Lord and find their satisfaction in learning of Him and meditating upon Him and in the spirit and act of prayer and praise. This is their inheritance. They have no one place in the well-ordered life, but pervade the whole. There is no part of our lives where there should not be "cities of the Levites," systems of thinking which relate that part to the Lord and His service. All parts of our lives should minister to this spirit of worship, as the tithes of all the people supported the Levites. We should not go to church on Sunday and forget the Lord the rest of the week. We should not have one place in our minds for religion and a separate compartment for everyday life. We should not read the Word each morning and refuse to test our conduct by it. "Take heed to thyself that thou forsake not the Levite as long as thou livest upon the earth." (Deuteronomy 12:19)

From the Writings of Swedenborg

Arcana Coelestia, n. 3913: "By the twelve sons of Jacob are here described the twelve general or cardinal things by means of which while being regenerated or made a church, man is initiated into what is spiritual and celestial. For when a man is being regenerated, or made a church (that is, when from a dead man he is becoming alive, or from corporeal heavenly), he is led by the Lord through many states. These general states are what are designated by the 'twelve sons,' and afterwards by the 'twelve tribes'; for which reason the 'twelve tribes' signify all things of faith and love . . . for generals involve all the particulars and singulars, and these latter bear relation to the former. When a man is being regenerated, the internal man is to be conjoined with the external, consequently the goods and truths of the internal man with the goods and truths of the external; for from truths and goods man is man. These cannot be conjoined without means. Means are such things as derive something from the one side, and something from the other, and which are attended with the effect that in so far as the man accedes to the one, the other becomes subordinate. These means are what are signified by the 'handmaids,' the means on the part of the internal man by the handmaids of Rachel; and the means on the part of the external man by the handmaids of Leah."

Suggested Questions on the Lesson

J. In how many campaigns did Joshua conquer the Holy Land? *three*
J. What was the order of these campaigns? *center, south, north*
J. What familiar stories are connected with the first? *Jericho, Ai, Gibeon*
J. Were all the enemies in the land conquered? *no*
P. Where was the tabernacle set up permanently? *Shiloh*
P. What does *Shiloh* mean? *peace*
J. Who marked out the divisions of the land? *three men from each tribe*
P. How was it decided which tribe should have which division? *by casting lots*
P. When lots are cast, who really makes the decision? *the Lord*
J. What tribes had the center of the land? *Joseph, Benjamin, Dan*
J. Why were there two tribes of Joseph? *Joseph's sons were "adopted" by Jacob*
J. What tribes had the cross-Jordan country? *Reuben, Gad, half Manasseh*
J. What tribes had the southern part of the land? *Judah, Simeon*
J. What city was given to Caleb? *Hebron*
J. Why were the Levites not given one of the divisions of the land? *in charge of worship*
P. What were they given instead? *forty-eight cities*
I. What do the twelve tribes represent? *all our mental faculties*
S. What is pictured by the setting up of the tabernacle at Shiloh? *putting worship in a central and settled (i.e., peaceful) part of our lives*

DEBORAH AND BARAK

Judges 4

In all classes some time should be spent on the accomplishments under Joshua and the character of the period of the Judges. Even the little children are not too young for the lesson that we never "know enough" to do right without constantly learning new truth from the Word.

Doctrinal Points

The Lord saves us through truths from the Word which are in our memories.

Whenever we think we know enough to do right without further study of the Word, we are sure to get into trouble.

Notes for Parents

Under Joshua's leadership the children of Israel carried on three campaigns in the Holy Land: one in the center of the land, one in the south, and one in the north. They won enough decisive victories so that the enemies in the land were subdued and permitted them to settle there. The land was divided into sections and then, by the casting of lots, these sections were assigned to the various tribes.

When we have mastered enough of our temptations so that we can feel safely established in regenerate living, all our faculties take their proper places in our scheme of life.

But the Israelites made a serious mistake at this point—a mistake which we also are likely to make. They did not completely destroy their enemies, but became overconfident and ceased to guard and fight against them. Presently they even began to intermarry with their former enemies and then to worship their gods. When once we begin to imagine we are "good enough" and stop examining and correcting ourselves in the light of the Lord's truth, we slip into careless ways.

Then suddenly some evil in us which we thought we had overcome crops up stronger than ever. Here and there, in one part of the land or another, old enemies of Israel one after another began to rise up and attack. Then, just as we are driven by trouble to remember the Lord and seek His help, so Israel turned to the Lord each time. And the Lord always helped them, as He always helps us. Against each enemy He raised up a leader to deliver Israel. These were local and temporary leaders, and were called Judges, and each one pictures some particular truth from the Word which the Lord, when we ask His help, can bring up out of our memory to show us the right way and give us courage to attack the enemy.

In our story for today the woman Judge Deborah did not fight, but she went with the leader Barak to direct and inspire him so that he overcame the enemy. In the same way, some simple affection for what is right in the Lord's sight will rise up in us to direct and inspire us when we realize suddenly how weak we are, and will cause us to exert ourselves to resist temptation and re-establish ourselves in heavenly living.

Does Jael's act in the last part of our story seem a fierce and cruel one? People in those days were often fierce and cruel—as some are today—but the Lord could use their deeds to teach us that we must show no mercy to the evil inclinations and wrong thoughts which rise up in our hearts and minds. We must strike them down promptly and finally. The "thou shalt not" of the commandments is like the tent peg in Jael's hand.

Primary

Begin by telling the class that the children of Israel have now reached the Promised Land and are finally settled in homes of their own. The people were so comfortable that they forgot to worship and obey the Lord. Tell them how one enemy after another rose up, and then go on to Deborah and her tent under the palm tree. Point out that the Lord again showed the Israelites that they could conquer only with His help. In telling the story of Jael and Sisera dwell on the friendship of Jael's people for Israel, and point out that the people of that time lived a rough life and were accustomed to violent deaths.

The children of Israel had to fight a great many battles before they proved to their enemies in the Holy Land that the Lord was really with them and intended them to rule there. But finally they were able to disband the army and scatter through the land to make homes for themselves and sow the fields and plant fruit trees.

Joshua had led them faithfully, and the Lord showed him how to divide the country among them so that each of the twelve tribes would have a settled home. Ever since they left Egypt, this was what the people had been looking forward to—a country of their own, where they would not be ruled by strangers. As long as Joshua lived, they got along very well because he kept them reminded of the Lord, and before he died, they promised him that they would always do as the Lord told them to do.

But they soon forgot and then the Lord permitted their enemies to become strong again.
The Israelites now had no one leader.
"Every man did that which was right in his own eyes." (17:6)

Did you ever promise to be good and then get so busy doing what you wanted to do that you forgot your promise? This was what the Israelites did. And when they forgot to obey the Lord, the Lord could not help them.

You know that when you get into trouble, you look around for someone to help you. The Israelites did not now have any one person like Joshua to lead them, but whenever they told the Lord they were sorry and asked Him to help them, He raised up someone to show them the way out of the particular trouble they were in. This person was called a Judge. There were sixteen* of them

---

*This total can be achieved only by counting *both* Deborah and Barak. In the order of their naming the judges are:

1. Othniel (Jud. 3:9)
2. Ehud (Jud. 3:15)
3. Shamgar (Jud. 3:31)
4. Deborah (Jud. 4:5)
5. Gideon (Jud. 6:36)
6. Abimelech (Jud. 9:1)
7. Tola (Jud. 10:1)
8. Jair (Jud. 10:3)
9. Jephthah (Jud. 11:11)
10. Ibzan (Jud. 12:8)
11. Elon (Jud. 12:11)
12. Abdon (Jud. 12:13)
13. Samson (Jud. 16:30)
14. Eli (I Sam. 4:18)
15. Samuel (I Sam. 7:15)

altogether.

The first three Judges were Othniel, Ehud, and Shamgar.
In our lesson for today, what enemy is attacking?
Who was the leader of his army?
Who was the Judge in Israel at this time?
Where did she live?
Whom did Deborah call to lead the battle?
From what tribe did the army come?
Near what river did the battle take place?
Verse 21 of chapter 5 tells of another way in which the Lord helped Barak to win.
It says that the river Kishon swept the enemy away.
Who won the battle?
Who killed Sisera?
How did she kill him?
The Kenites were descendants of Jethro the Midianite, the father-in-law of Moses.

After the victory Deborah and Barak sang a song of praise and thanksgiving to the Lord for saving the nation.

Junior

The geography will interest the Juniors. Have them locate on a map all the places named and look up the Bible references. They can be told more than the younger children about Jael and Sisera and the reason why such stories appear in the Word. The Lord judges people in every age by their motives and by how far they do right according to what they may be expected to know.

Joshua led the people until they had conquered the Holy Land and divided it among the tribes. On a map, find the names of the tribes in their proper places. Two and a half tribes had chosen to make their homes on the east side of the Jordan. The Holy Land itself was surveyed by a company of men picked from all the tribes and was marked out into ten parts. Then they cast lots to see which tribe should have each part; so you see the Lord actually determined where each tribe should make its home. Before Joshua's death they all promised him that they would serve the Lord faithfully and would continue fighting, each in his own territory, until all their enemies were completely overcome. The tribes of Judah and Simeon did continue to make conquests as they had promised, but the other tribes were too much interested in settling their own homes to go on fighting, and after Joshua's death there was no one great leader to keep them reminded of their duty to the Lord. So, many of the enemies remained in some strength. The Israelites began to associate with them, and soon they were intermarrying with them and even worshiping their gods. Do we ever find it easier to do as other people do than to think for ourselves what is really right?

When the people began to worship the gods of their enemies, these enemies gained strength and eventually tried again to overcome the interlopers. The Lord permitted each of these enemies to prevail until the people in that particular part of the country remembered Him and turned to Him for help. Then in each case He raised up some individual to lead them out of their difficulty. These individuals were not set over all the people as Moses and Joshua had been, but were local and temporary leaders. They were called Judges. The Lord does the same thing for us when we are in trouble and turn to Him for help. He brings up in our memories the particular truth we need to lead us against the present temptation. The Lord never lets trouble come to us unless we need it to show us our weaknesses and to rouse us up to fight them. We can see this truth when we read verses 20-23 of chapter 2.

The first three Judges were Othniel, who led the people against the king of Mesopotamia; Ehud of the tribe of Benjamin, who saved them from Eglon king of Moab; and Shamgar, who won victories over the Philistines.

In our lesson today what enemy is threatening?
In what general section of the land did he live?
Who was the captain of his army?
Who was the Judge raised up at this time?
Where did she live?

Look up Bethel and Ramah on the map. Bethel was Abraham's second stop when he first came into the Holy Land, and also the place where Jacob had his wonderful dream of the ladder. Ramah was the town where Samuel was born and made his home.

Whom did Deborah call to lead the battle against Jabin?
From what tribes was he to draw his army?

Find the place of these tribes on the map.

What did Barak insist that Deborah should do?
What did she tell him would happen?

The battle took place in the plain of Esdraelon. On the map you will see a point of land which breaks the line of the coast at the southern boundary of the tribe of Zebulun. This is Mount Carmel. From this mountain the river Kishon flows southeastward through the plain of Esdraelon. This plain is a natural meeting place for armies trying to take possession of the Holy Land, and many battles have been fought there. There was even a battle there in our own century during the first World War. The plain is drained by the River Kishon, and in chapter 5, which is Deborah's song of triumph, verse 21 tells how the Lord helped the Israelites by means of the Kishon.

From what people did Jael come?

Read Numbers 10:29-32 and Judges 1:16 to learn about her ancestry and how her family happened to be living in the Holy Land and to be friendly to Israel.

How did she help Israel this time?

The "nail" was a wooden tent peg or stake. Perhaps this seems a very cruel thing for a woman to do, but we must remember that the people of that time were cruel. The Lord could use these harsh facts in the Word because of their correspondence. And we must remember that He does not blame people for doing wrong things when they do not know any better. He always judges us by our motives. Jael's motive was to help Israel. Read verses 6-9 and see if you can find a reason for the Lord's allowing Jael to kill Sisera. The Lord always tried to show the Israelites that it was not their own strength and wisdom which gave them victory. He wants us to see this, too.

Intermediate

The general lesson of the period of the Judges is the thing to be emphasized in this class, and the fact that if we are not wise enough to obey the Lord readily and willingly, we often have to be taught by hard experiences. The difference between the mind and the will should be made clear, and the part each plays in meeting our temptations.

The history of the children of Israel up to the time of the book of Judges may be said to describe, in its large general outline, our spiritual development from infancy to the time when we begin our independent lives away from the direct guidance of our parents. Abraham, Isaac, Jacob, Moses, and Joshua had been with the people to judge and intercede, and had directed their life much as our parents direct our lives. But now the people were established in their own homes in the land, and were to stand on their own feet.

So with the death of Joshua we pass into the period of our independent life. We have to make our own decisions. However sure we may be that we intend to follow the Lord, there is always a period here when, missing the strong leadership of our parents and teachers, we make many mistakes. We find our temptations unexpectedly strong. We go out into new fields "on our own" as the twelve tribes did when they scattered to take possession of their lands, and we find it much easier to do as the people around us do than to follow the strict line of duty as our religious training has marked it out for us. The idols of the land–success, money, pleasure–begin to influence us. Our natural selfish tendencies, which we never wholly conquer, grow stronger and at last rise up and attack us openly.

The period of the Judges was a time when "every man did that which was right in his own eyes" because "there was no king in Israel." (17:6) This is the time when we think we know enough about what is right without looking to the Lord and learning more all the time. It is a time of temptation and trouble. For the Lord has to permit us to make mistakes and to suffer for them, in order that we may recognize our weaknesses and turn to Him for guidance.

The Judges were temporary leaders raised up here and there in the land to lead the people against particular enemies. They represent individual truths which the Lord calls to our minds when we need them. Chapter 3 tells of the first three Judges: Othniel—the nephew and son-in-law of Caleb—who won a victory over the king of Mesopotamia; Ehud, of the tribe of Benjamin, who killed Eglon king of Moab by a ruse and then led his people in the slaughter of Eglon's army; and Shamgar, who slew six hundred of the Philistines with an ox-goad.

Then in our chapter for today we have the story of a woman Judge, Deborah. She is described as making her home under a palm tree between Bethel and Ramah in the tribe of Benjamin. Bethel pictures knowledge of celestial things; Ramah, spiritual knowledge; and the palm tree, the principle that all goodness and all salvation are from the Lord alone. So here we have a situation in which the Judge who is to govern us is an affection for heavenly knowledges living in recognition of the fact that the Lord alone can save us.

The enemy this time is not near the home of the Judge—not in the central or southern part of the land, but in the north. That is, the temptation threatening us is the temptation to yield to falsity in the understanding. Deborah appoints as leader for the army Barak, from the tribe of Naphtali in the north, and tells him to gather an army from his own tribe and that of Zebulun, also in the north. False reasoning must be met by true reasoning, for the battle is to be fought in the mind. But Barak refuses to fight unless Deborah will go with him; and when she does, the battle is won with the direct help of the Lord, who sweeps away the horses and chariots of the enemy in the river Kishon (Judges 5:21-22). So our affection for the Lord and heavenly things must always be there to back up our efforts to reason against falsity, and it is the Lord who gives the victory.

Then comes the powerful story of the destruction of Sisera, leader of Jabin's army, who represents the false principle which was directing our false reasoning and which sometimes eludes us even when we think we have won the battle. The woman Jael was a Kenite. The Kenites were a good remnant of the Ancient Church, and represent those simple good impulses in our hearts which go back to our early religious teaching. The tent pictures a childlike state of worship, and the tent pins which fasten it to the ground are the simple truths from the Word which connect our worship with our daily life. So Jael's apparently cruel act pictures our ability to overcome the basic principle behind of false reasoning by "knocking it on the head" with the simple commandments we learned as children.

In chapter 5 we have the song of praise which Deborah and Barak together sang to the Lord after the victory. Both our hearts and our minds should acknowledge the Lord as our Savior in every victory over temptation.

Basic Correspondences

Bethel = knowledge of celestial things
Ramah = knowledge of spiritual things
a tent = a childlike state of worship

Senior

The finer points of the correspondence can be discussed with this class. Some effort should be made to define what Deborah in her surroundings pictures. The history of the Kenites and their meaning should be stressed, and the nature and outcome of the battle should be illustrated as it applies to our own experience.

The conquest of the Holy Land and the settlement there pictures our final years of preparation for adult life. Joshua's death is like the withdrawal of our parents from control of our lives. Our characters are "formed." Our intentions are good: that is pictured by the fact that in the southern part of the land, as the first chapter of Judges tells us, the tribes of Simeon and Judah under Caleb's direction had overcome all their enemies, even the three sons of the giant Anak.

But in the northern part of the land, which pictures the understanding, the Israelites had won only a partial victory. Although in some places they were sufficiently strong to exact tribute from their enemies, they did not drive them out, but settled down to live among them and very soon were led away into the worship of their idols. When we are young, our minds do not have sufficient knowledge and independence to recognize and condemn the many fallacies in the current thought of our community. We compromise with worldly reasoning and are easily led astray by it.

Verse 7 of Judges 2 tells us that "the people served the Lord all the days of Joshua, and all the days of the elders that outlived Joshua, who had seen all the great works of the Lord, that he did for Israel." For a time in our new independent state we are still under the sway of our early training. But when this influence recedes, it is with us as with the Israelites, "the children of Israel did evil in the sight of the Lord, and served Baalim."

The key note of the period of the Judges is found in the statement in verse 6 of chapter 17: "In those days there was no king in Israel, but every man did that which was right in his own eyes." Many people, older as well as younger, are in this state. They say, "If I do what I think is right, what more can be expected of me?" And it takes repeated experience, as it did with Israel, to prove that one's own idea of right is not necessarily a safe guide. When Israel settled back in comfort with the idea that all its conquests were won, its old enemies, only partially overcome, began to regain strength and one by one rose up and attacked.

The Judges were individuals raised up by the Lord here and there in the land to lead Israel against particular enemies. When we recognize a temptation, realize our weakness, and turn to the Lord for help, He will always call up out of our memory some particular truth which can help us. Each enemy and each Judge is a study in itself.

The enemy in the northern part of the land who is attacking in our chapter for today pictures some false reasoning, and this time Israel is saved by two women. The first is the prophetess Deborah, who lived under a palm tree between Bethel and Ramah in the territory of Benjamin. Benjamin, the youngest son of Jacob, pictures our faculty for spiritual thought, and a palm tree is the symbol of the principle that goodness is of the Lord alone and that His truth should rule us. Women represent affections. So the Judge raised up in us to meet the temptation to accede to false reasoning is our affection for looking to the Lord for leadership in our thinking.

Deborah calls two of the northernmost tribes to fight the battle. The combat against false reasoning must be waged in the mind rather than in the heart, but if the affection for the Lord's guidance is present, the Lord can help us. Our enemy is caught in the flood and his horses and chariots are overwhelmed. Read chapter 5, verse 21, a part of Deborah's song of triumph.

In the heat of battle Sisera, the leader of the enemy forces, escapes. He pictures the selfish principle that prompts and directs false reasoning. We sometimes become involved in argument and imagine we have won a victory, when we have not really traced the temptation to its source and overcome that.

Jael was the wife of Heber the Kenite, a descendant of the father-in-law of Moses, who helped Moses in the wilderness. Moses' father-in-law Jethro—also called Reuel and Raguel (Hobab was Reuel's son)—pictures the remains of simple goodness which are preserved in our minds as the result of our early religious faith, for Midian was the son of Abraham by Keturah, whom Abraham married after Sarah's death. Most of the Midianites turned against Israel, but one good remnant, the Kenites, not only remained friendly but came with Israel into the Holy Land (see Numbers 10:29-32 and Judges 1:16 and 4:11). The tent is the symbol of worship from this simple faith, and the "nail" or wooden tent pin, which fastened the tent to the ground, is one of those simple commandments which relate our worship directly to our daily living. So Jael's apparently cruel act pictures our final disposal of the root of false reasoning by means of the simple "thou shalt not" of our childhood, always the final effective answer to the enemy. Notice that it is said that when Jael drove the tent pin through Sisera's temple, she "fastened it into the ground." Our "thou shalt not" must be driven home in the daily life.

Without Deborah and Jael, Barak and the two northern tribes could not have won the victory. Our intelligence alone is not sufficient to combat the assaults of worldly reasoning. Indeed Israel, forgetting its worship of Jehovah, had fallen subject to the king of Hazor. The story repeats itself over and over again in the Word and in our life: self-satisfaction, slavery, remembrance of the Lord, deliverance. "Then they called unto the Lord in their trouble, and he delivered them out of their distresses." (Psalm 107:6)

Adult

This story in its internal meaning connects with the experience of all of us. Cover the story and its interpretation briefly. Then read Judges 17:6, pointing out that this is the keynote of the period of the Judges, and base the discussion on the danger of thinking we know what is right without constant study of the Word in the light of the writings. Too many people even to old age remain in the period of the Judges as to their spiritual life. They recognize the necessity of constant study in connection with their business or profession and, in the case of housewives, of learning new methods and new recipes, but in their religious life they are content with a minimum of knowledge.

In Deuteronomy 6:10-12 we read: "And it shall be, when the Lord thy God shall have brought thee into the land which he sware unto they fathers, to Abraham, to Isaac, and to Jacob, to give thee great and goodly cities, which thou buildest not, and houses full of all good things, which thou filledst not, and wells digged, which thou diggedst not, vineyards and olive trees, which thou plantedst not; when thou shalt have eaten and be full; then beware lest thou forget the Lord, which brought thee forth out of the land of Egypt, from the house of bondage."

The time of the Judges is the time foretold in these verses. The children of Israel have come into the land promised to their fathers, and through the power of the Lord have taken possession of it. Their conquests under Joshua were sufficient to give them peace for a time, freedom to settle down in homes and enjoy the fruits of the land. This was the reward to which they had been looking forward, and in their enjoyment of it they fell into just the temptation which the Lord had prophesied. So long as Joshua lived or any of the elders who had been eyewitnesses of the miracles which the Lord had performed for their salvation, they remained faithful, but as soon as these were gone, they began to mingle with the evil people of the land, to intermarry with them, and finally to worship their idols.

This is a picture of a temptation which comes to every regenerating man and woman. Our first efforts to lead a spiritual life have a certain zeal which carries us along. Joshua—the truth fighting—is alive in us, our leader; the many instances in which the Lord has helped us in temptation are fresh in our memories. Then we gain a measure of victory; we taste the satisfaction of living from spiritual motives; we feel that we are settled in the right way and may relax our vigilance. We forget that we have not completely destroyed the enemies we have been fighting, but have merely put them to tribute. And while we rest on our laurels, confident in our new-found security and peace, these enemies begin to stir again and to gain strength. We feel so sure that we have mastered them that we allow ourselves to yield a little here and there to the old uncharitable feelings, to compromise with the worldly reasonings; and presently we are setting up instead of the Lord our God the very idols which the world about us worships—success, pleasure, money, power.

This is the period of the Judges. We go along about so far and then we wake to the fact that we have fallen prey to some enemy we thought we had crushed. We struggle against it for a time in vain and then, when we have realized our weakness, the Lord recalls to our mind the needed truth which alone can save us from this particular temptation; this is the Judge raised up. Under its leadership we conquer, and again have peace for a time until some other slumbering foe awakes, gains strength, and masters us.

So long as we are in this world, we never gain a complete victory. Indeed some of our evil tendencies we can never destroy, although in the other life the Lord will keep them quiescent for us and we shall not have to struggle against them. In Judges 2:22 we have the reason given why enemies were allowed to remain in the Holy Land: "That through them I may prove Israel, whether they will keep the way of the Lord to walk therein, as their fathers did keep it, or not." It is through victory in temptations that we gain strength of character. In Psalm 55:19 it is said of the wicked, "Because they have no changes, therefore they fear not God." Our souls grow strong by exercise just as our bodies do. When we are tempted, our weaknesses come to light and we can seek the Lord's help to overcome them. Swedenborg agrees with the apostle Paul that the Lord never permits us to be tempted beyond our strength (I Corinthians 10:13), and further tells us that those who have no temptations are kept from them because the Lord sees that they would not resist them. We should look upon our temptations as opportunities to gain strength of character, and we should not be discouraged because as we grow older we see deeper and deeper evils in ourselves.

Swedenborg does not tell us much directly about this battle between Deborah and Barak on the one hand and Sisera on the other. In AE 447[4] he says that it represents the "combat of truth from good against falsity from evil," and in AE 434[13] he says that Sisera represents "falsity from evil destroying the church." The enemies in the north were falsities in the understanding. These falsities crop up again and again in one form or another and often gain control of us before we realize it. Take, for example, the falsity that we do not need to go to church. This is a very obvious falsity to anyone who has acquired the habit of church attendance. But even such a person may perhaps move away from the church he loves. He does not immediately decide what church to attend, or he attends one and does not like it. He says, "It irritates me to hear preaching which does not agree with my belief and so it does me no good to go to church." Another may say, "I have to work hard all week and I need to sleep or to be out of doors on Sunday in order to do my work properly." What we actually mean is that other things are really more important than going to church, that we can get along without it. In our story Deborah is the Judge. She was a prophetess and lived "under the palm tree of Deborah between Ramah and Bethel." We are told that Ramah represents the things which belong to spiritual truth from the celestial, and that Bethel represents knowledges of internal things. The palm tree is the symbol of the principle that the Lord is our Savior. Thus all that we know of Deborah points to the fact that she represents our affection for inner, spiritual truths which look to the Lord as our Savior. This is indeed the affection which leads us to fight against falsities. The military leader, however, and the two tribes chosen to furnish the fighting men are from the north, truths in the understanding which can most easily meet the attacking falsities.

The death of Sisera at the hands of Jael is one of the striking and terrible pictures from the letter of the Word such as the old painters used to love to portray. It is also one of the stumbling blocks to those who see nothing but the literal sense. In the song of Deborah in chapter 5, Jael is represented as blessed above women and the details of her deed are rehearsed with seeming delight. The Lord does not commend nor offer us as examples to be followed the cruel practices of a cruel day. Swedenborg tells us that He purposely spoke through people who had departed farthest from Him so that the letter of His Word might reach men in their lowest states. There are always people who need to be reached through fear—shocked into thinking—and we all have states in which this is true of us. But for our higher states there is the internal sense. Jael, the wife of Heber the Kenite, a descendant of the priest of Midian who was the father-in-law of Moses, pictures an affection surviving from our childhood states even in the midst of falsity. In the example we have used, this final blow may well be given by some Jael in us, perhaps the remains of our childhood affection for going to church and Sunday school. Since a tent represents what is holy, the tent peg would be some particular truth which has served to anchor this general state of holiness to the earth of good living, such as one of the commandments or some other verse we have learned in childhood. And the blow is struck in a quiet moment when the threatening falsity has been temporarily lulled to sleep. If we can form the habit of always thinking of the enemies in the letter of the Word as evils and falsities within ourselves, the stories of battle and conquest, of extermination of the enemy and destroying his cities will not only cease to trouble our modern civilized attitude toward violence, but they will offer us specific instruction and help in meeting our temptations and overcoming them.

From the Writings of Swedenborg

Arcana Coelestia, n. 5280: "In order that man may be regenerated he must first be reformed, and this is done by means of the truths of faith; for he has to learn from the Word and from doctrine therefrom what good is. The knowledges of good from the Word, or from doctrine therefrom, are called the truths of faith, because all the truths of faith spring from good, and flow to good, for they look to good as an end. This is the first state, and is called the state of reformation. During their childhood and youth most of those who are in the church, are introduced into this state, and yet few are regenerated; for most in the church learn the truths of faith or the knowledges of good for the sake of reputation and honor, and also for gain; and when the truths of faith have been introduced by means of these loves, the man cannot be born anew or regenerated until these loves have been removed. In order that they may be removed, the man is let into a state of temptation, and this in the following manner. The loves referred to are excited by the infernal crew . . . but the affections of truth and good that have been insinuated from infancy . . . are then excited by angels. The result is a conflict . . . which is felt in the man as temptation."

Suggested Questions on the Lesson

J. What did Joshua accomplish during his lifetime? *conquered Holy Land*

J. How was the Holy Land divided among the tribes? *by lot*

J. Did another great leader immediately follow Joshua? *no*

P. After Joshua died, what mistake did the children of Israel make? *forgot the Lord*

J. What was the result? *various enemies troubled them*

J. What did the Lord do for them each time they turned to Him for help? *called a leader*

P. What did they call the leaders whom the Lord raised up for them? *Judges*

P. What woman was a Judge? *Deborah*

J. What enemy was attacking at this time? *Jabin*

J. Who was the leader of the army of the enemy? *Sisera*

P. What man did Deborah call to lead the army of Israel? *Barak*

J. On what condition did he agree to lead it? *if she also went*

J. From what tribes did he draw his forces? *Naphtali, Zebulun*

J. Where was the battle fought? *near Kishon*

J. Who won? *Israel*

J. To whom did Sisera flee? *Jael*

J. What did she do to him? *killed him*

S. What does the period of the Judges picture in our lives? *a time when we think we know enough not to have to learn more from the Lord*

I. What does an enemy from the north picture? *temptation to yield to false ideas*

S. What is represented by the tent pin? *a simple truth from the Word which binds or "nails" our worship to our daily life*

THE STORY OF GIDEON

Judges 6; 7

In every class above the Primary, the teacher should read aloud Judges 17:6 as the keynote of the period of the Judges and explain the difference between looking to self and looking to the Lord for knowledge of what is right. Be sure to point out the difference between the Judges and the patriarchs and Moses and Joshua, and also the kings, who are to come later. The Judges were local and temporary leaders.

Doctrinal Points

We never in this world reach a state in which we should consider ourselves "saved."

Humility and courage are both essential in our fight against evil.

Notes for Parents

Gideon was one of the Judges. The period of the Judges came between the time of Joshua—under whom the Israelites conquered the Holy Land and divided it by lot among the tribes—and the period of the kings. The Judges were not rulers over the whole land. They were individuals raised up from time to time by the Lord in one or another locality in the Holy Land to lead an attack upon a particular enemy. The enemies in Gideon's time were the Midianites, who were overrunning the land "like grasshoppers" and stealing the crops before the Israelites could harvest them. The whole story of Gideon is a striking one and is given in the Bible to teach us that the power to gain victory over our temptations is not in ourselves, but comes to us from the Lord as we learn His truths from the Word and obey them.

If the Israelites, after they reached the Holy Land and conquered it, had remained faithful to the Lord and continued to keep their enemies in check, they could have been happy and prosperous.

The troubles they got into in the time of the Judges were the result of their becoming self-satisfied and yielding to the great temptation of prosperity—the temptation to forget the Lord. Whenever we get to thinking that we know enough to do right without trying to learn any more, we are sure to get into trouble.

Primary

The little ones will enjoy the story, especially the way in which the three hundred were chosen and the way in which the lamps and trumpets were used. Tell them that Gideon did not think much of his own abilities, but that he won the victory because he was willing to obey the Lord and was not afraid. All the details of the story will be interesting to the class, especially those concerning Gideon's call, his destroying the altar of Baal, and the signs given him. The Midianite's dream will also interest them.

Under Joshua the Israelites conquered the whole land.
Then it was divided among the tribes by lot.
They set up the tabernacle at Shiloh, in the center of the land, halfway between Shechem and Bethel.
Then they settled down in their new homes and became prosperous, and they began to forget the Lord.
Joshua died, and for a time they had no great leader.
Their enemies began to grow strong again and to trouble and attack them.
Each time an enemy attacked, they suddenly remembered to ask the Lord's help, and each time He raised up someone to lead them to victory again.
These people were called Judges.
They did not rule over all the people, but each had one special task to do.

In our story for today, the enemies who are attacking them are the Midianites. They came into the country in hordes, just like grasshoppers, and destroyed the crops of the Israelites and drove away their cattle.

Then the Israelites began to think about the Lord again and begged Him to save them, and the Lord did save them. He sent an angel to a man named Gideon and told him to raise an army and fight the Midianites. Gideon, just like Moses at the burning bush, thought at first that he was not great enough to lead the people, but the Lord promised to be with him.

You see, Gideon was modest about himself just like Moses and Joshua.
But the Lord proved to Gideon that He would be with him and give him victory.
Then Gideon was able to raise a great army of thirty-two thousand men.
Why did the Lord tell him he had too many men?
Who were first sent home?
What further test was given?
How many were there in the army finally?
What "weapons" did they have?
What did Gideon tell them to do?
What were they to shout?
What happened to the Midianites?

If we forget the Lord and do not obey Him, He cannot help us. But if we do obey Him and trust Him, then it does not matter how weak and small we are or how few there are of us, for the Lord is with us and gives us power.

Junior

Show the Juniors a map of the land as it was divided among the tribes and have them find the tribe of Manasseh, from which Gideon came; and the tribes of Asher, Zebulun, and Naphtali, who sent men for Gideon's army. Then locate the place of the battle, with the place where each army was drawn up. Stress Gideon's humility, his obedience, and the reason given for the reduction of the army (7:2), as well as the point emphasized in the pupils' notes that it takes courage to do right when those about you are doing wrong, but that such courage is one of the essentials of real leadership.

Under Joshua the Israelites conquered all of the Holy Land. Then it was divided by lot among the twelve tribes, and all the people settled down and built homes. The tabernacle was set up at Shiloh, which was about halfway between Bethel and Shechem. Then Joshua died. Read Judges 2:6-13. Joshua had charged the tribes to complete the conquest of their enemies, each within its own borders, but the tribes of Judah and Simeon were the only ones who obeyed. The others were all too much interested in becoming prosperous themselves. So the Lord allowed their enemies to become strong again and to rise up and attack them. Of course when they were in trouble, the people always begged the Lord to save them. They had no one leader, but each time they asked Him, the Lord raised up someone to lead them against the particular enemy who was attacking. These leaders were called Judges.

At the time of our lesson for today, an enemy from the cross-Jordan country is attacking Israel.

Who were these enemies?

You may remember from our lesson about Moses at the burning bush that Midian was a son of Abraham by Keturah, whom he married after Sarah's death. His descendants had helped Israel in the wilderness (Exodus 18; Numbers 10:29-32; Judges 1:16), but now, except for the family of the Kenites, they have become enemies.

Gideon of the tribe of Manasseh was chosen and prepared to lead Israel against the Midianites.

What was he doing when he was called to serve the Lord?
Who called him?
He was humble and willing to obey. These are the two qualities in us which the Lord needs to find in order to use us for His work in the world.
How did the Lord test Gideon's willingness to obey?
What other name was given to him?
What two signs did he ask of the Lord?

Look on a map at the plain of Esdraelon. Part of its western boundary is the hill of Morah. The Midianites were camped in the valley at the foot of this mountain. A little further south is the well of Harod, which was later called "Gideon's spring" because Gideon's army was gathered there. Esdraelon is the Greek form of the Hebrew name Jezreel. Jezreel is mentioned many times in the Old Testament, but we usually call it "the plain of Esdraelon" because under that name it has become a famous battlefield.

What tribes furnished the men for Gideon's army?
Why did the Lord say the army was too big?
Who were first sent home?

When we are trying to fight a temptation, we must first get rid of the fear of being defeated. And there was another kind of man who had to be sent home.

How many men did Gideon finally have?
What assurance of victory did the Lord give him?
How did he divide his army?
What did they have instead of weapons?

The lamps in the pitchers picture truth from the Lord hidden within the letter of the Word. Blowing on trumpets pictures declaring the power of obedience to the commandments. Truth from the Lord and obedience to the commandments are all the "weapons" we need in order to overcome our temptations. In the face of them, evil and falsity become confused and destroy themselves, just as the Midianites did.

Intermediate

The correspondence of the Midianites, the altar of Baal, the two tests by which the army was reduced, and the lamps, pitchers, and trumpets should all be discussed. The need of humility, obedience, and courage and the fact that the power to overcome is in the Word are the important lessons.

Under Joshua the Israelites conquered the land and settled in it. The country was divided among the tribes by lot, and the tabernacle was set up at Shiloh near the center of the land. Shiloh means "peace." But the people, with the exception of the tribes of Simeon and Judah, did not obey Joshua's injunction to complete the conquest of the enemies within their own borders and to make no terms with them (Joshua 23:4-13), and they were led away into the worship of the gods of their enemies, the worship of Baal and other idols. The Lord had warned them in the wilderness against just this evil (Deuteronomy 6:10-12).

After Joshua's death they had for a time no one leader. The characteristic of the period is described in the words: "In those days there was no king in Israel, but every man did that which was right in his own eyes." (Judges 17:6) When we look to ourselves for the knowledge of what is right, we are setting ourselves up above the Lord; this is worshiping Baal. Because of this unfaithfulness the Lord permitted their enemies to increase in strength and to attack them. Then, whenever they were sufficiently frightened to turn to Him for help, He would raise up some person to lead them against the particular enemy who was troubling them. These leaders were called Judges. Only the last one, Samuel, had more than a temporary and local authority. They picture the particular truths which the Lord calls to our memory when we need them to fight against particular temptations.

In our lesson for today, the particular enemies are the Midianites. You may remember that they also were descended from Abraham and had been friends of the Israelites at the time of the Exodus, protecting Moses for forty years and later giving him good advice. One family of Midianites, the Kenites, joined the Israelites and settled with them in the Holy Land. But the rest of the Midianites had become enemies. The Midianites picture the kind of thoughts we had about the Lord when we were children. These were holy and good, and so long as they are used to protect our worship, they are friends to our spiritual life. But they can become enemies. For example, when we were little children, our thoughts about the birth of the Lord centered in the little baby in the manger with the animals nearby and the shepherds and wise men coming in. But as we grow older, our thoughts of the Lord's Advent should grow greater and deeper. If we think only of the infant Jesus, the thoughts of the external and superficial surroundings of His birth will fill our minds, as the Midianites overran the fields of Israel, and will take away the real spiritual food which we need at Christmas time. They may even become false thoughts if they lead us to think of the Lord as a mere man and to doubt that the Divine could have come into the world as a helpless baby.

Gideon told the angel sent to call him that his family was the lowliest in the tribe of Manasseh, and that he was the least in his family. Yet when he was assured that he was really called to lead his people against its overwhelming foe, he obeyed immediately and fearlessly. These two qualities, humility and courage, were the same ones enjoined upon Joshua, and they are essential to a fight against evil because the only power which can overcome evil is the Lord's, and we can use the Lord's power only when we recognize our own weakness and are willing to obey Him wholly.

Gideon's first assignment was the overthrow of the altar of Baal in the face of the certain displeasure of everyone he knew. We must be able to pass this test of ability to do right bravely when everyone around us is doing wrong. It takes real courage to face the ridicule and disapproval of the people we live with every day. The result of this first act of bravery on the part of Gideon has a lesson for us, too. Although his neighbors at first wanted to kill him for throwing down their altar, his bravery before them made such an impression on them that afterward they accepted his leadership and followed him to battle. Moral courage always in the end inspires respect.

The reduction of Gideon's army was another lesson to Israel in the truth that their strength was in the Lord alone. For us it pictures the fact that when we set out to fight our temptations, we must first get rid of the fear of failure and then of all the tendencies to hesitation and self-indulgence; these were the two tests by which Gideon's army was reduced. We must always meet the enemy not in our own strength or with our own arguments, but with simple truth from the Word—the lamps in the pitchers—and with obedience to the commandments, which is pictured by the blowing of the trumpets. The division of the three hundred men into three companies represents the simultaneous attack upon our temptations in our hearts, our minds, and our conduct. The enemy camped in the valley pictures the false reasonings in favor of having our own way which have filled the lower part of our minds. We all know how easy it is to find excuses for doing what we want to do. These false reasonings all fall into confusion when we flash upon them the truths we get from the Lord in the Word and when we make ourselves remember and obey the commandments. The next chapter tells how Gideon chased the enemy across the Jordan and beyond; he then destroyed them with their kings. After we have conquered a temptation, we need to clear out of our hearts and minds all the wrong feelings and thoughts that have been connected with it.

Basic Correspondences

the Judges = particular truths which help us to overcome particular temptations

---

Senior

The necessity of looking to the Lord instead of to our own intelligence for the knowledge of what is right is an important point to make with this class. Every detail of the story can be seen to add to the force of this lesson. After suggesting the use of quotations from the Word as weapons against temptation, the teacher might read to the class the quotations found at the end of the Adult notes, and then ask the class to suggest others.

We recall from our previous knowledge of the Bible that the book of Joshua covers the period of conquest of the Holy Land and its division among the tribes. This is a picture of coming into a state of regeneration with all our faculties ordered in their proper relation to our service of the Lord and the neighbor. The tabernacle was set up at Shiloh (which means "peace") in the center of the land. But it is a great mistake to think that we ever come into a state when we can consider ourselves regenerate and, as some churches express it, "saved." Again and again the Bible teaches us that our enemies are always with us and that we must be constantly on our guard against them or we shall surely slip back. In Deuteronomy 6:10-12 the Lord had warned Israel against this danger which would be inherent in their victory, and in Joshua 23:4-13 the tribes are charged to maintain their worship of the Lord and to make no terms with the enemies that remained within their borders. But all the tribes except Simeon and Judah disregarded both the warning and the charge, and turned to the worship of the gods of their enemies. Then the enemies regained strength and rose against them.

This is the picture presented in the book of Judges. "In those days there was no king in Israel, but every man did that which was right in his own eyes." (Judges 17:6) This is not the way to spiritual success. It is the way to danger and destruction. Only as the Lord raised up people to lead them was it possible for the Israelites to be saved. These people, the Judges, were not rulers over the whole country or for long periods of time. They represent particular truths which the Lord raises up from our memories when we realize that we are in grave danger and turn to Him for help. Each enemy represents a particular temptation.

The story of Gideon is the description of our battle against superficiality, for the Midianites, as enemies, represent superficial and hence false thoughts about religious things. Midian, the son of Abraham by Keturah, the wife of his old age, originally pictures our childish concept of religious truth, innocent and good at the time when it is formed. Moses, after his first flight from Egypt, was protected for forty years in the land of Midian by Jethro the priest, whose daughter he married. So long as there is innocence in the heart and our minds have not developed enough to be troubled by arguments against our faith, this childish thinking is helpful. But as we grow older and come in contact with worldly reasoning, it begins to stand in the way of our spiritual growth. A host of inconsequential thoughts, like the Midianites, overrun our minds when we should instead be growing in depth of understanding of the Lord and of spiritual living. In the animal kingdom grasshoppers and locusts represent this indulgence in childish and superficial thinking. So the Midianites were likened to them. We should remember that all thinking which is based on the testimony of sense experience alone is superficial and childish. Our minds are given us to use in religion as well as in everything else.

Gideon, threshing wheat in the winepress to hide it from the Midianites, pictures our higher self trying to discover what is really good in a time of temptation. His humility and his willingness to obey the Lord made it possible for the Lord to use him to save Israel.

The two signs which he asked are interesting. The fleece pictures a good external life from a principle of innocence. The ground pictures the mind in general. The dew, which comes in the morning, pictures truth from the Lord refreshing us at the time of a new beginning. Sometimes our efforts to do right are rewarded with this sense of renewal and understanding. Sometimes they are not apparently rewarded. Both conditions are under the Lord's providence. Gideon wanted to be sure the Lord was leading him, whatever the appearance. We need this same assurance to protect us against discouragement.

Gideon naturally called out a large army to battle, as we sometimes use time and effort in thinking just what we are going to say and do in the face of some expected attack upon our principles. The Lord told His Apostles: "But when they shall lead you, and deliver you up, take no thought beforehand what ye shall speak, neither do ye premeditate: but whatsoever shall be given you in that hour, that speak ye: for it is not ye that speak, but the Holy Ghost." (Mark 13:11) If we constantly read and meditate upon the Word of God and are determined to obey it, we shall be enabled to meet temptation with the Lord's words rather than with our own.

From Gideon's army the Lord removed first all who were fearful, and then all who were slothful and self-indulgent. Our answers to the tempter should not be given fearfully or with hesitation. Gideon was given an experience to encourage him. We all have had the experience of seeing in people we know the triumph of simple goodness over the superficial reasonings of the self-assured. These experiences, like Gideon's overhearing the story of the dream of the cake of barley bread which overturned the Midianite tent, are granted us by the Lord to strengthen our faith.

And Israel was saved not by its own weapons. The three hundred were divided into three companies, picturing effort on all three planes of life; so they appeared on three sides of the enemy at once. And the attack was made with the lamps and trumpets, just as we can be led in our temptation battles by the sudden flashing of truth out of the letter of the Word and the proclamation of the determination to obey the Lord. These were the "sword of the

Lord and of Gideon," before which the enemy was confounded. It is a matter of experience that nothing so confuses one who is using selfish and worldly arguments as an unexpected quotation from the Word and the simple determination to obey it.

Adult

There are any number of interesting discussion topics in this story: the characteristics of the period of the Judges, the altar to Baal, the dew on the fleece, and the Midianite's dream, as well as the immediately obvious ones.

The division of the Holy Land by lot among the tribes pictures the well-rounded spiritual life, and also the well-rounded spiritual society, in which good men and women of all types and gifts have their proper places and work together harmoniously in the Lord's service.

But the Israelites in their new prosperity forgot their duty to the Lord. So long as Joshua lived or any of the elders who had been eyewitnesses of the miracles which the Lord had performed for their salvation, they remained faithful; but as soon as these were gone, they began to have dealings with the evil peoples of the land, to intermarry with them, and presently even to worship their idols. Our first efforts to lead a spiritual life have a certain zeal which carries us along. Joshua—the truth fighting—is alive in us, our leader; the many instances in which the Lord has helped us in temptation are fresh in our memories. Then we gain a measure of victory; we taste the satisfaction of living from spiritual motives; we feel that we are settled in the right way and may relax our vigilance. We forget that we have not completely destroyed the enemies which we have subdued, but have merely, as it were, put them to tribute. And while we rest on our laurels, confident in our new-found security and peace, these enemies begin to stir again and to gain strength. This is the period of the Judges. The keynote of this period is found in Judges 17:6: "In those days there was no king in Israel, but every man did that which was right in his own eyes."

In the story of Gideon, we have again impressed upon us—though in a new form, the lesson of the necessity of humility, obedience, and courage. The enemy this time is Midian. Swedenborg links Midian in a good sense with those of his own day who were brought up in the doctrine of faith alone and believed it because it was taught them by the church, and yet were in a good state of life. In a bad sense the Midianites, he says, are those who are in "truth which was not truth because there was no good of life." Sometimes, after a period of apparent security in our relations to the Lord, we are suddenly overwhelmed by an attack from without. This may perhaps take the form of ridicule from some person who seems to know a great deal more about the Bible than we do and uses the very stories which we have loved and reverenced against us as weapons to break down our faith, appealing to so-called "common sense" to support his attack. Thus our childhood's knowledge is made to raise doubts in our minds. Those of us who have skeptics among our acquaintances become very familiar with the attacks of the Midianites.

The angel of the Lord came to Gideon as he was threshing wheat in the winepress to hide it from the Midianites. Gideon was of the tribe of Manasseh, the tribe which represents love of the neighbor coming from its true source, the Lord, and expressing itself in the outward life. Gideon acknowledged himself to be the least in the tribe, but he was found trying to preserve some wheat—some genuine good—from the Midianites. Even a very small amount of such genuine love can be used by the Lord to destroy the Midianites "as one man" if we will be faithful and brave. Gideon received the sign of fire from heaven consuming his offering as a proof that the Lord's power would be with him. His first act after that was to destroy the altar of Baal (Baal, like Babylon, represents the love of dominion from the love of self) which had been set up by his own father. Next he built an altar to the Lord in its place. After this he received the further signs of the dew on the fleece and on the ground, which picture the fact that the Lord is with all our genuine efforts to be good, whether these efforts seem to succeed or not. When we are attacked by the Midianites, the first thing necessary is the admission of our own weakness and need of help from the Lord. The second is that we see that what stands in our way is the altar to Baal in our minds; that is, when we find it hard to meet and overcome ridicule and worldly reasoning, it is because we really care more about what people around us think of us than we do about what the Lord thinks of us. Once we see and overthrow this altar, the Lord can show us the truths we need for our defense. If we can bring ourselves to think of ridicule as a test of our sincerity and courage, the battle is half won, and if we can be armed with truths from the Word with which to meet ridicule, we can go the rest of the way.

It is obvious, even in the letter, that the victory of Gideon teaches the lesson that the power to conquer in temptation comes from the Lord and not from ourselves. The details of the victory suggest the means by which the Lord's power is made effective in us. In addition to his own tribe, Gideon summoned men from the three northernmost tribes–representing truth to fight against falsity. Then all those who were afraid were sent home; we must put aside fear of failure and fear of consequences when we enter upon the Lord's battles. Finally only those who stooped and drank hastily at the spring, lapping water from their hands as a dog laps, were chosen to win the victory. This suggests that the battle with the Midianites calls for speed and zeal and our quickest wits to select hastily the truths which will answer our present external need for arguments. The army was divided into three parts, picturing attack on all three planes of heart, mind, and conduct; and it was placed so as to surround the enemy and made use of no ordinary weapons of warfare. The ordinary campaign of argument and reasoning cannot be used against those who employ ridicule or against the influence of such attacks in our own minds. These enemies must be attacked suddenly, upon all sides, and with weapons which are not generally thought of as weapons. Trumpets represent the power of the Lord speaking through the Word, and the torches within the pitchers are the truth which is hidden within the letter of the Word, truth which can flash out suddenly from an apparently dark or obscure verse.

The Midianites were thrown into confusion and destroyed each other in the darkness. The attack of those who ridicule faith in the Lord and the Word as childish can often be routed by a bombardment of simple quotations from the Scriptures which come from different angles of thought. Such an attack is always unexpected. The Lord's truth shines forth where they were convinced all was darkness; His power is manifest in one they thought an easy prey. They are thrown into confusion, and if they try to answer they destroy their own strength by self-contradiction.

We have the Lord's own example to follow here. Three times He answered the tempter by a simple quotation from the Scriptures, and again and again He put the scribes and Pharisees to rout in the same way. Study Matthew 22:23-46 for a wonderful illustration of this method. If we will think about what we read in the Word and memorize striking verses, we can all arm ourselves with Gideon's lamps and pitchers and trumpets. Verses like the following come to mind:

> The fool hath said in his heart, There is no God. (Psalm 14:1)
>
> For lo, the wicked bend their bow, they make ready their arrow upon the string, that they may privily shoot at the upright in heart. (Psalm 11:2)
>
> For my thoughts are not your thoughts, neither are my ways your ways, saith the Lord. (Isaiah 55:8)

From the Writings of Swedenborg

Apocalypse Explained, n. 455[9]: "'Midian' here means those who do not care for truth, because they are merely natural and external: therefore Midian was smitten by those who 'lapped the waters in the hand with the tongue like a dog'; these mean such as have an appetite for truths, thus who from some natural affection seek to know truths, a 'dog' signifying appetite and eagerness, 'waters' truths, and 'lapping them with the tongue' to have an appetite for and eagerly seek. So it was by these that Midian was smitten. Anyone can see that such things would not have been commanded unless they had been significative."

Arcana Coelestia, n. 8815: "The Divine truth which passes through heaven is also represented by . . . the trumpets with which the three hundred men who were with Gideon sounded round about the camp of Midian, Amalek, and the sons of the east (Judges 7). The reason why the trumpets produced this effect was that they represented the truth Divine through the heavens, which is such that it perfects the good, but destroys the evil; the reason why it perfects the good is that these receive the Divine good which is in the truth; but that it destroys the evil is because these do not receive the Divine good which is in it. . . . 'Midian, Amalek, and the sons of the east,' round about whose camp the three hundred men of Gideon sounded the trumpets, signified those who were in evils and in the derivative falsities."

Suggested Questions on the Lesson

P. From what book of the Bible is our lesson for today? *Judges*

J. Who were the Judges? *temporary local leaders*

J. In what way were the Judges different from Moses and Joshua as leaders? *not great leaders of entire people*

J. What was the trouble with the people in the period of the Judges? *forgot God*

P. Which Judge is our lesson about today? *Gideon*

J. From what tribe did he come? *Manasseh*

P. What enemy was attacking Israel? *Midian (also Amalek)*

J. What was the first thing Gideon did after he was called? *humbled himself*

J. What assurance did he ask of the Lord? *fleece*

J. From what tribes did he gather his army? *Asher, Zebulun, Naphtali, Manasseh*

P. Why did the army have to be reduced in numbers? *God to give victory*

P. Who were first sent home? *fearful*

P. What was the second test? *water drinking*

P. How large was the army finally? *three hundred*

P. What did they have instead of weapons? *lamps, pitchers, trumpets*

J. How was the attack made? *surrounded enemy, broke jars, shouted*

J. What was the result? *confusion, victory*

I. What do the Judges represent? *particular truths needed in time of trouble*

S. What do you think are the important lessons taught in this story? *trust the Lord, get rid of fearful thoughts, be prepared to face ridicule, ask the Lord what is right*

JEPHTHAH

Judges 11

The lesson should be prefaced by a reminder of Joshua's conquest of the whole land and its division among the tribes. Then should follow a statement of the conditions which prevailed during the period of the Judges, emphasizing the reason why the enemies in the land gained in strength. In the lesson for the day, Jephthah's rash vow may be compared with Joshua's hasty acceptance of the Gibeonites. Teachers of all classes should study the Adult notes as a preparation for answering questions which may be asked concerning Jephthah's daughter.

Doctrinal Points

We cannot safely bargain with the Lord.
The spiritual sense of the Word is sometimes the very opposite of the apparent meaning in the letter.
True faith involves willingness to give up anything of our own when it is required of us by the Lord.
Charity always involves obedience.

Notes for Parents

The book of Judges contains many interesting stories. Up to this time the children of Israel have had a series of outstanding leaders—Abraham, Isaac, Jacob, Joseph, Moses, and Joshua—each one recognized by all the people as their divinely appointed head. But after Joshua's death, when they had come into possession of their long-desired homes in the Holy Land, each family settled down to build and plant for itself, and they became overconfident. Of this period it is said: "In those days there was no king in Israel, but every man did that which was right in his own eyes." (21:25) We may hear people today say, "If I do what I think is right, that is all that can be expected of me." This sounds good, but it overlooks the fact that people often think things are right which are actually wrong, and that we all need constant study of the Lord's truth to keep us in the right way.

The Israelites forgot the warning Moses had given them that they must be especially careful when they were prosperous not to forget the Lord. We all need the same warning. When we think we can rely on ourselves for guidance, the evils that are in us rise up and get the upper hand as the enemies of Israel did. We can be saved only by the Lord's help. He is always ready to show us the right way and to help us overcome our temptations if we ask Him. But we must be willing, as Jephthah was, to go all the way and really give up our own desires when we find that it is required of us.

Primary

The lesson drawn from the general character of the period of the Judges is an easy one to present, Jephthah's vow and its result can be discussed with the class. The faithfulness of Jephthah and his daughter to a promise made to the Lord should be stressed.

The Lord gave Joshua victory over all the enemies in the Holy Land, and then the whole country was marked out into sections. The tribes—all but the tribes of Reuben and Gad and half the tribe of Manasseh—cast lots to see which part of the land they should have. Those two and a half tribes had already been given land on the other side of the Jordan River.

After that each tribe took possession of its land and settled down in comfort. And they did just what Moses had told them to be sure not to do: they forgot all about the Lord. They even began to worship the gods of their enemies. So of course their enemies became strong again. And every time their enemies attacked them, they expected the Lord to help them. The Lord did help them over and over again. Each time He raised up some strong leader and gave him the victory. These leaders were called Judges.

Wouldn't you think the Israelites would have learned to be sensible and obey the Lord? Are you ever naughty? Doesn't being naughty always get you into trouble? And then you expect your mother to forgive you, don't you? And she does. And then are you always good after that? You see, we are very much like the children of Israel, aren't we?

One time the enemy was making trouble on the other side of the Jordan. This enemy was the Ammonites. When the Israelites turned to the Lord for help, He raised up a man named Jephthah, who lived on that other side of the Jordan to be their leader.

What rash vow did Jephthah make?
What did he have to give up as a result?

When Jephthah made his vow, he did not think that he was going to have to give up his only daughter, whom he loved. But he kept his promise, and his daughter helped him keep it. We should keep our promises, and we should never try to make anyone else break a promise either.

Junior

For this class the Bible references are important, as they impress upon the children the historical sequence of the Word. Map work is important this time also, and another connection can be made through the home of Jephthah and the settlement of the two and a half tribes in that region. The moral lessons to be stressed are summed up at the end of the Junior notes.

Look up Deuteronomy 6:10-15 and read the warning the Lord had given Israel which they should have then remembered. But Israel was very prone to forget the Lord except when they were in trouble. Aren't we likely to do the same thing? When everything is going well with us, we become self-satisfied and self-confident. Then the Lord has to let trouble come to us to show us how weak we really are and how much we need Him.

After Joshua and all the people who had fought to conquer the land had died, the Israelites let themselves mingle with the people they thought they had overcome and even intermarried with them, which they had been strictly commanded not to do. Presently they were worshiping the gods of the land instead of their own

God, who had done so much for them. When we have overcome a bad habit, we have to keep it under control or we may find that we have slipped back into it.

Whenever their enemies began to attack and oppress them, the Israelites remembered the Lord and cried to Him for help, and each time He raised up someone to deliver them. These leaders were called Judges. They did not rule the whole country or lead all the people, but they overcame a particular enemy in a particular place. The book of Judges tells about them. You may remember the stories of Deborah, Gideon, Samson, Eli, and Samuel.

What was the name of the Judge in our chapter for today?
Where did he live?
What enemy was attacking Israel?
Look at a map to see where the Ammonites lived and where Gilead is.
What rash vow did Jephthah make?
What did he find he had to sacrifice?
Did his daughter try to make him break his vow?
What favor did she ask?
To what custom did this lead?

We must remember that human sacrifices were very common among the idolatrous people of those days. It was apparently not against Jephthah's conscience to sacrifice his daughter, just as it was not against Abraham's conscience to sacrifice Isaac. What seems a crime to us did not seem a crime to them. This does not mean that it was right, but that they did not know it was wrong. We all do many wrong things ignorantly from good motives, and the Lord forgives us. Jephthah and his daughter both believed that they were doing right, and the Lord could have said to Jephthah what He said to Abraham in Genesis 22:16-17.

We may learn three lessons from this story. One is that we should think carefully before we make a promise. The second is that we should do our best to keep our promises and should also help other people to keep theirs. And the third is that when we promise to obey the Lord we must be prepared to be asked to give up some things which may seem very dear to us.

Intermediate

Probably the most interesting lesson for the Intermediates is the correspondence of the sacrifice of Jephthah's daughter, but the class should also have a clear idea of the meaning of the period of the Judges.

The Judges were men raised up one after another by the Lord to lead the people against their enemies after the original conquest of the Holy Land was over.

You remember that the conquest of the Holy Land pictures in our lives the period of regeneration, the time when we have learned to enjoy living an orderly outward life and are beginning our real battle against the inherited evils in our hearts. Under Joshua the Israelites conquered the land and brought their enemies under control. Then the land was divided by lot among the tribes and each tribe was supposed to complete the conquest within its own territory. But only in the southernmost part of the land–especially in the region around Hebron, which had been given to Caleb and his descendants–did the people fulfill this duty. Most of the tribes were too anxious to settle down, build their homes, plant their fields, and begin to enjoy their new land.

This is very much what we all do. When we think we have our bad tendencies pretty well under control, we become overconfident of our own goodness and fall into the habit of excusing our little weaknesses. The Israelites began to mingle with the people of the land and even to intermarry with them, which they had been strictly charged not to do. Joshua had died and so had "all the elders who outlived Joshua." So we sometimes forget all our former eagerness to overcome our evils. Finally the Israelites actually began to worship the gods of the land. We find it more and more easy to think and act as the people around us in the world do.

Then the enemies began to gain strength and to attack, and in places they gained the upper hand over the Israelites and oppressed them. So our evils, which we imagined we had overcome, crop up again, and suddenly we find that we are in the grip of some old temptation. "Then they cried unto the Lord in their trouble, and he saved them out of their distresses," as we read in Psalm 107.

When they were in trouble, they always remembered the Lord, just as we do. The Judge whom the Lord each time raised up pictures some particular truth from the Word called up out of our memory to lead us in the fight against the particular temptation which is upon us.

Most of the enemies were within the land itself, but after a while even one of the enemies on the other side of the Jordan gained strength and tried to reconquer that country. The tribes of Reuben and Gad and half the tribe of Manasseh had been given their inheritance on the east side of the Jordan. This was a country which had been taken from the Amorites before the crossing of the Jordan. It included the rich mountainous pasture land of Gilead. The country east of the Jordan represents our outward conduct, and the enemies there are the temptations which come to us from our worldly environment. After we reach the Holy Land of regenerate living, we sometimes feel that we have put behind us all need of watching our external conduct to keep it in order, and this is never true. As long as we live we shall be tempted to say and do things which are not right. The attack by the Ammonites pictures such a temptation.

Swedenborg tells us that the Ammonites represent the "falsification of truth." This means the temptation, once we have acknowledged some truth of the Word, to twist this truth to suit our convenience, as some people, for example, acknowledge the truth that we should worship the Lord on the sabbath day, and then say, "I can worship the Lord better on the golf links than in church." This is an external type of temptation, and the Lord brings to our mind to meet it some simple statement from the letter of the Word, such as the statement about the Lord in Luke 4:16: ". . . as his custom was, he went into the synagogue on the sabbath day." Such a truth is pictured by Jephthah the Gileadite, for Gilead represents good in the external life.

Then we have the story of Jephthah's rash vow. It reminds us of Jacob's promise to serve the Lord if the Lord would prosper him. We should not pray to the Lord in the spirit of bargaining. We should recognize that whatever the Lord permits to happen to us is permitted in love and with a view to our good. So what happened to Jephthah was permitted in order to teach us what genuine service of the Lord requires: the readiness to give up our own desires.

This is one of the cases in which the spiritual sense of the Word is almost the opposite of the literal sense. In the letter we have what is to us a horrible instance of human sacrifice apparently required of Jephthah by the Lord. We must remember, of course, that with the people about Jephthah human sacrifices were not at all uncommon, and Jephthah had no feeling that they were wrong. Both he and his daughter undoubtedly thought of human sacrifices as the sign of supreme devotion to God, just as Abraham did when he thought he was required to sacrifice Isaac. And the Lord permitted the sacrifice, as He permits us to do many wrong things which we believe to be right. The Lord "looketh upon the heart."

But in the internal sense we have a different picture. Daughters represent affections, and Jephthah's only daughter pictures the only affection he had up to that time—the affection for success because of the feeling of satisfaction it gave him. This he was required to give up, and we remember that burnt offerings made to the Lord represent acknowledgment that all the good qualities we seem to have are not really ours but the Lord's. The two months allowed for Jephthah's daughter to go "up and down upon the mountains" picture the time it takes for the thought of this sacrifice of our self-satisfaction to work itself out in our minds so that we are completely ready to make it. And the custom to which it gave rise among the daughters of Israel pictures the effect in our lives ever afterward of having once made this offering to the Lord. So the story of Jephthah really teaches us a beautiful lesson which we all need.

Basic Correspondences

a Judge = some particular truth from the Word
Gilead = good on the external plane of life

Senior

The lessons of particular importance for the Seniors in this story are the danger of overconfidence and the need of recognizing that without the Lord we can do nothing. The Seniors are approaching the time when they will go out into the world "on their own," and should be impressed with the necessity of being always watchful against the weakening of the good principles they have adopted as theirs.

Our lesson for today is the strange and to us forbidding story of Jephthah and his daughter. The book of Judges presents a sort of interlude between the period of the development of the Jewish nation and the period of its history as the recognized possessor of the Holy Land. It is a stage through which all of us pass—not a very creditable stage, but one which teaches us a great deal about ourselves and about our need of the Lord.

In our lives the conquest of the Holy Land represents the beginning of regeneration, that state in which with the Lord's help we are eagerly trying to find and overcome weaknesses and evils which are within us by heredity. Under Joshua the Israelites did conquer the land. Then it was divided by lot among the tribes, and each tribe was told to enter upon its inheritance and to complete the conquest of the enemies within its own borders. This pictures a time when we feel that we have really won the victory over our weaknesses and can begin to enjoy the fruits of this victory. We know that we are not perfect, that there will be further temptations, but we feel confident of our ability to meet them. And in this confidence is our danger.

In the first chapter of Judges we learn that in the south the tribes of Judah and Simeon actually did complete their conquest. This means that at heart we wish to be wholly good. But the chapter goes on to say that none of the other tribes won a full victory. Each left certain enemies unconquered. Then we read that as long as Joshua lived and the elders who outlived Joshua, the people continued to serve the Lord; but after that they forgot the Lord and began to mingle with the people of the land and to intermarry with them and finally to worship their gods. This is a picture of how our first enthusiasm for the truly spiritual life is liable to cool as we go about our everyday occupations. We begin to do as others do, then to think as they think, and finally to seek our own advantage instead of serving the Lord and the neighbor as we started out to do.

Then we find suddenly that the evils within us which we thought we had overcome are not only still there, but have gained strength and are threatening to control us again. One after another the enemies in the different parts of the Holy Land rose up and harassed the Israelites. Each time, when they were hard pressed, the Israelites turned to the Lord for help, and each time He raised up a Judge in the particular part of the land where the trouble was, to lead the men of that land against the enemy. These Judges represent particular truths from the Word which the Lord, when we ask Him for help, brings up out of our memory to show us how to fight particular temptations.

We think of the Holy Land as the strip of country which lies between the Jordan River and the Mediterranean Sea. But the Jordan valley on the east side of the river was also a part of the Holy Land in its wider sense; it was the rich country which Lot had chosen to live in when he separated from Abram. It represents the natural plane of our lives with all its good and pleasant things, and with its many temptations also. When the Israelites were nearing the Holy Land under Moses, they bypassed the lands of Edom and of Moab and Ammon, but took this rich valley from the Amorites by conquering their king Sihon and also Og, the giant king of Bashan. At that time the tribes of Reuben and Gad asked if they might have their inheritance in that valley instead of in the land west of Jordan, and their request was granted on condition that their fighting men would first go over with the others and help conquer the Holy Land proper.

Half of the tribe of Manasseh was also settled in this "cross-Jordan" country. The richest part of this land was the part called *Gilead*, which, Swedenborg tells us, represents "the first good, which is that of the senses of the body." There are many people who want to be good men and women, obeying the Lord and being kind to the neighbor, who nevertheless do not care for any higher kind of enjoyment than the enjoyment of the good things of the world. They are the people who after death are completely happy in the "natural" heavens, knowing that there are higher heavens above them, but not wishing to go higher themselves.

The scene of the story of Jephthah is laid in this land of Gilead. Jephthah was a Gileadite. The Judge just before him, Jair, was also a Gileadite. We are told very little about Jair and nothing about any wars or conquests in the twenty-two years of his judgeship, but as he and Jephthah were the only two Judges who did not come from the Holy Land proper, we may assume that trouble was brewing in Gilead before Jephthah's call and that Jair's judgeship served as a preparation for meeting it when it broke out.

After our regeneration begins, most of our enemies are our hereditary evils, the tribes in the Holy Land proper. But we never reach the point when we do not still need to be on our guard also against a resurgence of our external temptations. The enemies in our story today are the Ammonites. Ammon was one of the two sons of Lot, and represents those who, because they are in merely natural good, are easily led astray and falsify the truth. It is not hard to see what the uprising of the Ammonites is in us. When we fall into the habit of thinking of good in terms of merely earthly comfort and happiness, we interpret everything in the Word in its application to such things. Swedenborg points out that the person who is in merely natural good gives his benefactions to the good and to the evil alike, not stopping to think that when he gives to the evil, he is encouraging evil. He says in one place, "To do good to the evil is to do evil to the good." (AC 3820²)

Jephthah as Judge stands for some simple truth from the letter of the Word raised up in our minds to contradict this false interpretation of truth—in our example it might be such a phrase as that in Luke 6:34: "for sinners also lend to sinners." Like Jacob, Jephthah has an idea that he can bargain with the Lord, as his rash vow shows. He thinks of doing good in terms of self-merit and rewards.

This is, as we have seen before, where we often begin, but when we have once crossed the Jordan, we should have put this idea behind us. Through the story of Jephthah we are taught that what we must give up is our natural affection for thinking ourselves good. This affection is Jephthah's daughter. The picture of this only daughter coming out of his house with timbrels and dances to meet him when he returns victorious reminds us immediately of the self-congratulation with which we hail our own spiritual as well as natural victories. But the regenerating man, when he feels this emotion, immediately recognizes it as the thing he must give up. We remember that the burnt sacrifice was the symbol of the acknowledgment that whatever goodness we have is not our own, but the Lord's working in and through us. So we must overcome our natural reluctance—pictured by the two months' mourning on the mountains—and make the sacrifice.

Adult

Probably the best line of discussion is that of the constant pressure of the world about us and the ease with which we sometimes are led astray. The mistakes into which we may be led by thinking of *good* in terms of merely external benefactions is an important point also. The whole problem of Jephthah's daughter is interesting both in the letter and in the internal sense. The teacher will find various approaches to it in the notes for the other classes.

The period of the Judges is that time in our lives when we have set our outward conduct in order and made enough headway against our deeper temptations so that we feel that we are well established in spiritual living. Our tendency then is to relax our vigilance, to yield a little here and there to the thought and practice of the world about us. We do not realize how easy it is to slip back gradually into evils once we have begun to compromise. After the Israelites had conquered and divided the land and settled down every man under his own vine and fig tree, they stopped fighting the enemies around them and began to mingle with them instead. So they grew weaker and their enemies grew stronger. One after another they rose up and tried to throw off the yoke which

Israel under Joshua had imposed upon them. The Judges whom the Lord raised up to meet these enemies were local leaders—Deborah, Gideon, Samson, and others. They represent particular truths from the Word which the Lord calls up from our memories when we are tempted, realize our own weakness, and turn to Him for help.

Most of the enemies and most of the Judges were in the Holy Land proper, but in our lesson for today the enemy comes from the cross-Jordan country. The Judge is from that country also, and the fighting is done there. This would indicate that the temptation pictured is an external one, and one which may be met and overcome by means of the simple truths of the letter of the Word. As we learn in Jephthah's message to the king of the children of Ammon, the Israelites took this land from the Amorites (see also Numbers 21:21-24), who represent evil in general. Between this country and the desert, on the southeastern and eastern borders of Reuben and Gad, lived the Moabites and the Ammonites, the descendants of Lot (Genesis 19). We remember that when Abraham and Lot came up out of Egypt to settle in the land, Lot, who represents the sensuous or, as Swedenborg puts it in AC 1547, "the external man and his pleasures which are of sensuous things," chose the Jordan valley as his home, and this led him into serious dangers. Like Lot, the sensuous plane of our minds stands in a precarious position. It is closely related to the higher planes and is a necessary part of us, but it is always attracted by external beauties and pleasures and is easily led astray through them. Moab and Ammon, the incestuous sons of Lot, represent departures from the true order of the sensuous, the adulteration of good and truth on the sensuous plane. In AC 2468 Swedenborg speaks of them as denoting "those who are in an external worship which appears in a manner holy, but who are not in internal worship; and who readily learn as being goods and truths the things that belong to external worship, but reject and despise those of internal worship." He makes the further enlightening statement that "such worship and such religion fall to the lot of those who are in natural good, but despise others in comparison with themselves."

In our story they are now attacking Gilead. Gilead is the name given to a considerable portion of the more mountainous country east of the Jordan and parallel to it, from the Sea of Galilee to the Dead Sea, the inheritance of the tribe of Gad. Gad, we are told, represents in a good sense the "good of life," or good conduct springing from love to the Lord and based upon true doctrine (AE 435). In AC 4117[3] it is said that Gilead signifies "the first good, which is that of the senses of the body; for it is the good or the pleasure of these into which the man who is being regenerated is first of all initiated." In AE 654[44] we are told that Gilead signifies, among other things, "reasonings from the sense of the letter of the Word." Thus in the chapter we are studying we have a picture of the outward life of the man who is regenerating, his conduct, his pleasures, and his worship all open to view and constantly subject to attack and especially subject to the temptation to compromise with evil, that "adulteration of truth" represented by the sons of Ammon (SS 18[3]).

This temptation takes countless forms, but in substance it is perhaps this: So long as I support the church, attend worship regularly, give to the poor, etc., I'm a pretty good sort of person; standards of morality and of taste change; things that would have shocked people fifty years ago are perfectly all right now; one can't be prudish and have a good time; if I don't get ahead of the other fellow in business, he'll get ahead of me; why, doesn't even the Bible say, "Make to yourselves friends of the mammon of unrighteousness"? We argue with ourselves and with others in this way and presently we find that we have lost the power to judge clearly as to what is really right and wrong in conduct—we are helpless before the Ammonites. The man who is raised up as Judge in our story is not even a legitimate son of Gilead, but is one who has been cast out by his brethren and has gone to live apart. Swedenborg gives us no interpretation for Jephthah. The name itself means "an opposer" or "one who opens." We can think of him perhaps as representing some simple truth which has come to us through our sense experiences in their contact with false and worldly standards which the Lord can disentangle from the network of worldly reasonings into which we have fallen and can make the instrument of our deliverance.

Jephthah's oath pictures a recognition of what victory over the Ammonites involves. When we are fighting the temptation to compromise with worldly standards of conduct, we cannot hope for victory unless we are willing to give up particular indulgences which the Lord shows us to be wrong. Jephthah vowed to sacrifice as a burnt offering to the Lord "whatsoever cometh forth of the doors of my house to meet me, when I return in peace from the children of Ammon." Jephthah, the mighty man of valor, performed his vow, even though it cost the life of his only daughter. When we enter the conflict with the Ammonites genuinely, it often seems as though the one sacrifice required of us is the thing dearest of all to our hearts. The same lesson in a less external conflict is taught in the story of Abraham's temptation to sacrifice Isaac (Genesis 22). The fact that Abraham's sacrifice was prevented and Jephthah's was not* suggests that Jephthah's daughter pictures an affection of self-love, which should be given up—although of course the burnt offering itself is in the internal sense an act not of destruction but of consecration through love to the Lord.

The moral question involved in the letter of the story of Jeph thah is paramount in most non-New Church commentaries. Did Jephthah do right in keeping a rash vow? The first and most obvious comment is that we should not make rash promises. The Lord says: "But I say unto you, Swear not at all . . . But let your communication be, Yea, yea; Nay, nay: for whatsoever is more than these cometh of evil." (Matthew 5:32, 37) In AE 608 Swedenborg tells us that "Oaths are made by those who are not interior, but exterior men," and that the angels regard an oath as abhorrent, since it insults the integrity of one's motives. A promise is a serious thing, not to be lightly made and not to be lightly broken. But if

*Samuel Noble argued against this conclusion. See his *Plenary Inspiration*, pp. 475ff. and Appendix VI. See also his *Sermons on Judges*, sermons 18-20. —*Ed.*

one has been made which proves to be a foolish one, we have the problem of choosing, not between right and wrong, but between two evils; and it is right to choose the lesser. If keeping the promise involves only inconvenience to ourselves, it will perhaps serve us as a lesson and keep us from trouble later. But if it involves danger, injury, or even inconvenience to others, we may do less harm if we acknowledge our folly frankly and accept the blame and the loss of confidence resulting from a broken promise. Parents should not form the habit of constantly exacting promises from their children, and they should not allow their children to enter into pledges which they do not fully understand and whose consequences they cannot possibly foresee.

[*Note:* There is only one passing mention of Jephthah in all the writings—AE 811[29]—which probably accounts for the omission of the usual quotation from Swedenborg at the end of this lesson.]

Suggested Questions on the Lesson

J. What happened after Joshua and the elders died? *people forgot the Lord*
J. How did the Lord help the people whenever they turned to Him again? *raised Judges*
P. Which Judge is our lesson about today? *Jephthah*
P. Where was his home? *across the Jordan*
P. What enemy was attacking Israel? *Ammon*
J. What did Jephthah vow? *to sacrifice first who greeted him*
P. What was the first thing that came out of his house when he returned? *daughter*
P. Did his daughter try to make him break his vow? *no*
J. What favor did she ask? *two months' time*
J. To what custom did this lead? *annual four-day lament*
I. What do the Judges represent? *particular truths to meet needs*
I. What does the land of Gilead represent? *enjoyment of world*
S. What is pictured by the sacrifice of Jephthah's daughter? *giving up affection for thinking ourselves to be good*

SAMSON

Judges 14

There is a very practical lesson in this lesson for every age, and the story of Samson himself illustrates the danger of carelessness and self-confidence, and our constant need of the Lord's guidance and protection. All the classes should be taught that Samson's strength was in his hair, and even the little ones can get some idea of the meaning of Samson's riddle. There is happiness in doing right.

Doctrinal Points

Samson represents the power of the Lord in our outward life.
The Word is in its power in the sense of the letter.
The Philistines represent knowing spiritual truth but not caring to live according to it. This is what is called "faith alone."
There is no real strength apart from love in the heart.

Notes for Parents

Almost everyone thinks of Samson as a synonym for strength and Delilah for treachery, but many have not read the whole story of Samson and so do not know that he had his strength only so long as he obeyed the Lord, and that if he had not yielded to his lower desires, he could not have been overcome by Delilah's wiles.

The last verse of the book of Judges gives us the key to the meaning of the whole book, as well as of the story of Samson: "In those days there was no king in Israel: every man did that which was right in his own eyes." You may have heard people say, "If I do what I think is right, that is all that can be expected of me." That *sounds* reasonable, but it is really just an excuse for doing what we want to do without testing our desires and thoughts by the Lord's truth. We should have a king–the Lord Jesus Christ–by whose laws we intend to be governed. When each man is a law unto himself, there is anarchy, and only trouble and conflict result.

Samson was a Nazarite, a man set apart for the service of God. The principal sign of a Nazarite was that he never cut his hair. As long as Samson kept this sign, the Lord could be with him and give him strength to overcome any enemy. So his strength was in his hair. The first victory given him—over a lion—means to us that the Lord can give us strength to resist any temptation, and the honey he afterward found in the carcass represents the happiness which comes from overcoming temptation. Anyone who steadily tries to learn truth from the Word and to obey the commandments has had this experience and knows the answer to Samson's riddle. Our strength is in keeping the letter of the law of the Lord, which is the outmost form of the Lord's truth, as the hair is the outmost manifestation of the body's life.

Primary

Teach the children the general background of the book of Judges and the difference between a Judge and a national leader or king. They should also learn what a Nazarite was—the word means "separated"—and why Samson's strength left him when his hair was cut. Tell the whole story of Samson briefly.

Who gave the Israelites power over their enemies?
After Joshua died, the people forgot this.
They thought they were strong and wise enough to get along without the Lord.
So their enemies became strong again and one by one attacked them.
When real trouble came, the Israelites always called on the Lord for help.
Each time He raised up someone to lead them against the attacking enemy.
These leaders were called Judges.
At the time of our lesson the Philistines had gained control of Israel.
The Judge the Lord raised up was Samson.

The Philistines, who lived in the Holy Land along the seacoast, had become so strong that the Israelites were having to do just what the Philistines told them to do. Before Samson was born the Lord had told his mother and father that he was to be a Nazarite, which meant a man singled out to serve the Lord in a special way. The principal sign of a Nazarite was that he allowed his hair and beard to grow, and never cut or trimmed them.

The Lord could give Samson great strength as long as he kept this rule. So his strength was in his hair.

Why did he go into the Philistine country?

What feat of strength did he perform on the way?

What did he find the next time he went down?

What riddle did he ask the Philistines?

Samson's wife coaxed the answer from him and then told her people the answer.

Samson kept his promise, but he was very angry.

From that time on he did many great deeds against the Philistines.

Finally, however, Delilah found out where his great strength lay, and she cut off his hair while he slept.

The Philistines took him prisoner and put out his eyes. But after a while his hair grew again and his strength came back. He did not tell the Philistines that he was strong again. Then one day when a great crowd of Philistines were gathered in one of their temples, and they brought Samson in so that they could enjoy making fun of him, he pushed down the pillars of the temple and the roof fell in and killed them all. Samson knew he would be killed with them, and he was. But he was doing his people a final great service.

Junior

Remind the Juniors that they heard of the Philistines in our lesson about Isaac and Abimelech, and show them the Philistine country on a map. Then point out the territory of Dan from which Samson came. They will be interested in Samson's feats of strength. The teacher should list them beforehand and tell them to the class. They are all found in chapters 14, 15, and 16.

All through the conquest of the Holy Land, the Lord had performed miracles to help the Israelites. You remember how He had told Joshua to study and obey the Law continually if he wished to succeed. Joshua obeyed this charge, but after he died the people forgot it. Read Judges 2:6-13. The Lord could not be with them when they ceased to obey Him, and so the enemies in the land began to gain strength again. The Israelites were so settled in their new homes and busy with their private affairs that they imagined they were wise and strong enough to get along without paying any attention to the law of the Lord. The last verse of the book of Judges shows what their fault was: "In those days there was no king in Israel: every man did that which was right in his own eyes." The Lord should be our king, and we should direct our lives according to His commandments.

Scattered in their homes throughout the country, the Israelites were really weak instead of strong, and after a while here and there an enemy would begin to annoy them, then to oppress them, and finally to rule them completely. When this happened, the Israelites always at last called on the Lord for help. And the Lord always helped them, just as He always helps us when we are ready to acknowledge our own weakness and turn to Him. In the part of the country where the enemy was attacking, the Lord would raise up some strong person to lead the people of that region against that particular enemy. These leaders were called Judges, and the book of Judges tells about them.

At the time of this lesson the Israelites in the southwestern part of the land had fallen under the dominion of the Philistines, who lived along the coast of the Mediterranean. Look at a map and see where they lived and also where the tribe of Dan was settled. Your teacher can show you the town of Zorah near the border of Judah, and southwest of it the town of Timnath. Zorah belonged to Dan, and Timnath was a town of the Philistines. Chapter 13 tells us how an angel of the Lord appeared to the wife of Manoah, a man of Zorah, and promised her a son, who should begin to deliver Israel out of the hand of the Philistines. The woman called her husband and they made a sacrifice to the Lord and saw the angel ascend in the flame from their altar; so they knew the message was from the Lord. The angel had told them that the child must be brought up as a Nazarite; that is, a man especially dedicated to the service of the Lord. The signs of a Nazarite were that he should not touch wine or strong drink, and that he should never cut his hair. In due time the child was born and named Samson.

When he grew up, what did he want to do which displeased his parents?
What threatened Samson as they went down to Timnath?

How did Samson kill the lion?
What did he find when he came down the second time?
What riddle did he ask the Philistines?
How did they finally get the answer?
How did Samson keep his bargain?

Chapter 15 tells further exploits of Samson. If you read it, you will see what good reason the Philistines had to fear and hate him. They knew he had more than human strength, and they tried to trap him through the woman he loved, as they had done the first time. The woman who betrayed Samson this second time was a Philistine named Delilah. She coaxed Samson to tell her why he was so strong, and he finally was persuaded to tell her. As long as Samson was faithful to his Nazariteship and did not cut his hair, the Lord could give him strength. One night while Samson was asleep, Delilah cut his hair. To learn what happened when he awoke and the rest of his story, read Judges 16:20-31.

Intermediate

The correspondence of the tribe of Dan, of the Philistines, and of Samson and his hair are basic for this class. They will be interested also in the meaning of Samson's riddle, which can be illustrated from their own experience.

After Joshua there was no one ruler over all Israel and therefore no general organization of their forces. But whenever any enemy in any part of the land became so oppressive that the Israelites turned again to the Lord for help, the Lord would raise up someone strong from one of the tribes in that region to lead them in their resistance. These local leaders were called Judges, and they picture particular truths called to our minds by the Lord to strengthen us against particular temptations.

If we rely on the Lord and obey Him, He will always give us strength to conquer in temptation. Our troubles come from the weakness of our faith in the Lord and not from the strength of the evils in us. When the Israelites obeyed the Lord, His power was with them and their enemies became weak. The story of Samson teaches this lesson. So long as he obeyed the Lord he was given strength to meet many enemies and overcame each of them single-handed, as he overcame the lion in our chapter. When he let his lower desires beguile him, he lost his strength. Read chapter 13 to learn of his birth and the conditions he was told to observe. He came from the tribe of Dan, which represents among other things the acknowledgment of the truth of revelation.

Samson represents simple obedience to the letter of the Word. He was to have nothing to do with wine and strong drink—which symbolize an intellectual grasp of the truth—and he was to let his hair grow. The hair, which has the least life of any part of the body, pictures what is most external: in this case, the letter of the Word. We learn from Samson that if we obey even the literal commands of the Word from a motive of obedience to the Lord, we shall have strength to meet and overcome every enemy which threatens us.

Swedenborg tells us that the Philistines—the only enemy never fully conquered by Israel at one time or another—picture an affection for learning the truth without any desire to live according to it. This is one of our persistent enemies—the temptation to be satisfied with knowing what is right. We go to Sunday school, for example, and are interested in the lesson. What do we do with it when we go home? How far do we really apply it in our own life?

Samson wanted a Philistine wife. He was tempted by this desire for knowledge for its own sake. It was of the Lord's providence, as we see in verse 4 of our chapter, that he was allowed to make this attempt. The young lion in the Philistine vineyard pictures the powerful temptation which is hidden in this superficial intellectual approach to life. Samson overcame the lion, and afterward found honey in its carcass. Honey, a wholesome and natural sweet, is a symbol of the delight which comes from doing what is right. The riddle which the Philistines could not solve without Samson's help asks, spiritually: "Is it possible to draw good out of trial, happiness out of struggle?" Only those who use the strength the Lord gives them to overcome their temptations really know the answer.

In spite of Samson's experience of the treachery of the Philistines, he still desired a Philistine wife. The story of Samson and Delilah, found in chapter 16, is so powerful that Delilah has come to be recognized as the symbol of anything which beguiles in order to betray. The thing which betrays us more than any other is the love of learning without doing. So long as Samson's hair was uncut, no Philistine bonds could hold him. So long as we keep the commandments, we are safe. But once we reject the commandments, evil captures us, blinds us to the right, and eventually destroys us. Read chapter 16.

Basic Correspondences

the Judges	=	particular truths called to our minds by the Lord to strengthen us against particular temptations
Samson	=	judgment, and in a good sense acknowledgment of the truth of revelation
the Philistines	=	the affection for knowing the truth without any desire to live according to it
the hair	=	the outmost form of life; the letter of the Word
a lion	=	power
honey	=	sweetness, or the delight which comes in doing right

Senior

The story of Samson should be used to put the Seniors on their guard against two things: the folly of overconfidence in one's own goodness and spiritual strength, and the ever-present danger of being beguiled by the allurements of the world about us and the reasonings in favor of them. Stress also the importance of the letter of the Word.

We are told in Judges 2:7 that the Israelites served the Lord all the days of Joshua and of the elders who outlived Joshua, who had seen the wonderful works of the Lord in the wilderness journey and in the conquest. Then they began to mingle with the evil people in the land whom, you remember, they had not wholly conquered, and finally even to worship their gods. When we are just beginning the regenerate life, we are eager and enthusiastic in serving the Lord; but after we think we are established in the new pattern, we are liable to become self-satisfied and careless, to give way a little here and there to the pressure of worldly thinking and selfish feeling. Our inner spiritual enemies gain strength and threaten to resume control of our character.

The Judges, who were raised up from time to time by the Lord in one or another part of the land, represent particular truths which the Lord recalls to our minds in time of need to strengthen and lead us in our resistance to particular temptations. The period of the Judges pictures a time of vacillation in our lives before we have learned through experience the extent of our own weakness and our need of continual direction by the Lord.

The enemy now threatening Israel in the southwestern part of the country was the Philistines, and Samson—the Judge in this story—was of the tribe of Dan. Dan in a good sense represents the affirmation and acknowledgment that we should believe in God and live a good life. Samson was also a Nazarite, a man "separated" or set apart for special service of the Lord. The signs of Nazariteship were to abstain from wine and strong drink and not to cut the hair. As long as these signs were observed, the Lord could be with the man. A fuller explanation of this will be found in the quotation at the end of this lesson. The Philistines represent the affection for knowing the truth without any desire to live according to it. So we can easily see why Samson of the tribe of Dan was the chosen Judge.

The story of Samson is a very simple and striking one. Samson's strength was in his hair: that is, in obedience to the law which had been laid down for his life. His was a simple character. Temptation came to him in the form of two women—both Philistines. Women represent the will side of our lives. In both cases Samson's integrity was worn down by repeated appeals to his affections.

The lion which attacked him when Samson first went down into the Philistine country pictures the strength of the temptation to which he was subjecting himself. His victory over the lion was given to show him that it was possible for him with the Lord's help to withstand temptation, and his finding the honey in the carcass of the lion the second time he came down was a reminder that overcoming temptation always brings satisfaction. Honey is a symbol of delight in doing right. Heaven is a state in which we both know the truth and delight in living according to it. So the Holy Land is described as a land "flowing with milk and honey." Samson should have learned his lesson from this experience and from the events which follow in the rest of our chapter.

But we remember that later he yielded again, with far more serious results. We all know the story of Samson and Delilah, which is told in chapter 16. Delilah beguiled him into disclosing to her the secret of his strength and cut off his hair while he slept. Then the Philistines captured him and put out his eyes. When we allow ourselves to be betrayed into giving up obedience to the commandments in their letter, we fall captive to false reasonings of every kind and lose our power to see what is truly right and wrong. There is much of this confusion in the world today simply because some people are being taught that the Bible is the product of men and that the commandments were written for an earlier time and are not binding upon "modern" men and women. A whole structure of philosophy and psychology has been built up, like the temple of Dagon the fish-god in Philistia, in honor of the human intellect and its achievements. Those who accept this philosophy make sport of the "simple-minded" people who still believe in the Word of God, just as the Philistines made sport of the blind Samson.

But Samson's hair began to grow again. The moment we see our folly and return to the acceptance of the commandments as our rule of life and exert ourselves to keep them again, the very central pillars of the house of Dagon are knocked out, and the whole structure comes tumbling down.

Adult

Good discussion topics are the meaning of the period of the Judges, Samson's riddle, Samson's strength and weakness, and the Philistine temptation. Swedenborg's teaching that the letter of the Word is the "basis, containant, and support" of all our spiritual knowledge and power is one which we particularly need.

The Israelites, before they moved out to take possession of their allotted homes in the Holy Land, had been charged by Joshua to continue in their own territories the fight against the enemies who remained there, and to root them out. The first chapter of the book of Judges tells us how far short all the tribes fell of fulfilling this charge. Only one individual–Caleb–seems to have made a complete conquest of his inheritance. In AE 768[21] we learn that Caleb represents "those who are to be introduced into the church." (In AC 2909 we find a brief and very interesting summary of the history of Hebron and its meaning.) The rest of the people were too much interested in making themselves comfortable in their new homes to worry about enemies who appeared to be no longer threatening. The book of Judges teaches us that even after we have begun to regenerate, we cannot assume that we have reached a state in which we can settle down confident of our own spiritual security. Read Matthew 24:43. Self-confidence always betrays us. "Pride goeth before destruction, and an haughty spirit before a fall." (Proverbs 16:18) Our inner foes gain strength, and we suddenly find ourselves in the throes of temptation again. It may take us some time to learn this lesson. The period of the Judges lasted about two hundred years. We recall that the Judges were not rulers of the whole people but local leaders raised up by the Lord to meet the various enemies in one part of the country or another. They represent particular truths called to our attention by the Lord to help us fight particular temptations. We have already studied Deborah, Gideon, and Jephthah.

Our lesson today is about Samson, one of the Judges, and his exploits against the Philistines. The Philistines, as we recall from our lesson on Isaac and Abimelech, were a people who lived along the western border of the Holy Land. Authorities differ as to their origin. One suggests that they were pirates of ancient Aryan stock, who forced themselves upon the Canaanites and settled permanently in the land. Genesis 10:14 makes them descendants of Ham, and they were a settled people in the time of Abraham. Abraham and Isaac both spent some time in the Philistine country and made treaties with them. At the time of the Exodus the Israelites were not allowed to go by the "way of the Philistines" (Exodus 13:17). From time to time throughout the history of Israel, the Philistines caused trouble. The Israelites often chastised them and even captured some of their strong cities, but never wholly overcame them. The story suggests an ever-present enemy to our spiritual peace, one with whom we are often tempted to compromise and against whom we must always be on our guard.

Swedenborg leaves us in no doubt as to what this enemy is. The Philistines, he says, represent those who are in the "knowledge of the knowledges of faith and charity," those in faith separated from charity, with whom "the knowledge of the knowledges of faith is the principal thing, but not a life according to it; consequently those who teach and believe that faith alone saves" (AC 8093). The doctrine of faith alone was a widely accepted doctrine of the Protestant Reformation. Even Luther felt forced to adopt it in order to have a basis for separation from the Roman system, and in the course of time apparently argued himself into a belief in it. It has wrought tremendous havoc in the Christian world, and Swedenborg has much to say of its effects both in this world and in the spiritual world. Practically, it means that it makes no difference what we do so long as we acknowledge Christ and look to Him for salvation. We sometimes hear it said that this doctrine is no longer held today, but this is not true. Many still hold it even in its bald general form. But further than this, there are many less obvious manifestations of it, and none of us is wholly free from some form of it. For instance, whenever we go to church and come away critical of others and not equally dissatisfied with ourselves, we may know that the Philistines are upon us. Self-righteousness and the pride of self-intelligence are the earmarks of faith alone. For the more we know of the Lord and His ways, the more conscious we should be of our own shortcomings; if we are not, it is a sign that we are not genuinely trying to live the truth we learn, that we are satisfied to know without doing. This is the Philistine temptation.

It is significant that Samson, the Judge raised up against the Philistines, was from the tribe of Dan, for Dan represents the "affirmation and acknowledgment" that we should believe in God and live a good life, which "is the first general principle with the man who is being regenerated." Samson won notable victories over the Philistines. In SS 49[2] Swedenborg says: "The Lord's power from the ultimate things of truth was represented by the Nazirites in the Jewish Church; and by Samson, of whom it is said that he was a Nazirite from his mother's womb, and that his power lay in his hair." AE 619[18] and AE 1086[2] elaborate this idea, with particular reference to Samson, and specify the sense of the letter of the Word as the ultimate in which the power of divine truth resides. Samson was tempted to ally himself with the Philistines, and was more than once overcome by them. In the same way, our affection for knowledge often leads us astray. We learn a great many things without due thought as to the use this knowledge should perform. This temptation is like the young lion which threatened Samson, and if we overcome it, we are given the joy pictured by the honey which Samson found in the carcass of the lion. This is a joy which comes only from carrying out in life the truth we learn. The Philistines could never have guessed Samson's riddle. No one who is not trying to do right can believe that he would find pleasure in it. Samson fell as a result of his desire for a wife from among the Philistines. We may think he was easily beguiled, but how often we ourselves feel the attraction of "the world, the flesh, and the devil," and take the easy way instead of the right way!

All the details of the story of Samson are interesting in their correspondence and useful in adding point to the lesson. But the principal truth with which we should be impressed is the fact that Samson's power was in his hair. The hair corresponds to the "ultimates of the Divine truth," and thus to the sense of the letter of the Word in which the Lord's power is in its fullness. It was on account of this correspondence that the Israelites were led to think of baldness as a disgrace; that the children who called Elisha "thou baldhead" were torn by bears; that the prophets, including John the Baptist, wore hairy garments; and that the Lord's hair is described so beautifully in the vision of John in Revelation 1:14. The letter of the Word is our only means of conjunction with the Lord and of receiving power from Him. It is through the knowledge of the letter of the Word which we store in our minds that the Lord can speak to us; it is through our reading of the Word that His presence and power can come into our daily lives. The Lord in His Second Coming has opened the Word and made it possible for us by prayerful study and constant application in our lives to understand more and more of the spiritual and celestial things which lie within it. But it is still the letter of the Word which is "the basis, containant, and support" of all we learn. We cannot substitute the spiritual sense for the letter, as Swedenborg himself tells us more than once. Samson's strength went from him when his hair was shaved. So his story contains a special warning for us of the New Church. We should not allow our delight in the new knowledge which is given us to beguile us into becoming separated from the source of all our spiritual strength.

From the Writings of Swedenborg

Doctrine of the Holy Scripture, n. 49: "The power of Divine truth is directed especially against falsities and evils, thus against the hells. The fight against these must be waged by means of truths from the sense of the letter of the Word. Moreover it is by means of the truths in a man that the Lord has the power to save him; for man is reformed and regenerated and is at the same time taken out of hell and introduced into heaven, by means of truths from the sense of the letter of the Word . . . The Lord's power from the ultimate things of truth was represented by the Nazirites in the Jewish Church; and by Samson, of whom it is said that he was a Nazirite from his mother's womb, and that his power lay in his hair . . . No one can know why the Naziriteship (by which is meant the hair) was instituted, or whence it came that Samson's strength was from the hair, unless he knows what is signified in the Word by the 'head.' The 'head' signifies the heavenly wisdom which angels and men have from the Lord by means of Divine truth; consequently the 'hair of the head' signifies heavenly wisdom in ultimate things, and also Divine truth in ultimate things . . . In short, the reason why the power of Divine truth or of the Word is in the sense of the letter, is that there the Word is in its fullness; and it is also because in that sense are, at the same time and together [*simul*], the angels of both the Lord's kingdoms and men on earth."

Suggestion Questions on the Lesson

J. What mistake did the Israelites make after Joshua's death? *forgot God*
J. What was the result? *enemies rose up*
P. How did the Lord help them when they turned to Him? *Judges*
J. What tribe did Samson belong to? *Dan*
P. What were his parents told he should be? *Nazarite*
P. What was the special sign of a Nazarite? *uncut hair*
J. What enemy was threatening Israel in Samson's part of the country? *Philistines*
P. What was the secret of Samson's strength? *his hair*
J. What was his weakness? *women, pride*
P. What feat of strength did he perform when he first went into Philistia? *killed lion*
P. What did he find the second time he went down? *honey*
J. What riddle did he ask the Philistines? *"Out of the eater . . ."*
J. What can you tell about Samson's later life and his death? *hair cut, blinded . . .*
I. What do the Philistines represent? *desire to know truth but not live according to it*
I. What is meant by Samson's strength being in his hair? *power in ultimates*
S. What does Samson's riddle teach us? *happiness can come from struggle*